The Grey Album _ _ _ _ _ _ _ _ _ _ _ _ _ _ _ _ _

Other Books by Kevin Young

POETRY

Ardency: A Chronicle of the Amistad *Rebels*
Dear Darkness
For the Confederate Dead
Black Maria
Jelly Roll: A Blues
To Repel Ghosts
Most Way Home

EDITOR

Best American Poetry 2011
The Art of Losing: Poems of Grief and Healing
Jazz Poems
John Berryman: Selected Poems
Blues Poems
Giant Steps: The New Generation of African American Writers

The
Grey Album

ON THE BLACKNESS OF BLACKNESS

KEVIN YOUNG

Text and image permission acknowledgments begin on page 409.

This publication is made possible in part by a grant from the Minnesota State Arts Board, through an appropriation by the Minnesota State Legislature from the Minnesota general fund and its art and cultural heritage fund with money from the vote of the people of Minnesota on November 4, 2008, and a grant from the Wells Fargo Foundation Minnesota. Significant support has also been provided by the National Endowment for the Arts; Target; the McKnight Foundation; and other generous contributions from foundations, corporations, and individuals. To these organizations and individuals we offer our heartfelt thanks.

ART WORKS.
arts.gov

MINNESOTA
STATE ARTS BOARD

CLEAN
WATER
LAND &
LEGACY
AMENDMENT

WELLS
FARGO

TARGET.

Published by Graywolf Press
250 Third Avenue North, Suite 600
Minneapolis, Minnesota 55401

www.graywolfpress.org

Published in the United States of America

ISBN 978-1-55597-607-1

2 4 6 8 9 7 5 3

Library of Congress Control Number: 2011944858

Cover design: Kyle G. Hunter
Cover art: Jennie C. Jones, from the "Breathless Series." Audiotape pressed under glass, 2010. Courtesy of the artist.

This book is for

COLSON WHITEHEAD

my brother

And you keep writing—all it takes is ——it, grit and motherwit—
and a good strong tendency towards lying (in the Negro sense
of the term).

—RALPH ELLISON TO ALBERT MURRAY
January 24, 1950

"Zora," George Thomas informed me, "you come to de right place
if lies is what you want. Ah'm gointer lie up a nation."

—ZORA NEALE HURSTON
Mules and Men

Contents

BOOK THREE: Heaven Is Negro

BOOK FOUR: Cosmic Slop

Illustrations

The Grey Album _ _ _ _ _ _ _ _ _ _ _ _ _ _ _ _ _

Overture

Storying: animal tales; the spirituals as codes for runaway slaves; runaway slaves themselves; maroons; the blues code of life, tragic and comic, "laughing to keep from crying"; nothing but a good man feeling bad; nothing but a bad woman feeling good. "Sell the Shadow to support the Substance."

Frederick Douglass finding a *root* to defeat his master; High John de Conquer; learning to write on the sly; writing yourself free passes to leave the plantation; Henry Box Brown mailing himself to freedom; Phillis Wheatley's letters to Obour, a code to her poems; pretending to be an owner and traveling north with your husband disguised as a slave; writing letters from the South that pretend to be from the North, so no one will look for you; freeing oneself from the fact of slavery with the fiction of song; the River Jordan is really the Ohio; slaves composing poems for money to buy their freedom; basket names; Dave the Slave's pottery and poetry. Elsewhere.

Langston Hughes's autobiography; novels by slaves that aren't really but barely masked autobiography; *The Bondwoman's Narrative*; masks and modernity; jungle music; the primitivism of Picasso and the Picasso-esque qualities of primitivism; Zora Neale Hurston pretending she's a bootlegger to record ("bootleg") the lies of her neighbors; the blues singer, the numbers writer, the rootworker, and the conjure woman.

Not the Confederate bill; nor the contraband of slaves; passing, sometimes; sometimes "The Blue-Tailed Fly"; not Sally Hemmings but the story of Sally Hemmings and her descendants we always knew 'bout;

Clotel; or, The President's Daughter; not Strom Thurmond but his black daughter we'd heard of for years, mm-hmm, told you so.

Richard Wright forging his own library card he'd have a white man sign so he could check out books; *The Lost Zoo; Giovanni's Room;* Anne Spencer's garden; Louis Armstrong's solos; his letters; his collages; bebop's borrowings; "Salt Peanuts"; Rent-a-Beatnik; Abomunism; the hesitation pitch; "The Hesitation Blues"; fake books; dreambooks; *Omeros;* hoodoo, neo or no; Miles Davis kicking smack; Krazy Kat; SAMO©; draft dodging; *Vibration* Cooking; highlife; Otis Redding covering "Satisfaction"; Aretha Franklin covering Otis Redding's "Respect" so that everyone thinks of her even before Otis; "A-Tisket A-Tasket"; the whistling in "Sittin' on the Dock of the Bay"; scatting; the human beatbox; the lindy hop; hip-hop from 1983 to 1993; De La Soul's *Three Feet High and Rising;* Black Star Line; Black Ark; Lucille Clifton's spirit writing; *Curtis Live!;* SAMO© IS DEAD; *De La Soul Is Dead;* "Hip Hop Is Dead"; Charlie Parker Lives.

"The Payback." The Groove. "The Crazy Blues." Not the Rolling Stones; not "Rock N Roll Nigger" but Jimi Hendrix playing the National Anthem on his guitar; yearning; wordlessness; deep desire; Deep Deuce; artist Adrian Piper's card reading "I am black" to give to those who say racist things not suspecting she is; Adrian Piper dressing as a man and recording the reactions; Adrian Piper's self-portrait "with her Negro features exaggerated"; trickeration; the rope-a-dope; the put-on; Basquiat's drawings of money as conjure, cause then he made it; bling, sometimes; WIT; "UFO" by ESG; Afronauts; Afro wigs; *The Wig;* Richard Pryor's Mudbone; his deciding not to use the word "nigger" again. *A Feast of Scraps.* Nigerian money scams.

"The Exquisite"; The Silver Surfer; Dick Gregory's dollars; Thelonious Monk's stamps; Bob Kaufman's silence, started after Kennedy was shot, only ending at the announcement of the end of the Vietnam War; his silence broken by declaiming T. S. Eliot's *Murder in the Cathedral* mashed up with his own poem "All the Ships That Never Sailed"; Mlle Bourgeoise Noire; "Girl You Know It's True"; *Angela's Mixtape; Orpheus in the Bronx;* Drexciya, the underwater utopia; "We Can Dance

Underwater and Not Get Wet"; The Robot; wildstyle; to frink, to clown, to krump; getting crunk. Mingering Mike, who invented mingering and then did it, painting and drawing his own Fake records and selling millions in his own bedroom;

and, selling snowballs on the street.

BOOK ONE
Elsewhere _

I sell the Shadow to support the Substance.

—SOJOURNER TRUTH

I SELL THE SHADOW TO SUPPORT THE SUBSTANCE.

SOJOURNER TRUTH.

The Shadow Book

ONE

Lately I have been thinking about the idea of a shadow book—a book that we don't have, but know of, a book that may haunt the very book we have in our hands. I have even begun to think that there are three kinds of shadow books in the tradition, and hope to provide a brief taxonomy of them. *Like to hear it, here it go—*

First are the kinds of shadow books that fail to be written: the *Africana Encyclopedia* by Du Bois; the second novels of Jean Toomer or Ralph Ellison that never appeared, at least in recognizable form; the failed attempt at a novel by Anatole Broyard, who passed for white. As readers eager for such shadow books, we search among the fragments of a life unlived; there's also a suspicion that this book, at least in the case of Toomer, Ellison, and Broyard, is the real result of a psychological block from actual or black life—of living some form of lie. This writer's block is often seen as a troubled relation to blackness itself. In this way, the shadow books' very unwrittenness becomes a metaphor, and argu-ably a too easy one, for race in the United States. Comfort with yourself is equated with being able to write—despite the fact that not writing is actually the norm and we should perhaps applaud what is there, rather than what ain't.

Still, this *unwritten* form of the shadow book fascinates. This un-written shadow book haunts not just the reader—what could have been—it haunts every writer each time she or he sits down to write. It is part of the vast unwritten that threatens us all, and that in the case of the African American writer, seems too much like the life denied him or her, the black literature denied existence. It is, in some way, the price of the ticket.

Second is the *removed* book, the book that's a shadow of the one we do have. If the first threatens all writers, either from death or despair or difficulty, then the threat of the removed book is the secret book found just behind all the others, its meaning never to be fully revealed.

The first is blues; the second, jazz. By blues I mean that the first, unwritten shadow book is a recognizing of and reckoning with existence, however tragic, even (or especially) in its failings. Jazz on the other hand represents a willingness to recognize the unfinished, process-based quality of life and art, even taking pleasure in the incompleteness of being.

Recent examples of this second, jazzlike shadow book include Toi Derricotte's *Black Notebooks,* which regularly mentions things removed from the text; Natasha Trethewey's *Bellocq's Ophelia,* which in taking the once anonymous, defaced, even half-erased photos of Hillaire Bellocq, tries to reconstruct a life—and a quadroon, prostitute life at that; and Colson Whitehead's *The Intuitionist* with its book within a book, "Theoretical Elevators," the pseudophilosophical guide to Intuitionism penned by a shadowy figure within his novel. These books suggest more that's beyond even our knowing; and, in the case of Whitehead, suggest that all knowing is somehow involved in knowing just that.

It also strikes me now that passing is at the heart of all Derricotte's, Trethewey's, and Whitehead's books—if not literally, then symbolically. Ambiguity of the book matches that of race, it would seem—and why not? Other recent books that deal with the lacunae of life on the color line include *One Drop,* the book by Bliss Broyard, Anatole's daughter, about her father's origins; and *Where Did You Sleep Last Night?* by Danzy Senna. Both of these include the search for a father's past and take the narrators to Louisiana to locate what could be called their Creole origins. Such origins question the very idea of passing, of simple racial opposites or identities—African American and Louisianan and American—in a way that also speaks to the black and Creole and New World origins of jazz.

While Broyard's and Senna's two nonfictions don't necessarily involve textual removals, they do speak to the losses inherent in black inheritance—and leave us, in each case, with fathers at a remove and whose different responses to race could be said to mirror a jazz aesthetic. The fathers improvise, shade, dissemble, distance; it feels in reading both books there are shadow books behind them—if not those unwritten by Senna or Broyard *père,* then those actually written by the daughters, mostly in the form of their semi-autobiographical fiction before these memoirs.

The removed book is also suggested by poetry titles like Amiri Baraka's *Preface to a Twenty Volume Suicide Note . . .* or Elizabeth Alexander's "Ars Poetica" series with gaps in its numbering; these works suggest, in their form and very naming, the ways African American utterance is fleeting and even in Baraka's case, potentially fatal. There's always something missing, the removed book suggests—with the distinct and hopeful possibility that there's always something more.

This second shadow book (not to mention its Creoleness) may remind us of the late artist Jean-Michel Basquiat, who said he crossed out words in his paintings so you saw them more. Life in all these works, black life I suppose, is necessarily analog, a mixtape of sorts that seeks to approximate life itself—practicing the exacting art of inexactness.

The removed shadow book doesn't so much represent loss as it recognizes it. As Jean Genet says about George Jackson's *Soledad Brother,* any "book from prison" is marked by what is left out, either from the censors or by the self who speaks in code:

> It is therefore prudent that any text which reaches us from
> this infernal place should reach us as though mutilated, pruned
> of its overly tumultuous adornments.
>   It is thus behind bars, bars accepted by them alone, that
> its readers, if they dare, will discover the infamy of a situation
> which a respectable vocabulary cannot reinstate—but behind
> the permitted words, listen for the others!

This shadow book is particularly important to us, situated on the cusp of fiction and history—and trying to find the truth in both.

The first book is a form of reconstruction; the second, of resistance. In this way these shadow books mirror the measure of our literature and our history, which could be said over the course of the twentieth century to have moved from reconstruction to resistance.

The last shadow book is the *lost.* These shadow books are at once the rarest and most common—written and now gone. Rather than those never written, these books were lost because their authors' lives were cut too short; and because the oral book of black culture is at times not passed down, at others simply passed over.

Elusive as beauty and as necessary, these lost shadow books include the autobiography of Joe Wood, the complete writings of Philippe Wamba, the lost second book of Phillis Wheatley, James Baldwin's no longer extant first book about storefront churches in Harlem, the accidentally burned writings of Fenton Johnson, the purposefully burned writings of Lucille Clifton's mother—and others not so literal, lost to time, from the recording of the sound of Buddy Bolden's horn, and the first jazz in New Orleans, and later, in many senses, the actual autobiography of Billie Holiday. These shadow books are what keep me up at night, ghost limbs, books that could be and have been, but aren't anymore.

I am reminded of the ways Lucille Clifton made brilliant poems about having been born with extra fingers, polydactyly being a sign of the poet's unique birthright, of something witchy yet lost that is now part of the poetry. The shadow books go, then, from the unwritten or untold ones; to the removed or unspoken ones (often because they are themselves wordless); to the shadow book as ghost story, disallowed, vanished. Still, at times—such as Hurston and Hughes's mythic collaboration *Mule Bone*—these lost shadow books turn up. They are invoked, too, by a book like Toni Morrison's *Beloved* and its idea of *rememory*. Such a process, the willed recovery of what's been lost, often forcibly, I suppose is what keeps me going.

In some crucial ways, the lost shadow book is the book that blackness writes every day. The book that memory, time, accident, and the more active forms of oppression prevent from being read.

It is this symbolic book that slavery really banned—a book of belief. It is this book we lose daily, when the storm sweeps it all away, whenever someone is silenced, or an elder dies or is otherwise lost to us, quilts gone out the door, actual books left on the stoop for dead. Not to mention the secret recipes—and I don't just mean for food—that our ancestors managed to keep secret. It is the scrap of paper I found my father's barbeque sauce recipe on, which I'm tempted to frame but instead attempted to re-create. It is this reason I found myself a poet and a collector and now a curator: to save what we didn't even know needed saving.

As African Americans, we have gone over the past century and a half from Reconstruction, to resistance, to recovery—and today, to a real need for reclamation. Forget reparations—we need to rescue aspects of black culture abandoned even by black folks, whether it is the blues or home cookin' or broader forms of not just survival, but triumph.

TWO

There's the book that could have been, and the book that each day threatened to leave unfinished. I am reminded of our departed Lucille Clifton again, specifically her untitled poem from *The Book of Light*, the collection's very title combating the shadow book:

> won't you celebrate with me
> what i have shaped into
> a kind of life? i had no model.
> born in babylon
> both nonwhite and woman
> what did i see to be except myself?
> i made it up
> here on this bridge between
> starshine and clay,
> my one hand holding tight
> my one hand; come celebrate
> with me that everyday
> something has tried to kill me
> and has failed.

As a measure of its own stubborn survival, *The Grey Album* has come to seem like three books in one. A mash-up. The first is a book about literature and what I have found there, the pleasures and mysteries of reading while also discovering disparate ancestors, from Phillis Wheatley to Billie Holiday, from groundbreaking poet Paul Laurence Dunbar to overlooked Beat poet Bob Kaufman.

The second is a book about music—especially the way that the spirituals, blues, jazz, soul music, and hip-hop can each be thought of as emblematic of their eras, from slavery to the present day. In this book,

chiefly as a series of "Choruses," I am interested not just in the wonders of music but in the ways in which black folks make music art, and
their own, in a world that often still manages to ignore them. One of
my main convictions throughout this book is the centrality of black
people to the American experience, to the dream of America. As jazz
composer Duke Ellington says, "We play more than a minority role, in
singing 'America.' . . . I say our 10 per cent is the very heart of the chorus: the sopranos, so to speak, carrying the melody, the rhythm section
of the band, the violins, pointing the way." The choruses in this book
are the heart of this exploration.

Which brings me to the last book that makes up *The Grey Album*,
a book that is here chiefly as an echo, a shadow book of its own—a
book that may be impossible to write. For a time, after starting with
poetry and ending up with music, it seems I was attempting to write a
unified theory, a book that would encompass most everything. Such is
the promise of modernity, at least in poetry: books like William Carlos
Williams's *Paterson* or Ezra Pound's *Cantos* seemed to wonder, if only
by their form, can the poem, can any one book, contain everything?
Often, in an attempt to write "news that stays news" or to "make it new,"
modernists created a poem that includes not everything but *anything*,
from letters to news reports to the weather to other poets' poems:

> Look at
> what passes for the new.
> You will not find it there but in
> despised poems.
> It is difficult
> to get the news from poems
> yet men die miserably every day
> for lack
> of what is found there.
>
> (WILLIAMS, "ASPHODEL, THAT GREENY FLOWER")

It is this rough inheritance that has led me to include a range of
artistic ancestors, from bebop to postmodernism to P-Funk to Public
Enemy. All these are what I think of when I think of blackness, so I
suppose it's natural in a book about black creativity that I would be
interested in naming all I thought. The books I admire, from James

Baldwin's *Price of the Ticket* to Susan Sontag's *Against Interpretation*—
not to mention the "verse journalism" pioneered by Gwendolyn Brooks—
attempt to do just that. However, while inspired by the spirit of Brooks's
precision, rather than trying to fit everything under one tidy roof I've
settled for "Tearing the Roof Off the Sucker"—which of course may not
mean settling at all.

THREE

The thread that binds all these books together is the notion of *lying*—
the artful dodge, faking it till you make it—the forging of black lives
and selves in all their forms. Of what, "visiting home" in Louisiana,
where both sides of my family are from, we called *storying*. You see,
growing up, a child would never say to someone, "You lie," especially
to an adult; if you happened to, it was a serious accusation tantamount
to cursing (which we didn't dare get caught doing either). Instead, we'd
say, "You story."

To me, then, *storying* is both a tradition and a form; it is what links
artfulness as diverse as a solo by Louis Armstrong—which, as any jazz-
head will tell you, brilliantly tells a story—with any of the number of
stories (or tall tales or "lies" or literature) black folks tell among and
about themselves. Storying connects African American "story quilts"
with the animal tales and spirituals that provided a code for runaway
slaves. Such "black codes" are exactly the kind I explore here. Whether
in the chapter-portraits of specific writers, or in the choruses that take
on music, throughout this book I'm interested in the ways the fabric of
black life has often meant its very fabrication, making a way out of no
way, and making it up as you go along.

Storying means the "lies" black folks tell to amuse themselves and
to explain their origins, many of which are recorded by Hurston in her
collection *Mules and Men;* storying is also Hurston herself lying about
being a bootlegger in order to better hear those "lies" in the first place.
Storying is what Alice Walker does when she claims she's Hurston's
kinfolk in order to locate her grave and provide a headstone, literally
reclaiming her for future generations. Like Walker's "womanism" or
Henry Louis Gates's "signifyin(g)," storying takes a folk term from
black culture—a term first used to demonize or at least dismiss—and
turns it on its head. Such reversals are crucial to black culture.

Storying is a term also taken in part from jazz, where it is a way of describing the desirable, necessary discipline required by a soloist—it is a form of saying the music must move, and must move you. Each good solo tells a story, one that while collective in nature—a calling out—must also be unique, your own. Otherwise, you yourself can be called out. An anecdote from Robert G. O'Meally's *The Jazz Cadence of American Culture* helps illustrate this:

> Among this music's most magical words are those reminding its players to "tell the story." This is jazz's profoundest invocation, its most deep-voiced invitation and witness, amen-ing those who have achieved more than technical fluency and tricks of the trade; exhorting and high-praising those who have reached jazz's highest goal of attaining a personal artistic voice. Max Roach tells one on himself, the young drummer, new in town from North Carolina, the teenage virtuoso sitting in with elder statesman Lester Young and showing off his talent by playing master drummer Jo Jones's style to a fare-thee-well, a perfect copy. When the set broke, Max waited for a good word from Prez, who at first remained silent as he packed his horn, his face a distracted mask. Then he turned to look at Max and shook his head as he sing-songed his warning: "You can't join the throng . . . till you got your own song."

Pres's critique is one I came to later, after I'd already been considering the place of storying in the tradition—but it echoes the ways that storying provides a communal vision of individual achievement and collective standards of excellence. A vision based not on mere technical expertise, but feeling, purpose, presence. You could say that this is not just musical but architectural—as with a tall building's many "stories," the goal with storying is to reach the heights.

FOUR

By storying, or what I sometimes call here "the counterfeit tradition," I don't mean falsehood or some kind of fake blackness; nor do I mean to champion the recently prevalent bending of truth to make money or avoid trouble, as practiced by government officials and writers from Jayson Blair to Margaret Seltzer to James Frey, in the manner lately called "truthiness." For where these faux journalists and worse seem to exhibit imagination, they in fact mark the failure of it. They bend the truth, instead of taking it apart to explore or expand it—*or does it explode?*—and usually in the service of cash's cold comfort. The storying artist's job is to dance on and in the breaks. Poet Bob Kaufman riffs off one such incarnation of the artist, the Abominable Snowman, crafting an "Abomunist Manifesto" that declares "Abomunists do not write for money, they write the money itself." Kaufman's mock manifesto views the artist as the ultimate outsider, a mythic beast barely glimpsed, insisting on parody and myth as its main currency.

Such storying also counters the ongoing, reflexive desire in our culture for "realness" in all its forms. From reality television to keeping it real, what we most desire is an experience beyond the phony or the phoned in, beyond the mode of pretense that daily life insists upon. While admirable, this urge ignores the valences of black life—an insistence on and nervousness over a constantly tested black reality denies the ways black folks have found their escape where they can, often as not in the imagination—not as mere distraction from oppression but as a derailing of it.

The black imagination conducts its escape by way of underground railroads of meaning—a practice we could call the black art of escape. In contrast, both realness and truthiness—distinct from a funky, vernacular "troof" that's part proof and part story—miss the ineffable, lyric quality found in the imagination, and in the tradition traced here. Throughout, I am interested in the ways in which black folks use fiction in its various forms to free themselves from the bounds of fact.

Uh, I'm sorry, I lied—this book, then, is indeed an attempt at a unifying theory, or evidence of my search for one. It is the story of what I read, heard, and saw at the crossroads of African American and American culture, which, as we shall see, may be much the same rocky road.

Ultimately it is my wish, as a storyteller in Hurston's *Mules and Men* has it, "to lie up a nation"—by taking up not arms but the imagination.

How Not to Be a Slave
On the Black Art of Escape _ _ _ _ _ _ _ _ _ _ _ _ _ _ _ _ _

We can think of traditional views of slavery as being the conversation between two slave masters: one, "I lock mine up because they are dangerous"; the other, "No, they are harmless, subservient, and I lock them up because that's what they need, how they feel most comfortable." We are the ones on the plantation speaking and singing to each other in *code,* to let others know our intent—such art and artfulness precede what sets us free, and more often than not, are the code by which that freedom is achieved. If we cannot first imagine freedom, we cannot actually achieve it. Freedom, like fiction and all art, is a process in which the dream of freedom is only the first part.

Rather than stay in their place, the slaves imagined a new one. Remapping was for the slave a necessary form of survival—reconfiguring the American landscape as Egypt or Canaan in order to shore up (and keep secret) their search for freedom. At times allegorical, always coded, such remappings—a kind of storying—provided a set of radical metaphors for the slave's exile.

Critic and poet Melvin Dixon indicates the ways in which African American use of the valley, the wilderness, and the mountain provided "images of physical and spiritual landscapes that reveal over time a changing topography in black American quests for selfhood."[1] Likewise, Henry Louis Gates Jr. reveals that when the spirituals speak of "down," it is not a literal place but a significant, symbolic one:

> "Down" is the Afro-American "Fourth Stage," that place where Yahweh told Moses exactly what to say to ole Pharaoh, "way down in Egypt land," to "let my people go." Almost as strongly, "down" also implies the not-so-mythic (but mythically recalled)

land from which black people were severed, the Africa of their fathers where people were people and people were free.[2]

No wonder the slang phrase "He's down" is not an insult, but an indication of belonging. For, while corresponding to the outside world, the slave's map was chiefly an interior one—which all too often has left it unread, misplaced, or denied.

Would you rather be misread, or unread?

The captive African's compass pointed Elsewhere and served as a measure of a boundless desire for freedom. This jerry-rigging black imagination runs directly counter to the gerrymandering of white oppression. Even an expression as seemingly familiar as "jerry-rigging" contains at least two other, shadow ideas: first, that the phrase is actually "jury-rigged," which contains a notion of judging and justice all too important to the slave; and second, in Louisiana my family jokingly calls it "nigger-rigging," which, in its very self-deprecation, admires black innovation.

Those who doubt the slave's inner compass, or the remapping the newly American African performed, do so at their peril—or at least will find themselves surprised tomorrow when the slave's not there no mo. The Negro spirituals are not just songs of the everlasting but also of imminent disappearance: *Steal Away. Dere's a Han' Writin' on de Wall. Tell Ole Pha-raoh, Let My People Go. Oh, I want two wings to veil my face, Oh, I want two wings to fly away.* They are maps charting the black art of escape.

What's more, this remapping wasn't just about survival but also a kind of African survival in its own right. We now know, for instance, that slaves in the colonies kept their African cosmologies alive, as was discovered in a New York City attic[3] and beneath a Maryland hearth:

> They are the secrets of the early American slave culture. While the white family upstairs went about their transplanted English lives, practicing conventional Christianity, African-Americans downstairs cooked, did the laundry and, though baptized, still practiced rituals of their former West African religions. They might be slaves in the New World, but a vital part of them steadfastly clung to their old world, to Africa.
>
> The evidence, archeologists and other scholars say, lay

> beneath the bricks of the hearths and hidden in the northeast corners of the rooms. . . .
>
> With these rituals and amulets, they sought protection from overbearing masters, overseers or mistresses. They resorted to secret cures, casting healing spells with roots, herbs and charms, because professional doctors were rarely called in to care for slaves. A third purpose of these practices was divination of the future.[4]

Easily overlooked, and even more often suppressed, the continued presence of such African belief systems indicates how important they were to black life in the New World—and how slaves in the North and South often preserved a symbolic, spiritual place in a hidden one.

No wonder the black imagination involves much that is hidden, squirreled away, storied. Rather than the madwoman, ours is the cosmology in the attic. Much of that inner life takes its form in what Elizabeth Alexander calls "the black interior"—for hiding was a tradition not just of the body but of the mind. As the folk saying has it, "Got one mind for me and another for the master to see."[5]

I mean this notion of a "hiding tradition" in both senses—that in African American culture, there is a tradition of hiding one's self, life, loves, and more, often in plain sight; and that there is also a sense of the black imaginative tradition being overlooked. The two are related, if not in the way they may seem at first. The tradition of hiding (versus the hidden tradition) emerged as a defense long before it was lost: an underground railroad of meaning to survive, a second sight to redress freedom in a culture designed to destroy any remnants of Africa or inherent humanity of an African being.

We should not blame the methods of survival for their being ignored, or repressed; it is our job—not as detectives but as readers and lovers of what needs to be read—to uncover the tradition on our own. Forget cosmopolitanism: let's discuss the trapped black mind as a cosmos.

WHAT IS THE WHAT (NEGATION)

Take Langston Hughes. In his poetry and even his memoir *The Big Sea*, Hughes recognizes the tension between form and content, as well as a blues tension between personality and impersonality, between private

pain and public performance. By doing so, Hughes participates in storying and what could be called the *counterfeit tradition:* one in which the
freedom of fiction, of crafting one's own identity (much like the man-
ufacture of money), allows the author a literal freedom. As Frederick
Douglass relates, even in an oppressive system such as slavery blacks
forged for themselves "free passes" taking another "counterfeit" identity as freedmen or -women, even counterfeiting the master's signature.

It is through telling lies to get at a larger freedom—and truth—that
the counterfeit is born. Of necessity.

To put it simply, and to distinguish it a bit from mere fiction, *counterfeit* is a term I use to discuss ways in which black writers create their
own authority in order to craft their own, alternative system of literary
currency and value, so to speak, functioning both within and without
the dominant, supposed gold-standard system of American culture.
Counterfeit I also see as a literary counterpart to the long-standing tradition of the trickster. There are many other names for the black artist, who, like the trickster—just one prototype African Americans have
embraced—seeks to go beyond expectations, both black and white. For
the black author, and even the ex-slave narrator,[6] creativity has often
lain with the lie—*forging* an identity, "making" one, but "lying" about
one too.

I take this term directly from slave narratives, speaking to the everyday insurrections of those in bondage, whether Douglass's own learning
to write or black folks' falsifying their own "papers" to set themselves
free. The counterfeit is written; black; subversive; often hidden: it does
not so much participate in white authentication systems of papers that
could somehow decide freedom as mock and mark them, allowing
black folks to literally go free, as well as to move literarily within and
beyond what Toni Morrison calls "the master narrative."

Like the forged free passes that inaugurate it, one crucial aspect of
the counterfeit is a renegotiation of borders—and a freedom from an
insular identity itself. And like runaway slaves, the black writer in the
counterfeit tradition crosses, then questions, all bounds—of fact and
fiction, between "real" bills and fake ones. Counterfeit is the way in
which black folks forge—both "create" and "fake"—black authority in a
world not necessarily of their making.

'Cause, as we all know, the trickster may lie to get over, to save his or her rusty behind, and may leave a few of us tar babies behind in the proverbial briar patch. One of these briar patches may be the link between fiction and fact; another may be between right and white, black and back. Of course, we know freedom ain't free—one of America's biggest ironies is that it was only after Emancipation, once black folks had no literal, monetary value to whites, that lynching began. You don't lynch your mule; you just whip him, or perhaps, if he keeps trying to get loose, you hobble him, or clip the Flying African's wings. The caged bird sings—or stories—a way out.

My notion of counterfeit is quite distinct from, though related to, notions of the dehumanizing images of black people in American fiction. Consider Ralph Ellison's description, writing at the twentieth century's midpoint, of such stereotypical depictions: "Despite their billings as images of reality, these Negroes of fiction are counterfeits. They are projected aspects of an internal symbolic process through which, like a primitive tribesman dancing himself into the group frenzy necessary for battle, the white American prepares himself emotionally to perform a social role."[7]

The black artist uses the counterfeit to battle exactly these stereotypes. Ironically this is sometimes done after first "putting on" or parodying these white-made masks—not only does Ellison do so in *Invisible Man,* he does so in the preceding passage, turning the tables on the idea of the primitive by calling the white a "tribesman," by treating whites with the sort of sociological and ethnographic distancing to which the dark natives usually are subjected.

Ellison's writing neatly delineates what amounts to the complexities and interrelatedness of African Americans' and white Americans' images of themselves, and the masks both wear. To this I would add that the tradition of the trickster—a tradition of counterfeit and fiction, of storying—has just as much place in African American letters as our rituals of church or prayer or music. Though for Ellison the trickster was overdetermined, and not uniquely African American, Ellison importantly articulates the notion of black influence on white culture— that whites took the mask of blackness in order to say something about themselves. And not without cost: "Here another ironic facet of the old American problem of identity crops up. For out of the counterfeiting of the black American's identity there arises a profound doubt in the white man's mind as to the authenticity of his own image of himself."[8] Let's place the power of the counterfeit back in the black hands where it originated.

As Leslie Fiedler put it, we are all "imaginary Americans" for whom the ranges of ethnicity represent not so much facts as roles, or what might be best called "necessary fictions." Ultimately, this imaginary America that is as much black as anything else violates the simple notion that authenticity is a process of white authentication of black books and their authors. Instead, whether through the fetish of the desired black body or through the *fetiche* of the black mask, it is often a case of white culture looking to black culture to authenticate, and even question, itself.

WHAT I SAY (RENAMING)

Just as freed slaves renamed themselves Sojourner Truth or Frederick Douglass, naming in slave narratives often involved some of the techniques of invention, participating in the process (and the continuity) we call fiction. Whether through renaming or remapping, such second sight was as much about revision as vision.

Even if we ignore the semiautobiographical pseudonovels that serve as a transition between autobiography and fiction—such as the pseudonymous *Our Nig* or the *Bondswoman's Narrative*—we still must recognize that the more orthodox slave narratives start to fictionalize as early as the name on their title page. For example, in Harriet Jacobs's groundbreaking narrative *Incidents in the Life of a Slave Girl,* the book's first page—its very title—immediately introduces to the contemporary reader a pseudonymous narrator in Linda Brent.[9] As a result, the reader should recognize its self-conscious author substituting (at least on a naming level) the fictional for the real or factual life, a "slave girl" whose life is bounded by "incidents" and yet not quite defined by them.[10]

In a similar move, though with quite different effect, the ex-slave author regularly renamed other characters in the narrative, particularly the master, often in highly symbolic terms; Jacobs's book renames the white masters Dr. Flint and Mr. Sands, while Frederick Douglass's *Narrative* of 1845 ironically dubs the master Freeland, then self-consciously puns upon it: "I began to want to live *upon free land,* as well as *with Freeland;* and I was no longer content, therefore, to live with him or any other slaveholder."[11] William Andrews has also convincingly argued that the "literal" dialogue between master and slave, written years later, is a point of fictionalization and contention with the slavocracy's master narrative.[12] Fictionalizing also liberates black autobiographers and authors by providing "a living contact with unfinished, still-evolving contemporary reality,"[13] critiquing white-dominated past and present realities while substituting an alternate black one.

This is the counterfeit, the written, textual "counter fit," which inverts the white-based construction of authentication. Instead of relying on the authority (and resulting authenticity) of white "fact," the black author counterfeits such authority by way of fiction. Since previously conceived notions of truth have often oppressed black people, the counterfeit is a literary tool that fictionalizes a black "troof." Such a black, vernacular-based reality proves quite different from a white-dominated historical, factual, and authenticated one. In short, since even fact-based, "objectively scientific truth" has been used to oppress black people and their authors, their authors have often sought counterfeit or fictional or alternate realities. Such "troof" also has resonances of "spoof," parody, and basic exaggeration. As readers, then, we should not make the master's classic mistake: believing that a Good Negro is incapable of fictionalization or outright lying.

In no way do I mean to suggest that slave narratives are lies. Nor do I mean to make the mistake, parodied by Ishmael Reed in his slave-satire *Flight to Canada,* that "slavery [is] a state of mind, metaphysical."[14] Rather, the slaves' varied narratives gave chattel slavery's very real and persistent horrors a shape and name—rendering them as *story.*

Counterfeit might help us recognize that critics who read simply in terms of authenticity do two quite damaging things: first, they read (white) skepticism back into the slave's writing and thus limit the "freedom" of black authorship; second, they ignore or downplay the African American trickster tradition, itself related to black rhetorical strategies like lying. The critic's emphasis on white authentication—and attendant black attempts at achieving such authentication—seems at once to privilege and perpetuate the master's idea that black authors depended on white folks for their authority. Even Gates falls into this authenticity fallacy, arguing that "the primal scene" of African American literature was not Phillis Wheatley's picking up a pen; nor publishing her book; nor writing to and about General Washington; nor writing poems about the Boston Massacre and inscribing her own postcolonial identity; nor even her death in poverty, with a second book completed but never finding its way into print: but rather, is the testing and then authenticating by colonial figures of her first (and only) published book.[15]

When confronted with African American writing, too many seem to focus on its reception, on how many men signed Phillis Wheatley's proof of authorship, without examining the myriad ways in which black writers, even Wheatley herself, predict, parody, and make possible white authentication of their own work. What if Wheatley's meeting with the men who judged her writing was not the primal moment of black literature? What if it was instead the moment Wheatley, a slave in a foreign land who couldn't fly home, dared to pick up the quill?

What if it was the writing, in other words, and not the judging?

Not merely negating authentication or merely substituting constructions of fiction for those of fact, the black author goes further, storying his or her way out of the very bounds of fact and fiction. This often tense "fictional freedom" comes from what Harriet Jacobs called the "loophole of retreat," crafted by the African or African American slave herself. The chapter "Competition in Cunning" shows Jacobs writing false "letters from the north" from that self-described physical "loophole of retreat"—a nine-foot-long, seven-foot-wide, and three-foot-high hiding place in her grandmother's attic in the South—in which Jacobs stories a series of letters telling her master she is up north, ironically giving her more freedom in the South. In doing so, Jacobs creates a counterfeit epistolary "loophole" to match her physical one; this in turn increases her physical freedom, allowing her to move about in her grandmother's house.[16] Much like the cosmologies found buried in the attic, such symbolic retreat resembles *Invisible Man*'s hideout in that book's prologue: "Please, a definition: A hibernation is a covert preparation for a more overt action."

Brent's letters, like Ellison's protagonist's invisibility, participate in the African American counterfeit tradition of the "'protection'—

Frederick Douglass's term for a pass usually written by a slave's master that allows him, almost paradoxically, to travel while in bondage."[17] While still a slave Douglass forges such a protection, allowing him to travel and ultimately gain freedom.[18] For Douglass the counterfeit provides an opportunity to first attempt journeying north; for Jacobs, "It was a great object to keep up this delusion, for it made me and my friends feel less anxious, and it would be very convenient whenever there was a chance to escape."[19] Perhaps most important, for authors in slavery and after, the counterfeit freedom precedes and in many ways provides for the personal, factual, and actual freedom that follows.

And that's the troof.

WHAT IT IS (THE LESSON)

If, in what Ellison called "the unwritten dictionary of American Negro usage,"[20] the lie may mean another name for story—and lies are simply stories, and to story is in fact to lie—then this euphemistic inversion tells us plenty about the nature of counterfeit, and the black culture it comes from. It also may provide one map to being a writer. We may take Ellison's advice to fellow writer Albert Murray to heart: "And you keep writing—all it takes is ——it, grit and motherwit—and a good strong tendency towards lying (in the Negro sense of the term)."[21]

Much like *womanism,* coined by Alice Walker, storying also takes what once was a transgressive behavior—in Walker's case, acting "womanish"; in this case, "lying"—and redeems it as a literary virtue. In her book *In Search of Our Mothers' Gardens,* where she defines "'big old lies,' i.e. folk tales," Alice Walker honors and seeks out the original collector (and maker) of lies herself: Miss Hurston. In doing so, she encounters not only Hurston's storying inheritance but the storying tradition as found in the broader community.

"Looking for Zora," Walker lies to find out the truth, journeying to Eatonville, Florida, Hurston's all-black hometown, to see if she can locate Hurston's burying place:

> Inside the Eatonville City Hall half of the building, a slender,
> dark-brown-skin woman sits looking through letters on a desk.
> When she hears we are searching for anyone who might have

known Zora Neale Hurston, she leans back in thought. Because I don't wish to inspire foot-dragging in people who might know something about Zora they're not sure they should tell, I have decided on a simple, but I feel profoundly *useful,* lie.

"I am Miss Hurston's niece," I prompt the young woman, who brings her head down with a smile.

"I think Mrs. Moseley is about the only one still living who might remember her," she says.

"Do you mean *Mathilda* Moseley, the woman who tells those 'woman-is-smarter-than-man' lies in Zora's book?"

"Yes," says the young woman. "Mrs. Moseley is real old now, of course. But this time of day, she should be at home."[22]

Such an exchange might seem all the more remarkable for what is not remarked on. The "smile" that the young woman gives—is it knowing? She certainly seems an incarnation of motherwit, a "woman-is-smarter" knowledge that both women, as well as Mrs. Moseley, share.

Like other forms of storying, the lie provides an easing of passage. Not that it works fully—there's a sense in her smile that the young woman at City Hall, like the Little Man at Chehaw Station, is also in on it. And that in some real sense, Walker is Hurston's spiritual "niece," knowing the town well enough through Hurston's words that she can craft her own. The encounter also is an encounter with history in the form of Mrs. Moseley, who we learn soon enough is a real character in every important sense.

The inheritance Walker seeks, and that she finds all along the way, takes its form in her essay through a subtle renaming. Up till now, the essay has referred to Hurston as Zora Hurston, always using her last name, while in Eatonville Walker adds the honorific *Miss* when she tells her "useful lie" about being Hurston's niece. But from this point on in the narrative, both "because of Zora's books" and her newfound familiarity, suddenly Walker—in the essay and the dialogue in Eatonville alike—refers to her simply as "Zora."

Such renaming is not a form of fiction but of family. Now, a whole book itself could be written on black naming, and even just about those times when the use of the honorific proves a sign of both familiarity and respect (such as calling poet Gwendolyn Brooks "Miss Brooks") and those times when such respect is signaled yet made intimate by the use of first names only (as in saying Bessie or Billie or Aretha). But here it is mostly important to note how family is as much a form of invention as a matter of blood. More than any other cultures I know, black folks are always calling someone close but not technically kin "aunt"; and then there's that moment, if it ever occurs, when you call those once strictly your elders by their first names.

This is the first lesson about the tradition: *What we claim, we are.*

Walker continues to say to Mrs. Moseley and to others, from the black funeral home director to the "monument man" in Florida, that she is "Zora's niece"; it is its own honorific. "By this time I am, of course, completely into being Zora's niece, and the lie comes with perfect naturalness to my lips. Besides, as far as I'm concerned, she *is* my aunt—and that of all black people as well." The naturalness of such artifice is telling. But later, when Walker encounters one of Hurston's childhood friends, Dr. Benton—"one of those old, good-looking men whom I always have trouble not liking"—she feels guilty about the lie but continues it nonetheless. Walker even suspects that "if he knows anything at all about Zora Hurston, he will not believe I am her niece."

Instead, "I say with shy dignity, yet with some tinge, I hope, of a nineteenth-century blush, 'I'm illegitimate. That's why I never knew Aunt Zora.'"[23] This awareness of inheritance and its insider/outsider status parallels the *counterfeit* itself: as with money, the language of the counterfeit is both circulating within a dominant power system and also resistant to it. It is an inheritance we too often are told is illegitimate or illegal. It is a fiction not simply meant to pass along, but also to ease passage.

Perhaps just as telling about the tradition is Dr. Benton's response:

"You're *not* illegitimate!" he cries, his eyes resting on me fondly. "All of us are God's children! Don't you even *think* such a thing!"

And I hate myself for lying to him. Still, I ask myself, would I have gotten this far toward getting the headstone and finding out about Zora Hurston's last days without telling my lie? Actually, I probably would have. But I don't like taking chances that could get me stranded in central Florida.[24]

Call this *Lesson Two:* Accepting even the stranded, strange, and seemingly illegitimate is the black elder's aim.

Walker's ease and questioning, her manifold roles, symptomatic of a trickster mentality, were presaged by Hurston herself, who not only collected "lies" as a folklorist but lied just to get by. She too didn't mean to be stranded in central Florida any more than Walker did! As Michael North relates in *The Dialect of Modernism,* Hurston's brilliant essay "How It Feels to Be Colored Me" is a virtual manifesto of shifting identities, of a sense of herself as "not always feeling colored" and even "feeling most colored when thrown against a white background."[25] It is both modern and, if we didn't know better because of its being written in 1928, postmodern. More pointedly, and poetically to my mind, in her brilliant *Mules and Men* Hurston herself has to "lie" in order to get in with the local townspeople—nearby in her own Florida hometown no less—not only notoriously changing out of a fancy dress into a "simpler" one (symbolically leaving her citified ways) but also declaring that she's a bootlegger.

In this moment of shifting identities (and by wearing a simple shift), Hurston performs a counterfeit by storying that she's a bootlegger—an identity that itself is involved in counterfeiting, if only of liquor. This counterfeit of a counterfeiter tells us worlds more about the "reality" of black existence and expression than a simplistic view of what is art and what is not—not to mention what is *truth* and how we uncover it. Simply put, we may have to don a "simple" dress to get a complex set of stories ("lies") from folks, just as we may have to lie to join the liars in order to find out the truth about them. And us.

The whole of *Mules and Men,* with its collection of folktales or lies, organized by Hurston in an almost novelistic framework, serves as a brilliant incarnation of the counterfeit. A *bootleg,* if you will. A stitching together of the folktales in *Mules and Men* to tell a larger (I'm tempted to say "taller") tale of black culture, Hurston symbolizing the relations between mules and men, women and motherwit, herself and her community. While some see the book as somehow compromised by its narrative framework, this very interleaving is what enlivens the lies it contains, what makes the folktales neither independent from their tellers (as a more academic study might) nor divorced from their communal source. Hurston is a recorder without a recording device, apart from participatory memory; her method mimics the ways the folktales are passed down in the first place—and in this way not less scientifically but more. Memory, for Hurston, is a form of technology and another instance of storying.

Let's put it another way then: the counterfeit is the "literary lie."

Which is to say, it is, in that way, *useful*.

There is another way in which storying proved useful for Hurston: she lied about her age throughout her life, shaving a decade off her years. Constantly shaded, unknowable even to those supposedly close to her, Hurston even lied about her age on one of her marriage certificates; until recently, biographers did not admit this marriage took place, finding no records of it at all.[26] (Ellison too, his biographer Arnold Rampersad reveals, took a year off his age; indeed, after you start looking in the tradition, lying about one's age becomes an oddly familiar strategy in black autobiography, from Satchmo to Sweetness: might such small fictions speak to the need for a larger, improvisatory storying?) In the great mix of mystery and necessity that governs all great art, Hurston clearly falls on the side of mystery—though perhaps it is not her work but her life that remains mysterious and that, out of some unknowable necessity, she turned into art.

Storying, then, can be a specific moment of counterfeit in a text (forging free passes in Douglass's *Narrative*), or a larger counterfeit text itself (James Weldon Johnson's pseudonymous and fictional *Autobiography of an Ex-Coloured Man*), or, as I have come to see, a way of approaching the world.

These uses of storying are not only historical, memorable, and pervasive, but were also made real upon the death of critic Nellie McKay, whose groundbreaking work certainly influenced this very book and many others before it. Only after she died in 2006 did McKay let it be known that she had been "living a lie": that the woman she claimed as sister all her life, even to her closest friends, was in fact her daughter;

and that she herself was some twenty years older than anyone had thought. This unnerved many, both close to her and within the field, who understandably felt deceived—yet who, in understanding the source of this untruth, knew all too well that in her applying to attend graduate school at Harvard in the early 1970s (McKay receiving her PhD from there in 1977), it was less than advantageous to be seen as a single mother and scholar. Not to mention African American. Indeed, these were all paradoxes not to be embodied. And so, we can imagine, a choice was made; a secret begun; the trickster tradition rolls on.

Professor McKay's storying is less a story about her, though it is certainly that, than about the Great White Lie about black inhumanity, however defined—here about being at once black and female and a mother and a scholar—and rejecting it in order to fulfill life's possibilities. One may be reminded of Wheatley's testifying before the committee to allow her to publish her book: the need for outside approval is often said to deform the work, but I'm more interested in the writer than the audience—in the ways these mothers, out of necessity, reinvented themselves in order to reinvent our world.

WHAT IT BE (DEFINITIONS)

Drum signals; the spirituals as codes for escape from slavery; folktales or lies; the mask of dialect in capable hands; "the Black Rimbaud"; the Black Atlantic; "the black electric"; *The Big Sea;* Charlie Parker turning "Cherokee" into "Ko Ko" as the birth of bebop; Richard Wright forging a note from a white man, thus allowing him to use the segregated public library; James Baldwin's *Giovanni's Room* and its mask of whiteness (a mask also used in his essay "Ten Thousand Gone"); jazz riffs and inversions; Jimi Hendrix's feedback during his "Star-Spangled Banner"; Lucille Clifton's *Two-Headed Woman;* artist Jean-Michel Basquiat's alchemical paintings of money that then earned him money; the fugitive slave, the trickster, the rootworker, blues people, the bootlegger, the numbers writer, the diva; some might even say the pimp, the gangsta, the addict, and other outlaw identities that violate and transform traditional codes of behavior: all are examples of the storying tradition, of the self invented and pursued through a profound act of imagination.

So too the slave's "free pass," often forged to ease passage; even "passing" to escape the bounds of racism (and the vagaries of race); and a "passing on" of these acts of resistance, these "lies," as a collective inheritance. *This is not a story to pass on.* Perhaps we should refer to this not as the counterfeit tradition but as a "counterfeit inheritance" that indicates the manner of its being passed on down. For while it may seem derogatory or even a contradiction in terms—would you really want a "false inheritance"?—the counterfeit tradition indicates something of the subtle ways by which black inheritance is transmitted and received. And that tradition, no matter your color or culture, is not simply something you inherit, but what you choose to keep, and even more, invent: just because you need to invent it, or forge and find it, after all, does not mean it's not there.

Struggle is the third lesson of the tradition.[27]

James Baldwin perhaps embodies this best in his account of meeting painter Beauford Delaney, whom, in Baldwin's collected essays, *The Price of the Ticket,* he calls "the first walking, living proof, for me, that a black man could be an artist":

> I had grown up with music, but now, on Beauford's small black record player, I began to hear what I had never dared or been able to hear. Beauford never gave me any lectures. But, in his studio and because of his presence, I really began to *hear* Ella Fitzgerald, Ma Rainey, Louis Armstrong, Bessie Smith, Ethel Waters, Paul Robeson, Lena Horne, Fats Waller. He could inform me about Duke Ellington and W. C. Handy, and Josh White, introduce me to Frankie Newton and tell tall tales about Ethel Waters. And these people were not meant to be looked on by me as celebrities, but as a part of Beauford's life and as part of my inheritance.[28]

Such an inheritance, tall tales and all, is more than mere instruction in music. A paragraph later, Baldwin helps us further understand the ways in which, trudging to Manhattan after a poorly paying job in Jersey "working for the Army—or the Yankee dollar!," he learned from both Beauford Delaney and Miss Anderson (that is, Delaney's friend, the famous opera singer Marian Anderson), the high cost involved in transforming oneself:

> Not only was I not born to be a slave: I was not born to hope
> to become the equal of the slave-master. They had, the masters,
> incontestably, the rope—in time, with enough, they would hang
> themselves with it. They were not to hang *me: I* was to see to that.
> If Beauford and Miss Anderson were a part of my inheritance, I
> was part of their hope.[29]

In his introduction to this incredible gathering of essays, Baldwin indicates both the power of the tradition and the great cost of failing to discover it. He also indicates the ways in which the tradition is an active one: this birthright ("not born to be a slave") is one that requires black folks' own action and imagination. Or the hope of the rope-a-dope. (Note too the difference in the honorific for Miss Anderson, while Baldwin refers to Delaney simply as Beauford.) For the elders seeing "the kid," as he is called, become part of this inheritance is both reward and hope enough. Baldwin's very newness provides hope for what went before—providing, that is, a kind of folk corollary to Eliot's notion of "Tradition and the Individual Talent," in which the tradition can be changed by what comes after.

This is *Lesson Four:* not only does the tradition ennoble those who come after, but by following in it, one honors those who went before. In that way, we are "their hope."

WHO DAT? (ANCESTRY)

If the counterfeit represents a moment of masking—or the entire text itself as a self-conscious, playful, even unreliable persona—then the fetish is an extension of that moment of power. I use this term *fetish* in the manner evoked in Douglass's second autobiography: meaning a physical, visual, even private totem that provides power to its carrier. As with the counterfeit or the free pass, the fetish is a feigned freedom that itself provides, and paves the way for, actual freedom. *Free Your Mind and Your Ass Will Follow.*

But the fetish steps in where words fail. With fetish, the author need not say anything, need not even be literate; far more than its counterfeit counterpart, which requires some form of literacy even as it questions that literacy, the fetish need only be seen and understood. Fetish is the readerly text, personified—or better, "thingified"—if only to counter the thingification of black people by a society that saw them as mere fractions. This wasn't a feeling but the law. The damage of such "thingification" Douglass charts in describing in seeing his own appearance after what turns out to be the last flogging by an overseer, a beating that causes him to flee into the woods: "I was an object of horror, even to myself."[30]

In his *Narrative,* Douglass relates his freedom not just through literacy or a "protection" but also through the help of a *root* he obtains from a fellow slave and "old adviser," Sandy Jenkins, when Douglass flees his violent overseer, Covey. As a fetish, this *root* allows him to battle Covey: "The circumstances leading to the change in Mr. Covey's course toward me form an epoch in my humble history," Douglass writes. "You have seen how a man was made a slave; you shall see how a slave was made a man."

Douglass then relates obtaining the *root* from Sandy; interestingly Douglass is already in a tenuous, limbo-like kind of freedom, having run away from Covey following a whipping:

> I spent that day mostly in the woods, having the alternative before me,—to go home and be whipped to death, or stay in the woods and be starved to death. That night, I fell in with Sandy Jenkins, a slave with whom I was somewhat acquainted. Sandy had a free wife who lived about four miles from Mr. Covey's; and it being Saturday, he was on his way to see her. . . . I found Sandy an old adviser. He told me, with great solemnity, I must go back to Mr. Covey; but that before I went, I must go with him into another part of the woods, where there was a certain *root,* which, if I would take some of it with me, carrying it *always on my right side,* would render it impossible for Mr. Covey,

> or any other white man, to whip me. He said he had carried
> it for years; and since he had done so, he had never received a
> blow, and never expected to while he carried it. I at first rejected
> the idea, that the simple carrying of a root in my pocket would
> have any such effect as he had said, and was not disposed to
> take it; but Sandy impressed the necessity with much earnest-
> ness, telling me it could do no harm, if it did no good.[31]

This interesting logic—that there's no harm, if no good, in the *root,*
which is italicized in the original—seems to speak to the ambiguity of
the fetish if not its power. The *root* serves to empower Douglass: its mere
possession allows him to no longer be a possession.

This key chapter in Douglass's narrative—containing "the turning-
point in [his] career as a slave"—is worth reading in full. Certainly,
as others have noted, Sandy Jenkins stands as a connection to old ways
and to folkways, serving an example of ancestor. Toni Morrison defines
ancestors as "not just parents, they are sort of timeless people whose
relationship to the characters are benevolent, instructive, and protective, and they provide a certain kind of wisdom."[32] In *My Bondage and
My Freedom,* where Douglass re-creates the incident, he terms Sandy
"a genuine African, [who] had inherited some of the so called magical powers, said to be possessed by African and eastern nations. He
told me that he could help me; that, in those very woods, there was an
herb, which in the morning might be found, possessing all the powers
required for my protection, (I put his thoughts in my own language);
and that, if I would take his advice, he would procure me the root of the
herb of which he spoke."

Sandy proves a liminal figure, if not free, then a key link to freedom, both because of his free wife and his liberated manner. As critic
Robert G. O'Meally notes, even his name "Sandy," which Douglass
likely assigned him, "seems to reinforce his identity as a man of the spirit
and of the earth—perhaps of the seashore."[33] (In Douglass, "renaming"
serves not only to signal significance and signifyin' but also to protect
the innocent and damn the damnable.) I want to note here something
about the text itself: Douglass's use of italics further emphasizes the
ways in which the *root* is ever mysterious, even in his writing of the
Narrative years later. *Root* is both italicized for emphasis and foreign-

ness; if not actually in another language or "his thoughts in my own language," the *root* is suggestive of another tongue and another world, untranslatable.[34]

It also stands in contrast to a phrase the *Narrative* chapter repeats almost as much as *root*: Douglass says that the cruel overseer Covey, as well as his own Master Thomas, threatens to *"get hold of me,"* meaning to whip Douglass. Throughout, Douglass sets up a counterpoint between the phrases *"get hold of me"* and *"always on my right side"* that subtly emphasizes that the "holding" is not an embrace and the "right side" is not just on the body but on the correct side of history. What's more, the very fetish nature, as it were, of the *root* counters Covey as a "professor of religion—a pious soul—a member and a class-leader in the Methodist church. All of this added weight to his reputation as a 'nigger-breaker.'"[35] He is a "professor," meaning both teacher and faker.

Against this idea of Covey as faker, Douglass becomes a kind of fakir, reveling in his own kind of mastery. Douglass's *root* and writing point out the limits of false piety and slavery's hypocrisy more generally: "Mr Covey's *forte* consisted in his power to deceive. His life was devoted to planning and perpetrating the grossest deceptions. Every thing he possessed in the shape of learning or religion, he made conform to his disposition to deceive. He seemed to think himself equal to deceiving the Almighty."[36] The Big Lie of slavery, its racial ironies, are no match for Douglass—the fetish points out the difference between storying and mere lying, speaking in ways mere words cannot.

The fetish asserts itself too against such white conjuring and professing of Christianity. Upon returning to the plantation, Mister Covey, a "nigger-breaker" by profession and a "professor of religion," is surprisingly calm when first seeing Douglass, which leads him "half inclined to think the *root* to be something more than I at first had taken it to be." Later, "the virtue of the *root* was fully tested" when Covey ambushes Douglass in the stable and Douglass fights back for nearly two hours. The standoff is really a victory: "The truth was, that he had not whipped me at all. I considered him as getting entirely the worst end of the bargain; for he had drawn no blood from me, but I had from him. The whole six months afterwards, that I spent with Mr. Covey, he never laid the weight of his finger upon me in anger." Douglass learns an object lesson in how not to be an object.

"It was a glorious resurrection, from the tomb of slavery, to the heaven of freedom," Douglass elegantly asserts after his defeat of Covey. Can we imagine any of this at Douglass's mere age of sixteen? "My long-crushed spirit rose, cowardice departed, bold defiance took its place; and I now, resolved that, however long I might remain a slave in form, the day had passed forever when I could be a slave in fact."[37] This denial of being "a slave in fact" requires the triumph of fiction—in the form of Elsewhere, and the fetish. As he describes it in *My Bondage,* "When a slave cannot be flogged he is more than half free. He has a domain as broad as his own manly heart to defend, and he is really *'a power on earth.'*"[38] This domain is found well inside, a wellspring not just of feeling but of freedom, fictional and newfound and filled with power.

The fetish, in true trickster fashion, takes the counterfeit and runs with it, violating not just simple notions of good and bad but also the dichotomies of written and spoken, made and unmade. "The fight with Covey indicates that to survive slavery Douglass needs the strategies of both trickster and strongman—'the hare and the bear,' as Ralph Ellison once put it."[39] The fetish fights even the bounds of literacy and freedom that are the hallmarks of the slave narrative; Douglass himself suggests how "with all my learning—it was precious little—Sandy was more than a match for me. 'My book learning,' he said, 'had not kept Covey off me.'" Just as Douglass and his *root* were no match for Covey, Sandy and his taproot of knowledge are no match for the book learning that freed Douglass in so many other crucial ways.

In many ways, this freedom is the storying spirit of folk figure and "hope-bringer" High John de Conquer, lyrically described by Hurston: "High John de Conquer came to be a man, and a mighty man at that. But he was not a natural man in the beginning. First off, he was a whisper, a will to hope, a wish to find something worthy of laughter and song. . . . The sign of this man was a laugh, and his singing-symbol was a drumbeat. No parading drum-shout like soldiers out for show. It did not call to the feet of those who were fixed to hear it. *It was an inside thing to live by.*"[40] The "secret laughter" he provided exemplified the spirit of resistance, also found in the fabled High John de Conquer root. Sandy's, and then Douglass's, *root* further embodies the secrecy and invulnerability of this black folk culture, challenging what Albert Murray calls the "folklore of white supremacy"—with its seeming knowledge and "power to deceive"—in a way that furthers the counterfeit, bringing it into the physical, and not just written, realm.[41]

Identifiable and elusive, these survivals of African ritual often found their form in terms of "perforated disks," much like "a dime with a hole in it" or plug nickel, carried or worn by black folks who ascribed to it higher forms of value. The uncovering of such ritual objects, in the course of archaeological digs, say, invokes their history: the objects themselves are a form of recovery and of resistance. But it also indicates how easily such tokens can be overlooked. "Brass pins, buttons and beads, rock crystals, a piece of a crab claw, disks pierced with holes, a brass ring and bell, pieces of glass and bone, and the arms and legs of a small doll":[42] these assemblages are no Joseph Cornell box but rather a ritualistic grouping that attests to the life of the slave; denied the right to assembly or selfhood, slaves use these objects to craft their own story. The fetish is this ritual of power, of belief, of higher value hidden under the hearth of a Maryland house, in the kitchen where no one would look for what was really cooking. It is also the slave's cooking itself.

A key question with the fetish is, who's reading whom? The authority of the fetish, after all, is granted by the reader of the fetish, rather than by its "author": as with Douglass's *root,* you don't have to have made the fetish to relish (or fear) its power. In the case of rootwork, the power may be from nature—not human nature, but something far larger, supernatural. We could say that for black folks, the fetish represents a way of viewing tradition as a site of living power, dependent on being well read for its full meaning. And that this "reading" is not simply literary or even literate, but a matter of folk-faith—of carrying it *on the right side.*

In Alice Walker we may see the power of conjuring and its relation to tradition in a modern context. When searching for Hurston's unmarked grave in an overgrown cemetery, Walker's fear among the weeds is ostensibly about snakes, though we as audience know such an admission hides a deeper fear of never finding her play-aunt and literary ancestor. In fact, Walker is without luck locating Hurston's grave till she "fusses" out loud with Zora: almost immediately she stumbles across the mere indention, a "sunken spot" where Hurston lies. The solution, Walker suggests, is a literal calling out to the ancestors—not in a merely pleasant way, mind you, but one at times a forceful fussing—in order to discover where they rest.

Or, should I say, lie.

WHAT THE . . . ? (THE FETISH)

In thinking of fetish, we must remember how one person's prototype is another's stereotype. For just as with counterfeit, there is another meaning of fetish, which is "negative"—representing, at least, blackness as "other," as something viewed with a mixture of horror and desire. Both exotic and erotic, fetish for many white or nonblack viewers represents a confluence of fears, anxieties, and repressed desires.

This sense of the fetish, of course, has some commonality with Freud's sexualized (and undeniably masculinized) version. As Freud envisioned it, the fetish represented a substitute: it was a stand-in for staving off the male fear of castration, and emerged from the instant the young (male) child realized his mother did not have a penis. As a result, the male child "looks away"—partially in horror—and sees instead an object that would become fixed in memory and desire (hence the prominence of shoe fetishes, or fetishes for the accoutrements of motherhood or fragmented femaleness, such as stockings).

While in the early 1990s the fetish was "feminized" by many critics wanting to expand and explore Freud's male-centered vision of sexuality and identity formation, few have properly or successfully "racialized" it. Unlike Freud's later discussion of fetish, which is most commonly referenced, his earliest discussions of fetish in *Three Essays on the Theory of Sexuality* (1905) not only reveal him as far less dogmatic and judgmental about the fetish—allowing that "a certain degree of fetishism is thus habitually present in normal love"[43]—but also hint at the racialized, "primitive" past of the term:

> What is substituted for the sexual object is some part of the body (such as the foot or hair) which is in general very inappropriate for sexual purposes, or some inanimate object which bears an assignable relation to the person whom it replaces and preferably to that person's sexuality (e.g. a piece of clothing or underlinen). Such substitutes are with some justice

likened to the fetishes in which savages believe that their gods are embodied.[44]

This Africanist meaning of fetish has a long history, well explored in Christopher L. Miller's *Blank Darkness* or by critic Valerie Steele in her *Fetish: Fashion, Sex & Power*. While Steele briefly notes that the fetish has a "dual meaning, denoting a magic charm and also a '*fabrication, an artifact, a labour of appearances and signs*,'"[45] I want to talk about exactly this doubleness—to reconsider fetish not just as African totem but as European fear and fantasy. Somehow, this all adds up to American—which is to say a fabrication dependent on African American labor.

Where the counterfeit provides a means of black acquisition of authority (even as so-called authenticity is called into question), the fetish represents the "real deal": a confrontation with "pure" blackness, as seen by a viewer who is either black or white. While both views encounter a totem of black power, the fetish may yield different results: for the black viewer, like Douglass, this power is one to be used, harnessed, and often seen as an extension of tradition; while for many a white viewer, this is a power not simply feared but desired and ultimately to be harvested, hemmed in, used. For one, the fetish provides, or can provide, a black self; for the other, it often provides a sense of blackness as other.

Both views of fetish operate on a sense of black community. For the black viewer, as we've seen, the fetish can provide a sense of such community, ancestry, and the viewer's closeness to tradition—think of Baldwin, not just listening to Bessie Smith in Beauford Delaney's apartment but *hearing* her. For the white viewer, too often the fetish seems far off yet far too close, not just a sign of community but of an entire dark history that can no longer be denied. "Mumbo-Jumbo will hoo-doo you." "Mistah Kurtz—he dead." Think of the fetish found in LeRoi Jones's (Amiri Baraka) *Black Art,* whose cover featured a white voodoo doll pierced with pins, and whose eponymous poem's opening lines declared: "Poems are bullshit unless they are / trees or lemons piled / on a step." The thingness of the thing—something demanded by modernism and almost as often by the Black Arts movement of the 1960s, usually in opposition to the thingness modernism had made the Negro endure. As one of Valerie Steele's chapter titles tells us, "A fetish is a story masquerading as an object."[46]

The fetish represents then the moment in white cultural development when the onlooker realizes that black power has a penis, a vagina, a sweet sweet jelly roll, and looks away. *Look away, Dixieland.*

Or perhaps more accurately, the fetish, much as in Freud's formulation, offers a moment of simultaneity: except, where for Freud the child (who, it goes without saying, is white as well as male) sees a "female absence," the white viewer of the fetish realizes the culture itself is emasculated, then looks away (and toward "Africa"). In other words, seeing the black mask—as Picasso did with his *Les Demoiselles d'Avignon* (1907)—can result in a potent combination of fear and pleasure, the viewer simultaneously looking away from European (or white American) culture and fixating on the black object of power.

THEN I SAW THE CONGO CREEPING THROUGH THE BLACK,
CUTTING THROUGH THE JUNGLE WITH A GOLDEN TRACK.

This is a fancy way of telling the oldest story in the (European) book: boy sees black icon, boy wants black icon, boy loses whiteness, then gets whiteness back—precisely through acquiring this black icon. The fetish for the white viewer becomes the totem of this process. In Freud's formulation at its most insightful, the fetish object simultaneously dispels the anxiety and represents a failure to conquer it. As parallel, the racialized fetish both dispels the anxiety over blackness and maintains it; the fetish ain't nothing if not ambiguous, both symbol of anxiety and substitute for it.[47] *It don't mean a thing if it ain't got that swing.* The fetish is both a cure for, and an expression of, anxiety over black influence.

The fetish represents what's *left out* of traditional white culture, its black absence—while also holding that absence at bay by incorporating it into paintings, sculpture, prose, and poetry. No wonder fetish and the blackness it represents fuel much of the modernist enterprise.

For now, let's skip any further thinking about the fetish and focus instead on a prime example of it in the history of art: the doubleness of the fetish mirrored in Picasso's *Demoiselles*, "a bridge between modernist and premodernist painting, a primal scene of modern primitivism." Hal Foster describes brilliantly how "the painting presents an encounter in which are inscribed two scenes: the depicted one of the brothel and the projected one of the heralded 1907 visit of Picasso to the collection of tribal artifacts in the Musée d'Ethnographie du Trocadéro. This *double encounter* is tellingly situated: the prostitutes in the bordello, the African masks in the Trocadéro, both disposed for recognition, for use. There is, to be sure, both fear and desire of this other figured here, but is it not desire for mastery and fear of its frustration?"[48]

Recognition, use: these are the very poles of the fetish, and arguably only different takes on the same object. It is indeed a double encounter; one overseer's frightened recognition is another slave's use. While Foster sees *Desmoiselles* as inscribing the primitive onto the woman as Other, representing both "decentering and its defense," he also notes the ways in which Picasso does intuit the tribal masks as weapons.[49] Foster's quote from Picasso himself will help us see what's at stake in the fetish:

> They [the tribal artifacts] were against everything—against un-known threatening spirits. . . . I, too, I am against everything. I, too, believe that everything is unknown, that everything is an enemy! . . . women, children . . . the whole of it! I understood what the Negroes used their sculptures for. . . . All fetishes . . . were weapons. To help people avoid coming under the influence of spirits again, to help them become independent. Spirits, the unconscious . . . they are all the same thing. I understood why I was a painter. All alone in that awful museum with the masks . . . the dusty manikins. *Les Demoiselles d'Avignon* must have been born that day, but not at all because of the forms; because it was my first exorcism painting—yes, absolutely![50]

Certainly not everyone has this reaction, but fetish is a useful way of talking about the ways blackness influences (and makes anxious) certain white forms of vision. Seeing the painting certainly confirms the painting's unique and powerful role as "exorcism," if not Picasso's getting exercised over seeing the tribal and the sexual (and placing both tantalizingly together). Picasso's literal view of the fetish is symbolic and arguably accurate: the fetish is not so much misread as over-read, made raw material by the viewer, moving quickly from awe to "awful" in its current, negative sense. The mingling of inspiration and perspiration found in Picasso's account, the mix of Freudian unconscious and African spirits, meet in the fetish.

But the fetish is also at work earlier, in the framing of African folktales into Joel Chandler Harris's *Uncle Remus,* and later in many of the classics of postmodernism, such as Thom Demijohn's 1968 novel *Black Alice* or *The Tar Baby* written in 1973 by Jerome Charyn. We may contrast this view with Hurston's depiction of the animal tales in *Mules and Men,* where the mules outsmart men, and the black men and women outsmart Massa and each other. One's a counterfeit, the other a kind of *contraband,* taken from black mouths that are then ventriloquized for white pleasure and profit. Ironically, the Uncle Remus tales served as a kind of matrix, as critic Michael North notes, for the private correspondence of Ezra Pound and T. S. Eliot, in which the former was "Uncle Ez," the latter "Old Possum." For them, blacktalk served as "against everything." You can see this, too, in the fiction of Margaret Seltzer, better known as Margaret B. Jones, in her false memoir in which she claimed to be a Native American and white child raised in a black L.A. gang. Just as with Picasso, Old Possum, and Uncle Ez (if without their artistry), for Seltzer the fetish is employed to escape whiteness while simultaneously enforcing it.[51] As Joel Chandler Harris puts it (or should we say, garbles it) in his "Plantation Proverbs": *Youk'n hide de fier, but w'at you gwine do wid de smoke?*

WHAT NOW (QUESTIONS)

Would you rather be misread or unread? Would you rather be a credit or a counterfeit to the race?

These are the questions all too often posed to the black artist, particularly the black writer, for whom struggle may be the primary point—not mere survival or suffering. And just as the fetish can provide strength against the elements and against one's enemies, perhaps one's writing might serve as a fetish in just this way.

But the fetish can also be complicated for its black carrier. Think of James Baldwin, who says it was Bessie Smith (and, it should be said, exile) that spurred him on to finish his first novel, *Go Tell It on the Mountain,* while in Switzerland:

There, in that absolutely alabaster landscape, armed with two
Bessie Smith records and a typewriter, I began to try to recreate
the life that I had first known as a child and from which I had
spent so many years in flight.

It was Bessie Smith, through her tone and her cadence, who
helped me to dig back to the way I myself must have spoken
when I was a pickaninny, and to remember the things I had
heard and seen and felt. I had buried them very deep. I had
never listened to Bessie Smith in America (in the same way
that, for years, I would not touch watermelon), but in Europe
she helped to reconcile me to being a "nigger."[52]

This is a remarkable passage—Bessie Smith reconciles Baldwin both to
his Americanness (the passage is taken from the piece "The Discovery
of What It Means to Be an American") and to blackness, or at least to
being a "nigger." Baldwin suggests that Smith's records and his typewriter are both weapons, or perhaps totems, that "arm" him on his journey. The duality of the records (each a kind of arm, not to mention the
record player's) alongside the typewriter's literary face provides a fascinating, almost sculptural image—something we might imagine in the
constructions of, say, the black visual artist Bettye Saar. For Baldwin,
Bessie's voice is itself a kind of memory and recovery, a fetish that leads
him back across the pond at least symbolically, a middle passage not of
pain but perception.

But we might also recall that Baldwin himself is storying—or at
least contradicting himself. After all, we've already seen how Baldwin,
writing later, includes Bessie Smith as a crucial part of his first artistic awakening in America, spurred on by Beauford Delaney (whom
Baldwin often called his spiritual "father"). While contradictory, all
these versions of listening to Smith—as a weapon he is "armed with"
abroad, as anathema as watermelon or his first exposure to tradition at
home—are true, at least in the sense that they are equally important to
highlight. The difference depends only on Baldwin's need.

Both sides of the story in fact deal with the uses of memory, with
the ways Bessie Smith both terrifies and comforts Baldwin, in the true
manner of the blues; Smith's voice is a figure of power, and of *transport*.
But Baldwin's association of Smith with watermelon—both delicious,

but somehow (well, we know how) made stereotypical and shameful—says something about the difficulty of embracing the fetish, or its plentiful portion of the black tradition.

A critique of embracing the blues is evoked by the Black Arts movement (itself a name of conjure). Amiri Baraka (then LeRoi Jones) details the oppressiveness of the past—much the same one as finally accepted by Baldwin through Bessie Smith, whether downtown or abroad—in his play *Dutchman*. In this Obie Award–winning drama, the character of Clay launches into a rebellious monologue, citing Bessie Smith's blues in rebuffing his white companion's advances:

> Old bald-headed four-eyed ofays popping their fingers . . . and don't know yet what they're doing. They say, "I love Bessie Smith." And don't even understand that Bessie Smith is saying, "Kiss my ass, kiss my black unruly ass." Before love, suffering, desire, anything you can explain, she's saying, and very plainly, "Kiss my black ass." And if you don't know that, it's you that's doing the kissing.
>
> Charlie Parker? Charlie Parker. All the hip white boys scream for Bird. And Bird saying, "Up your ass, feeble-minded ofay! Up your ass." And they sit there talking about the tortured genius of Charlie Parker. Bird would've played not a note of music if he just walked up to East Sixty-seventh Street and killed the first ten white people he saw. Not a note! And I'm the great would-be poet. Yes. That's right! Poet. Some kind of bastard literature . . . all it needs is a simple knife thrust.[53]

For Clay, the blues are not a cure for repression but a symptom of it. (We might as well call it a fetish and be done with it.) What some would say is clearly coded in Smith and Parker, Clay sees as merely hiding—less playing possum than acting chicken.

Clay's identification of Bessie's blues and Parker's bop as an outlet for murder, the result not just of oppression but suppression; Baldwin's association of Bessie with watermelon; the evocation of a mere "bastard literature": these wrestlings are exactly the black experience of tradition that can be most difficult to reconcile. But also the most necessary—for it is not so much the tradition that is furtive, or so coded as to be unspoken, as our relation to it.

In other words, is soul food a remedy for what ails you, a coming home, if you grew up with it as I did? Or, if it is all too familiar, might you want to take leave of it entirely? Is nostalgia a productive part of memory, or the exile's condition, fitting nostalgia's original meaning of "homesickness"?

Perhaps then the fetish of memory troubles us all?

"Our *relation* to it" is right: the phrase "bastard literature" is one that rings across the years—if not in phrasing then in fear—both before and after *Dutchman*'s off-Broadway debut. Clay's muttering echoes a simplified version of Baraka's own critique of the tradition in "Myth of a 'Negro Literature'" (1962), which he later disavowed; it is tempting to read Clay as Baraka's own thinly veiled self, the Poet set loose, at least in this monologue. This, however, is a misreading as flawed as Baraka's apparent unreading: the long-held, if wrongheaded, belief that there is no black tradition is one no amount of evidence to the contrary can contravene. It is the chauvinist's myopia and mantra: *If I don't know it, it must not exist.*

But Baraka himself might be saying something less about the self or the tradition than about the white literature around it. You could say that Baraka is calling out so-called whiteness as "some kind of bastard literature," saying "all it needs is a simple knife thrust" to achieve freedom. The violence in Baraka is a substitute for the fetish as a totem, but doesn't render the fetish any less important. Any journey past "Kiss my ass" requires it.

Still, Clay's invoking "bastard literature" does echo the notion of illegitimacy that figures in the tradition—while mirroring Baldwin's writing of his own personal "illegitimacy," not as a sign of his lack of belonging but rather as a metaphor for exactly "love, suffering, desire, anything you can explain." Baldwin's finding a father in Delaney mirrors and reconfigures his own father—whom later he would learn was actually his stepfather, and whose self-hate and bitterness we are led to believe literally drove the man mad. Such a symbolic set of mirrors is shattered on the day of his father's funeral, ironically Baldwin's nineteenth birthday and the day after the Harlem Riot of 1943. His re-markable essay "Notes of a Native Son" evokes that day this way:

> On the twenty-ninth of July, in 1943, my father died. On the
> same day, a few hours later, his last child was born. Over a
> month before this, while all our energies were concentrated
> in waiting for these events, there had been, in Detroit, one of
> the bloodiest race riots of the century. A few hours after my
> father's funeral, while he lay in state in the undertaker's chapel,
> a race riot broke out in Harlem. On the morning of the third of
> August, we drove my father to the graveyard through a wilder-
> ness of smashed plate glass.[54]

This "wilderness" Baldwin reads as apocalyptic, in evocation of biblical and black tradition: "It seemed to me that God himself had devised, to mark my father's end, the most sustained and brutally dissonant of codas." Such a coda is the constant threat to the tradition, to one's right-ful inheritance, not despite, but precisely because of, claims of illegiti-macy. It is our duty, within this wilderness, to recognize and reconcile beauty and ugly and belonging, to seek the very being of blackness.

Baldwin himself does so, even in his essay's title, which riffs off Richard Wright's own *Native Son*. But between that very complex "na-tiveness" and "son" there's not irony, or paradox, so much as a reifica-tion of belonging to a tradition, one both fathered and inherited. Just because belonging is contested, or rioted over, does not mean it is any less vital. Being a "native son" or Hurston's "lost niece" is not unlike ex-periencing double consciousness, itself echoed in the remarkable end-ing to Baldwin's essay:

> It began to seem that one would have to hold in the mind
> forever two ideas which seemed to be in opposition. The first
> idea was acceptance, the acceptance, totally without rancor, of
> life as it is, and men as they are: in the light of this idea, it goes
> without saying that injustice is a commonplace. But this did not
> mean that one could be complacent, for the second idea was of
> equal power: that one must never in one's own life, accept those
> injustices as commonplace but must fight them with all one's

strength. This fight begins, however, in the heart and it now had been laid to my charge to keep my own heart free of hatred and despair. This intimation made my heart heavy and, now that my father was irrecoverable, I wished that he had been beside me so that I could have searched his face for the answers which only the future would give me now.[55]

Such a future depends on a relation to the past—one that is not static but fluid and free. The future, then, is the code the black art of escape hopes to crack.

These cracks, the imperceptible ruptures, come from many sources—and rarely from a knife in the gut. Rather, as with Baldwin's father's death, Baldwin's own death would inspire the future: Baldwin's funeral was the starting point of the Dark Room Collective, the Boston-based black writers group founded after the funeral. Several soon-to-be founders made a pilgrimage to the funeral, declaring afterward that they themselves would make sure the future would bring no writers they would not know, or seek, and find. The collective was born, a group I was lucky enough to join a few years later: we only wished that Baldwin was beside us, but in a way, through his writing and his vision, he was and still is.

WHY FOR? (INNOVATION)

To reframe: we might think of tradition not just as inheritance but as devotion—one measured by fetish as well as by other religion—and even invention. Tradition is not what you inherit, but what you seek, and then seek to keep.

Such invention can be troubling. Nor can it be measured by the dutiful trotting out of "black firsts" during Black History Month. (See, even I am bowing to tradition, calling it what it was called in my youth, and not the awkward "African American Identity Roundup" or whatever we call it these days. Perhaps we should return to Carter G. Woodson's "Negro History Week" and start all over again.) Yet invention is as crucial as it is elusive: we may not point to its origin so easily.

Tradition is what we take, but also what we make of it. That is the fifth and final lesson.

Perhaps we should go further and refer to the counterfeit not as a tradition, which may imply a fundamentally conservative inheritance, but as an *innovation*. The counterfeit, the innovation of storying, then, is a subset of both the ever-growing black tradition and a seemingly shrinking American one, while also a subversion of those traditions. With such fascinating artistic "parents" as Delaney and Anderson, Smith and Waters, how could it not be—either for Baldwin or the rest of us?

Such a storying "innovation" also calls into question our very notion of progress, central to modernity and the postindustrial age—instead, it focuses on *process*. As might be expected, storying in this way is an ever-shifting definition, like jazz, or even definitions of race, or America, with improvisation its way and aim.

Here's a handy-dandy diagram to illustrate what I mean:

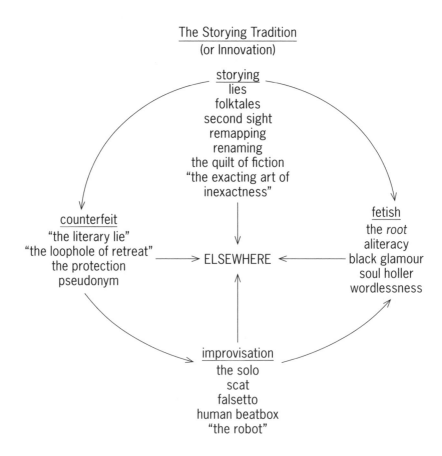

The Storying Tradition
(or Innovation)

storying
lies
folktales
second sight
remapping
renaming
the quilt of fiction
"the exacting art of
inexactness"

counterfeit
"the literary lie"
"the loophole of retreat"
the protection
pseudonym

ELSEWHERE

fetish
the *root*
aliteracy
black glamour
soul holler
wordlessness

improvisation
the solo
scat
falsetto
human beatbox
"the robot"

While I've conceptualized this as essentially a circle, with most roads leading to Elsewhere, we might also think this as a kind of crossroads, with Elsewhere a choice facing the tradition. And us.

However we conceive of it, Elsewhere is central to the African American tradition. Conjured again and again in the spirituals, simultaneously ethereal and earthbound, Canaan and Canada, heaven and Harriet Tubman heading north, Elsewhere is the goal of going—framed in the remapping of what's here. A cosmology that is simultaneously exterior and internal, and what's more, eternally hopeful, however hidden.

It may even be hidden from me: only later, after I completed this circle, did I observe my diagram's resemblance to those perforated disks used in African and African American religious tradition. "In the Kongo religion," writes art historian Robert Farris Thompson, "the shape of the soul is round, like a miniature sun. Parents fashioned a small round disk from wood or a seed and tied it around the neck or waist or ankle of a child as a prayer to 'keep the circle of the child complete.'"[56]

As good a definition of tradition as any.

Alice Walker's *In Search of Our Mothers' Gardens* makes further sense of Elsewhere and of invention—both of which are contained in her very title, if not mentioned explicitly in her actual book. "It has been said that someone asked Toni Morrison why she writes the kind of books she writes," Walker says, "and that she replied: Because they are the kind of books I want to read." Later on, in her essay "Saving the Life That Is Your Own," Walker revises this notion: "To take Toni Morrison's statement further, if that is possible, in my own work I write not only what I want to read—understanding fully and indelibly that if I don't do it no one else is so vitally interested, or capable of doing it to my satisfaction—I write all the things *I should have been able to read*."[57]

For Walker this means writing a kind of ancestry of herself, "Consulting, as belatedly discovered models, those writers—most of whom, not surprisingly, are women—who understood that their experience as ordinary human beings was also valuable, and in danger of being misrepresented, distorted, or lost." Such invention, even of the past, accompanies our search for it; it also requires serving double duty, both as a writer and of being your own model of one. We raise ourselves up as we raise others by our praise. "It is, in the end, the saving of lives that we writers are about." Such a life might be invented as much as lived, improvised as much as dictated, filled with struggle, rather than suffering—seeking among the weeds to find *what might be*. I am telling you this to spare you the struggle, and to prepare you for it when it comes at you anyway.

The true test of fiction is its usefulness.

WHAT WILL BE (USEFULNESS)

Ultimately, storying is the space such useful fiction occupies in both our lives and our writing. When one's life is on the line, invention may demand a lie as a lifeline. Forging free papers to get off the plantation or get out of an occupied Europe is far more serious, needless to say, than forging or plagiarizing a dissertation, or simply pretending to be something one is not. This is not homework we are talking about; we are forging for our lives.

This is one notion of usefulness—writing as survival. But there's a broader notion that I take from philosopher Emanuel Swedenborg, in which usefulness is our proper response to the very beauty of the universe, and of creation itself. (This from an eighteenth-century European thinker whose visions included and even elevated Africans, saying "of non-Christians, the Africans are especially valued in heaven." He elsewhere notes that Africans "are more interiorly rational," possessing "an interior sight"—rather than an inferior one.)[58] Creation might be the impetus of Swedenborgian usefulness;[59] but usefulness is also, I argue here, creation's result.

Fiction protects and preserves many truths. But we are scared of fiction. Or at least confused by it. We—and here I mean Americans in general—confuse public personae with people, thinking we can relate to those renamed (and one-named) stars, from 50 Cent to Ice Cube to even Queen Latifah, all of whose names have been conflated with on-screen images.

Let's face it, fiction comprises a continuum (or at least a dialectic) rather than a dichotomy with "fact." I'd even argue that the opposite of "fiction"—if such a search for opposites is required—is not fact, or even nonfiction; it certainly is not "truth." Rather, we should be prepared to see the truth *in* fiction and the fiction in truth, not to mention the fiction in what we have already "authenticated" as nonfiction. Not only are these categories not "natural" to writing, but they are often assigned and entrenched after the fact, by bookstores and the very act of consumption. They are, in short, by-products of our literacy and our literary conventions.

These "either-or" categories of fiction and non- do not exist in poetry, my first home—no one asks if "Prufrock" is real, after all, or whether the women actually talked of Michelangelo. We recognize instead its truth, however slant.

I must say I am suspicious of those concordances, or certain kinds of literary biographies, that find correlations between every character in, say, Joyce's writing with someone in the author's life, or that insist in overlaying Faulkner's fictional landscape with a real, Southern one. Such a mistaking of fiction's borders is particularly dangerous for the black writer whose remapping of American landscape is such a crucial part of the storied and storying tradition we have inherited—a tradition that's proved far more reliable than those promised forty acres and a mule.

Is it better to be misread, or unread?

If Roland Barthes's famous "Death of the Author" once promised to take care of this assumption by declaring that the author is no longer there, his or her intentions irrelevant, it too has been overread, and of course misread. (Though these days it is perhaps mostly unread.) In denying the author's intent, it was the critic—that convention of someone interpreting for the public what a text says—not necessarily the author whom Barthes was trying to eliminate. He wanted to render the Reader powerful, uppercase, giving us a vernacular text in contrast to the critic's high-priest high jinks. Not to mention the critic's frequent role in categorizing and thereby separating fact and fiction.

Nowhere is this more harmful than in black autobiography. While at times a somewhat beleaguered genre in American literature, autobiography has remained a go-to form for African American writers through the years. Autobiography informs much of our best literature, as many have noted—not only everything from slave narratives, Booker T. Washington's *Up from Slavery*, *Malcolm X* as life and autobiography, but also fictions modeled on the form, from *Autobiography of an Ex-Coloured Man* and *The Bluest Eye,* to *The Autobiography of Miss Jane Pittman* and *Invisible Man.*

Even "actual" autobiographies, however, feature a certain element of fiction. Should it matter that Douglass's owner was not really named Freeland? Or that *Roots* may not have been entirely "factual"? Fact is, could any black ancestral research *not* include a sense of fiction in a country where black births were rarely recorded? Or, more to the point, could we as black people be satisfied with a history that was simply factual, devoid of the magic and mystery (and yes, the fact) of religion, superstition, family legends, *the root,* and storying?

SAY WHO (THE TROOF)

We don't need proof that we exist and can write and *are* literature; we need "troof," a funky, vernacular "truth" that doesn't answer to white-based or any other preconceptions of black reality. What that white view once translated into was the overwhelming sense of the invalidity of black life, if not a downright disbelief in black humanity—an understandable desire to correct this Big Lie has often resulted only in authentication, whether the need for the "social realism" of a Richard Wright in *Native Son* or gangsta rap of *Straight Outta Compton.* And despite its self-contained claims for strictly "black art by, about, and *for* black folks," a central goal of Black Nationalism and Black Arts has been to shock folks awake to black reality—especially white folks. (Such shock still occurs, whether in horrorcore or gangsta rap.) We can even say that too often earlier movements have spent too much time focusing on white limits and not on black levels of meaning.

This is true of even Wright himself, who represented his writing in ways it actually wasn't. Following in that African American tradition of "keeping it real," Wright, you could say, authenticated himself: in his now classic essay "How Bigger Was Born" (1940), Wright indicates the ways in which Bigger Thomas, the protagonist of *Native Son,* while fictional, is in fact based on real models. In an ironic twist on Walker's idea of Morrison having to provide her own model of a writer—birthing herself, as it were—these models of Bigger spawned a whole litter: "The birth of Bigger Thomas goes back to my childhood, and there was not just one Bigger, but many of them, more than I could count and more than you suspect." While Wright's essay constitutes a fascinating enumeration of black rage and accommodation—not to mention an unacknowledged anxiety over multiple paternity—it is strange to me the way it is now effectively a permanent part of *Native Son,* appearing today as a literal introduction for anyone setting about reading the novel itself. (This authentication occurred early on, as I have a later edition from 1940—the same year as the first—in which "How Bigger" already appears as prefatory matter.) Apart from characterizing blues, jazz, and swing as "naïve and mundane forms," Wright's denial of not just folk remedies, but the art of fiction itself, proves troubling.

Wright's emphasis, it would seem, is less on his own imagination than on Bigger's factual basis:

> In a fundamental sense, an imaginative novel represents the merging of two extremes; it is an intensely intimate expression on the part of a consciousness couched in terms of the most objective and commonly known events. It is at once something private and public by its very nature and texture. Confounding the author who is trying to lay his cards on the table is the dogging knowledge that his imagination is a kind of community medium of exchange: what he has read, felt, thought, seen, and remembered is translated into extensions as impersonal as a worn dollar bill.
>
> The more closely the author thinks of why he wrote, the more he comes to regard his imagination as a kind of self-generating cement which glued his facts together, and his emotions as a kind of dark and obscure designer of those facts. Always there is something that is just beyond the tip of the tongue that could explain it all.[60]

While Wright admits to the mystery "just beyond the tip of the tongue," he chooses mainly to focus on the conscious choices he made, the "facts" he glued together. For Wright, "his imagination is a kind of community medium of exchange . . . translated into extensions as impersonal as a worn dollar bill."

Why? Why is it this wearying "worn dollar bill," whose value still accrues but surely less so? Why this deficit of tongue, rather than speaking in many tongues all at once? In such a conception the imagination is beholden to the facts it glues together, or to speech as a form of explanation. And so the artist in Wright, while in some interesting sense a collagist, is lost in his own darkness (not to say blackness), which, like the imagination, is but "cement." Sturdy it may be; flexible it most certainly is not.

It is tempting to claim, as Ralph Ellison does, that the issue with *Native Son* is that "Richard Wright could imagine Bigger Thomas but Bigger Thomas could not imagine Richard Wright"—but that is too easy. The larger problem is the value Wright places (or doesn't place) on imagination, at least "consciously." For him it is just a worn bill, an exchange that holds not so much promise as potential danger—after all, the writer "who is trying to lay his cards on the table" is inevitably dogged by community, as well as the unknown. Wright has stacked the deck against the imagination, as it were, and declared any of the spoils it may win merely worn.

Here's a tip: like many writers, Wright values here what may actually be the most overdetermined and least interesting aspect of his work. We need not follow. Instead of the "birth" of Bigger, might we see the true moment of artistic conception as when a young Wright forges, in counterfeit style, a note from a white man in order to check out books from a segregated library? For here, wearing the mask of his own assumed illiteracy, Wright forges his own freedom, garnering access to further literacy. His imagination, his act of counterfeiting, wins Wright not just a library of books but the boundlessness of imagination—and leads to a freedom beyond that found in all the Bigger Thomases he has known, a storying sense he might better invoke to explain himself and his art. Storying is not just a form of escape but of rescue.

Richard Wright's concept of the imagination as "cement" mirrors his view of the South as a whole, which he regularly refers to as "Dixie." By doing so, "Dixie" remains all the more received, an "environment," as he puts it, rather than a place. Wright is almost as much a victim of the *idea* of the South—and note I say *almost*—as he is victim to the degradations of Dixie. The imagination as I conceive it is, and surely always was, far more freeing, even for Wright himself, than the cement he suggests it as being.

We can look to Wright's own writing in his last years, namely, his haiku, as further proof of the power of storying. Wright wrote thousands of poems in the form; it was even, as he was writing it, posthumous work seemingly meant to be read only after his passing. This wasn't mere distraction but a real craft he worked in almost religiously—it exists not just as counterfeit but as a fetish to stave off impending death. His daughter writes of the endeavor: "I believe his haiku were self-developed antidotes against illness, and that breaking down words into syllables matched the shortness of his breath, especially on the bad days when his inability to sit up at the typewriter restricted the very breadth of writing."[61]

Apart from his dying before it saw print, why did Wright leave this vast work out of his living canon? Could he not imagine his haiku as part of his full writing life, as the public part of the private dichotomy he discusses in "How Bigger Was Born"? As part of the breadth of his writing? As his *blues*print rather than his restrictive "Blueprint for Negro Writing," which insisted on the black writer's social responsibility? Julia Wright's fine introduction also discusses her father's increased monitoring by U.S. intelligence agencies during this time; might his haiku be black codes, either to or from a self under surveillance? In three lines much like the blues, filled with hesitations, Wright's haiku are certainly both forms of silence and disobedient of it: "They lie somewhere in that transitional twilight area between the loss for words and the few charmed syllables that can heal the loss."[62]

The truth is, Bigger himself sang, shouted, loved, and sometimes wrote poetry; it is this that Wright did not allow for—not necessarily in his best-known novel, which is its own world and form—but in his idea of his own writing. Revelation is one of storying's key functions.

Don't get me wrong—both the social realism of Wright and the Black Arts and Aesthetic movement that followed it deserve their dap; certainly they had a profound effect on black culture and writing, not to mention the fact that they opened the doors for other black writers, including me. But the aesthetic that looks only to truth and finds it in race denies race's many falsehoods as well as our culture's many strengths; and, as such, may not help us read Morrison or Baldwin or Hurston or Walker or Baraka, or even Wright or any other of the writers who have been ennobling forces here, in their unauthorized, iconoclastic invention of a black self.

Neither does social realism nor the Black Aesthetic provide the most useful tool for analyzing the full pleasures of a book like *Autobiography of an Ex-Coloured Man,* a fiction masquerading as an autobiography so effectively that long after its once anonymous author has been revealed to be James Weldon Johnson, I still know people and students who think of it as "true." Of course the book *is* "true," even if it is not fact—that Johnson did not actually pass for white does not eliminate the "troof" of the text's observations and fictions. The book is the ultimate passing subject.

People—and I would add, particularly Americans—confuse the personal, which is necessary in fiction and poetry of any quality, with the strictly autobiographical. Perhaps it is the limit we put on that word "personal," which for me connotes not just actual, factual events, but also a believable persona, someone we feel comfortable with (or perhaps reliably disturbed by), something we believe. Thus, we can read Baldwin's majestic novel *Giovanni's Room* as personal, as well as psychological, while not worrying overmuch about the fact that Baldwin was not, in fact, a blond white man.

Yet Baldwin's novel works because he is nonetheless inside his character, as well as gay culture and desire; a feat less of identification than of imagination, his writing is neither appropriation nor contraband. Rather, he achieves his counterfeit by fictionalizing in order to get at a "troof" that is beyond what we might consider "realism," whether social, political, or, ultimately, black. We may well remember Baldwin's own responses to social realism in his groundbreaking *Notes of a Native Son.*

I'm not saying that race does not matter, or that it does not provide a critical reality in Baldwin's writing; nor am I simply saying people should pretend to be what they are not. But people should stop trying to be "good" or "bad"—that goes for hair too—or at least stop denying the poses involved in either. The only thing black folks should require to be good or bad is the quality of their art—not whether some image is "positive" or "negative," kinky or straight, explicit or implicit. This not only goes for our literature but also our lives.

Otherwise, we get caught not just in the shallowness of easy evaluation, of what's good or bad, but also in reflexive acceptance and simple, often merely cosmetic solutions. I just don't think writing (and certainly not television) is the realm for upholding "reality" as we perceive it, but rather a place to confront reality, and even fictionalize it, in the process remaking it in our image—not necessarily as we live, but as we would like to. Things we *should have been able to read.* For the thing the African American writer might be most interested in, and might ultimately be confronting most often, is the American Dream.

Black authors, and others of course, for years have described the downsides of the dream, its contradictions and far worse its presence as promise unfulfilled—not to mention the nightmare it can become. *Native Son, Autobiography of an Ex-Coloured Man, Montage of a Dream Deferred,* Gwendolyn Brooks's *In the Mecca,* Coltrane's "Alabama," Nicolás Guillén's *Grand Zoo,* James Brown's "Payback": all show us ways in which the dream may be deferred.

But all these, we should note, reveal this through fiction, through performance, through storying—the very stuff of dream and art. And folklore: "Black folklore has a dream form, and it should be deciphered by the same means used to decipher dreams, that is, by symbols," writer Cecil Brown says. "Symbols in dreams are displacement, condensation, and distortion. Indeed, black narrative folklore is a 'dream plot.'"[63] We story, therefore we be.

TAKE IT FROM ME (SOMEDAY)

It would seem the very denial of dreaming that society seems to impose on black folks, while it hasn't made us dream less, does seem to punish us for what dreams we do have.

To wit, a story: a few years ago, before the Great Recession made such things rarer, I was fortunate enough to be sent on an extended book tour for my fourth book. In an interview a well-meaning reporter asked me to recite my résumé in order: Harvard, Stanford, Brown, who my parents were, blasé, blasé. Besides being boring, the line of questioning and its necessarily factual yet soulless answers led him to predictably assume that I'd grown up privileged. I can only assume he didn't recall that the goal of an education is to go where you can find out the most.

Mine is not any special pleading—this instead is a small complaint about the continual explanation of the ways in which my parents suffered and struggled and achieved and survived. I thought I'd write my first book, *Most Way Home*, about our rural Louisiana roots—how I carried them *on my right side*—and be done with it. But interviewers read less than other folks, so a book is of little aid—though it has long been my feeling that books and art can tell us more about folks than facts might.

Autobiography is almost always speculative and authenticity a trap door into further and further tests no one can pass. But here are the facts: my folks grew up so poor that, in the words of Redd Foxx, there were twenty *o*'s between the *p* and the *r*. They were so po' they couldn't afford the last *o* and *r*. Rural life in the segregated South was no picnic, I had to remind my interlocutor. *You must be out your cotton-pickin' mind,* I wanted to say—but he'd never picked cotton like my folks did.

If he had, he'd have known that doing so makes you never want to again.

In fact, doing so might make you want to dream of Elsewhere. This is the "dream" that Dr. King spoke about: not an assimilationist, easily invoked dream that since King's assassination has at times been diluted into a comforting, often unrecognizable fiction; but instead, in its more complex readings and proper context, proves a stand-in for the "future," the ultimate fictional place. For if we cannot imagine being there, free at last, then how are we to actually get there? And how will we recognize it when we do?

This dream is not, however, a denial of the possibilities and constraints of the present, or the pleasures and pain of the past. We have done that for too long—denying the blues, impatient with the spirituals, relinquishing our claim to our own culture.

If we found, as my grandparents and parents did, the scales weighted against us at counting time, we also knew we grew the crops ourselves, literally dining at our dinner table every single day on our own strength, innovation, and pluck. Around such a table we were less concerned with "the Man" than with belonging, and with becoming a man or a woman.

Such a rural, all-black context—where all you can see is the land you or your neighbor or your kin own—or that you rightly claimed once, either through sweat equity or actual money—provides an experience familiar to many African American families. In such a space, there is a stability, humor, and scale of being not warped by the outside world; if everybody you know is poor, more or less, you don't really know how poor you yourself are—and remain all the richer for it.

This is not a call for isolationism nor a return to some mythic purity—only to say that, as my family in Louisiana did, having roots in an American soil with a French tongue for two centuries prevents any number of quick assumptions as to how blackness looks, tastes, or talks. It is instead a breadth of being, a fullness that is part and parcel of freedom that we farmed and would not sell for anything. It is ourselves we knew as renewable, sustainable, and not just black, but evergreen.

While Ralph Ellison's question "What Would America Be Like Without Blacks?" is a crucial one, a more pressing question to me may be: "What Are Black Folks Like When No One Else Is Looking?" In those moments, which are many, we might feel like our Zora, having grown up in an all-black town—feeling both colored and not, a Zora both "everybody's" and "cosmic." A black cosmos. Most of the universe is made up of dark matter.

I don't mean to taxonomize but to rhapsodize. Take it from me— *mean mean mean to be free.*

RAN AWAY, Glenn, a black male, 5'8", very short hair cut, nearly completely shaved, stocky build, 155-165 lbs., medium complexion (not "light skinned," not "dark skinned," slightly orange). Wearing faded blue jeans, short sleeve button-down 50's style shirt, nice glasses (small, oval shaped), no socks. Very articulate, seemingly well-educated, does not look at you straight in the eye when talking to you. He's socially very adept, yet, paradoxically, he's somewhat of a loner.

17/45   Glenn Ligon '93

Chorus One: Steal Away
Slavery and Its Discontents _ _ _ _ _ _ _ _ _ _ _ _ _ _ _ _ _ _

It is difficult being a problem. Sho'nuff. To paraphrase comedian Bert Williams, "There's nothing wrong with being black, but it sure is inconvenient." This from a man who could only perform in blackface, darkening his light skin for the crowd to accept—and accept they did, making Williams the first black performer in the Ziegfeld Follies. Yet, even as he was making more money than most folks, black or white, he had to come in the back way. No wonder, his terrific definition of the difference between tragedy and comedy: "One of the funniest sights in the world is a man whose hat has been knocked in or ruined by being blown off—provided, of course, it be the other fellow's hat!"[1] Williams himself has come to embody both sides of this dilemma, or tragicomic divide, as in W. C. Fields's reported description of him: "The funniest man I ever saw, and the saddest man I ever knew."

Contradictions of race (and success) run throughout American life and, not coincidentally, African American thought. Such contradictions inform W. E. B. Du Bois's description of "double consciousness"—of life "behind the veil"—in his groundbreaking *Souls of Black Folk* (1903). Du Bois begins his study with a discussion of "the other world"—a phrase he uses as a shorthand for the white world, making *it* strange rather than him the stranger. As a result, he is speaking within the veil when he asks how whites at all costs avoid the question too often posed to black folks: "How does it feel to be a problem?" And when Du Bois further declared "the problem of the Twentieth Century is the problem of the color-line,"[2] more prophetic lines have not been written.

Yet we also have Zora Neale Hurston's liberating declaration that she doesn't feel like a problem: "But I am not tragically colored. There is no great sorrow dammed up in my soul, nor lurking behind my eyes.

I do not mind at all. . . . No, I do not weep at the world—I am too busy sharpening my oyster knife."[3] Not even Du Bois, in describing the perils of the veil, thinks of "double consciousness" merely as a hindrance:

> After the Egyptian and Indian, the Greek and Roman, the
> Teuton and Mongolian, the Negro is a sort of seventh son,
> born with a veil, and gifted with second-sight in this American
> world,—a world which yields him no true self-consciousness,
> but only lets him see himself through the revelation of the other
> world. It is a peculiar sensation, this double-consciousness, this
> sense of always looking at one's self through the eyes of others,
> of measuring one's soul by the tape of a world that looks on in
> amused contempt and pity. One ever feels his two-ness,—an
> American, a Negro; two souls, two thoughts, two unreconciled
> strivings; two warring ideals in one dark body, whose dogged
> strength alone keeps it from being torn asunder.[4]

The second sight such a veil affords can be just as powerful as the forces that tear it apart. But we need not believe in the folk power of the caul to understand that, in cultures where the veil exists, while the veil is to outsiders a curtain—or a divide, or an oppressive force—to those wearing the veil, "behind" is a vantage point that may protect or mask emotion, that may only heighten the performance the curtain covers.

This became all the more poignant to me after my father died. At his funeral my father's close, "double cousin," Leo Paul—and fellow namesake after a shared ancestor, Paul—revealed, or unveiled, that my father always had second sight and had told this cousin before he died he had seen something too terrible to name. What function does pain perform, does testimony?

It is performance Hurston celebrates, denying pain: "Sometimes, I feel discriminated against, but it does not make me angry. It merely astonishes me. How *can* any deny themselves the pleasure of my company? It's beyond me."[5] The fact of pleasure almost eclipsing pain may be a good definition of the blues; but in the era of slavery we must also consider the pain, the "sunder," not just the Sunday prayer. We must remember that in calling the spirituals "the sorrow songs," Du Bois, like Frederick Douglass before him, provides a corrective to the "happy darky" stereotype of the plantation slave. Even in the face of despair, however, the sorrow songs contain a transforming hope in the mere act of creating art out of slavery; in offering alternative, subversive readings of the Bible; and in the lyrics of the songs themselves. *I've got a home in dat Rock, don't you see?*

Hurston in turn disliked the term "sorrow songs," rejecting it as too limiting: "The idea that the whole body of spirituals are 'sorrow songs' is ridiculous. They cover a wide range of subjects from a peeve at gossipers to Death and Judgment."[6] One of my favorites, "Ezekiel Saw the Wheel"—especially in the version recorded by the Fisk Jubilee singers—reveals exactly this mix within the song itself, alternating between the verses and the chorus. Such variety of topics is mirrored in the very variety of these responses to the songs. Yet Douglass and Du Bois, Hurston and Langston Hughes all take the songs seriously; all tell us how to read the spirituals as the subversive, subtle, and ultimately coded forms they are.

The spaces between performance and pain, between blackness as a problem and as possibility, illuminate the *storying* tradition. Giving slavery a shape and freedom a form, slave narratives still are read as faithful documents, which of course they are, yet too often at the expense of their artfulness. In failing to recognize their potential, or to focus on their "double consciousness" or white authentication, is to ignore what Du Bois himself calls, mere moments after double consciousness, the "double-aimed struggle of the black artisan."[7] Such double-aimed struggle is the counterfeit's claim.

The gift may also be a curse, but second sight is one of the qualities necessary for being a black artist in America, and, I would argue, critical in our reading of the culture all around us. It is important for us not just to lift the veil, or look behind the curtain, but also to embrace the powerful notion of vision and the vantage the caul provides—otherwise we are left with art as mere epitaph, or sorrow song, rather than as a way of finding and fighting and freeing ourselves.

MARK OF CAIN

Storying describes the way in which black writers have forged their own traditions, their own identities, even their own freedom. Whether in the free passes "illiterate" slaves would write to allow them to travel, or the garments supposedly male or female slaves would don to change their gender and buy them time to escape, the counterfeit tradition originates in slavery as a form of written—or rewritten, or re-visionary—resistance.

In thinking of Phillis Wheatley, the originator of black letters in the United States (though, as is fitting in our problematizing of the idea of originality, *not* the first published black poet in the Americas; that distinction goes to Lucy Terry and Wheatley's contemporary Jupiter Hammon), many past critics have done two quite opposite things. Most emphasize her relation to slavery—usually seeing her as submissive, as J. Saunders Redding does in *To Make a Poet Black* (1939), viewing her as insufficiently critical of slavery. (Ironically, later poets and prose writers are seen by Redding as too propagandistic, in a "damned if you do, damned if you don't" proposition, a double standard far worse than double consciousness.) In contrast, Robert Hayden in *Kaleidoscope* (1967) critiques her as a mockingbird of sorts, less an artist than a copyist; in this set of thinking, Wheatley is damned for being merely imitative. Such an accusation has often been made of black folks—painted as being mere copyists of white culture, mimics who are not inventive or "too white" in their aesthetic (a charge Hayden himself, ironically, would fall prey to).

Along these very lines, in the 2002 Jefferson Lecture in the Humanities, Henry Louis Gates lays out the bounds of Wheatley's place in our imagination: too white for some, too black for others. But *The Trials of Phillis Wheatley* goes one further: in a troubling, if tongue-in-cheek turn, Gates calls Thomas Jefferson—who famously dismissed Wheatley's talent outright—the "midwife" of black literature. In overemphasizing the "distinguished men" who judged her work and praising Jefferson (at Jefferson's namesake lecture no less), Gates inadvertently points out the need for Wheatley to be rescued from our own agendas and simply to be *read*. She delivers her own self.

Critic and scholar Frances Foster has written wonderfully on the ways in which Wheatley was very involved in rewriting the figures of eighteenth-century verse for her own terms.[8] I too hear a rich ambiguity in Wheatley's work, even in her oft-quoted lyric about being brought from Africa to America: rather than thanking her captors for her enslavement ("'Twas mercy brought me from my *Pagan* land"), the poem ends with what could be thought to be an admonishment to those who claim purity and wrongly judge her as "black as Cain":

> Some view our sable race with scornful eye,
> "Their colour is a diabolic dye."
> Remember, *Christians, Negros,* black as *Cain,*
> May be refin'd, and join th' angelic train.[9]

Am I wrong to hear, in the italics found in the original printed text, not so much a "chain of being"—a hierarchy among Christians, Negros, and Cain, in that order—as a kind of "equality" among all three? In her final couplet, Wheatley isn't merely claiming that Negroes can be refined; she is also saying that Christians *are* Negroes, and Negroes Christians, yoking them together in a universal notion of sin, of shared origin. (In this, she differs from say, Robert Lowell, Wheatley's fellow Bostonian, who some two hundred years later in poems such as "A Mad Negro Soldier Confined at Munich" takes Negroes and makes them not so much Christians as merely signs of sin, even if it is his own.)[10] Wheatley is also saying that Christians, "black as Cain"—a biblical figure after all—*sho cain't* claim to be beyond sin themselves, a fact witnessed in Wheatley's being a slave in the first place, and in her very name: her last being her putative master's; her first, "Christian," name bearing the name of the slave ship that brought her to America.

The notion of the author as master is a familiar one, linking as it does in Western culture *author, father, master*—and even the Lord. I was recently at a wedding where the prayer, not atypically, referred to an Almighty by a number of names, including "Author" of our lives. Still, we need not rely on Sandra Gilbert and Susan Gubar's brilliant *Madwoman in the Attic* (1979) to see the way a male-based "master" can limit possibilities for female authorship—it should be said the ways in which the concept of author as "master" may have proved (and still proves) not only impossible for African American authors of any gender but also distasteful. *Who wants to be a master over one's book?* And yet this is not only how slave writers were read by their contemporaries—who, in the case of Wheatley, meant the white men who juried and judged her writing as "written by herself" and not a forgery, thus allowing it to be published—but also by present-day critics who overread such (white) receptions and standards of mastery back onto black works.

While certainly poets like Wheatley—indeed, all writers, of any stripe—are influenced by circumstance, and while being a slave poet is a peculiar institution if ever there was one, I simply cannot read the audience back onto her writing of the poems. In other words, what the writing itself does and what critics say about the writing differ in significant ways. It is our job, then, to understand some sense of the process of writing, not just the reading. In focusing on storying, we might see a further option, not "bound" by competing strictures: on the one hand, thinking we're better off than Wheatley and thus expecting her (subtle) protest in our (explicit) terms, a fault that yields ham-fisted readings of this daughter of Ham; and, on the other, allowing our opinions to be based on an amazement at her achievement, as if we too sit on her jury of skeptical, prominent, dubious, white gentlemen.

Rather, we should examine the ways in which Wheatley's writing protests her condition on her own terms—terms her public poetry relied on, terms made all the more explicit in her private letters to other black writers, poets, and artists. We must remember that even Wheatley, though that all-too-rare figure of "public poet," enjoyed a private community of black voices and words, including Jupiter Hammon and her beloved friend Obour Tanner. Such a sense of community, and all the untold undertow of her private letters, are wonderfully echoed in Hayden's own *American Journal* in the form of "A Letter from Phillis Wheatley." With Wheatley, why do we expect private thoughts in a public poetry?

Instead, with the writings of Wheatley, as with other artistic slave endeavors, it is often a matter of hiding in plain sight. In other words, *storying.*

SING LOW

In reading Wheatley, we would do well to heed the kind of sophistication involved in the composition of the spirituals, which also were thought (chiefly by white hearers) as signs of complacency, even happiness, showing no concern but for the world beyond. Now we can't help but hear such songs as "Swing Low, Sweet Chariot" as sophisticated allegories of freedom—not to mention as specific instructions for how and when to escape. Not only do the spirituals give the lie to the supposed simplicity of black art or the complacency of black folks under slavery, they directly answer Jefferson's declaration that "among the blacks is misery enough, God knows, but no poetry." The spirituals caution us against being lazy, Jeffersonian readers.

This is true for plenty of other aspects of black culture once thought to be expressive and even decorative. Ralph Ellison cautions against mistaking decorousness for mere decoration: "The effectiveness of Negro music and dance is first recorded in the journals and letters of travelers but it is important to remember that they saw and understood only that which they were prepared to accept. Thus a Negro dancing a courtly dance appeared comic from the outside simply because the dancer was a slave. But to the Negro dancing it—and there is ample evidence that he danced it well—burlesque or satire might have been the point, which might have been difficult for a white observer to even imagine."[11] The inability to see layers of meaning is a failure of the outside (often "white") observer's imagination, not of the black performer or poet. For instance, during the Civil War white listeners first wrote down many of the spirituals overheard in "contraband camps"— those essentially refugee camps housing fugitive slaves who had run away seeking their freedom across Union lines—not always noticing the limbo of their black makers, not to mention the full freedom the songs still sought.[12]

Even with Wheatley, while it did not allow her immediate freedom, her writing did afford her a kind of public currency and literal freedom unimaginable to her without it. Wheatley's poems literally carried her across the sea, allowing her to travel from the colonies, on the eve of their independence, to visit Britain; in many ways, this foremother became a kind of Eve of Independence herself.[13] And we do well to remember, as evidenced by signed copies of her book, Wheatley's status as that most modern of things: an author on tour.

It is tempting to read Wheatley as merely an exception, and thus not "quite a slave" (as Redding does), implying that she has not endured the humiliations afforded "normal" slaves, or worse, the suffering believed necessary to produce great art. But isn't "not being a slave" the point? *Ain't she a woman?* Isn't the desire of all art, particularly that of African

Americans, for freedom of various sorts? By any means necessary? In focusing on Wheatley's being an exception we keep her the kind of freak she was regarded as in her own time, if regarded at all.

The counterfeit is the literary feint that allows Wheatley, if not to return to "Afric's dark seat," then to make a literal and symbolic journey across what Langston Hughes would call "the big sea" in the title of his autobiography. And it is exactly Wheatley's words that allow her to travel, that buy her a crucial kind of freedom. Rather than see her as buffeted by various forces, in a kind of triangular trade between enslaved Africa, colonizing Britain, and revolutionary America, perhaps we can see how Wheatley rode the trade winds among all three, forging her own Black Atlantic. Wheatley escaped in the only way she could—by traveling to Britain where she could be published and was both legally and metaphorically free.

At the very least, we can admire the ways Wheatley negotiated the various shifting forces and allegiances of her turbulent times—certainly we are in a better position to recognize this than her panel of *American Idol*-style celebrity judges. Gates reminds us that many of the men who judged Wheatley have, in turn, been judged by history as Tory sympathizers or traitors or slave masters themselves, including, of course, Jefferson—many of them forced into exile or far from the popular imagination and memory. Might we say that in fact it is Wheatley who authenticates them? That it is not, as Gates argues, a case of Wheatley "auditioning for the humanity of the entire African people" but rather of Wheatley testing her supposed judges' humanity?

In contrast, lowly Wheatley earned audiences with then-General Washington and not a few members of the British aristocracy, including the Countess of Huntingdon, to whom Wheatley dedicated her book to help get it published. Like a jazz musician, Wheatley found Europe more open to her artistically, but at the same time, had to balance the political shifting sands of a nascent revolution. Even while she solicited British royalty, Wheatley wrote in praise of the emerging revolution as it was happening, including the Boston Massacre that occurred just doors down from where she lived.[14] Does it matter if it was a house she tended to as well as lived in?

Even her "master," John Wheatley, grants Phillis Wheatley enough independence to say, "As to her Writing, her own Curiosity led her to it; and this she learnt in so short a time, that in the Year 1765 [when she was roughly eleven] she wrote a letter to the Reverend Mr. Occom, the Indian Minister, while in England."[15] It seems more than mere coincidence that in her first letter ever, Wheatley would write not just to a dignitary—how many of us today would presume that, let alone at age eleven?—but to one who is Native American, Christian, and abroad, another American at the crossroads of several identities. If such crossroads is a cross to bear, it is certainly not without redemption.

Wheatley's overseas correspondence hints at how early America was, as Leslie Fiedler notes, largely imaginary, with whites wanting to be Indians (à la the Boston Tea Party) or to be blacks (as in later blackface minstrelsy); and blacks and Indians wanting to be anything they wanted to be, even in an America that treated them simultaneously as bondswomen and exiles, or abroad, where only one of these was true. The rest of Wheatley's poetry may be read as culminating her letters' understated but unequivocal desire to be free—not to mention Christian in the sense her community insisted on, using the Bible and spirituals as declarations of equality. As with the epistles in *Incidents in the Life of a Slave Girl,* or the letters of the *Amistad* rebels written from jail, the literate and literary freedom of the storying tradition leads to actual liberty.

Can slave girl Wheatley, writing on the eve of independence, on the cusp of the invention of America, help but issue protests—some literal, some subtle? As a line of her poetry indicates, and critic Frances Foster points out, "Sometimes by Simile, a Victory's Won": winning don't always have to mean shouting, "Give It Up or Turn It Loose"; though sometimes I think that's exactly what Wheatley's work was saying. The counterfeit allows us to pay the piper without too high a price.

GO DOWN, MOSES

Notions of economics and writing become even more entwined in the era of slavery—not only are black people recorded and accorded value as property, they are not allowed, you will recall, to read or write. Where these repressions ironically allowed some folks to forge their own freedoms in the forms of free passes, whether literal or literary, in the case of the nineteenth-century slave poet George Moses Horton the combination gives him another freedom. For Horton freedom was tied intimately to economics, a key part of the counterfeit tradition.

While many others wrote their slave narratives after reaching freedom, Horton composed his verse while still in bondage. Born in Northampton County, North Carolina, then moved to Chatham County in 1800, Horton was never a native African but rather a "native son" like Frederick Douglass, born in the United States. And as that newest of inventions, the African American, Horton was also the first American slave to directly protest his condition in verse, decades before Douglass put pen to paper.

The uniqueness of this achievement cannot be overstated and seems all the greater for the sheer number of protest poems Horton wrote. One poem, published in *Freedom's Journal* on July 18, 1828, is called simply "Slavery":

> Is it because my skin is black,
> That thou should'st be so dull and slack,
>   And scorn to set me free?
> Then let me hasten to the grave,
> The only refuge for the slave,
>   Who mourns for liberty.[16]

This excerpt gives some indication of Horton's early verse, which, in disobeying many of the laws and limits of what a black person *should* be—illiterate for one thing—still obeys many of the poetic conventions of the time. Yet it also shares the profound wish found in the spirituals: *Before I'd be a slave, I'd be buried in my grave.*

Most interestingly, Horton was not yet literate in 1828, at least in the strictest sense of being able to read and write. Later he would teach himself to do both by studying the Bible by the faintness of a fire. Earlier on, others would transcribe poems he had composed in his head while working before venturing on weekends to Chapel Hill, where he would sell his poems to students for money. Counterfeit indeed.

Horton's appearance in the back of the fourth edition of Wheatley's poems in 1832 binds the poets together in more than one way. Like Wheatley, Horton was an occasional poet—yet he was also "paid" for being a poet, as his first incarnation as a poet was in writing love poems and other verses for the gentlemen of Chapel Hill. In other words, Horton was a surrogate for the emotions of those in need of words—it was Horton to whom, out of convenience and surely of some novelty, students would turn. This may not be the best place to explore the full implications of white students paying a black man—still, strictly speaking illiterate, yet literary—to write for them. Certainly we could see them taking Horton's words as *contraband,* a term originally used to describe "runaway property" from the South.[17]

For the time being it might prove fruitful if we think of Horton's verse for hire as a kind of counterfeit, at least on Horton's part. Such writing for hire, as with Wheatley's tributes to Washington and the burgeoning revolution (while also balancing the impending British publication of her book), allowed him a kind of freedom—the journeyman "freedom" given to some slaves, who, if skilled labor, got "rented," the profits from their labor usually not accruing to them but to their masters. Such limited freedom of movement should not be confused with actual freedom (as is done by a recent editor of Horton's verse).[18] Often it was granted to certain slaves to quell unrest, if not simply to provide profit to the slave owners, with the false promise that the slaves might someday purchase their freedom—something Horton and his supporters spent most of his life trying to do, with little success.

Not only was Horton's poetry about freedom and the horrors of slavery, his *Hope of Liberty* (1829) was being sold to make money so he could literally buy his own freedom. This gives us a sense of the stakes of black writing, stakes indicated by the monetary meanings of counterfeit. In Horton's case, this promise was only a promise, as his so-called masters would "re-nig" when the money was provided by Horton or his abolitionist supporters.

More important, the idea of "mild bondage" seems contradicted by the poems themselves—from "A Slave's Complaint" to "A Slave's Reflections the Eve before His Sale"—which repeatedly contest captivity. He even named his son Free. The fact that Horton wrote another poem called "Slavery" again as late as 1865 reveals his continuing commitment to freedom even after the Emancipation Proclamation.

In such a devastating, absurd economic system as slavery—a system in which running away meant literally stealing yourself—we may see the benefit and full implications of the counterfeit. While many slaves

did "steal away," they sang of this freedom first. If you can't imagine a
Canaan, you can't get to a Canada—the two are inextricably entwined
in the black imagination.

What may surprise most of all is not Horton's one-man abolition-
ism—and this in the South long before the Fugitive Slave Act of 1850
rallied that movement—but rather that many poems he wrote are committed to love. This stems not just from his work as an occasional poet,
writing on events such as Lincoln's death or "The Graduate Leaving
College," but also from the fact that Horton was that rarest of beings—a
poet who writes for money. *Black Bard,* Horton's recently collected
poems, contains many love poems, some found in the three volumes
published during Horton's lifetime (and two of those while he was still
a slave), and many more in the invaluable section titled "Uncollected
Poems." Intriguingly in a love poem of 1843, "Lines to My ——,"[19]
Horton seems not to be ventriloquizing for a white buyer (much less
a white tradition), but rather encoding his own emotions about an
unnamed lover. Its mystery is reminiscent of the "Master Letters" of
Emily Dickinson—three missives addressed to "Master" or addressee
unknown, thought to be a lover or God or perhaps both. Horton writes:

> Let me be thine, altho' I take
>   My exit from this world;
> And when the heavens with thunder shake,
> And all the wheels of time shall break,
>   With globes to nothing hurl'd,
>   I would be thine.[20]

Like Dickinson's conflation of the Beloved and God (not to mention her constant companion, Death), Horton often composes his love
poems using the language of bondage. For while certainly a poetic convention to declare oneself a prisoner of love, Horton's constant writing
of love combating bonds serves as more than mere metaphor, instead
symbolizing the near impossibility of love during bondage—as well as
its necessity. Nowhere is this storying power explored more than in an
early poem, likely composed in the 1820s: "Excited from Reading the
Obedience of Nature to Her Lord in the Vessel on the Sea." A poem
about power and reading and "obedience," it not only addresses the

Lord and nature (topics Horton turns to frequently), it also dares to speak in the Lord's voice, much like James Weldon Johnson's "The Creation" nearly a century later. Devoid of quotation marks, this poem's power is enhanced by its directness:

> My smile is but the death of harm,
> Whilst riding on the wind,
> My power restrains the thunder's arm,
> Which dies in chains confined.[21]

The slant rhyme, the exegesis of the Bible verse, and more poignantly, the irony and metaphor of the last two lines, mark the best of what Horton has to offer. Speaking to and for the Lord in bondage, Horton well earns his middle name of Moses.

In true counterfeit fashion, Horton's writing imagines not only a literary freedom but a literal one to follow. That much of this freedom involves love should be no surprise. It is this freedom of feeling that the black writer, particularly the black slave writer, seeks; it is this freedom of art that we as readers would do well to examine in order to fully understand the black imagination and its emancipation.

A CAKEWALK

To the slave, slavery—despite its many insults and scars, both literal and symbolic—is not an entirely closed system. For if it were, it would not require Fugitive Slave Acts, slave codes, and various other reinforcements of repression. As Ralph Ellison reminds us:

> There is no sociology of ideas in this country. You cannot tell who is thinking what or where he gets the ideas. This was vaguely understood back during the Haitian Revolution early in the nineteenth century, when Southern governors and politicians became distraught because the ideas of the French Revolution had surfaced among the slaves. This tells you something about the availability of ideas beyond the levels of literacy. In our society, modes of conduct, styles, ideas, and even the most esoteric intellectual concepts find their ways into strange

places, and even the most unfree or illiterate American is aware of ideas and will act on them.[22]

To critique the freedom of art or ideas as being merely partial may be to miss a larger point—one that, as we've seen with the spirituals, not only "serves" as an expression of freedom's possibilities but also maps out ways to achieve such freedom. The jug we are bottled in is not opaque, but transparent, after all. Douglass noted clearly that these songs were not just about Canaan or the afterlife, but about Canada and the life after slavery:

> We were at times remarkably buoyant, singing hymns, and
> making joyous exclamations, almost as triumphant in their
> tone as if we had reached a land of freedom and safety. A
> keen observer might have detected in our repeated singing of
> "O Canaan, sweet Canaan, I am bound for the land of Canaan,"
> something more than a hope of reaching heaven. We meant to
> reach the *North,* and the *North* was our Canaan.[23]

A true North for which the slave songs, even in their sorrow, provide a joyous map, Canaan is a crucial kind of counterfeit—a black market of meaning for those bought and sold at whim, but who never bought into the bunk they were sold each day.

Spirituals have by now entered the mainstream enough to be both signs of popular protest ("We Shall Overcome" in the 1960s); of popular pastiche ("Swing Low, Sweet Chariot" made secular, referenced by rock bands like Hole); or even parodied (as "Swing Low, Sweet Cadillac").[24] For me, this is sacred music not to be taken lightly—the Hollywood-ization and co-opting of the spirituals deny their continued power, whether in contemporary concert performances or in their gospel descendants.[25] Just as important, secularized reading does not just tend to lose the spiritual's initial power but also to erase their delicate balance of protest and prayer, their second layer of meaning as Old Testament comeuppance for those who can see. And hear.

Such layers prevail on the secular side too. Take the *cakewalk,* an example of parody originally misperceived by white viewers. When blacks strutted in imitation of their masters, their masters found it amusing and so had the slaves imitate them all the more; soon this led to one of the first American dance crazes: whites doing a cakewalk in imitation of blacks themselves imitating whites. Like so much of popular culture, it began as black and ended up "white"; and like so many white folks before and after, the white cakewalkers did not know they were doing an imitation of an imitation, a dull copy of a parody. We may remember what Hurston observed about such imitation and originality (and their frequent misperception) in her essay "Characteristics of Negro Expression," critiquing those who saw black culture as mere parroting of white culture rather than instances not only of song but of the mockingbird's satire.

We could say that with the cakewalk, as with blackface, white folks projected back onto blacks the kind of pastiche or "blank copy" that Fredric Jameson saw as one of the fundamental qualities of postmodernism—a full century before the idea took hold. In this, those of us in the postmodern era may glimpse a fascinating, racialized aspect of the postmodern—its possible black origins.

The parody and popularity of the cakewalk are roughly contemporaneous with the popularization of the spirituals after Emancipation, which was largely the result of the formation of the Fisk Jubilee Singers and their wildly successful tours. The spirituals themselves provide a nice trope for this era, acting as *allegory*. Such allegory dominates the period and is necessary for reading on several layers the various worlds, the double consciousness of slavery found in the Negro spirituals or animal tales. We may now realize that the codes created by the slaves are also literary—we must be aware, and on the lookout, in our reading of both the writing and the oral literature of the slaves and freedmen, to recognize this double voicedness when we encounter it.

In part this is a result of the allusive nature of the African song that inspired them.[26] Such doublings are sometimes also in order to face a white public—continuing from slavery through questions of white patronage until today—but chiefly this storying is a function of circumstance caught in the creative act of art. If you are forbidden to dance, and dancing means crossing your feet, you invent a ring shout (or you modify your dance from Africa); if you can't use a drum, then the body (and the voice) becomes one, percussive to the very bone.

In considering the spirituals, animal tales, and the cakewalk, it must occur to us to ask (or *axe*): What else haven't we read correctly? How many underground railroads of meaning are there, unacknowledged, left just beneath the surface?

SWEET CANAAN

For every Canaan in the African American imagination, there is a countertradition intent on imagining "Ole Virginny"—a place of contentment that does not exist. Never did. Where Canaan may provide a code for an actual Canada, the myth of Ole Virginny crafted chiefly after Emancipation is all the more pernicious because it operates in the opposite direction, moving from a real place to a mythic one.[27] It is all the harder to combat a myth that is seemingly real. Still, we may think of Ole Virginny as the last of the failed utopias—"utopia" meaning, of course, "no place."

Don't tell that to the folks who made the film *Shadrach* (1998), which embodies the myth of a peaceful Ole Virginny completely. The film, with Harvey Keitel and Andie MacDowell, shows the ways in which Shadrach represents the "happy darky" and more specifically, the permanent past. Whether known as Ole Virginny, "My 'Tucky Home," or even Jefferson's Monticello, such fictionalized "songs of the South" align the region with the past—replacing a place with a time—an invented, distant one that is all but imaginary. (Like blackface, these Southern myths are all the more powerful for, and popular in, the North.) Unlike the fluid, imagined future of the spirituals, Ole Virginny's static past has the advantage of constantly being extended—we constantly gain ever more past to mythify even as we lose the future (and ground). In such a conception, the good old days are always yesterday, our best always behind us.

Like outer and inner space, Canaan is a place of the future. Where Canaan ultimately proved real—a powerful locale of possibility in the slave imagination, later translated into actual freedom—Virginny never existed, a vain pastoral projected large. The fact that it was a fantasy, however, makes Ole Virginny no less troubling. If blackface, as Ellison reminds us, "constituted a ritual of exorcism"[28] during slavery for the white mind confronting not black inhumanity but its own, then Ole Virginny remains one chief method of reconciling the persistent horrors and contradictions of slavery long after its abolition.

Populated with loyal slaves, grateful mammies, singing field hands, and contented, storytelling Uncles—*There's where the cotton and corn and taters grow, There's where the birds warble sweet in the springtime, There's where this old darkey's heart am long'd to go*—Ole Virginny maintains a powerful pull on our national imagination, no less so for being a place filled with ghosts, however friendly. But it raises the question: if slaves were so devoted to their masters, why didn't their owners free them before they were dead, rather than after?

Ole Virginny's imaginary Negroes are chiefly a way of solidifying an imaginary (and threatened) whiteness, just as the imaginary Indian embodied and addressed the violent contradictions of frontier life. (The real Negroes in Jefferson's Virginia are too often left out of the story, almost as much as they were lusted after.) To catalog the number and kinds of these imaginary Negroes is not my chief charge, though in many ways this is exactly what many of today's African American artists have done, whether through the parody suffusing Alice Randall's *The Wind Done Gone* and Ishmael Reed's *Flight to Canada* or the visual codings of Robert Colescott and Kara Walker. Gone with *What* Wind?

Here I'm more interested in Canaan. To call Canaan imaginary is to ignore its very real power in the life and afterlife of the slave. More important, to ignore Canaan's reality in slave life is to underestimate the powerful liberational rereading of the Bible the slaves *performed*. The slave wasn't merely illiterate but was instead a terrific reader in a metaphoric sense: with their spirituals, slaves provided a powerful exegesis of the biblical story of Moses and Pharaoh, Israel and bondage, in order to identify with, and aspire to, freedom. To ignore Canaan is to ignore the African American slave's intimate, intuitive, but no less strategic, remapping of the American landscape.

Such remappings are ongoing, and familiar to anyone with a radio or record player. Canaan continues in any number of black incarnations, whether as utopian "Ethiopia" in the early twentieth century, or its opposite—the slaves' allegorical "Egypt," later rendered as Rastafari's "Babylon." Critic Greg Tate discusses the various kinds of recent remappings in terms of music, in an essay about the abstract artist Ellen Gallagher and her recent work visualizing Detroit techno artists' invention of a Black Atlantic utopia called Drexciya, "a marine maroon colony." This underwater utopia is the ultimate reclamation of what's

unseen. Though Tate traces such conversions of "blighted urban con-
claves into places where liberatory dreamings could form: cf. Public
Enemy transforming Long Island into Strong Island, the Wu-Tang Clan
changing Staten Island into Shaolin, OutKast recasting Atlanta as the
homebase of ATLiens" as strictly contemporary, going back "at least as
far as Sun Ra,"[29] we can easily see the continuity between Canaan and
more recent African American escape.

Not only do the spirituals propose a paradise just beyond reach—
and this for folks with a collective memory of another real and mythic
homeland, Africa, itself often Canaan—but by extension, they offer up
a critique of current conditions. The field holler, the ring shout, animal
tales: all are adaptations, as well as protests and guides, not just to an
African past but to an African American future. No wonder that in this
future, descendants of slaves and freedmen would envision Drexciya,
a place where those thrown overboard in the Middle Passage actually
survived and gave birth to those who could breathe underwater. Going
beyond even P-Funk's notion of dancing underwater and not getting
wet, Drexciya is Dixie turned on its head—and as likely a place.

While Canaan crafts a state of mind in order to remake reality, Ole
Virginny is a slave state made fantasy. It might be said that this Ole
Virginny was as much a Northern pastoral fiction as it was a Southern
one, just as blackface's chief practitioners were Northerners (and new
immigrants) singing of a South they'd rarely if ever seen. This difference in trajectory—not just South versus North, or past versus future,
but moving back from real to imaginary, in direct opposition to the
ways the slaves succeeded in turning the imaginary into the real—
provides the crucial difference between Virginny and Canaan.

That, and time: for the black slave, Canaan was both tomorrow and
ever after; it was a place (Canada) they hoped to literally dwell in, and
also a release (crossing the river) into an afterlife they had more than
earned. If some of this is Christian imagery, much of it also is an African
conception of Great Time in which one's ancestors are ever present.
Canaan is Elsewhere; Virginny, Once Upon a Time: in Ole Virginny it
is always yesterday, a permanent past seen through the scrim of nostalgia, not the light of experience. It is this fog, not the slave's veil, that
needs lifting.

Canaan and other such sites of black imagination offer a form of second sight, necessary for the slave—and for us—in order to see the full extent of the burgeoning black imagination. To do so we must use this sight to read in ways that perhaps have more to do with reading music than reading literature. Or we must read in the physical ways you can literally grasp the pottery of Dave the Slave, a master (or should I say slave) potter whose pots are admired both for their form and for the verses he inscribed on their surfaces, making his jug the world:

> I wonder where is all my relations
> Friendship to all—and every nation.[30]

Whether it is lying up a nation, wondering about relations dispersed by slavery, or traveling to every nation, the domain being surveyed here is one of imagination.

BOOK TWO

Strange Fruit

The American artist whose will is to join in the tristful litany over the dissolving body of European culture does well, like T. S. Eliot, to live abroad. The American artist who feels within himself the power to add to the intricate glosses of that culture does well, like Ezra Pound or Henry James, to live abroad. But the artist who is tempted to the task of forging new organic life from chaos may bless his stars if America is his home. For in all the world there is no symbol of this chaos so potent and so pregnant as our American jungle.

—WALDO FRANK
In the American Jungle

Broken Tongue

Paul Laurence Dunbar, His Descendants,
and the Dance of Dialect _ _ _ _ _ _ _ _ _ _ _ _ _ _ _ _ _ _ _

As the first widely popular black poet, Paul Laurence Dunbar occupies the unenviable position of being at once extremely influential and strangely invisible. Such lack of acknowledgment of a writer's influence is, ironically, often a symptom of success: our repetition of the phrases and snippets of Dunbar without quite knowing their origin actually stems from their primacy in our minds. Most people use the Shakespearean phrase "star-crossed lovers" without knowing where it comes from; similarly, we offer up "We wear the mask that grins and lies" without knowing who wrote it, if it was written at all. Today, these phrases are no longer so much lines of crafted verse as easily won truths, even platitudes—they are the photographs we have hold of without knowing the names of the subjects in the image.

The photograph—whether tintype or daguerreotype—proves an apt metaphor for Paul Laurence Dunbar. Take its use by poet Robert Hayden in the second half of his stunning elegy for the poet:

> Poet of our youth—
> his "cri du coeur" our own,
> his verses "in a broken tongue"
>
> beguiling as an elder
> brother's antic lore.
> Their sad blackface lilt and croon
> survive him like
>
> The happy look (subliminal
> of victim, dying man)
> a summer's tintypes hold.

The roses flutter in the wind;
we weight their stems
with stones, then drive away.

Hayden's lines, while commenting on Dunbar's tragic, short life—the speaker is, after all, at the poet's grave—also reveal something of Dunbar's music. We have here much of Dunbar's doubling: Hayden's use of quotes and parentheticals indicates the ways in which he requires other tongues (French), lower registers ("subliminal / of victim, dying man") and Dunbar himself ("a broken tongue") to conjure up an image of the late poet. Such an image is related to the daguerreotype—which I have argued elsewhere was a way for African Americans to represent themselves in a world that didn't always regard them with care.[1] Here, in Hayden's hands, "summer's tintypes"—made doubly impermanent by impending autumn and unsturdy materials—cast and capture Dunbar's "blackface lilt and croon."

It is not simply that Dunbar's author's portrait seems inextricably linked with his work, though it certainly is, much like the drawing of an otherwise anonymous Whitman as "one of the roughs" in the first edition of *Leaves of Grass,* or the etching of Wheatley, likely by the black artist Scipio Moorhead, that accompanies her book. If the mournful photograph that serves as frontispiece to Dunbar's *Complete Poems* seems linked as much to the verse as to his young death, it is at least in part because Dunbar's poems often appeared alongside photographs, often from the Hampton Institute, rendering both the poems and the pictures as documents, rather than creations. They stand there as evidence of black invention captured, so to speak, on film.

Yet it is Dunbar's music, over and above popular notions of his work as dialect, "blackface croon," or personal formalism, that I wish to explore—what arguably, even in the "croon," audiences white and black have responded to.

And respond they did. At the turn of the twentieth century, Dunbar proved one of the most popular American poets of any stripe. His first, self-published book, *Oak and Ivy* (1893), reportedly sold out in a month; all his books went through many editions in his lifetime and after.

From his first book and mythologized death on, Dunbar's name would be recalled with reverence—largely, it should be said, because of the efforts of his widow, Alice Dunbar, a fine writer in her own right (this, despite Dunbar's alcoholism and troubling mistreatment of her). Alice Dunbar's gathering of the *Dunbar Reader & Entertainer* was a way of providing black content for black folks, both as signs of excellence and as aspirational texts. The Dunbar name went on to grace many African American institutions, from societies to high schools, across the country. "Dunbar" almost came to be synonymous with black, much like "Lincoln"; though arguably, while the word Lincoln above a hotel simply conveyed that it served blacks (and blacks only), Dunbar above a door suggested race pride and achievement.

For while other black poets like Wheatley, Jupiter Hammon, and George Moses Horton had preceded him in terms of publication, they remained chiefly locally or literarily influential. What's worse, to certain readers, they too often remained mere curiosities, literary Hottentot Venuses at some literary sideshow. Entertainments, distractions: such were the bounds of the black poetic bodies at work before Dunbar. But, then, what else could their "work" be, in antebellum slave labor society?

The son of slaves himself, Dunbar's influence is still felt, however invisibly. When younger, I must admit, it took me some time to realize that "I know why the caged bird sings" was not just a common phrase, or one coined by Maya Angelou, who took it as the title of her first autobiography. In contrast, we have a sense, even in Lorraine Hansberry's famous play *Raisin in the Sun,* that she is taking her title from somewhere else—and this I daresay is not just because of the recency of Hansberry or the phrase's original source, Langston Hughes's *Montage of a Dream Deferred.* Even with a title as ubiquitous as "The Road Less Traveled," we have a sense that it stems from a poem, even if we don't know its author, Robert Frost, or what exactly the poem says.

With Dunbar, it is not so much that the phrase seems allusive as elusive. Apart from the pervasiveness of his influence within both the literary and popular realms—his phrases even appearing in the R.E.M. song "Be Mine"—I would argue that what contributes to Dunbar's seeming invisibility is the lack of any clear personal language. Rather than too private or hermetic, in the way, say, of Gerard Manley Hopkins,

Dunbar's poems, if anything, seem too public, too filled with oratory. Dunbar presents us with a persona not of everyman but of "no body," disembodied, unwritten, nameless.

This is not a failure so much as a key to understanding Dunbar as the first black modern poet, and an advance guard in naming the modern condition. Dunbar's own anonymity surely anticipates and arguably even leads to the modern era's use of impersonality and persona, championed by T. S. Eliot and Ezra Pound, respectively, as a way to resist and represent the difficulties of the modernist moment.

In a sense, this modern condition is exactly what's embodied—or should I say disembodied—by the "blackface lilt and croon" Hayden speaks of. Blackface has long been used by the white modern artist— whether in Eliot's *Sweeney Agonistes;* or in his original scheme for *The Waste Land* as "He Do the Police in Different Voices"; or, decades later in John Berryman's *Dream Songs*—as a way to access a distinct, "deracinated" voice that symbolizes the tragic failures of modern life.

But we need not look to white writers to see blackface and its ritual power: performer Bert Williams may provide a useful contrast. His song "Nobody" (1905), later covered by the late great Johnny Cash, provides a kind of protoblues that Dunbar himself might have appreciated, if not heard:

> Well, one time when things was looking bright
> I started whittling on a stick one night
> Who said, "Hey, that's dynamite"?
> Nobody.
>
> Oh, I never done nothing to Nobody
> I ain't never got nothing from Nobody
> No time
> And until I get something from somebody
> Sometime
> I don't intend to do nothing for Nobody
> No time.[2]

The song's refusal, which in the narrator's terms is one of survival, proves both tragic and comic. Like Dunbar, the narrator here seeks sympathy—

and faced (or blackfaced) with not getting it, he will turn away, and inward. This seriocomic effect is precisely what makes "Nobody" a protoblues. It also makes the song all the more American: Jamaican-born Williams captured the public imagination in his role as "Jonah Man" who constantly faces trouble largely because he revels in a kind of American anonymity, a "nobodyness" that we can relate to whether we're "just a gigolo" (singing "I ain't got nobody") or spinster poet (declaring "I'm nobody—who are you?"). Or the black poet, whose *Majors and Minors* appeared "dateless, placeless, without a publisher."[3]

If Dunbar could not or did not express the dilemmas of race and recognition using the blues or a more "natural" sense of speech—a vernacular both in language and in form—then at least he has the stoic grace of Bert Williams's "Nobody" and the possibility of tragicomic praise. For if the blues were unavailable to Dunbar as a form, I suspect he knew the feeling of the blues all too well.

With Dunbar we have modernism's not-so-modest beginnings. Perhaps it is not that Dunbar is natural but "neutral"—the musical term for the tones that some would call blue. "Neutral tones are variously but similarly defined as 'wild notes,' quarter steps, 'blues' notes, minor-major thirds and sevenths. As Milton Metfessel has graphically demonstrated by means of the oscilloscope, they are a 'region' between minor and major intervals."[4] Dunbar provides not just the crossroads between pathos and humor, Standard English and dialect, he is the beginning of the intermingling of tragedy and comedy that would be mined by the blues—and by most every modernist from Langston Hughes to Samuel Beckett. *Dunbar is not modern despite dialect, but because of it.* At a certain slant of light (or dark), of meaning and rhyme, you could even call Dunbar's many dialects futuristic.

EMANCIPATION DAY

The connection between Dunbar and Williams is not merely coincidental but actual: the two were collaborators, inasmuch as Dunbar wrote lyrics for two of Williams's most famous stage appearances, *Clorindy; or, The Origin of the Cakewalk* (1898) and *In Dahomey* (1903). Williams then was mostly identified with being half of Williams and Walker, one the most famous stage duos of the time, with George Walker especially known for his cakewalk. Dunbar wrote the two musicals (at least the lyrics, not the book) with William Marion Cook, a black composer trained at Oberlin and at the National Conservatory of Music. There he studied with Antonín Dvořák, whose view of the New World (and use of African American material) influenced generations of American composers. Cook's compositions, not unlike Dunbar's, heralded something new.

"When Bert Williams and George Walker met in California, the Negro god of comedy and drama must have opened his thick lips and wide mouth and laughed loud, long, raucously!" writes Cook about composing *Clorindy*. This meeting of comedy and what might be called tragedy parallels not just the blues but Cook's meeting Williams and Walker: "Since I had come to New York to learn to write good music, I met Williams and Walker and gave them my ideas on creating a story of how the cakewalk came about in Louisiana in the early Eighteen Eighties. *Clorindy, the Origin of the Cakewalk* was the result and though, when the time came, Williams and Walker were unable to play in it, it was for them I wrote the show."[5] The storying Cook proposes is twofold, rewriting the story of the cakewalk—a form itself of parody.

Cook's account of writing the musical *Clorindy* indicates his own facility with both comedy and tragedy. He is continuously "hungry, mad with the world and heartbroken at such a failure" in a world where whites tell him he "must be crazy to believe any Broadway audience would listen to Negroes singing Negro opera."

> After a long siege of persuasion, I finally got Paul Laurence Dunbar to consent to write the *Clorindy* libretto (which was never used) and a few of the lyrics. We got together in the basement of my brother John's rented house on Sixth Street, just below Howard University, one night about eight o'clock. We had two dozen bottles of beer, a quart of whiskey, and we took my brother's porterhouse steak, cut it up with onions and red peppers and ate it raw. Without a piano or anything but the kitchen table, we finished all songs, all the libretto and all but a few bars of the ensembles by four o'clock the next morning. By that time Paul and I were happy, so happy that we were ready to cry "Eureka!" only we couldn't make any noise at that hour

so both of us sneaked off to bed, Paul to his house three blocks away and I to my room.

The following morning or rather later that morning I was at John's piano trying to learn to play my most Negroid song, "Who Dat Say Chicken in Dis Crowd?" My mother, who was cooking my breakfast, came into the parlor, tears streaming from her eyes, and said:

"Oh Will! Will! I've sent you all over the world to study and become a great musician, and you return such a *nigger!*" My mother was a graduate of Oberlin in the class of 1865 and thought that a Negro composer should write just like a white man. They all loved the Dunbar lyrics but weren't ready for Negro songs.[6]

His educated mother may seem no different in her reaction from the whites who also were not "ready for Negro songs"—though hers is a very different complaint about the stereotyping in Cook and Dunbar's title. But by Dunbar's "lyrics" does Cook mean both Dunbar's poems as well as his song lyrics? Or does Cook imply it is Negro music— *his* music, which ultimately would incorporate ragtime and other African American forms—that is offensive?

The account of composition conjures a drunken, carnivalesque— even cannibalistic—night. I can't help but think of the modernist Anthropophagia movement over a generation later in Brazil, which embraced the cannibalism the natives there had been accused of. Here, in devouring a raw porterhouse, Cook provides an apt if bloody metaphor for his hunger for new forms; the transformation of what could be said to be a raw or emergent black culture; and risk. (He also gives the lie to the notion that Dunbar began drinking only after he was diagnosed with tuberculosis a few years later.) Cook's hunger to write a "Negro operetta" is one shared by Dunbar, both onstage and on the page. And one that plays on Cook's very name.

While it may contain some leftover, as it were, "coon songs" and minstrelsy—songs like "Who Dat Say Chicken?" and "Darktown Is Out Tonight"—the play ends with a cakewalk and a strange kind of uplift. As the first black-written and black-performed production on Broadway, *Clorindy* sought its origins in folk music and theme, with Cook also becoming the first black leader of a white orchestra—rare even today. "I started the opening chorus, an orchestral and choral development of 'Darktown Is Out Tonight.' Remember, reader, I had twenty-six of the finest Negro voices in America, twenty-six happy, gifted Negroes who saw maybe weeks of work and money before them. Remember, too, that they were singing a new style of music. Like a mighty anthem, these voices rang out."[7] Despite its title, you can see in the lyrics how the finery of "Darktown" might be freeing: it is a song about coming out after all. This mix of anthem and ambush is rife in this period, not just from Cook and Dunbar but from J. Rosamond Johnson, who would compose broad vaudeville but also write "Lift Every Voice and Sing," often called "The Negro National Anthem," with his brother James Weldon Johnson.

Just like the line between tragedy and comedy, that between liberation and libertine can be blurred—and as blurry as Cook and Dunbar's night of composing and carousing. In part blurring is the very nature of collaboration, which is one key aspect of all these productions—and even in the interplay between Dunbar's dialect and other poems.

Such blurred, blue notes are found in Dunbar and Cook's later Negro operetta, *In Dahomey*. Walker and Williams debuted the piece on Broadway and took it to England with rousing success; the play is credited with reintroducing the cakewalk there, and furthered the cause for black drama abroad and in the United States—all with the theme of a return to Africa. Seriocomic or not, *Dahomey* boxes the compass of the Black Atlantic. This would seem especially poignant given that Williams and Walker reportedly met playing "Dahomeyans" at a California expo. The gods were laughing then, and later when they went on to bill themselves as "Two Real Coons"—the nickname as much a parody of whites' black masks as the cakewalk for which Walker and Williams were famous.

The opera's rousing song "On Emancipation Day," with words by Dunbar and music by Cook, avoids a minstrelsy theme despite its use of words like "darkies" and "coons":

> On Emancipation day
> All you whitefolks clear de way
> Brass ban' playin sev'ral tunes,

Darkies eyes look jes' lak moons,
Marshall of de day a struttin'
Lord but he is gay

Coons dressed up lak Masqueraders
Porters armed lak rude invaders
When dey hear dem ragtime tunes
White folks try to pass fo' coons
On Emancipation day.[8]

Is it possible to look past the language and see the ways in which there is another level of passing going on? Masqueraders, "masked raiders," rude invaders: the black threat, if comical, is still serious (just as later, when faced with the high seriousness of gangsta rap listeners didn't always see the humor). *Whitefolks clear de way*—but here it is whites who, amidst the masked black menace, will put on other masks to "pass" as black. Isn't this what white audiences and performers had done already on the minstrel stage, in the cakewalk craze, hearing ragtime—trying to pass not for Negroes but for "niggers," not for African Americans but "fo' coons"?

The "Emancipation" being sought by the operetta is also liberation for the national stage, where actual black performers couldn't appear for much of the nineteenth century—and where African Americans could eventually appear on Broadway in their own productions only thanks to Cook and Dunbar, and, soon enough, not just in blackface. In Williams and Walker, only Williams played in blackface; we were halfway there. One of the other hit all-black productions of the time actually featured blacks in whiteface, widely praised by the press for their mimicry.[9]

"Evah Dahkey Is a King," another song from *In Dahomey*, declared: *Ef yo' social life's a bungle, / Jes' you go back to yo' jun-gle, / An' remember dat a yo' daddy was a king.* However comical, the jungle's wilderness proved preferable to the plantation's topiary order. Soon enough Dunbar and Cook would not simply claim royalty: this and other songs were likely among those Williams and Walker performed for the King of England during *In Dahomey*'s successful overseas run.[10]

But could the language of dialect be "looked past"? Or was dialect itself a language of the past that ultimately could not bring about Emancipation in Dahomey, England, America, or the English language itself?

PLANTATION AMERICA

Just as the musicals moved from Darktown to Dahomey, Dunbar can be seen as working both in and away from the plantation tradition and its diminished sense of black dialect—which, while not quite English as such, is not a separate language either. This diminished dialect constitutes a sort of slave quarters on the grounds of the master's faux-British estate. The pastoral, plantation tradition took its cues from England or the ideas of England (and Eden), extending its idyll even to language, which it saw it as "natural" and God-given—rather than a series of clashes of cultures and tongues.

How little has changed! As the stilted Ebonics debate of the 1990s pointed out, we Americans still conceive that there is such a thing as proper English (and just who speaks this? newscasters? politicians? British people? Presumably whoever is speaking, or posing the question); that dialects of all stripes are lesser forms, evolved out of lack of intelligence, rather than need; and an especially unshakable view that black vernacular in particular is a broken, mutilated, ahistorical, insufficient, pidgin English. At our peril we ignore the fact that black vernacular, like the blues, both has a form and performs.

It should be enough to cite James Baldwin in his assessment of these perennial issues, summed up in the title of his essay "If Black English Is Not a Language, Then What Is?" Besides noting black vernacular's historic causes, and its similarity to, for example, the English of the invaded Irish—an idea that bears more exploration elsewhere—Baldwin also asserts the black idiom's uniqueness. Such inventiveness I believe should be seen as sharing with and shaping the blues, jazz, rock and roll, and in fact the entire music of American English. For just as there would be no American music without black folks, there would be very little of our American language.

But is what Dunbar was writing over a century ago "our language"? Is it a tongue at all? Dunbar himself wondered this, creating a dialectic with his dialect poems by also writing formal, traditional English verse—not to mention the stories of his hating dialect and feeling trapped by it. How is this verse different from the dialect poems, one must ask—and does this dialectic ever resolve itself, either directly in Dunbar or later, in the twentieth or twenty-first century?

While till now I have used them a bit interchangeably, I want to make clear a distinction between black "dialect"—a product of the plantation tradition, largely written—and African American "vernacular," something spoken, sung, in an everyday tongue. No one but Joel Chandler Harris, "inventor" of the Uncle Remus tales (who often would "translate" whole passages into "negro"), actually spoke dialect in this sense. "Speaking of dialect, it is almost a despairing task to write it. . . . The fact is there is no such thing as a Negro dialect,"[11] writes the fiction writer Charles Chesnutt, Dunbar's contemporary and fellow Ohioan.

Dialect's being one of the worst of nineteenth-century fictions has hardly stopped it from persisting to this day. Those in doubt need only consult a book like Margaret B. Seltzer's fake memoir *Love and Consequences* (2008), whose replacement of *c*'s with *k*'s throughout leads to some fascinating dialect—and whose "truthiness" caused it to be pulled from the shelves by the publisher.[12] This is no accident: like Seltzer's faux memoir, dialect is a fiction posing as the real thing. Much like the melodramatic dialogue of nineteenth-century Victorian novels or the misspelled titles of gangsta movies of the 1990s, dialect is a literary convention, a shorthand. On its own, such shorthand is not much of a problem; however, when matched with the excesses of the minstrel show, the inanities of naturalism, and worse, with a pseudoscientific and -linguistic need to explain and maintain racial difference, dialect reveals itself as pernicious.

Form as deformed. Tintypes turned stereotypes, exaggerated and unmoving. A mask made of words.

You could say the fault lies not just with poor approximations like "gwine" for what's actually "gonna" (or better yet, "gon'"), but with an apostrophe—black dialect is never the radical syntax or an old way of talking it actually was, but always meant something missing, whether a letter or learnin'. "If we are to believe the majority of writers of Negro dialect and the burnt-cork artists," Hurston writes, "Negro speech is a weird thing, full of 'ams' and 'Ises.' Fortunately we don't have to believe them. We may go directly to the Negro and let him speak for himself. I know that I run the risk of being damned as an infidel for declaring that nowhere can be found the Negro who asks 'am it?' nor yet his brother who announces 'Ise uh gwinter.' He exists only for a certain type of writers and performers."[13]

Poet Kamau Brathwaite distinguishes between such debased dialect and what he calls "nation language"—roughly equivalent to what I call vernacular—in his essential *History of the Voice:*

> The word "dialect" has been bandied about for a long time,
> and it carries very pejorative overtones. Dialect is thought of
> as "bad English." Dialect is "inferior English." Dialect is the
> language used when you want to make fun of someone. Carica-
> ture speaks in dialect. Dialect has a long history coming from
> the plantation where people's dignity is distorted through their
> language and the descriptions which the dialect gave to them.
> Nation language, on the other hand is the *submerged* area of
> that dialect which is much more closely allied to the African
> aspect of experience in the Caribbean. It may be in English:
> but often it is in an English which is like a howl, or a shout or
> a machine-gun or the wind or a wave. It is also like the blues.
> And sometimes it is English and African at the same time.[14]

While he refers here chiefly to his native Caribbean, Brathwaite's description certainly rings true for most all of "Plantation America," a useful and unfortunately accurate term whereby Brathwaite unites the Americas under the lash. It is this Plantation America against which nation language (and the borderless Black Atlantic) pit themselves.

Dialect denies the sly, understated, submerged, and shifting qualities of actual African American vernacular. We need only look to the spirituals to see how black folks, in slavery and out, took English and made it their own, replete with codes and calls of which whites were largely unaware or did not know quite how to respond to. This private language is one aspect of vernacular not enough discussed; even in dissecting such language's "performative" aspects, we would do well to remember the ways it both codifies and consolidates community, African and English at the same time.

Such a language outsiders have found strange, mistaking unintelligible for unintelligent, since its advent. In their early and important collection of spirituals, *Slave Songs of the United States* (1867), the white editors describe hearing black talk:

> A stranger, upon first hearing these people talk, especially if there is a group of them in animated conversation, can hardly understand them better than if they spoke a foreign language, and might, indeed, easily suppose this to be the case. The strange words and pronunciations, and frequent abbreviations, disguise the familiar features of one's native tongue, while the rhythmical modulations, so characteristic of certain European languages, give it an utterly un-English sound. After six months' residence among them, there were scholars in my school, among the most constant in attendance, whom I could not understand at all, unless they happened to speak very slowly.
>
> With these people the process of "phonetic decay" appears to have gone as far, perhaps, as is possible.[15]

To think these are the same folks who first rendered the spirituals (in dialect, of course) in book form—these are whites who meant well—should let us know the difficulties and unreliability of transcribing such tongues.

The public aspects of language serve as the private building blocks of community. "In the beginning the word was largely a pass-word, granting admission to a nucleus of like speakers."[16] While true of all language, this private nature is all the more important with Black English because of its dual nature, its particular desire to preserve while also being communicative. Further, much of black speaking life results from performance, walking a blurry black line between teasing and signifyin', between the dozens and one-on-ones with friends and family, between woofin' as playing the clown for others and as simply clowning around for one's own pleasure.

It is this public face that drew Americans to blackface and made them want to jump Jim Crow. Joel Chandler Harris, Georgia's own, took the show on the road. Harris highlighted the performative aspects of black dialect instead of the communicative or private ones—much less those that were, in fact, coded. In "translating" into black speech, Harris denied any sense of black privacy while also relying on it: he simultaneously supposed these creatures among us are strange and incomprehensible; and that, like Dr. Doolittle (pre–Eddie Murphy) or Henry Higgins, it is he who holds the key.

In thinking of Harris's translations, I am reminded of Shakespeare's *A Midsummer Night's Dream*—a play I, like just about everyone else, put on in high school—wherein the character of Bottom is "translated" into an ass. (The black vernacular term "blackbottom" comes to the ever-punning mind.) While critic, poet, and composer James Weldon Johnson convincingly argued that "dialect has only two stops: pathos and humor," I have come to see that with dialect the problem is that pathos and humor both infiltrate, and ultimately undermine, the other. Where the blues engage high tragedy and low comedy, dialect like blackface minstrelsy meant the opposite: low tragedy and high comedy. Like Bottom and his fellow Rude Mechanical's performance of tragedy at the end of Shakespeare's comedy, dialect's attempt at pathos is too often lugubrious; the stab at comedy, too often fatal.

Dunbar himself grew to greatly dislike his dialect work, pigeonholed by one of his chosen idioms after being damned with praise by novelist and tastemaker William Dean Howells in his 1896 review of *Majors and Minors* in *Harper's Weekly*. There, Howells introduced Dunbar's work to a larger public while chiefly praising his dialect. To make matters worse, the piece soon appeared in edited form as an introduction to *Lyrics of Lowly Life,* which gathered Dunbar's first two books. Eventually reprinted yet again in Dunbar's *Complete Poems* (1913), Howells's simple if not simplistic review is still appended to most editions of Dunbar, making it impossible to get to Dunbar without the all-too-familiar fog of white authenticating.

The reverse occurs in the title of *Lyrics of Lowly Life,* which refers to the subtitle of Harriet Beecher Stowe's *Uncle Tom's Cabin; or, Life among the Lowly.* By Dunbar's time, "lowly" had become virtually synonymous with black—just as "urban" or "inner city" or "underclass" has become in ours. Witness Howells, who describes "the poems in literary English":

> Some of these I thought very good, and even more than very good, but not distinctively his contribution to the body of American poetry. What I mean is that several people might have written them; but I do not know any one else at present who could quite have written the dialect pieces. These are divinations and reports of *what passes in the hearts and minds of a lowly people* whose poetry had hitherto been inarticulately expressed in music, but now finds, for the first time in *our* tongue, literary interpretation of a very artistic completeness.[17]

We can only assume that by "inarticulately expressed in music" Howells means the spirituals of those selfsame lowly people. Needless to say, Howells and I differ here: it is Howells and Harris and others who cannot articulate the spirituals' (or other black forms') storying possibility. Our first job in reading Dunbar is to excise Howells, who overpraises dialect's apostrophe, using it as another form of possession.

In including the word *lowly* in his title, Dunbar is not so much capitulating as capitalizing and even riffing off Stowe's, making it his own. By granting the "lowly" their own lyrics, Dunbar lays claim not just to being "*among* the lowly," as Stowe claimed and Harris implied, but to being one of them. *Black like me.* Further, Dunbar's title declares that these are "lyrics," claiming one of the highest forms of language; if paradox, *Lyrics of Lowly Life* provides a musical, fruitful one. You could call it a blues—one that sees "down" not as a deadly fate but as a moral high ground.

Still it can prove hard to read Howells's introduction and Dunbar's now-famous lines without trepidation, especially after knowing his feeling of being trapped by his fame in his too-short life:

> I know why the caged bird sings, ah me,
>   When his wing is bruised and his bosom sore,—
> When he beats his bars and he would be free;
> It is not a carol of joy or glee,

But a prayer that he sends from his heart's deep core,
But a plea, that upward to Heaven he flings—
I know why the caged bird sings!

Beyond providing an interesting metaphor for slavery, and even for the sorrow songs made in the midst of bondage, these lines from "Sympathy" recall the idea of the poem's very form as caged—a container for the poet to sing in. Rather than stealing away, the speaker expresses "sympathy," seeking our empathy, if perhaps too plaintively.

But if "Sympathy" has a syntax that is formal, even artificial, I would argue that this is precisely the point. This formality goes beyond rhyme: Dunbar maintains his use of formal, Standard English verse in order to express the captivity he and his speaker feels—ironically, using the classical form as an implicit protest against the strictures of dialect.

Rather than try to capture true speech, Dunbar uses both Standard English and black vernacular to question any poem's relation to language—to, in fact, heighten its performative aspects. If, in order to reiterate how trapped he must have felt by his own poems, critics often focus on the fact that Dunbar did not really speak dialect, we must remember that in fact no one did—and that nobody speaks in metered, rhyming verse either. If Dunbar protests what could be called the dance of dialect, it is important to note how he uses "the prison of pentameter" to do so.

The artificialness of dialect, the artificialness of meter: Dunbar's inability, or more tellingly, his era's, to reconcile the two makes for a difficult life story but an interesting challenge for us as readers. To see Dunbar's dialect and traditional poetry as not just "warring bodies" of work, but as a functioning whole, we must hear with all our ears.

LOWLY LIFE

What works in Dunbar is the very tension between form and freedom—not between dialect on one hand and more typical, formal verse on the other, but rather the freedom within both forms. While distinct, dialect and Standard English verse are each a form, with tradition and rules and histories. We must listen for the caged bird's singing. Such tension between form and freedom—ignoring, for now, the possibilities of freedom within form (as in Hopkins)—dominates much of twentieth-century black writing.

We could read the Harlem Renaissance, then, as two camps descending from Dunbar's dividing line—Countee Cullen the proper formalist on one side, Hughes the vernacular innovator on the other. Certainly many critics have. Yet it may be more useful to look sidelong. From such an angle we can see Claude McKay, who employs form in unconventional ways; or a poet like Sterling A. Brown, who manages not only to merge vernacular and formal verse but sees in vernacular a form filled with possibility.

McKay's invention, the militant sonnet, may provide a more useful paradox than Cullen's ironic questioning of a God who would dare to "make a poet black, and bid him sing." With McKay, the king's "Island English" gets transformed, made Caribbean—an archipelago of one—and it would seem this tradition of freedom within form finds some of its best practitioners in Caribbean writers such as Aimé Césaire, Derek Walcott, Kamau Brathwaite, and even June Jordan, who was Harlem-born of Jamaican descent. All four embodied this struggle early on in their work: we see the ways a form can be turned inside out in the revolutionary sonnets of McKay and in Walcott's rewriting of Homeric epic; in the invention of a whole "Sycorax" system of syntax in Brathwaite; and in "vertical rhythm" as defined by Jordan. *We are the ones we have been waiting for.*

Perhaps we should think of not just these writers but Dunbar himself as postcolonial, wrestling with a mother tongue that we had adopted but too often refused us. Certainly Brathwaite's account of an emergent "nation language" could apply more broadly to the new world, and not just the Caribbean he mentions explicitly:

> And so Ashanti, Congo, Yoruba, all that mighty coast of western Africa was imported into the Caribbean. And we had the arrival in our area of a new language structure. It consisted of many languages but basically they had a common semantic and stylistic form. What these languages had to do, however, was to submerge themselves, because officially the conquering peoples—the Spaniards, the English, the French, and the Dutch—insisted that the language of public discourse and

conversation, of obedience, command and conception should be English, French, Spanish or Dutch. They did not wish to hear people speaking Ashanti or any of the Congolese languages. So there was a submergence of this imported language. Its status became one of inferiority. Similarly, its speakers were slaves. They were conceived of as inferiors—non-human, in fact. But this very submergence served an interesting interculturative purpose, because although people continued to speak English as it was spoken in Elizabethan times and on through the Romantic and Victorian ages, that English was, nonetheless, still being influenced by the underground language, the sub-merged language that the slaves had brought. And that under-ground language was itself constantly transforming itself into new forms.[18]

Nowhere is this process made clearer than in the forms of McKay, whose peripatetic poetics and past are worthy of more study than is possible here. Interestingly, Brathwaite sees McKay as exactly *not* an example of nation language, feeling he relies on pentameter too much.[19]

I would argue that even if McKay does not fully realize nation language, then he certainly embodies its very struggle to emerge. At the very least, Jamaican-born McKay expressed his own "Island English" that was both related to and quite different from England's—he did so early in his writing career, publishing several books of "patois" and "Standard English" alongside each other. These 1912 books—*Songs from Jamaica, Constab Ballads,* and the rare volume *Songs of Jamaica,*[20] which included some of the poems set to music, were a radically differ-ent kind of Island English, despite or actually because McKay's island may have included both Jamaica and the England that first printed his work. Yet, the Jamaican-English books and even his earliest militant sonnets in *Spring in New Hampshire* (1920), such as "If We Must Die," were prefaced by white-authored introductions that, like Dunbar be-fore him, reduced his work to "pure-blooded" racial expression. Even McKay's friend the white radical Max Eastman reeks of reductiveness in his introduction to *Harlem Shadows* (1922), a book that remains one of the high points of the Harlem Renaissance. The editor of McKay's recent *Complete Poems,* William J. Maxwell, accurately sums up Eastman's introduction as "a mixed bag of shrewd critical insight, minstrel-fed drivel, scientific antiracism, creative biography, and worried cheerleading for the pre-modernist lyric in an 'age of roar and advertising.'"[21]

McKay's solution and response to the pressures of dialect and the framing devices of white authentication are summed up fairly simply in the first paragraph of his "Author's Word" that follows Eastman's intro in *Harlem Shadows:* "In putting ideas and feelings into poetry, I have tried in each case to use the medium most adaptable to the specific purpose. I own allegiance to no master."[22]

No matter the medium or form, whether writing in "dialect" or "Standard English," McKay insists his verse is free. We should demand the same of Dunbar and our readings of him.

MAPLE LEAF RAG

Tradition is meant to be broken, an inherited tongue we must interrogate. But it is also a tongue that binds, that "governs," as Seamus Heaney would have it. In his remarkable essay collection, *The Government of the Tongue,* Heaney focuses on a dialectic between the tongue as governing—the inspirational, generating, freeing forms of poetry—and the tongue as governed, as "minded" by a tempering force. That second sense of "government" is one of tempering, of social or public forces; and while the two are related, Heaney tends to come down on the side of the unfettered freed tongue.

But what if that tongue is overdetermined? What if that governing is not freeing or confiding but rather oppressive, *confining?* What if the subject is less a speaking subject than a slave forbidden to talk? Or, what to make of someone like Angelou herself—an abuse survivor who for years was an elective mute—someone for whom silence is both a symptom of pain and a means of overcoming it? Heaney, ever aware of the political aspects of the tongue and times, does examine breaking away from this "government," chiefly in the person of Osip Mandelstam, the Russian dissident writer who paid for his anti-Stalinist stance with his life.

Naturalism, however, was both denied Dunbar in his formal work and overdetermined in his dialect poems. The latter were too often asked (or simply made) to bear a sociological weight, not least as a result of Howells's introduction.

The problem is not just that Howells sought realism, as he did, but that as Henry B. Wonham has convincingly argued, the age of realism that Howells introduced was also the age of caricature—a technique that realism resembled and was deeply dependent on. The result is what another critic of Howells calls "minstrel realism" or "racial realism," terms that seek "to begin illuminating the cultural cooperation of racialism and realism during the postbellum period."[23]

The poems were further pushed into "naturalism" by the production and popularity of pictorial Dunbar volumes such as *Poems of Cabin and Field* (1899), *Candle-Lightin' Time* (1901), or the very title *In Old Plantation Days* (1903). These volumes replace the fact of the poet's race or his photographic portrait with interleaved photographs that go far beyond that chimera, the photo-essay, into the realm of fact.[24]

Though highlighting the usually fine photography of the Hampton Institute, such volumes further popularized not just Dunbar's poetry but also the notion that the speakers were real people, rather than imagined, if believable, voices. The chemistry that created the photographs is not complete: within the books the photos transform further, moving from individual tintypes into "stock types," pulling the poems along with them. Tensions originating outside the poem are "fixed" like photographs are to stop what might develop.

For Dunbar's inheritors the problem wasn't dialect as black speech—which they knew was a flawed fiction—but dialect as a calcified form and genre. As James Weldon Johnson wrote in 1922's groundbreaking *Book of American Negro Poetry* about the new generation, "They are trying to break away from, not Negro dialect itself, but the limitations on Negro dialect imposed by the fixing effects of long convention." The change he and others sought is in dialect's clichéd history, not necessarily in its potential content; by the 1920s, the two had become inextricable. Writing again of the New Negro poet, Johnson could be speaking of Dunbar in particular:

He needs a form that is freer and larger than dialect, but which
will still hold the racial flavor; a form expressing the imagery,
the idioms, the peculiar turns of thought, and the distinctive
humor and pathos, too, of the Negro, but which will also be
capable of voicing the deepest and highest emotions and aspirations, and allow the widest range of subjects and the widest
scope of treatment.[25]

Johnson's is one of many attempts by modern American poets of all
stripes to get to actual speech—and to overthrow the influence of
Britain during what Ann Douglas calls the postcolonial moment of
the 1920s.

This didn't stop many, including the Johnson brothers, both onstage
and in print, from trying their hand at dialect first. You could say that
this was exactly their intent: black dialect, even as mask, proved better
than a British whiteface one. Despite or more likely because of Dunbar's
achievement as the reinventor of dialect, generations broke with Dunbar's
broken tongue, either rejecting it entirely or seeking a more accurate
black vernacular.

Fix, meaning to stay put; *fix*, meaning to repair; *fixin' to*, meaning
an imminent future action: all of these are at work in and after Dunbar.

Johnson's two stops of "pathos and humor" for dialect are the direct
descendants of the minstrel tradition, in which the black man's burdens
remained either romanticized ("I miss ole Massa") or made merely romantic ("Oh Susannah, don't you cry for me").[26] Rarely are we given the
shifting, vengeful perspective of *Jimmy crack corn, and I don't care*—the
song in the voice of a slave almost literally dancing on his dead master's
grave. Women, if found in minstrelsy, are even more grossly exaggerated, made either fair-skinned and fine, or dark and decidedly unlovely.
(*Norbit,* anyone?) Part of this could be said to be the premodern, Gilded
Age zeitgeist—one that focused on a romantic naturalism the fin de
siècle and modern era both necessitated and later debunked.[27] Howells's
own work has even recently been discussed in terms of his championing
of realism that included racial stereotype, he and other realists not seeing racist caricature as anomalous but analogous.[28]

Yet we should not, in the end, assign Dunbar these burdens as if he labored and wrote under them. They are not only part of the poems' reception, largely out of any writer's control, but they come from reading the work as divided (and not reading the work closely at all). Dunbar's poems and the black vernacular insist otherwise. Poems such as "An Ante-Bellum Sermon" provide a neat contrast to Johnson's own strong achievements in the sermon tradition. Just as the speaker in the poem comments on his slave-drivin' present by using biblical allusion, the postbellum black writer, by picking a situation "far ago" (in slavery), comments on the limitations of his contemporary, turn-of-the-century, sharecropping, dialect-writin' possibilities. Text and subtext: like any good one, the sermon revels in both.

For, as Sterling A. Brown (graduate, it turns out, of the famed Dunbar High School in Washington, D.C.) reminds us, black folks ain't nothing if not exegetical. Even in dialect, Dunbar stays true to the African American tradition of the sermon, of spiraling out from a text, and ultimately of understatement and Underground Railroad code. You could say that it is because of "the underground language, the submerged language that the slaves had brought" and subsequently wrought—not just the codes found in the Negro spirituals, but the English "nation language" itself. It is in this storying tradition that Dunbar is best experienced.

When read in tandem, his dialect and formal poems provide their own exegesis—much the way Phillis Wheatley's letters inform her poems, or the way the first African American novel, *Clotel,* authenticates itself through William Wells Brown's own nonfiction preface that often accompanies it.[29] Doing so, we begin to see Dunbar's poems not in terms of a divided life or Howells's damning praise but in terms of the poems' relations to one other. Dunbar's dialect and formal verse complement and complete each other.

The ultimate limit, of course, is that Dunbar is seemingly unable—either as a poet, or product of his time, or both—to interweave the two. The very titles of the first two volumes he published early on, with support from his mother and white patrons, seem to bear this division out. *Oak and Ivy* (1893); *Majors and Minors* (1895): the former, presumably the formal poems, are seen as the "major" ones, the chief achievement; the others lesser, clinging like ivy.[30] Lowly life indeed.

By dividing them as such, Dunbar has assigned them a hierarchy I have myself refrained from imposing, elevating oaken "Standard English" above the creeping ivy of "dialect." I have also avoided raising up the dialect poems, as Howells does; or focusing only on the non-dialect poems, as critics such as Ashley Bryan have, if largely in reaction to Howells. Instead, when we read in a manner more consistent with storying, we see the poems less as narrative than as nodal—in a way more like early blues or ragtime.

What I am calling for here is for us, as readers, to be effective code switchers, moving with ease, elegance, and recognition between Dunbar's twinned tongues. It is up to us to take up both of Dunbar's languages at once—the shifting understatement made present—to move between dialect and other forms on a dime, recognizing that a tension between the two is what drives black poetics, and in the end, the vernacular itself.

DARK VERSE

Under Dunbar's influence almost two generations of poets, black and white alike, would include separate but unequal sections of dialect poems to play off the more dully Victorian ones. You could call it a kind of "dark" verse in lieu of or as complement to a section of "light verse." The dialect craze Dunbar resurrected even swept up James Weldon Johnson, who included a dialect section in his book *Fifty Years and Other Poems* (1917).

Such framing of dialect verse as lesser, as afterthought, is enough of a trend to be said to be part of the form. One of the problems with Joel Chandler Harris, it has been widely noted, was his insertion of a framing device that stood between us and the African folktale itself—and a racist device at that, namely, the "authenticating" fiction of Uncle Remus, whose happy darky undermined the often subversive aspects of the Brer Rabbit tales he told.[31] It should not go unnoticed that Harris required a black storyteller to authenticate *his* tale in the first place—not to mention relying on his stated lifelong "familiarity" with Negroes, long the premise of white minstrels and "genuine Ethiopian delineators," to make his work genuine. We do well to remember that authenticity is not a one-way street serving only black authors; rather, it is often a sign of white anxiety.

Radically, Dunbar cast aside the frame, seeing the vernacular not just as a type but as a form to be used when it suited the mood he wanted to convey. This mood was not so much pathos and humor as ecstasy and sorrow:

> Standin' at de winder,
>   Feelin' kind o' glum,
> Listenin' to de raindrops
>   Play de kettle drum,
> Lookin' crost de medders
>   Swimmin' lak a sea;
> Lawd 'a' mussy on us,
>   What's de good o' me?
>
> Can't go out a-hoein',
>   Wouldn't ef I could;
> Groun' too wet fu' huntin',
>   Fishin' ain't no good.
> Too much noise fo' sleepin',
>   No one hyeah to chat;
> Des mus' stan' an' listen
>   To dat pit-a-pat.
>
> Hills is gittin' misty,
>   Valley's gittin' dahk;
> Watch-dog's 'mence a-howlin',
>   Rathah have 'em ba'k
> Dan a-moanin' solemn
>   Somewhaih out o' sight;
> Rain-crow des a chucklin'—
>   Dis is his delight.
>   ("BLUE")

By placing both kinds of poems in the same volume, Dunbar also elevated dialect poems to the level of "standard," metered verse—both as valid forms worth interweaving. I prefer to think of the titles *Majors and Minors* less in terms not of hierarchies, then, but rather as major and minor chords keys of music that allow Dunbar entry into different emotions. Including the blues moan.

Take these two differing views of death: as bitter, faltering "Compensation"; or as part of the natural course of things in "A Death Song":

> Because I had loved so deeply,
>   Because I had loved so long,
> God in His great compassion
>   Gave me the gift of song.
>
> Because I have loved so vainly,
>   And sung with such faltering breath,
> The Master in infinite mercy
>   Offers the boon of Death.
>   ("COMPENSATION")

> Lay me down beneaf de willers in de grass
> Whah de branch'll go a-singin' as it pass.
>   An' w'en I 's a-layin' low,
>   I kin hyeah it as it go
> Singin', "Sleep, my honey, tek yo' res' at las'."
>   ("A DEATH SONG")

Both are songs, implicitly or explicitly. But where "Compensation," quoted in full, is bitterly ironic—"infinite mercy" might anticipate the start of Cullen's own "Yet Do I Marvel"—the music is the message in "Death Song." Such difference is not incidental, but springs from their respective forms—not the rhyme schemes, which resemble each other, but their very choice of tongues implying, and corresponding to, a worldview. One resigned, one accepting of death: both black.

If we read "Death Song" as passive, accepting death in a fashion that would come to be seen as clichéd, or even stereotyped, this would be a misreading just as the spirituals were seen as examples of contentment. Heaven, the spirituals in fact remind us, is not just a far-off promise but also an indictment of a life of hell. While often in the broadest strokes possible, as if playing the piano with his elbows, Dunbar recognizes that "dialect" has a time and a place—and not merely the past as a place, a stereotyped Dixie or Ole Virginny.

"Death Song" doesn't see death as compensation, in fact, but as the last stanza indicates, a return to the earth: "Nigh enough to hyeah de noises in de road . . . layin' 'mong de t'ings I 's allus knowed."[32] Such a wish does not in fact rely on God, at least a specified, Christian one (as does "Compensation"). You could say instead there's a blues quality, one found more pointed in a song like Memphis Slim's "Mother Earth" a half century later:

> Don't care how great you are, don't care what you worth
> When it all ends up you got to go back to Mother Earth.

We see in Dunbar, finally, less the lilt and croon of blackface than the rustling, restless music of ragtime. One hand keeps the melody; the other plays and riffs.

If at first blush all this seems quite far from the poetry of jazz and jazz-based poetry, from "Ain't nobody's business if I do," it's not so far from the radical free verse of Fenton Johnson and its assertion of black fatalism a generation later. Others of Dunbar's literary descendants, especially writers of the Harlem Renaissance, continued to dispense with the frame; a little later yet, writers used the frame to subvert the form of the dialect poem, such as in Hughes's early "Weary Blues" and James Weldon Johnson's prefaces to *God's Trombones* and *The Book of American Negro Poetry*. The whole of Brown's work often includes frames in a fashion more familiar to daguerreotypes—providing a gilded witness as it were, to the black speech within. Brown's "Old Lem," warning of the racial violence in Southern life, speaks to an "I" who listens—and in turn tells Lem's story to us—to indicate both the narrator's familiarity with dialect and his distance from it.

Let's think then of the two sides of Dunbar's work not as "double consciousness" but as a form of *double-* or even *multiple-speak*, elaborate and elegant. Both metered English and eye dialect are artificial languages that mirror yet mask actual speech; through the machining of the voice in each, Dunbar was able to achieve something that went far beyond naturalism into experience from multiple, even cubist, viewpoints.

Can we read "Sympathy" then not just as an indictment of captivity, or of history, or slavery, but also as a caution against the very Du Boisian double consciousness that Dunbar's life is so often read as embodying? In other words, can the sympathy Dunbar seeks actually be split between "serious verse" and comedic dialect, as well as between white and black, between being American and forever foreign, no matter how native the Negro actually was?

Reading multiply, we mirror the ways critic bell hooks describes how she understood the works as a child—not seeing them as separate but equal:

> In part, attending all-black segregated schools with black teachers meant that I had come to understand black poets as being capable of speaking in many voices, that the Dunbar of a poem written in dialect was no more or less authentic than the Dunbar writing a sonnet. Yet it was listening to black musicians like Duke Ellington, Louis Armstrong, and later John Coltrane that impressed upon our consciousness a sense of versatility— they played all kinds of music, had multiple voices. So it was with poetry. The black poet, as exemplified by Gwendolyn Brooks and later Amiri Baraka, had many voices—with no single voice being identified as more or less authentic.[33]

All told, Brown and McKay, Hughes and Hurston, Brooks and Baraka, Fenton Johnson and James Weldon Johnson, liberate us from dialect by vindicating it, turning dialect into a black vernacular based not on lack but on nuance and need. In them, Black English at last proves something untranslatable. This transformation began with Dunbar.

DOUBLE DOWN

In reading this way—meanings not divided but doubled, not missing but multiple—we may get the elevator operator's revenge. The elevator—

that unerring symbol of elevation, of "movin' on up" as the 1970s sitcom *The Jeffersons* would have it—makes a surprising series of appearances in black literature. After Dunbar, and his history and myth as an elevator operator (mentioned by Howells), we also have Rita Dove's poem "Elevator Man, 1949," describing her father. Here he gives rides to some of the very white men he had bested in engineering school a short time before:

> *Not a cage but an organ:*
> if he thought about it, he'd go insane
> Yes, if he thought about it
> *philosophically,*
> he was a bubble of bad air
> in a closed system.[34]

This closed system—arguably a description of tradition, with exclusions either literary or segregationist (or both)—gets challenged further by Dove and her protagonist, who gets his revenge on the segregated success of his white colleagues "by letting out all the stops, / jostling them up and down / the scale of his bitterness / until they emerge queasy, rubbing / the backs of their necks, / feeling absolved and somehow / in need of a drink."

Such jostling and absolution course through Colson Whitehead's *The Intuitionist,* a novel whose protagonist's position as the first black female elevator inspector in an alternate Gotham provides a powerful metaphor for integration and advancement—or, as the novel puts it, going beyond the obviousness of "Empiricism" into the "intuition of what's not you." *Not a cage but an organ*—meaning not just muscle, that is, but music.

Likewise, Natasha Trethewey's *Domestic Work* reimagines and celebrates her grandmother's relation to labor, including her stint as an elevator operator. This takes the form of a fine poem called "Speculation, 1939," whose title of course refers not just to the idea of soothsaying about the future but speculating for gold; the two are linked by rhyme in the first two lines:

> First, the moles on each hand—
> *That's money by the pan—*

The poem then continues with the grandmother's taking up such folk symbols of luck and seeking them out even on her job as elevator operator; Trethewey revels in leaps of the poem's end, her grandmother considering self-employment, and "the signs": "her palms itching with promise, / . . . Her left-eye twitch / says she'll see the boon." We may admire here the way Trethewey employs the "racial symbol from within," Johnson's phrase for what had to be invented after Dunbar and the dead end of dialect. I want to point out that like other writers in the post-soul era, Trethewey not only assumes this "racial symbol" is possible but uses it effortlessly—the superstitious signs are part of the folkways, valued, described, integral to the poem—in a way Dunbar could only imagine, but also, I would argue, in a way Dunbar first made possible.

Trethewey's "racial symbol," this process of music and movement the poem charts, of course allows us to see how the grandmother—here a "character" in all senses of the word—thinks. The ending enacts through rhyme her leaps of faith and thought, replicating the lurching of the elevator, again a symbol of "uplift":

> What's to be gained from this New Deal?
> *Something finer* like beauty school
> or a milliner's shop—she loves the feel
> of marcelled hair, felt and tulle,
>
> not this all day standing around,
> not that elevator lurching up, then down.[35]

Full rhymes give way to slant, and to an enjambment that stands and lurches. It also inverts—not for classicism but colloquialism—saying "not this all day" rather than "this standing around all day." Trethewey's poem uses inversion, language, full and slant rhyme, as well as tension between the tightness of form and the slantness of breath, to help us imagine the emotion behind the veil.

The poem, it could be said, is speaking double—lurching between history (New Deal) and possibility (*Something finer*); between "the feel" as emotion and literally as touch; between this personal or at least physical aspect of feelings, and the impersonal yet reassuring "felt" of fabric. We are not left in the lurch between this future and the reality, but in the leap between stanzas—suddenly, like the grandmother, we are back in the elevator, seasick without the comfort of the waves. Descent.

And again, possibility. After all, in the blues aesthetic "down" can sure look like up; and, as we've seen, "down" in the Negro spirituals is less a fate than a vantage point. "The use of dialect in Afro-American poetry itself was a form of masking, a verbal descent underground to the Great Dis," Henry Louis Gates reminds us. "The poet has in this mutation—this dialect—an accessible linguistic system that turns the literate language upon itself, exploiting the metaphor against its master. Afro-American dialects exist between two poles, one English and one lost in some mythical linguistic kingdom now irrecoverable. Dialect is our only key to that unknown tongue, and in its obvious relation and reaction to English it contains, as does the Yoruban mask, a verbal dialectic, a dialectic between some form of an African *antithesis* all the while obviating the English *thesis*."[36] Invoking the "City of Dis," Gates refers to the mythic underworld also found in Dante's *Inferno,* while punning on the idea of "Dis and Dat" as found in dialect.

"Dis" might also echo our term *dis* for disrespect, disregard, a fate worse than death. The dis that dialect underwent is both earned and imposed, a kind of haunting. It is also the ultimate undoing. And yet, perhaps exactly because of its lowly status, vernacular could provide a kind of insurrection, or at least antithesis, uprising against the standard mode. Uplift. Certainly it did so for Dante. "Dis is his delight." It is such sightings—or soundings—that we find in Dunbar in its earliest form, condensed, coal-like, filled with possibility. Our job is to light the fire, and the way.

THE UNCALLED

Does Dunbar represent not just the power of dialect and its descent but also its ascent? "There are many procedures for placing the voice in variation, not only *Sprechgesang* (speech-song), which constantly leaves pitch behind by descent or ascent, but also circular breathing techniques and zones of resonance in which several voices seem to issue from the same mouth." Deleuze and Guattari's sense of the ways single voices can be many, literally, is useful. As does their collaborative writing. The duo continues by discussing "secret languages" in music:

> Certain ethnomusiciologists have found extraordinary cases
> (in Dahomey, for example) where a first, diatonic, vocal part
> is superseded by a chromatic descent into a secret language
> that slips from one sound to the next in a continuous fashion,
> modulating a sound continuum into smaller and smaller inter-
> vals until it becomes a "parlando" all of the intervals of which
> blur together . . . A secret language does not merely have a hid-
> den cipher or code still operating by constants and forming a
> subsystem; *it places the public language's system of variables in
> a state of variation.*[37]

Such public language is further questioned and critiqued by a secret language. English becomes a site of resistance in variation, the language itself—the vernacular—shifting from Darktown to Dahomey. Several voices from the same mouth. English in the sense of moving a pinball around, manhandling the machine to get the result you want.

If we simply look for a "true" or authentic self in Dunbar, we may find it. But we may spend quite a bit of time pursuing "feeling" as emotion, psychologizing, supposing, and not enough time with the "feeling" as physical, as texture "felt." If we take too much time trying to see behind the veil, that is, we may miss its texture, too busy trying to describe the face—Dunbar the photograph turned mug shot, some suspect in a police lineup—and not enough time admiring the mask he and the vernacular continually craft. Or seeing the ways in which he takes part in storying, telling tales both tall and out of school:

> We wear the mask that grins and lies,
> It hides our cheeks and shades our eyes,—
> This debt we pay to human guile;
> With torn and bleeding hearts we smile,
> And mouth with myriad subtleties.

It is crucial, in Dunbar, that we take note of the very phrase "myriad subtleties"—itself a subtle off-rhyme, to my ear, with "lies" and "eyes."

These "subtleties" are also subtle ties between masks and faces, emotion and persona, as well as between people. The "we" here is simultaneously black folks and all folks—guile is human, not black. But to deny the tradition of the mask as African (and arguably, of the concept of community, a specific African American "we") is to miss quite a lot.

What's more, "We Wear the Mask"—itself in a "formal," traditional form—cautions against a reading of even Dunbar's formal verse as his private thought. And, however indirectly, in "Mask" Dunbar critiques the mask of dialect and the plantation tradition. That he does so in the tone of the spirituals is significant (and signifyin'):

> We smile, but, O great Christ, our cries
> To thee from tortured souls arise.
> We sing, but oh the clay is vile
> Beneath our feet, and long the mile;
> But let the world dream otherwise,
>   We wear the mask.[38]

The mask, fittingly, does not fit: it is the only line, repeated in the second stanza and the title, that does not even slant rhyme. Stark, lonely, offset by sound and by indentation, the music here stumbles on purpose, highlighting the mask as a kind of jarring noise, not a strict music. You could call it a kind of vernacular—one that splits or exploits the difference between the two.

Dunbar's mask of language, whether in dialect or in his formal verse, is both self-conscious and an antidote to harsh realities. By foregrounding the poems' self-consciousness—played out in their personae and impersonalities—we can further see Dunbar's achievement as prototypically modern. Not to mention the way, like the spirituals, his poems remap a fallen world; a world in which a mask, as in Eliot's "The Hollow Men," is one means of survival, however troubling.

This modern tension between the clay and its creation, regret and redemption, may help us better understand Howells's racist, or at best essentializing, statement on his first reading Dunbar:

> So far as I could remember, Paul Dunbar was the only man
> of pure African blood and of American civilization to feel the

negro life aesthetically and express it lyrically. It seemed to me
that this had come to its most *modern consciousness* in him,
and that his brilliant and unique achievement was to have
studied the American negro objectively, and to have represented him as he found him to be, with humor, with sympathy,
and yet with what the reader must instinctively feel to be entire
truthfulness.[39]

I have added emphasis to Howells's notion of *modern consciousness*—as
aestheticism and lyricism—in order to reiterate the ways Dunbar was
absolutely modern. How do these come out of studying "the American negro objectively"? And how is the Negro, in Howells and other
modern writers, the white man's own objective correlative?

It is Howells's widespread belief in the lowercase negro's innate "humor"
and "sympathy"—a sympathy quite different from Dunbar's own—that
Johnson sought to correct by declaring dialect a "limited instrument."
Johnson himself rewrites and signifies on Howells by using and the-
matically slant-rhyming off Howells's terms, turning Howells's aestheticism and lyricism into humor and pathos. Similarly, Johnson inverts
Howells's faint praise of Dunbar to damn dialect in turn.

We must avoid being a Howells-type reader for whom a poem like
"An Ante-Bellum Sermon" provides a perfect harmony of sympathy and
humor, all the more delightful for its accuracy of dialect. Especially because the black slave persona, both in the poem and in the world before
the Civil War, proves far more complex and revels in its play of code.
Rather than directly violate code, "An Ante-Bellum Sermon" uses the allegory of far-off biblical times in order to protest modern slavery—and
arguably Dunbar's own time. Directly paralleling the work of Phillis
Wheatley or the spirituals, such a sermon not only promotes a kind of
reading—twofold, counterfeit. It also indicates a type of speaking that's
not just double but wordless, a howl valuable as language:

> We is gathahed hyeah, my brothahs,
>   In dis howlin' wildaness,
> Fu' to speak some words of comfo't
>   To each othah in distress.

The sermon continues further on with a vision of holy wrath upon one's enemies:

> An' de lan' shall hyeah his thundah
>   Lak a blas' from Gab'el's ho'n.
> Fu' de Lawd of hosts is mighty
>   When he girds his ahmor on.
> But fu' feah some one mistakes me,
>   I will pause right hyeah to say,
> Dat I'm still a-preachin' ancient,
>   I ain't talkin' 'bout to-day.[40]

Again, the poem denies its own power—while this may seem comical in some hands, here it seems like a harnessed righteousness, a double-speak of another kind. Pass it off as harmless fun and you miss its self-conscious use of form; if you believe it is entirely truthful, or uncoded, you are by definition excluded from it: you are, in fact, the literalism the poem protests against.

The yoke's on you.

CANARY IN BLOOM

As in Wheatley, classicism in Dunbar is a form of defense. Classicism leaves the preacher or poet free to say whatever he or she wants, so long as it is indirect. Or in a strange, stilted tongue. Or both.

The two, it would seem, are intimately tied and meet in dialect's chief emblem: the apostrophe. Ostensibly a signal of something missing, of malaprop and mispronunciation, the apostrophe is instead a sign of what can't be fully represented by the written word. We could call it *scat* and be done with it. But with dialect at its best—which is to say, with Dunbar—the apostrophe (') is not just an accent, but an accent with a twist ('), a winking intonation that suggests a whole host of intentions. "Preachin' ancient."

There is another meaning of an apostrophe: as a call to a God. Think of Dunbar's delicious "Alas!" in "We Wear the Mask." It is a moment of appeal shared by the "invisible church"—and by the tone and the undertow of "An Ante-Bellum Sermon"—one that can hardly be con-

tained by its form. Here it is also dangerous, the sermon's code always
threatening to be exposed:

> Now don't run an' tell yo' mastahs
>   Dat I's preachin' discontent.
>
> 'Cause I isn't; I'se a-judgin'
>   Bible people by deir ac's;
> I'se a-givin' you de Scriptuah,
>   I'se a-handin' you de fac's.
> Cose ole Pher'oh b'lieved in slav'ry,
>   But de Lawd he let him see,
> Dat de people he put bref in,—
>   Evah mothah's son was free.

Evah Dahkey Is a King. The judging here is, of course, implied and
rendered not just by de Lawd but by de preachin' of discontent, thinly
veiled. The apostrophe—here I mean in both senses—is itself the veil,
at least as much as the semicorny photographs of a preacher that accompany it.

"An Ante-Bellum Sermon" appears in the pictorial volume *Jogging
Erlong* (1905), whose title's alliteration, its strange, unsteady poetry,
indicates the wordplay and worldview found in Black English. Such a
view, transmitted in part by the dialect itself, is that English has many
registers, often lower, that we ignore at our peril. This register is implied even in a typo in the first edition of the book: the poems all have
half titles before them, and this one reads "An Anti-Bellum Sermon."
In a way, the poem is "anti" as in "against" and not just "ante" as in
"before"—there's a sense that the sermon is constantly being revised
and reversed, part of its pleasure no doubt for the listener. It ain't what
you say, but how you say it.

The poem is also antiliteral, and perhaps even antiwar (as "anti-
bellum" would etymologically mean) in its description of retribution,
fate, and God's power beyond the mortal plane. Despite or maybe because of the preacher's protestations to the contrary, the dialect offers
up a protest against the cage of black life, and even the limits of language itself.

Such a protest may be made against the renaming—or perhaps I should call it unnaming—that routinely occurs "in slav'ry." This continued into Dunbar's era, and happens with Dunbar himself: any number of his books misprint his name as "Paul *Lawrence* Dunbar." If for a collector this might be the mark of a first edition—as in the case of his novel *The Uncalled*—it is a slim consolation for being called out one's name. That such misspelling happens regularly with "Phyllis Wheatly" or others does not make it any less troubling. Would you rather be pseudonymous or anonymous? Your name false or lost?

But with the vernacular, as with the black musical traditions it spawned, renaming is part and parcel of its remapping of language. Dunbar's name, in the end, wouldn't remain pseudonymous or a misnomer for long, but would become synonymous with black excellence.

The only other modern poet I know who can work an exclamation point as well as Dunbar is Rita Dove. (Maybe Lorca.) Dove rises to Dunbar's challenge not just in her lithe use of form and free verse—as opposed to slave verse?—but in her frequent use of caged bird imagery.

Dove's poetic use of domestic birds first appears in *Yellow House on the Corner* in the form of a canary; then, in "Parsley," one of her most widely discussed poems, we find a parrot. (In the poem, as in the real-life massacre it describes, mere mispronunciation can lead to death.) The birds also become self-referential riffs off Dove's last name, as in "Agosta the Winged Man and Rasha the Black Dove." Ultimately all these poems share concerns about distinctions in language, or color, and how both bear the stakes of life and death. Most interestingly, Dove often genders her metaphorical bird as female: in *Thomas and Beulah* (1986), the Pulitzer Prize–winning collection about her grandparents that expanded the possibilities I saw as a young writer, Dove titles the section about the grandmother figure, Beulah, "Canary in Bloom."

By mastering a sort of third-person limited point of view, Dove's poems avoid the problem of personal testimony, broadening out to history. Dove creates a forceful, ultimately vernacular voice, both a comment on her fellow Ohioan Dunbar and as a nod to Hurston's free indirect discourse in *Their Eyes Were Watching God*, where Hurston crafts a narrator who speaks like the characters in the book.[41] Neither framed nor unframed, such a closely aligned if not identical narrator finds its first voicings in Dunbar, its fullest genius in Hurston, and its fulfillment in Dove.

We have a sense here not just of history's impact on Dove's people but of their impact on history: for instance, Thomas's working in a World War II aircraft factory, contemplating that if he were to do his job worse—a subtle subversion—would anyone notice? What would the deadly effect be? Would his failure to do his job—through his very inaction, through the very destructiveness of *not* acting—somehow be empowering? At home the canary as songbird provides a painful reminder to Thomas of loss: of his early life as a sort of traveling minstrel (though not of the blackface sort) playing his mandolin (which serves as the title of his section); of his friend Lem, who died on a dare on their way north, and who haunts Thomas throughout the volume; and of his masculinity in general, not allowed to fight a war, living in a house full of women between his wife, Beulah, and their four daughters ("Girl girl / girl girl").

The canary, then, becomes a sign of domesticity as well as captivity, one that Beulah embodies even more fully. For Beulah is both the bird and the cager of the bird; she wishes for freedom, and thinks on it, her desire to be "nothing, pure nothing in the middle of the day" at once limiting and liberating. Hers is Dickinson's and Bert Williams's nobody, Bob Kaufman's anonymity and Dunbar's invisibility—updated, female, heroic. *Nobody's blues but mine.*

This paradox of freedom is best embodied in one of Dove's finest poems, simply called "Canary." "Billie Holiday's burned voice / had as many shadows as light" the poem begins, in many ways embodying the range of language forecast by Dunbar. A shifting sense of the vernacular is found in parentheses, which Dove uses as a kind of aside and vamp— "(Now you're cooking, drummer to bass . . .)"—recognizing and reconciling the blurry distinctions between drugs and music, knowing that the vernacular for "cooking" applies equally to both.

The metaphoric connection between Dove's "Canary" and the figure of Billie Holiday is ultimately one of song. *Song* is the only word that appears in Dunbar's work (and titles) more than "God" (or "de Lawd")—it is what the caged bird is singing, what the lover sings when he declares, "Jump back, honey, jump back." Song is Dunbar's poetry itself—no wonder his work was a favorite of black composers. But this song is not always, or ever, purely natural. At times as raw as the uncooked porterhouse Dunbar and Cook devour, at others the artifice of classicism, such song is forged and not found.

Dove's work is suffused with classicism *as* song. Take her book, *Sonata Mulattica* (2009), which considers a historical biracial figure— the "mulatto" and musical genius of the title who played alongside Beethoven, and even had a sonata dedicated to him. Like the poems he's inspired, George Augustus Polgreen Bridgetower sits at the crossroads of classicism and expression. Dove and her Bridgetower both know black life as *Not a cage but an organ*—something musical and liturgical, filled with subtle ironies.

While the canary in *Thomas and Beulah* is "in bloom," and almost articulate, in "Canary" the bird is the unexpressed itself, as musical and organic as the vernacular. The poem's final line says volumes about Billie Holiday, as others have noted, but also about poetry and, I believe, Dunbar's work and too-short life: *If you can't be free, be a mystery.*

UN-ENGLISH

It may prove fruitful, and ultimately freeing, to consider Dunbar in the context of more radical fin de siècle and protomodernist literature a century before Dove. In "Time out of Motion: Looking Ahead to See Backward," Language poet Charles Bernstein looks back at the end of the nineteenth century, seeing there not the "Genteel Tradition" but the influx and influence of immigration. "For American poetry of the twentieth century, there is no more important fact than the fundamental alteration of the language base—who was speaking and how they spoke—that occurred in the 1880s and 1890s; indeed, it is perhaps that period's most lasting legacy for our literature."[42] Bernstein sees this process as the chief cause of the critical break from British "Island English," as he calls it, into the many Englishes we have today: "In America, the reverse has been the rule: far from colonizing the foreigners' consciousness, the foreigners colonized English. Island English—the language of the English people—was no longer the common yardstick but only one of a number of *inflected* variants of a decentered confederacy."⁴³ Whether nation language or Island English, these compounds are also the African American's.

Bernstein's ultimate championing of what he calls "eccentricity in poetry for its ability to rekindle writing and thinking" stands directly opposed to "centrism," or a false notion of unity of language; Bernstein in fact seeks to decenter the confederacy further yet, or rather, to more fully recognize its already disparate nature. With this in mind, then, we can easily see his admiration of Emily Dickinson and his reading of her in concert with the (not just black) dialect tradition. "If Dickinson can be said to have fashioned an idiolect, her work's publication in 1890 is also consonant with the liveliest poetic practice of the period, one quite distinct from Island-oriented literature: dialect writing."⁴⁴ Bernstein goes on to praise Dunbar:

> Here I would interject to say that the "confederacy" of language would not quite seem as decentered for a black writer. Unlike Dickinson, Dunbar had no "room of his own" to further his practice. And ironically, the Library of Congress job designed to support him may have literally killed him, the dusty shelves hastening his tubercular departure. The confederacy for us is far more fixed, and deadly. Breaking tongue we know was never "fixed" or whole, in order to show the fluidity of language.⁴⁵

Bernstein's idea of English as a "second tongue" influencing the recognition of language's artificiality fits well with the modernists he cites (William Carlos Williams, Gertrude Stein, Louis Zukofksy) who learned English as a "second tongue," as well as for several British writers (Oscar Wilde, William Morris) committed to artifice.

Bernstein stops short, however, at recognizing the *simultaneity* of the black experience in English—that is, Standard English learned not as a distant second or secondary tongue, but as a twinned tongue, a doppelgänger. In Bernstein's radical yet surprisingly restricted view, there is little room of our own for the doubling of Du Bois or even Dunbar, not to mention the ways language, especially for African Americans, was already decentered. We are, after all, not immigrants but *imports* to this experiment America, lending not just everyday artifice to our experience in English but true violence. Confederacy, indeed.

This ahistorical view has traditionally, in the representation of black dialect on the page, viewed even the vernacular as the "mauling" of the English language, perpetuating the notion that Black English is somehow broken or filled with "decay." (Dunbar himself echoed this view at the end of "The Poet": "But ah, the world, it turned to praise / A jingle in a broken tongue," lines alluded to in Hayden's elegy.) In reality, it was those brought to these shores as slaves who were mauled, broken by the language. Forced to speak English while banned from ever using it fully—either in writing or reading, not to mention the language of body and drum—we quite quickly, almost simultaneously, adopted it and made English our own.

Instead, we are told, words and books, the nation's library, killed Dunbar.

What recent and recurrent discussions of the validity of black vernacular have failed to recognize is that, in our very outsiderness to the language, we forged a sense of belonging. African American Vernacular English has always been both communication and code—but this paradoxical masking is not merely a function of blackness per se, but of American modern life. In America we do not recognize our different masks, instead expecting our social masks to be identical to our private selves. In America we see a synthesis of our lives, of language even, as our goal; whereas in Babel there was the dream of a common language, America dreams of assimilation not of just ethnic groups but of the various spheres of our lives. Work is home is play is office; we do not understand theater.

On the other hand, too often *drama* is all we understand—there is little room, on our screens, small and large, for understatement, much less irony. Even the distinction I am drawing here depends on my overstating it. It is not, after all, that there is never irony in films or television—only that it is too often overdetermined. Think of the difference between a "screen," or something that shields or projects, and a "mask," which has a multitude of functions, many as emotional—celebratory, fear-inducing—as unemotional or purely deceptive. We need only tune in to reality television and its refrain that should be a drinking game—"I am not here to make friends"—to see the ways in which behavior, even at the edges of supposed reality, is predetermined and in fact scripted.

We live in a culture where we expect to learn about the "lives" of the famous, to know people from screens as if they are more than just two-dimensional entertainments. In the case of hip-hop, we often have gone beyond the mask of, say, someone who raps as a persona (Ice Cube) with a name his momma did not give him who then "acts" as other characters (some of which once were admittedly close to the Ice Cube persona itself), using that same stage name. This, admittedly, may not prove fundamentally different from any stage name, but surely results in a form a bit more extreme and playful in its refractions of the real and represented. The mask puts on another mask, yet we expect to see a face.

You could say that with the mask we haven't gone far enough.

I am suggesting here not dialect as orthographic, naturalistic, and thus a sign of "phonetic decay," but black vernacular as a technological marvel—a machining, rejiggering, and at times rejection of English, from its use of time (you be illin), temperature (I'm chillin), to tone (motherfucker). This is un-English not as non- or ante- but anti-English.

All this is to say that the African American vernacular certainly has standard practices and purposes: not just renaming but masking. African American Vernacular English is often spoken to confuse as much as to communicate; it is "untranslatable" because it does not want to be. Rather, it seeks to divide: black from white, young from old, hip from square.

No wonder that to be "with it" you must be "down"—the vernacular speaks on the lower frequencies. No wonder then that Black English (or AAVE, as it's known by linguists) is filled with juncture and ruptures—it is, in fact, one of our key witnesses to the process of becoming American. Too often, we take Black English as a sign of our failure to understand, rather than a site of persistent resistance to some mythical "standard" English. For Black English is not just an example of a conquered tongue, though English was often literally forced down our throats. Black English is also itself a reversal: yet another means by which the supposedly conquered instead became the conqueror. A testament to black inventiveness and nativity, African American Vernacular English is not just a site of conflict but a sign of black folks' resolve.

The paradox of Dunbar as black popular poet parallels the paradox of African American Vernacular English, and the broader black experience, in America: influential and even indispensable to the language, yet not recognized by it; denied by the very thing he and we helped create. Bernstein himself misses Dunbar's and black dialect's influence on a seemingly white modernism. The fact is, William Carlos Williams was read Dunbar as a child, while whole generations of modernists, including Pound, Eliot, and Vachel Lindsay, were raised on Uncle Remus.[46] Their work, in ways little and large, refers not just to Brer Rabbit's tales but also to their talk: Black English, the ultimate tar baby.

Black influence in English can be tricky to spot sometimes, not just because of its trickster nature, but also because of its violent origin. Nevertheless, its influence is pervasive, subtle, and large scale: from everyday words, such as Africanisms like *tote* or *goober* (peanut), to vernacular like *hip, cool, chill, dis,* or *24/7.* When such terms enter the lexicon, it is strange how suddenly their origins are not only declared unknown by the dictionary, but seemingly unknowable. Fugitive and hotly pursued, words of unarguably African American origin or usage reflect the harsh treatment of the slaves and freedmen and -women who spoke it: borrow from them freely; deny their source (asserting that origins are unimportant) or declare them exotic while pooh-poohing their pedigree; patronize, fraternize, pillage, and burn them.

Yet it is Black English that has emerged the victor, changing the tongues around it. The black vernacular is not a site of marginalization but of imagination and even infiltration, helping invent the music and meaning of the language we might best call *American.* "And speaking of language," Ralph Ellison reminds us, "whenever anyone tells you you're outside the *framework* of American culture and when they deflect you into something called 'black English,' remember that the American version of the English language was born in rebellion against proper English usage, and that the music of the African voice and the imagery coming from the people who lived close to the soil under the condition of slavery added greatly to that language. And when you look for the spiritual context of that language you can be sure that some of the passion for the unfulfilled ideals of democracy comes from the voices of those black and unknown bards, as well as from my mama and papa and your mama and papa crying in church, protesting in pool halls, cussing in shine parlors, and celebrating Juneteenth (that's what we call emancipation). . . . There is no specifically American vernacular and language which has not been touched by us and our style."[47]

It is black culture that is the dominant culture.

English broken here.

CRAZY BLUES

By PERRY BRADFORD

MAMIE SMITH AND HER JAZZ HOUNDS

Get this number for your phonograph on Okeh Record No. 416?

PUBLISHED BY
PERRY BRADFORD
MUSIC PUB. CO.
1547 BROADWAY, N. Y. C.

Chorus Two: It Don't Mean a Thing
The Blues Mask of Modernism _ _ _ _ _ _ _ _ _ _ _ _ _ _ _

The blues contain multitudes. Among the last mysteries, blues music re-
sists not only sentimentality but also easy summary: just when you say
the blues are about one thing—lost love, say—here comes a song about
death, or about work, about canned heat or loose women, hard men or
harder times, to challenge your definitions. Urban and rural, tragic and
comic, modern as African America and primal as America, the blues
are as innovative in structure as they are in mood—they resurrect old
feelings even as they describe them in new ways. They are the definitive
statement of that new invention, the African American, though when
Langston Hughes first wrote on them and through them in the 1920s,
he felt as much resistance from black folks as white. Known by black
churchgoers as "devil's music," the blues are defiant and existential and
necessary. Blues singers describe walking with the devil, or "preachin'
the blues" as Son House did—

> Yes I'ma get me religion
> I'ma join the Baptist church
>
> Yes I'ma get me religion
> I say I'ma join the Baptist church
>
> You know I want to be a Baptist preacher
> So I won't have to work

—then turn round and sing of "John the Revelator." Both the bluesman and the preacher, whose own story often includes being called to

the pulpit after a life of sin, know full well that most folks choose both Saturday night and Sunday morning: one, after all, turns into the other.

Perhaps the best way to describe the blues is to say that they reveal and revel in all our holy and humane contradictions—and that this revelatory quality announces itself not with the book of the seven seals but rather the broken seal on a bottle of whiskey. The same bottle that, poisoned one way or another, will leave you barking at the moon. The same bottle that, broken, you can smooth down to slide over the neck of your guitar.

The blues will surely get you, but offer "Good Morning" when they do.

WHAT DID I DO (TO BE SO BLACK AND BLUE)?

The rise of modernism parallels the rise and reach of the blues. This is no coincidence—after all, what critic Fredric Jameson identifies as "the great modernist thematics of alienation, anomie, solitude, social fragmentation, and isolation,"[1] could be summed up as simply having them blues.

But as I have said elsewhere, the blues are both a form and a feeling, the one a cure for the other.[2] The blues are good-time music after all, meant to make you tap your feet and feel, if not better, then at least comforted by the fact that you are in good (or deliciously bad) hands. The blues offer company, even if only misery's.

It is in the face of alienation and anomie that the mask, modern and often racial, becomes necessary. This is why the dominant mode of the modernist era is the *persona*—the mask both as metaphor and means of production. But the mask is not just T. S. Eliot's blackface, Ezra Pound's love of Noh drama, or Edvard Munch's iconic rictus of despair in *The Scream,* but also the Janus mask of the blues, which laughs and cries at the same time.

The blues, then, are both an approach and a feeling—one that had to wait for former slaves to name. Virginia Woolf tried, declaring "On or about December 1910 human character changed."[3] Woolf's dating, even in hindsight, of what may be called the advent of modernism has become more true after it was said—just as when asked why his portrait of Gertrude Stein didn't look like her, Picasso reportedly answered: *It will.*

Such history as a form of fortune-telling was reflected and refracted in the first published blues, W. C. Handy's "St. Louis Blues" (1914), and in the first recorded blues, Mamie Smith's "The Crazy Blues" (1920). Smith's very title indicates the vector of this change of "human character" ten years after the fact. Just as Louis Armstrong's "West End Blues" would reinvent the jazz solo, forever changing music, ultimately history itself was reinvented by those too often seen as victims of it. From New Orleans on north up the Mississippi, the blues and their offspring, jazz, mark the modern moment as well as anything.

For the "St. Louis Blues" weren't just St. Louis–born T. S. Eliot's or Josephine Baker's; they were everyone's. When Handy wrote down the first blues lyrics, he was capturing and collaging the common oral culture of African Americans, the "floating verses" that amounted to a shared store of imagery, one as allusive and elusive as *The Waste Land,* published years later. "I hate to see de ev'nin' sun go down": even the iconic first line of the song looks west, and ahead to the "The Love Song of J. Alfred Prufrock" with its evening sky "like a patient etherized upon a table." Could hindsight as second sight help us recognize that the love song Prufrock proffers might in fact be a blues? Well before "Ash Wednesday" the "St. Louis Blues" announced

> Oh ashes to ashes and dust to dust,
> I said ashes to ashes and dust to dust
> If my blues don't get you my jazzing must.

Years later when Eliot placed black song in his *Waste Land,* "sampling" James Weldon Johnson, the emergence and merging of modernism—our "Shakespeherian Rag"—were complete.

However we date its start, by the early 1920s, the modernism that before and during World War I once proved strange and unsettling, with its many movements and "isms," and its use of metaphysical wit, irony, and collage, seemed to culminate in the high modernist moment. In literature alone, the publication of William Carlos Williams's *Spring and All* (1923), H. D.'s *Palimpsest* (1921), Eliot's *The Waste Land* (1922), Marianne Moore's *Observations* (1924), James Joyce's *Ulysses* (1922), and Wallace Stevens's *Harmonium* (1923) all signaled not just a new sheriff in town but that all the "low modernists" and populists who had begun the deputizing of modernism a decade or more before, now had till sunset to get out of town. As the twenties roared, high modernism was in full swing.

Swing would seem to be the operative word, describing not just the music that propelled the Jazz Age but also the quality of change in attitudes and culture that accompanied the advent of the New Negro—who had been agitating for change since at least the century's turn, and whose rise almost exactly parallels modernism's. What's commonly called the Harlem Renaissance had begun by the early 1920s, inaugurated by Claude McKay's *Harlem Shadows* (1922), Georgia Douglas Johnson's *Bronze* (1922), Jean Toomer's *Cane* (1923), and James Weldon Johnson's *The Book of American Negro Poetry* (1922); by the time of the second of *Opportunity*'s award dinners in 1925 (from the first had come the anthology *The New Negro*), the younger generation had been duly anointed.[4] This younger group, affiliated with heiress A'Lelia Walker's Dark Tower Salon—and with the house down the street that Hurston, Wallace Thurman, and others jokingly termed "Niggerati Manor"—simultaneously continued and rebelled against the strict desire for a "positive" image set forth by the older generation.[5] While the era and movement have been greatly explored in recent years, the Harlem or New Negro Renaissance's importance, intricacies, and intimacies cannot be overstated—if only to reemphasize how the achievement of these African American writers (and artists) should be thought of as one of the heights of modernism.

So, too, should the release of the first blues record in 1920. The popularity and passion of "Crazy Blues" by Mamie Smith (which, in its first year, sold over a million copies) provide the first full expression, still overlooked, of a black modernist presence previously hinted at by the dialect of Dunbar and realized in the 1910s by the work of Fenton Johnson, a poet equally worthy of further study. You could even say that the storying tradition serves as a true vernacular to the standard borne by modernism, however avant-garde modernism self-consciously (and congratulatorily) thought itself. For now, it seems to me that, alongside Modernism & All, we should place Blues & Thangs, in order to fully appreciate the new, modern consciousness—one urban and urbane, ironic and genuine, cosmopolitan and American, black and white. Mine is an attempt to unmask the blues and see in them a useful rootlessness—and the roots of modernism more generally.

SITTING ON TOP OF THE WORLD

This idea of blackness containing modernism, and vice versa, has been increasingly recognized by critics detailing Harlem's role in New York's emergence as a literary capital. But despite Houston Baker's *Modernism and the Harlem Renaissance* (1987), Ann Douglas's *Terrible Honesty* (1995), Susan Gubar's *Racechanges* (1997), Brent Edwards's *The Practice of Diaspora* (2003), and many other efforts to reveal the racial and international underpinnings of what Ann Douglas calls a "mongrel modernism," the whites-only view of modernism still persists.

Perhaps then we shouldn't be surprised when Peter Gay's otherwise thoughtful, large-scale study *Modernism* (2008)—completed after all the other aforementioned studies—fails to mention African Americans at all in its 610 pages. (That is, except for Baudelaire's "mulatto mistress.") It is a dizzying, disheartening thing to register such an absence, particularly when critic Christopher Miller's *Blank Darkness* has so endlessly detailed the "Africanist" presence in the array of early modernists Gay does consider, from Baudelaire to Rimbaud and beyond. *Vous êtes des faux nègres.*

Which leads us to the question: Is it better to be misread, as in Africanist, racist white texts? Or unread, as in Gay's study?

Such separate but unequal—and more or less invisible—divisions continue even in an influential anthology like *Modernism/Postmodernism,* which starts by declaring, "Both modernism and postmodernism are phenomena, primarily, of twentieth-century Anglo-American and European culture, though with a changing relation to that culture."[6] While there is some debate over terms—to some Anglo means "British," to others "white"—there is no doubt that for many the true locus of modernism remains far from the juke joint or coldwater flat where blues records spin, or far beyond Langston Hughes circulating the Black Atlantic, writing poems about the Negro and "his rivers." Though some have explored the interactions and interracialism of modernism, often in terms of racism, I want to go further—locating modernism's origins specifically in black culture. The change, the roar, the very swing in the "Anglo" culture, might well be said to be exactly this too-often invisible African American influence.

What's at stake is not just a representation of reality but also one of the counterfeit's chief aims: to give credit where credit is overdue.

The whites-only view of modernism cuts both ways, obscuring its origins while also leaving modernism open for critique as just another form of imperialism. Take this definition of modernism by art critic Thomas McEvilley:

> Modernism—here, let's describe it loosely as the ideology
> behind European colonialism and imperialism—involved a
> conviction that all cultures would ultimately be united, because
> they would all be Westernized. Their differences would be
> ironed out through assimilation to Europe. Post-Modernism
> has a different vision of the relation between sameness and
> difference: the hope that instead of difference being submerged
> in sameness, sameness and difference can somehow contain
> and maintain one another—that some state which might be
> described as a global unity can be attained without destroying
> the individuals of the various cultures within it.[7]

Critics like McEvilley see a dictum like "It is necessary to be completely modern" as akin to European colonialism. To him, "Make It New" might as well be American Western expansionism's "Go West, young man"—with the same devastating consequences. This anti-imperialist view sees the impulse to modernize in literature not as a response to industrialization but as a colonial desire to update art like just another export or exploit. Oppression is the real reason, or effect, of such an urge to "modernize," the result not so much fated as fatal.

Yet if the nineteenth century sought either to cure or kill the native, however noble, one crucial way the modern era consistently defines itself is in embracing primitivism. The Freudian modernists, both "high" and "low," went native precisely (and messily) to avoid being Victorian, separating themselves from the staid past or the chaotic present. Not only was modernism a reaction to the Victorian era and its distanced, defanged romanticism, it conducted much of this reaction in terms of black culture. In the case of an American modernism interested in an everyday language separate from a foreign, European past, the modern artist often turned to the Negro as both symbol and sustaining force.

This occurs not just in the work of high modernists but in that of the "low" or what I call "domestic" modernists quite popular at the time. Witness Pulitzer Prize winner Stephen Vincent Benét, whose epic *John Brown's Body* (1928) considers the Civil War, its very title a black spiritual; we may discern the telling mix of modernism and nativism in his poem "American Names," which ends with the famous line "Bury my heart at Wounded Knee":

> I have fallen in love with American names,
> The sharp names that never get fat,
> The snakeskin-titles of mining-claims,
> The plumed war-bonnet of Medicine Hat,
> Tucson and Deadwood and Lost Mule Flat.
> . . .
>
> I will fall in love with a Salem tree
> And a rawhide quirt from Santa Cruz,
> I will get me a bottle of Boston sea
> And a blue-gum nigger to sing me blues.
> I am tired of loving a foreign muse.[8]

Putting aside the ways in which "American Names" calls black folks out of theirs, for Benét the surefire antidote to a "foreign muse," in rhyme and source and sound, not accidentally turns out to be the blues.

Might the "it" in Pound's dictum "Make it new" mean not tradition but the Negro?

CONCRETE JUNGLE

By the Jazz Age of the third decade of the twentieth century, race had already become a metaphor for the modern era, much as Du Bois predicted—one in which black folks functioned as both signs of the changing times (how fresh and lively their music!), and signs of a primal, unchanging past in which history plays no part (how freeing to not be burdened by thought or history!). There is a strangely contradictory notion at play whereby blacks are simultaneously modern and primitive.

The double mask of this conception of blackness is revealed not just in "more literary" high modernists or in the domestic modernists, but in the popular literature of the time. Take *Black Sadie,* an attractive, art deco–covered 1928 volume I found in a used-book store; the troubling inside flap copy remains all too typical of the time:

> "Black Sadie" is a dusky imp who was borne in on the crest of the "negro fad" just before the War. Gradually she learned to speak like the whites, forsake her low-born Southern friends for high-class Harlem "yallers," pose as a model, and dance at a famous night-club named in her honor.
>
> Skin of soft ebony, eyes like coals, delicately poised head, she dominates this book as completely as she dominated the Black Sadie night-club. Her story is modern, elemental, compelling. The author, who was brought up on a Southern plantation, has flavored it with moments of humor and sharp irony. He has achieved an astounding *tour de force* which deserves to stand with the very best of the negro novels.[9]

The lowercase "negro" is here in full swing—low-born but high-class, black in name but "yaller" in appearance, simultaneously "elemental" and "modern." Such inherent, paradoxical features coexist with each other, separate but not equal. Sadie is not born, but "borne in on the crest of the 'negro fad' just before the War." (In this she seems a bit premature, and in her infancy to have somehow missed the Red Summer of 1919. You could say she Jes Grew.) The flap copy creates quite a flap, conflating not just modern and primitive, but Sadie the character, *Black Sadie* the novel, and Black Sadie the uptown club. The slippage between the three is only part of the pleasure—one presumes when one is in Black Sadie, who's to care! Same difference!

Of course, Sadie's similarities to Josephine Baker's own story (and storying) should not be overlooked—though we should recall Baker's fame required, if not exile, then the willed self-exile of expatriatism. Exile, all too familiar to the Negro, is to become arguably the chief condition of modernism. *La Bakair* both embodied this and disrobed it— her *La Revue Nègre* managed to be at once au courant, exhibitionistic, and coy. For amidst and in lieu of the ubiquitous, symbolic, and literal Waste Land that the Lost Generation found after the war, Baker offered a Dark Africa—or rather, a brown-skinded one—that you could visit safely, tantalizingly close. A sexual safari of sorts, her *danse banane*. But as she even participated in the show, Baker seemed to mock it— dancing on the tightrope of race in ways that echo or anticipate black artists from Bert Williams to Jean-Michel Basquiat.

A word here on the Jungle. Just as the idea of Ole Virginny provided a needed "once upon a time" for white Americans before and even long after the Civil War, the Jungle proved a place of refuge, refusal, and rejection of all things modern, while also providing a handy, if static, metaphor for the modern age itself. Eliot himself uses the jungle this way: while *The Waste Land* as book and place was one conception of the modern landscape, his *Sweeney Agonistes* is intimately tied to a foreign shore, or rather, an outlying place of foreignness, "a cannibal isle" that is Jungle for all intents and purposes.[10] Whether in a Tarzan matinee or "reality television,"[11] the Jungle remains a dangerous, alluring Eden that might swallow us up if we aren't careful.

This Never Never Land, lying in a direction almost opposite a slave-conjured Canaan, is a place rich in contraband. In the endpages of my copy of Michael North's *The Dialect of Modernism*, where he discusses Eliot and McKay and others in relation to race and representation, are notes I made a number of years back about the idea of contraband, scrawled in pencil:

> *Some contraband: Berryman, some swing, Cotton Club, minstrelsy, Elvis, Rolling Stones, Melanctha, Moynihan report, "voguing," Beat writing.*

Below this, there's a quick definition of contraband: *not just stealing culture or stealing an image, but mistaking an image for reality i.e. not realizing that many of these are parodies, taken at face value.* The problem here is not the "negative typing" of these works by whites, but rather their adopting of black masks and then mistaking them for a face.

The Western fascination with the Jungle can be seen in some of the most famous titles of the modern era, from Upton Sinclair's *The Jungle* to Rudyard Kipling's *The Jungle Book,* with its tabloid-like story of a boy raised by wolves (not to mention the Disney movie's wolf-ticket jazz). The Jungle was either symbolic of the unruliness of the city itself or indicative of what innocence the city had lost. French "outsider artist" (okay, let's call him *primitif*) Le Douanier's renderings of the Jungle are clearly imaginary, yet no less filled with a fertile danger. (This was later to be wrested from the modernists—or should I say the colonists—by the postcolonial, Afro-Asian Cuban artist Wifredo Lam in paintings such as *The Jungle.*) Just as he had celebrated the workers with drinking ballads, Kipling's *Jungle Book,* its very title a kind of paradox, was one response to a disappearing "Genteel Tradition" and the worried "White Man's Burden" he named in its wake.

We see this burden at large in the nostalgia found in the plantation tradition that preceded the modern era. Too rarely discussed in terms of the Genteel Tradition that follows and interacts with it, this Plantation America is the one Pound and Eliot turned to, writing to each other in the voices of Uncle Remus. By signing as "Possum" and "Uncle Ez," as North notes, the two undergo a deliberate if subconscious racial masquerade to get beyond the social masquerades and mores of their time. We might even say that in looking back at the Genteel Tradition and trying to rebel against it, the two architects of modernism required the somewhat rebellious energy that the plantation tradition, and the blackface of Uncle Remus in particular, provided. The "Jazz Age" as a whole could be said to be responding to this rebellious blackness.

Is it any wonder that—among the challenges and swift changes brought about by modernity—the mask was turned to as a means of resolution? And that the mask was so often black—as a reflection of change even as it was a refuge from that change and a retreat into a primal past?

JUNGLE BOOGIE

It's a short trip from the perfect plantation past to the scary, or symbolic, jungle-filled one. In venues such as Paris's *La Revue Nègre* or

Harlem's Cotton Club, the two were, if not directly conflated, then suggestively interchangeable. But what does the Jungle mean for African Americans, who have sometimes played into it, donning the mask of the primitive?

In part it may mean liberation.

Urban in origin, and often conflating the verticality of the skyscraper with that of the Jungle setting (as visualized, say, in the work of Aaron Douglas),[12] this idea of the Jungle, if not entirely accurate, is black-made and -masked not to express a real self or an imagined other but *to conjure an imagined self.* This Jungle self is not so much savage as freed; is not the paradoxical noble savage but a transport back to a lost heritage—the more aggressively or laughably artificial, the better. If not quite the Elsewhere of the Negro spirituals, this transformative Jungle does recognize that the mask is not a cover but a vehicle, a way for its spirit—let's call it swing—to enter you and your art or music or movement.

The Jungle's regenerative power is trumpeted by later black artists, from Kool & the Gang's "Jungle Boogie" to James Brown's album *In the Jungle Groove,* which introduced the world to the break on "Funky Drummer," and thus to hip-hop. Which in turn gave us the Jungle Brothers, not to mention the form of drum-and-bass music known as "jungle" (often based on a sample of a drum solo fittingly known as the "Amen Break"). The persistence of the Jungle into black-made art forms a half century or century later indicates its defiant appeal.

Much like its seeming opposite, the biblical desert, the Jungle is a place not of lifelessness but renewal. The Jungle is an oasis in a modern world come to resemble a less transcendent sort of desert, a virtual Waste Land; yet the Jungle also provides a metaphor for that same, out-of-control world. *Down in the jungle, way down by a creek, the Signifying Monkey hadn't eaten in a week.* We might not be surprised to learn that the word *jungle* in fact derives from "waste land": "[Skt. *jaṅgalam,* desert, wasteland, uncultivated area < *jangala-,* desert, waste.]"[13]

White readers often brought to the Jungle the image of the Forest, found in European fairy tales as a site of danger, of wolves and lost children, while the black audience and artist seem almost always to have found in Jungle the liberating notion of "going wild." (Though, of course, by accepting the Jungle, or going "wild about Harry," some whites in the 1920s would do the same.) As critic J. Lee Greene discusses, "In the wilderness, the English colonists felt a great urgency to destroy what historian [Winthrop] Jordan described as 'the living image of primitive aggression which they said was the Negro but was really their own.'"[14]

In contrast, wilderness for the African American in slavery had long meant a place preferable to the plantation and its ornate garden: "Slaves knew that as chattel they were considered part of the property and wilds of nature, which a smoothly functioning plantation could restrain. The nearby woods contained enough birds and roaming animals to provide slaves with geographical and naturalistic references for freedom. . . . Thus it was hardly a difficult choice for slaves to forsake the pastoral Eden for the unpredictable wilderness."[15] If the garden meant order, and order meant slavery, I'd take wilderness and its freedom too.

For the slave wilderness also meant praise. The slave songs (or should we say freedom songs) were often performed in the wilderness, in what's been termed "the invisible church": those services and worship that the slaves conducted in secret. (You might call it the "Amen break.") "A common practice was to meet in the deep woods, in remote ravines or gullies, or in secluded thickets (called 'brush arbors'). The preachers and exhorters would speak over a kettle of water in order to drown the sound, or the group would turn a kettle upside down in the center of the gathering so that the kettle would absorb the sound of the singing."[16]

> My name it is poor Pilgrim
> To Canaan I am bound
> Travellin' through this wilderness
> On-a this enchanted ground.

This remapping of the wilderness by African Americans, both in praise and in practice, was a direct rebuke of the ways white settlers saw the New World. From the start the colonists, bringing the Forest with them, had pitched their destiny upon the most primal of pasts, invoking either Eden or wilderness as an originating force. In his *Blacks in Eden,* Greene notes that for the Puritans America was wilderness, a "devil's land" they were sent to tame. In contrast, white Southerners saw the country as Eden, themselves as descendants of Adam and Eve (with blacks a sign of original sin). If one group saw the New World as after the Fall, the other before it, both worldviews required the conversion or ignoring of Native Americans and African slaves to continue.[17]

Such a dichotomy—Eden or wilderness—found its way into the contradictions of western expansionism and the frontier. No wonder the West needed conquering.

In contrast, for African Americans the Jungle means both Eden blackened and wilderness redeemed—or better yet, wilderness always proved an "enchanted ground," a form of home.

JUNGLE MAN BLUES

If the redemptive black view of Jungle persists, so did the racialized, racist, modern one, from at least the time "Mistah Kurtz—he dead" struck fear into readers of *Heart of Darkness* to later become a sign of phonetic and other decay as an epigraph to Eliot's "Hollow Men" (1925). Years later, in *Jungle Fever,* artist and photographer Jean-Paul Goude would account for his fascination with blacks (and before that Indians) growing up in Josephine Baker's Paris:

> I have been in love with Indians since before I could read or write. I had seen them first in comic books like *Tin-Tin* and later in Westerns. . . . I loved the brown color of their skin. Their teeth looked so white by comparison. This is true not only of Indians but also of blacks—of anyone with a color of skin darker than pink. . . . I'd have an army of Indians and an army of cowboys. To help you understand that the cowboys were crummy guys, I made them all look alike. The good guys, the Indians, were all different. They had nice ornaments. I made one drawing of Womba which is completely black, a black-faced Indian with white tribal marks. . . . Indians were the first brown people I liked. Black people came later.[18]

Even his beloved blacks are ornaments, racial profiles of a literal sort. Goude's entire book traces the way that not just Americans but Europeans spend their childhood as Imaginary Indians, and their adolescence, however extended, as Imaginary Negroes (or wishing to be among them). Goude's art book is less a personal history than a racial one: images depict not just Womba (drawn in 1947 when Goude was seven, a fascinating image); but also Goude's mother, a dancer, photographed among whites in blackface in 1927, and seven years later as part of the chorus surrounding a wide-mouthed Ethel Waters. Goude's often erotic drawings and photographs are "wishful thinking," as he labels one 1965 explicit depiction of interracial oral sex; he even goes so far as to include photographs he terms "from memory," made years later in the 1970s, that depict past visions of racial contact such as an Alvin Ailey dancer not so much eroticized as abstracted, literally manipulated, extended, blurred.

All this, no doubt, is meant as praise. So too is his description of his and his fellow audience's mix of horror and lust watching a black performer: "she was performing wearing just a prom skirt and nothing else. Her tits were bare. The strength of her image, then as now, is that it swings constantly from the near grotesque—from the organ grinder's monkey—to the great African beauty. You are constantly looking at her and wondering if she's beautiful or grotesque, or both, and how can she be one if she's the other?"[19] Same difference. The fact that he here is describing Grace Jones, not only one of Josephine Baker's clear inheritors but Goude's future common-law wife, should give us pause.

Are we again in the presence again of the fetish? Goude's manipulation of Grace Jones's literal image—"I cut her legs apart, lengthened them, turned her body completely to face the audience like an Egyptian painting, and of course, once it was all done, I had a print made which I used as my preliminary drawing. Then I started painting, joining up all those pieces to give the illusion that Grace Jones actually posed for the photograph and that only she was capable of assuming such a position"—is contraband that views the mask as reality, strains to convince us it is. Certainly Grace Jones herself played with her own image in fascinating ways and was as interested in artifice as anything else. But Goude goes further, rendering not just his own memories false but also hers: "The first picture you'll see of Grace is of her as a child exposing herself. Why not? I show her as the natural exhibitionist she probably was."[20]

It is not enough for Jones or Goude's other blacks (and Indians and Puerto Ricans and gays and Vietnamese who also appear) to be wild in the present, he must also imagine their wildness as primal, prima facie, and a "natural" part of their past. "Wild Things" he calls a photo shoot for *Harper's Bazaar* from 2009, with black supermodel Naomi Campbell depicted in jungle garb, racing alongside a cheetah (her weave flying) and even jumping rope spun by two monkeys.[21] *Me Tarzan, You Cheetah*: the fetishized white-placed Jungle persists to this day.

This is tricky terrain. In the wrong hands Jungle is reminiscent of Ole Virginny as a site of pernicious nostalgia; in others, it is a call to Africa.

LIBERTY HALL

The main idea behind the Jungle is that of home. The home the blues circle and mention, the rootlessness that jazz embodies: both take not just aspects of technique from African music but also solace from the very idea of Africa. *I sought my Lord in de wilderness, For I'm a-going home.* Basquiat put it this way: "I've never been to Africa. I'm an artist who has been influenced by his New York environment. But I have a cultural memory. I don't need to look for it; it exists. It's over there, in Africa. That doesn't mean that I have to go live there. Our cultural memory follows us everywhere, wherever you live."[22]

Just as the idea of Canaan proved a necessary part of the slave's liberation, an Elsewhere present in the spirituals, Africa persists in the freedperson's collective memory and as part of the slave's ever-present past. The danger, of course, is that Africa is a real place—not a mere country, as some still seem to think, but a diverse, populous continent. Even Marcus Garvey, whose agitation for black empowerment and a return to and "redemption of Africa" got him deported to his native Jamaica, offered stock certificates for his Universal Negro Improvement Association that read: "Africa: The Country of Possibility."[23]

At its best, Garveyism, which curator Randall Burkett terms a "form of civil religion,"[24] does not make this mistake: instead of a physical place, both literary and political Garveyism argues about and for the image of Africa, redeeming it from centuries of its dismissal (and fetishizing) as the Dark Continent. The remapping performed by the enslaved African and the freed artist—turning an Africa of memory, and even of recent experience, into utopia—was pitched against the notion of Africa as "no place" in the European imagination. In his desire to form a black nation, to form the Black Star Line (in direct contrast to the White Star Line), Marcus Garvey's is a wish to return across the Black Atlantic, boxing the compass by not being boxed in.

Such an image of free Africa is aligned not only with the past but also with the future. Garvey himself is said to have recognized this: "In one of his Liberty Hall speeches, the indefatigable leader of the 1920s warned opponents that he could not be tampered with or harmed because, as he said, 'I am a *modern.*'"[25]

In their more modern remappings—of Africa, of the Jungle—African Americans such as Baker or Duke Ellington or Hughes sought to fight the "colonial memory," as Deleuze and Guattari termed it, and the rampant "phantasy" found in Eliot's and other modernists' encounters with imaginary blackness. Given that the imagination is where the Negro was first questioned and dismissed, why wouldn't black folks also choose the imagination as the site of this struggle and reclamation?

And why not Harlem? While Harlem certainly does not include all the wings of what might best be called the New Negro Renaissance—which took place in Washington, D.C., Philadelphia, Paris, and other outposts as early as the 1890s—Harlem had by the end of the 1920s come to stand as a mythic as well as a literal home for those in the African Diaspora. Perhaps the Jungle is not actually found in Africa, then, but America. Or, is Jungle just another word for heaven? As Arna Bontemps put it, "In some places the autumn of 1924 may have been an unremarkable season. In Harlem it was like a foretaste of paradise."[26]

Paradise had been promised by the spirituals: *I am going to make heaven my home.* But the culture black folks made promised a kind of belonging in the idea of nativeness, even in the midst of exile. For black culture, "going native" was less a dangerous excursion than a reclaiming of the home they found themselves in. *Native Son, Notes of a Native Son,* Natasha Trethewey's *Native Guard,* the Native Tongues hip-hop collective: African American conceptions of nativeness mean belonging, a nativity holy and human. It is exactly this nativity that some would seek to deny our first black president.

HOME TO HARLEM

Taking the A Train meant to bring you home, to Harlem, again. As Cheryl Wall's *Women of the Harlem Renaissance* eloquently notes:

> The idea of "home" has a particular resonance in African-American expressive tradition, a resonance that reflects the

experience of dispossession that initiates it. In the spirituals, blacks had sung of themselves as motherless children "a long way from home." Images of homelessness—souls lost in the storm or the wilderness—abound. In the absence of an earthly home, the slaves envisioned a spiritual one, a home over Jordan, for example; or they laid claim defiantly to "a home in dat rock." . . . The efforts to claim Harlem as home found voice in texts such as James Weldon Johnson's *Black Manhattan* and McKay's *Harlem: Negro Metropolis.* In the political realm, Marcus Garvey sought through his visionary rhetoric to inspire a New Negro who would fight to redeem Africa, the ancestral home.[27]

While Wall mentions both McKay's study, *Harlem,* and his memoir *Long Way from Home,* she does not mention here his *Home to Harlem* (1928), McKay's first novel and the first best seller by an African American. Certainly the book's popularity stemmed in part from its tapping into the "Harlem vogue." Though seen as a misnomer by some, such a vogue is represented by a yellow sticker on the cover of the first edition (with its lovely Aaron Douglas illustration) advertising "A negro's own novel—for those who enjoyed NIGGER HEAVEN, PORGY and BLACK APRIL." As with *Black Sadie,* the selling point (though not necessarily the novel's) is the accessibility of Harlem, presumably not just for black folks, to cash in on and enjoy. "For those white Americans with the time, money, and sophistication to make the trip, Harlem at night seemed a world apart. In contrast to their own world, discipline, hard work, and frugality were counterfeit coin in the realm of imaginary Harlem. Nothing symbolized its otherness more than the cabaret."[28]

Yet Harlem was imaginary, too, at least in part, for the black folks who lived, loved, and visited there—who thought of it as a, if not *the,* "black mecca." For them it was counterfeit coin in the best, storying sense: Harlem meant being free both spiritually and economically. However temporary, the power of the migrant and the exoduster's ennobling dream of homesteading cannot be overstated. For black folks, Harlem/home remains expressive of a black self, however fictive: a place where Hurston could feel her color coming on like a mythic tribesman; or where Ellington could play "jungle music" that was jazz by another name. What the cabaret provides—like the Southern juke joint, or the

Harlem drag ball—is not mere tourism but also black agency, no matter how mediated.

In a way, Harlem itself represents a *recolonization* of Manhattan. Instead of merely breaking from the British Isles, as many American modernists sought to do culturally, black folks recaptured the Isle of Manhattan, and on their own terms. Traveling from the South and the Caribbean, black migrants came north and east to reclaim the island the Indians were lowballed for centuries before, recapturing a Harlem named by the Dutch who once lived there too. Recolonization meant a kind of coming home—rewriting the song Manhattan was sold for—keeping in mind that, especially for those of African descent in exile in the West, the exile finds home wherever she can.

Might we also say that the Great Migration, with its satisfying notion of "feeling at home" in a brand-new, cosmopolitan place, not only counters modernist exile but exemplifies it? Such exile provided less a sense of loss than a look-out. "The maroon community of 'Harlem,'" Houston Baker reminds us, "conceived as the *modern* capital of those 'capable of speaking' for themselves, is thus source (of insubordination)—haven (for fugitives)—base (for marauding expeditions)—and nucleus (of leadership for planned uprisings)."[29]

Just as Josephine Baker and jazz overtook Paris after taking Harlem by storm, the Jungle always threatened to spread. (Not that, a generation later, Jean-Paul Goude and others like him would seem to mind.) Such recolonization follows the remapping of the American landscape, and the reclaiming of black dialect by Dunbar and his Harlem Renaissance descendants from the jaws of the blackfaced, white-wide mouth. The transformation of the Island English of Britain into the "nation language" of McKay and company on the northern tip of the island of Manhattan could be said to be another part of this recolonization. Such recolonization may even result in or make use of what Susan Gubar calls "recoloring," or black artists taking over often restrictive roles that white artists had invented as black.

For now, let's say that in the hands of the author of *Black Sadie,* the real Josephine Baker's hard-won autonomy—much less any notion of Negro authority or autonomy—is quickly displaced by the notion of the "negro novel" as a blackface, "whites-only" form.[30] In this, *Sadie* contrasts only slightly with the *Home to Harlem* sticker's citing *Nigger*

Heaven, Porgy, and *Black April* as examples of similar blackface writing. In such a context, *Home to Harlem*'s being "A negro's own novel" is in fact quite novel.

We need only think for a moment of the contemporary young black writer, whether McKay or Hurston or Langston Hughes, wanting to write about "common" folk and Negro life and stepping into the minefield of assumptions created by books such as *Sadie.* Reading the back flap of Hughes's *Fine Clothes to the Jew* (1927), for example, and seeing that

> these poems, for the most part, interpret the more primitive types of American Negro, the bell-boys, the cabaret girls, the migratory workers, the singers of Blues and Spirituals, and the makers of folk-songs

one might better understand the uproar the book caused upon publication, among black as well as white reviewers, who mistakenly saw it in *Sadie*'s same dusky, "primitive typed" blackface light. It was a similar view that prompted many, most famously Du Bois, to be angry about Carl Van Vechten's *Nigger Heaven,* a book Hughes and other younger writers defended liking as a part of their artistic freedom and resistance to the burden of a narrowly positive, New Negro representation. Given the importance of heaven = home = Harlem in the black imagination, the outrage over the reductiveness of at least the title *Nigger Heaven,* a flip phrase that implied settling for far less, may be better understood.

It is in the midst of all the Black Sadies that Hughes's cry for unfettered expression in "The Negro Artist and the Racial Mountain" becomes important, and its perils (especially as seen by the older generation) more clear: for those dedicated to the New Negro, low class meant lowercase. For Du Bois, all art is propaganda, and artistic freedom a luxury the uppercase and uplifting Negro could ill afford.

For Hughes, the New Negro also meant the newness of modernism, a freedom to write about whatever he wished. This also meant a resistance—a poetics of refusal—that characterized Hughes's complex lifework.

CROSS ROAD BLUES

Not coincidentally, much like the people who made them did, the blues see the city as a place teeming with possibility. If in Harlem, black folks sensed "a foretaste of paradise," in this they were thoroughly modern, American-style—finding delight, even romance, in the challenges of city life. The blues also foresaw the postmodern reaction to the urban environs: the City that seems a "waste land" to Eliot becomes the heroic "Paterson" of William Carlos Williams after the war (or his "Pastoral" written before it); for Hughes, while the city would become a "dream deferred," it remained still a dream, not yet a nightmare. When, in his long poem *Montage of a Dream Deferred* (1951), Hughes goes on to experience nightmare it is a "Nightmare Boogie," art made from pain in the blues tradition.

Even in the 1920s the blues enact a citified two-step between acceptance and despair. As Hughes noted:

> The Spirituals are group songs, but the Blues are songs you
> sing alone. The Spirituals are religious songs, born in camp
> meetings and remote plantation districts. But the Blues are *city*
> songs rising from the crowded streets of big towns, or beat-
> ing against the lonely walls of hall bed-rooms where you can't
> sleep at night. The Spirituals are escape songs, looking toward
> heaven, tomorrow, and God. But the Blues are *today* songs, here
> and now, broke and broken-hearted, when you're troubled in
> mind and don't know what to do, and nobody cares.[31]

If at times, like Williams did, the blues find beauty in the city, the music also knows heartache can follow you wherever you go. As such, the blues are about the crossroads—between good and evil, tragedy and comedy—and also *are* the crossroads, the exact place where north meets south, city meets country. As befitting a crossroads, the blues shift between two sets of dueling impulses: first, seeing the city as a place of both welcome and betrayal—its landscape as haunted, even helpless—and second, seeing modern life as exile and black life in particular as a delightful survival.

"Poor man's heart disease," the blues also describes a particular American—or should I say African American—rootlessness. Where the spirituals used Elsewhere as a comfort, for the blues the very possibility of Elsewhere causes both pain and pleasure. As Hughes says, the blues are "sadder even than the spirituals because their sadness is not softened with tears but hardened with laughter, the absurd, incongruous laughter of a sadness without even a god to appeal to."[32] Even as what Hughes calls "songs of escape," the spirituals reiterate their own surety: *I've got a home in dat rock, don't you see?* But the blues offer an Elsewhere that may never be; even the escape of migration, one of the key subjects of the blues, is not always fully realized.

The difference between migration and exile can be slim. Think of Bessie Smith's "Backwater Blues," here transcribed by Angela Davis:

> *Then I went and stood upon some high old lonesome hill*
> *Then I went and stood upon some high old lonesome hill*
> *Then looked down on the house where I used to live*
>
> *Backwater blues done caused me to pack my things and go*
> *Backwater blues done caused me to pack my things and go*
> *'Cause my house fell down and I can't live there no mo'*
>
> *Mmmmmmmmmm, I can't move no mo'*
> *Mmmmmmmmmm, I can't move no mo'*
> *There ain't no place for a poor old girl to go.*[33]

The song, written by Bessie Smith after the disastrous 1927 flood of the Mississippi, not only describes a larger African American condition, but could apply today to the displaced people from Hurricane Katrina and the second Bush administration's failed infrastructures and sympathy. One hopes it is not still relevant in the wake of the 2010 toxic Gulf oil spill.

Rather than that creeping black, it is the structure of the blues that interests me here: the rootlessness of blues feeling is both mirrored and fought by the restlessness of the form; the form's constant recasting parallels the singer's search for meaning, and for home. In the blues the feeling of being displaced—also found in the spirituals—becomes a search for a safe haven rather than its guarantee. Whether "Sweet Home Chicago" or "Kansas City Here I Come," the blues seek an earthbound Elsewhere, extending the hope of the spirituals while arguing against such hope, foregrounding the here and now. The result is a sustained argument over existence.

Needless to say "the poor girl" in Bessie Smith and other singers' blues also offers a protest, however indirect, against both class and gender oppression in a city or country that often does not have much of a place for black women at all. Angela Davis's and Hazel Carby's studies of blueswomen prove indispensable in understanding this.[34] As Carby points out, different, gendered reactions to oppression are revealed by the famous blues lyric:

> When a woman gets the blues she goes to her room and hides,
> When a woman gets the blues she goes to her room and hides,
> When a man gets the blues he catch the freight train and rides.

Riding and *hiding*: these are not only gendered options but two crucial ways the blues make meaning. For alongside their almost exact contemporary the cinema, the blues provide a shifting space of identity. They provide not just a metaphor for migration—the "kicker" or last line inverting, or finding irony in, all that goes before—but also a migration of meanings.

This floating lyric about hiding and riding is echoed by the often-quoted opening of Hurston's *Their Eyes Are Watching God:*

> Ships at a distance have every man's wish on board. For some
> they come in with the tide. For others they sail forever on the
> horizon, never out of sight, never landing until the Watcher
> turns his eyes away in resignation, his dreams mocked to death
> by Time. That is the life of men.
>   Now, women forget all those things they don't want to
> remember, and remember everything they don't want to
> forget. The dream is the truth. Then they act and do things
> accordingly.[35]

This recasts the blues trope of the train in terms of the ship—heading where, I wonder? (But then again, I am a man.) Adrift, mocking, the dream as the truth: these are things the storying tradition knows well, and perhaps speaks of best in the blues.

The blues are revolutionary, not just because they are the invention of a black "I" in American culture—versus the powerful "we" of the Negro spirituals—but also because the blues upend our expectations both in the reversals of "kicker" and in their overall aesthetic of the unexpected. The blues revel in their and our dualistic nature, part tragedy, part comedy, all drama. *I got a kindhearted woman, she studies evil all the time.* Though often this can sound like two sides of the same tragedy: *See, see, rider, see what you done done, Lord, Lord, Lord—Made me love you, now your gal done come.*

Even the blues line is doubled and divided, filled with hesitation, caesuras, and, as I hear it, line breaks—note that Langston Hughes always wrote his blues as six-line stanzas, recognizing the importance of timing, and giving the lie, or shall we say counterfeit, to the three-line stanza. Son House's "Death Letter Blues" is haunting exactly because of its delays, its doubts, its very wordlessness. Perhaps we should say the blues are in constant dialogue—the words with the music, tragedy with comedy, uplift with outrage (and outrageousness), the singer with the audience and the audience with its own past and pain. These are all, as with any crossroads, a form of divining.

Where for Eliot the poet was the catalyst for the work of art, remaining unchanged by the process, the blues singer is forever changed and always changing—one hand on the elixir of hope or celebration or forgetfulness (or cheap wine), the other ready to stir in despair and a past the singer is forever naming, if only to forget. *The dream is the truth.* Such transformation extends to the audience, who shares in the blues singer's mad scientist scheme. Even if, as blues well knew, the broken-seal bottle could be poison—our thirst will kill us all.

Besides the revelatory quality of the songs and lives—the storying—of blueswomen well charted by Davis and Carby, the blues also reveal shifting meanings of maleness. Some have written of Hughes's writing in the voices of black women, but we can see such polyvocal expression even in bluesman Robert Johnson, the bad man of the blues. Despite the overemphasis by certain critics on his short life and death, Johnson may best be defined by double entendre as by elusive autobiography; and double consciousness may prove the true hellhound on his trail: "two warring ideals in one dark body, whose dogged strength alone keeps it from being torn asunder."[36]

For the bad man, as Johnson sings and Hughes points out, is but one side of a double consciousness in which "sad boy" or "poor girl" is its tragicomic counterpart. *The blues ain't nothin but a good man feelin bad.* This sad, less braggadocious side of manhood is clearly seen in Johnson's remarkable "Come On in My Kitchen" in which Johnson's plea is for a lover to come into the singer's "kitchen"—a place of warmth and comfort, nurturing and socializing. Johnson's remapping is personal and metaphoric: in the blues, where cookin' is usually a metaphor for much more, the kitchen is never only literal; here the kitchen is welcoming and even sexual, the base of happiness and the hair's nappiness. *If today was Christmas Eve, If Today was Christmas Eve, and tomorrow was Christmas Day:* Johnson's lines sing of possibility and pain.

The fact that the blues sing of pain at all helps them resist the sentimentality of the pop music of the times—not to mention the blackface crooners and plainfaced white contemporaries who would attempt to co-opt the blues. "Blues music . . . is neither negative nor sentimental," Albert Murray says. "It counterstates the torch singer's sob story, sometimes as if with the snap of two fingers!"[37] In short, blues do resist the popular, even as they represent the first modern popular black culture.

The idea of the blues as popular culture, it should be said, hasn't proved a very popular notion, largely because the blues are also an important folk tradition. It has proved irresistible for experts (as distinct from music lovers) to dismiss the "classic blues" in favor of "country blues," to reify the rural bad-ass bluesman over the Empresses, Queens, and cohort of Smiths who first broadened the blues' appeal. Such a narrow view, however, ignores the fact that the blues mark exactly the transition between the folk and the popular—not to mention that even country blues reject the pastoral mode with its idealized South. The blues care little for purity, except when drinking canned heat.

The blues insist upon the popular even as they reform the notion. Hughes, for instance, engages with the popular by fabricating folk songs at the last minute when Van Vechten could not obtain permission for reprinting the blues songs he wanted for *Nigger Heaven*. (Which raises a kind of question—is *Nigger Heaven* a further kind of contraband, not for its stolen images, but for the presence of Hughes's counterfeit blues? Why haven't we seen enough written about the ways, in jazz fashion, Hughes performed a sort of collaboration with Van Vechten?) Along with Williams's wheelbarrow and Lorca's deep song, Hughes's blues rebuff and reframe the purist, international notion of high modernism that soon came to be seen as the only forum for great art.

Certainly Hughes was drawn to blues because of their form: the unique ability of the blues to tell a single story (losing love, coming north, loneliness and mistresses and misters and mistrust) while making that story resonant and plural; to tell a simple story (my man left me, the flood took everything) and make it complex (referencing displacement, protesting conditions, echoing biblical undertones); the making of a fruitful music from loss; and in the end, often abandoning story altogether for sound. From their blurred notes to their tension between word and deed, between meaning and moaning, between writing and hiding, between the backing bottleneck sound and the up-front voice—in a word, irony—the blues recognize that even blurring posits its own claim to meaning, storying all the way home.

In Hughes, not to mention Bessie Smith and Robert Johnson, we can see just how the blues move from the "we" of the spirituals to the modern "I"—the blues, as Hughes reminds us, are to be sung alone. The blues are songs about loneliness that somehow, in our listening, turn their "I" into a form of "we": we listen to the blues so's not to feel alone. In this "I," the blues are Whitmanesque and profound—for a moment, the duration of the lyric at least, we experience what the "I" experiences. You could say both lyric poetry and the blues turn us into a city of one.

The blues do offer comfort, no matter how cold.

A STRONG BROWN GOD

As plain talk and local metaphor, the blues would go on to influence much of modern literature—if only as a useful example of, or contrast with, such a literature's own making and masking. While some might argue about the entertainment or popular value of *The Waste Land*, Eliot's poem, like the blues from Johnson to the host of Smiths, relies on an implied protest about the modern human condition. If we say one does so by collage, the other by refrain, we are apt to confuse which is which: "HURRY UP PLEASE IT'S TIME" quickly can seem like a blues lyric, while "I've got a kindhearted woman, she studies evil all the time" fits somewhere between the gossip of the old ladies and the quake of thunder.

As such, the chief difference between high and low modernism may be the mere borrowing of black material by the popular, domestic modernists, versus its outright theft by the more skilled, "high modernists." Originally called "He Do the Police in Different Voices," Eliot's *Waste Land* used the multiple voices found in the minstrel show, America's first popular entertainment.[38] But while Eliot was burying the blackface origins (as well as the autobiographical ones) of *The Waste Land,* they resurfaced as part of *Sweeney Agonistes,* not only in its characters Tambo and Bones but also in its being labeled as "melodrama" (which originally meant a drama "with music").

Not just black, this music was also jazz. Despite his brilliant critique of Eliot's use of race, Michael North neglects to note how the multifaceted, multivoiced structure of *The Waste Land*—and by extension the poets whose accolades, criticism, and own poetry cemented its place as the prototypical and certainly most influential modernist poem— could be said to mirror the multiplicity of jazz. Ralph Ellison certainly saw a correlation between Eliot's collage and the concerted *storying* of Satchmo: "Consider that at least as early as T. S. Eliot's creation of a new aesthetic for poetry through the artful juxtapositioning of earlier styles, Louis Armstrong, way down the river in New Orleans, was working out a similar technique for jazz."[39] Satchmo would also use collage not just in his music but on the road, as anyone viewing his recently published collages—not to mention his own collage-like letters—may discover.

In further observing Eliot's upriver technique, Ellison describes finding Eliot's transcription inclusion of a song written by James Weldon Johnson as transcendent:

> Somehow music was transcending the racial divisions. Listening to songs such as "I'm Just Wild About Harry" and knowing that it was the work of Negroes didn't change all our attitudes but it helped all kinds of people identify with Americanness or American music. Among all the allusions to earlier poetry that you find in Eliot's *The Waste Land* he still found a place to quote from "Under the Bamboo Tree," a lyric from a song by James Weldon Johnson, Bob Cole, and Rosamond Johnson. During the twenties when *The Waste Land* was published many readers made the connection.[40]

Other writers such as Kamau Brathwaite have noted connections across the Americas: "What T. S. Eliot did for Caribbean poetry and Caribbean literature was to introduce the notion of the speaking voice, the conversational tone." For Brathwaite and many more, Eliot's deformation of language was not a sign of the modern world's flaws but of a liberating step toward fully acknowledging an English influenced by blacks brought to the Americas—a "nation language" now emergent and pervasive.[41]

For many black writers, not just Eliot's poetry but his birth in St. Louis—home to Scott Joplin, Stagolee, and likely the Bamboo Tree—and his invoking of the "strong brown god" of the Mississippi, link him and his voice to a long history of race and music in the Americas. As Brathwaite notes, "For those who really made the breakthrough, it was Eliot's actual voice—or rather his recorded voice, property of the British Council—reading 'Preludes', 'The love song of J. Alfred Prufrock', *The Waste Land* and the *Four Quartets*—not the texts—which turned us on. In that dry deadpan delivery, the riddims of St Louis (though we didn't know the source then) were stark and clear for those of us who at the same time were listening to the dislocations of Bird, Dizzy and Klook. And it is interesting that on the whole, the Establishment couldn't stand Eliot's voice—far less jazz!"[42]

Yet why do Ellison, Brathwaite, and those "many readers" in "our segregated schools" see a connection between blackness and modernism, while for some critics and, no doubt, the popular imagination, there is little to none to speak of? And why does what, for Ellison, seems like love, to me feel at times like theft?

CRAZY BLUES

You say *Waste Land,* I say "Crazy Blues": both declare the madness of the modern moment, with Eliot disguising his personal breakdown as society's, while Mamie Smith breaks down a song into a breakthrough of black voice, echoing across the land.

We may measure modernism not just by the journey from domestic modernism to high modernism to New Criticism, or from Handy's "St. Louis Blues" to Eliot's "The river is a strong brown god," but also from "St. Louis Blues" to Louis Armstrong's "West End Blues," with its redefinition and virtual invention of the jazz solo. The journey from collective folk vision, recorded by Handy, to individual excellence and promise found and re-formed in Satchmo—who played behind Bessie Smith on her "St. Louis Blues"—is no less powerful than Eliot's notion that the modern era meant the disintegration of not just society but the self. Not to mention his startlingly corresponding view that any effective individual talent must function like a catalyst, as an escape from personality, changed by as well as changing tradition.

Mamie Smith solidified and started a new tradition, one that insists on if not personality, then swing. When she stepped into a studio in 1920, the "Crazy Blues" Smith recorded was in many ways a "recoding": Smith not only changes the chords, blurring them with the music provided by her Jazz Hounds, but also invents the new form of the blues recording. (Is this another kind of recolonizing?) Those who object to her vaudeville voice, or deny the song because it doesn't fit the purity of the blues, seem unaware of the blues' always syncretic nature. They almost certainly fail to hear the coded meanings and implied protest in the song, written by black songwriter Perry Bradford:

> Now I've got the crazy blues
> Since my baby went away
> I ain't got no time to lose
> I must find him today
> Now the doctor's gonna do all . . . that he can
> But what you gonna need is a undertaker man
> I ain't had nothin' but bad news
> Now I've got the crazy blues

Smith's high-pitched voice seems to me not a fault but a conduit. For with it she manages to convey simultaneous identification with both victim and perpetrator; its very eeriness evokes "crazy."

There is a technology at work here, black as wax, a virtual voice speaking for and to the masses who bought and borrowed it. "Crazy Blues" sings of disembodiment, a synthesis of folk and machine found not just in the recording but in Smith's warbling. Behind the vocal, her Jazz Hounds echo and engulf the singer (and listener) with a clarinet accompanying Smith almost phrase for phrase, the trombone practically looping and swooping behind her. These are the foundational instruments of jazz (before the trumpet and then the saxophone took over) singing their swan song as "Crazy Blues" gestures toward a new one. Much of it is in her tremulous tone: *I don't have any time to lose,* she sings, and we believe her. The urgency is palpable, an analogue to diasporic yearning.

Smith's narrator must find her lover "today" and the doctor's been called, either for her presumed heartache or for the violence implied against her "baby" or herself. In a way, her "baby" is the selfsame "undertaker man" "you gonna need": a man the narrator also can't help but desire; who may send her to the grave; or who, by mistreating her, unwittingly dooms himself. Not just a description of our heroine's feelings, the "Crazy Blues" is metaphor for modern life as vibrant as the notion of Jungle or Waste Land. Or home.

Critic Adam Gussow focuses on the last stanzas of the song, the first few lines of which incorporate a floating verse perhaps made most familiar in the song "Trouble in Mind":

> *I went to the railroad*
> *Hang my head on the track*
> *Thought about my daddy*
> *I gladly snatched it back*
> *Now my babe's gone*
> *And gave me the sack*
>
> *Now I've got the crazy blues*
> *Since my baby went away*
> *I ain't had no time to lose*
> *I must find him today*
> *I'm gonna do like a Chinaman . . . go and get some hop*
> *Get myself a gun . . . and shoot myself a cop*
> *I ain't had nothin' but bad news*
> *Now I've got the crazy blues*
>
> *Those blues*[43]

Where Eliot once wanted to "do the police in different voices," "Crazy Blues" would have you "do like a Chinaman," putting on yet another racial mask, and then shoot a cop. Gussow reads the floating verse "snatch my head back" as a reference to the practice of lynching or mutilation by train, and the ending of the song as a protest against police violence, however veiled.

I myself am interested here in several things: not only the way that "Crazy Blues" tapped into an underground set of meanings but also the way it tapped into an underground economy. The two were no coincidence. Many reports have it that the record was distributed informally by black Pullman porters who bought the record in the North for a dollar and sold it along their routes south and west for two or even three dollars. Certainly each copy was listened to by more than just the purchaser and, like any underground classic, got passed around like gossip.

If it might be a protest against lynching, the song is certainly a symbol of the railroad as empowering the porters; as a symbolic means of escaping the South (and distributing the blues, quite literally); and also as an implied protest of working conditions where a railroad, like a bad lover, could up and "give you the sack," especially if you were a black worker unlucky enough to be hurt on the job.

The train needless to say courses through black and folk expression, where it occupies many stations of meaning. Chief among them for black culture may be the locomotive as a sign of motion and freedom; the Underground Railroad is itself an elegant metaphor for escape. Call it the *blues correlative:* when DeFord Bailey or Robert Johnson or Bessie Smith refers to the train through lyrics or music, they need not explain the history of railroad imagery, from the Underground Railroad to John Henry's hammer, in order to embody the locomotive's crucial complexities as a metaphor for leaving and for life itself. *The blue light was my blues, the red light was my mind.* Even a song like "The Midnight Special" was originally not the defanged bar-band singalong it has become but rather the words of a prisoner from his cell watching the light of the midnight train go by, and wishing it carried him—and his very wishes—along with it.

Where most modernism sought an objective correlative to describe emotions through the apt symbol, the black artist sought a subjective, blues correlative from the store of shared imagery inherited, changed, and reinvigorated by the latest artist in the tradition. Much the way an abstract artist drawing a horizontal line calls up centuries of landscape painting, the black and blues artist invoking a train—or river or mountain or valley or other remapped landscape—conjures a host and history of meanings. The task is to make it your own, internal and eternal.

The railroad links not just country blues to city blues but also black struggle to the "Chinaman's chance." For the railroad, symbol of modernization and East meeting West, was also the site of cultural connection, with black railroad workers literally connecting with Asian American ones. Although it's troubling that "Chinamen" here represent being "hopped up," "Crazy Blues" borrows Asianness not merely to signify "crazy" but to help transform the narrator into a "crazy nigger" who would shoot a cop. Smith's song, then, suggests the shifting identities of the modern era—and of a patently racialized, if masked, rebellion. From the Boston Tea Party onward, American rebellion and rewriting tradition have required not reality but such a mask.

Crazy, as everyone from Gussow to Richard Pryor knows, may not necessarily mean insanity so much as a fierce recognition of the craziness of the world. The "Crazy Blues" of the title may not be the narrator's view but the view of authorities for whom any uncompromising black (or Asian) response left the colored folks deemed crazy and killable. "Crazy" is another outlaw identity black folks have championed—along with the bootlegger, the numbers writer, the hustler, and the graffiti writer—because when normal means kowtowing to figures of power, "crazy" may not be insane in the least. *Where I come from,* as I recently said in "Ode to Homemade Wine," *crazy is a compliment.*[44] Crazy is the tonic in which misbehavior mixes with outright rebellion; *the blues ain't nothin but a bad woman feelin good.*

In a crucial sense, Mamie Smith's achievement mirrors Langston Hughes's much-remarked-upon innovation in his *Fine Clothes*—that is, removing the framing device so that instead of being listened to by a narrator ("I heard a Negro play" in his "Weary Blues"), the bellboys, bad men, and sad girls speak or sing directly to us. Smith, as it happens, stepped in to replace a "popular" white singer to sing another song, which then prompted black songwriter Perry Bradford to convince Okeh records to let him record "Crazy Blues" at the session. The recording went on to reveal to record companies a black audience hungry for the blues, and for black song.

Without the removal of the white star's frame Smith might never have sung Bradford's blues as the blues, instead keeping it mere novelty. For Smith's rendition not only begat "race records"—and the promotion of records for a black audience—it also cemented a blues craze first seen in sheet music of the 1910s; from ragtime to cakewalks to boogie-woogie to "Ethiopian Airs" to the blues, sheet music traces the ways in which whites used black forms not just for profit but pleasure.[45] This often required, at least on the covers, erasure of the blues' black origins—substituting white faces on the covers of songs called "blues" in a way later familiar to rhythm and blues and even jazz albums—or defacing those origins enough that they are no longer recognizable, blacking up like "coon songs" that do not picture people but a degraded image. The blackface and white masks the blues and jazz were made to wear also appear among much of the literature of the time. The real framing device that Mamie Smith and Langston Hughes cast off was not only black mores or blackface but whitewash and white pleasure.

BLACK AND TAN FANTASY

Such pleasure often masked a form of anxiety. Rather than a comfort with progress—that American ideal—modernism itself may represent an apprehension about precisely that progress. Part of the blues' brood, jazz was and remains for many a site of this anxiety. While the music is seen as hectic, jumpy, and symptomatic, jazz is actually the diagnosis: we've all come down with a serious case of modernism. In its self-consciousness jazz mirrors modernism; in its willingness to refer to itself (especially later, in bebop), jazz foreshadows the growing self-reflexivity found in the postmodern era and art over the course of the last century.

One example of jazz's anxiety—and, by extension, modernism's—is Marie Cardinal's interestingly titled *The Words to Say It*. This "autobiographical novel," mentioned by Toni Morrison in her *Playing in the Dark,* describes Cardinal's lifelong bouts of depression and nervous breakdowns—what she calls "the Thing"—a condition first precipitated by hearing Louis Armstrong play live:

My first anxiety attack occurred during a Louis Armstrong concert. I was nineteen or twenty. Armstrong was going to improvise with his trumpet, to build a whole composition in which each note would be important and would contain within itself the essence of the whole. I was not disappointed: the atmosphere warmed up very fast. The scaffolding and flying buttresses of the jazz instruments supported Armstrong's trumpet, creating spaces which were adequate enough for it to climb higher, establish itself, and take off again. The sounds of the trumpet sometimes piled up together, fusing a new musical base, a sort of matrix which gave birth to one precise, unique note, tracing a sound whose path was almost painful, so absolutely necessary had its equilibrium and duration become; it tore at the nerves of those who followed it. . . . Gripped by panic at the idea of dying there in the middle of spasms, stomping feet, and the crowd howling, I ran into the street like someone possessed.[46]

It would seem the Thing is not only the author's own anxiety but the modern world's—the threat of possession tearing at the nerves till fleeing is the only response worth having. (Where for someone like Vachel Lindsay, mislabeled "The Jazz Poet," the only impulse was to fight.) There's that Thing, an uneasy "It" again: black and modern and possessed; or should we say dispossessed.

The passage describes Armstrong's ability so wonderfully, even fetishizing it—but where I see achievement, remapping, a storying tradition, Armstrong's flights of sound lead the protagonist merely to flee. Faced with such freedom, could she be said to have another choice?

A similar, fetishized feeling courses through the opening of Blair Niles's 1931 novel, *Strange Brother,* an important early novel concerning a gay white man exploring Harlem. In its opening paragraphs we find the cabaret as tourist attraction, capturing the venue's unsettling of the white viewer through a jazz song's suggestiveness:

Colored lights hung under the low ceiling—red, blue, and yellow lights. There was a dance floor in the center of the room, with tables surrounding it on three sides, and on the fourth side an orchestra. There were saxophones, trombones, trumpets and fiddles, banjos and flutes and drums—a great jazz orchestra. At the tables there were white men and women; and alone on the dance floor there was Glory, standing straight and slender, with the spotlight full upon her, Glory singing the Creole Love Call.

There were no words in Glory's song. Glory seemed simply to open her mouth and let her heart find expression in wordless sounds which fluttered up from the dark column of her throat and floated through the thick smoke-blue air of the crowded night club.

It was said in Harlem that Glory was the sort of girl who can make a man "see the City," make a man know joy.

But to June Westbrook, Glory's voice brought unrest.[47]

Knowing joy, bringing unrest: these seem the typical, if here well put, poles of jazz for the white viewer. Considering Glory and the "unrest" she and the "colored lights" call forth in the white viewer, we might recall Black Sadie—and her other incarnations whom the scene also evokes.

Actually an Ellington composition, "Creole Love Call" has no words, but is a kind of scatting wordlessness, a blend of language (and love) that is overwhelmingly suggestive, and that little else can name. Unlike the French my grandparents and their entire generation spoke in southern Louisiana, "Creole" in Ellington is not necessarily a tongue but a stand-in for a high-pitched, unsettling, dare I say primitive, wail. *Strange Brother*'s all-too familiar witnessing of such wordlessness echoes other instances of a white audience used to viewing black art through the scrim of racism—taken to an extreme in minstrelsy's *nonsense,* which as Houston Baker recounts, isn't just linguistic. And yet, the nonsense of minstrelsy did provide meaning, even if it was only to demean.

With Ellington's "jungle music"—a name reportedly first given it by George Gershwin[48]—the music provides a pathway far more irreducible and fluid than many white listeners may have first thought. Standing as it does between blues gossip and spiritual thunder, jazz offers not just freedom but another, radical tradition—instead of progress, jazz emphasizes *process*. Most interested in the past only as a way of riffing toward the future, jazz seems to say we "make it new" only when we make it our own. Negotiating between modern individuality and community, both in its actual form and its ongoing history, jazz and its birth parents, the blues, are in many ways the collective unconscious of African America—and by extension America—offering a firsthand account of risk, redemption, and yearning. No wonder, then, with its sound alone jazz provided both a cure and a cause for anxiety.

If the blues don't get you, my jazzing must: the conclusion of the "St. Louis Blues" proved less a threat than a promise, the black seduction of modern culture coming true just as did Virginia Woolf's declaration or Picasso's portrait of Stein. Still, despite their inventions and predictions—or perhaps because of them—African Americans were often reduced to "It," a Thing. Such forms of objectification black music would playfully and subversively contest in the very title of one of Duke Ellington's key numbers, "It Don't Mean a Thing (If It Ain't Got that Swing)." In its very title the song, which would name swing music, wrested African American music away from the nonsense that threatened us all. Its "It" had no antecedent. Both the "It" and the music, the song insisted, were sui generis. It was not a love call but a battle cry about the direction and meaningfulness of the art.

The "It" here I like to think of as the same "It" in "MAKE IT NEW"— which I take to mean the tradition—but also further, and funkier, a black body, which, for the black storyteller or author, became a body of work. This "It" also happens to be the slippery pronoun Mamie Smith recorded as the other side of "Crazy Blues": "It's Right Here for You, If You Don't Get It, 'Tain't No Fault of Mine." At once plainly sexual and more elusively suggestive, the taint is faultless, and right here for you to engage, as tradition. And to make, like the Negro, new.

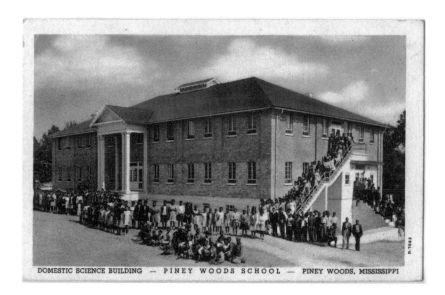

DOMESTIC SCIENCE BUILDING — PINEY WOODS SCHOOL — PINEY WOODS, MISSISSIPPI

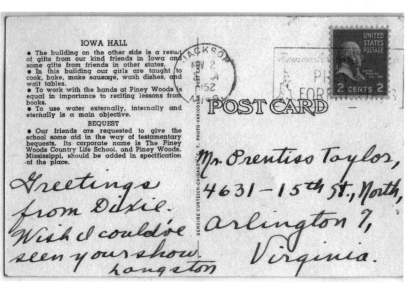

IOWA HALL

● The building on the other side is a result of gifts from our kind friends in Iowa and some gifts from friends in other states.
● In this building our girls are taught to cook, bake, make sausage, wash dishes, and wait tables.
● To work with the hands at Piney Woods is equal in importance to reciting lessons from books.
● To use water externally, internally and eternally is a main objective.

BEQUEST

● Our friends are requested to give the school some aid in the way of testamentary bequests. Its corporate name is The Piney Woods Country Life School, and Piney Woods, Mississippi, should be added in specification of the place.

Greetings
from Dixie.
Wish I could've
seen your show.
Langston

POST CARD

Mr. Prentiss Taylor,
4631 – 15th St., North,
Arlington 7,
Virginia.

"If You Can't Read, Run Anyhow!"
Langston Hughes and the Poetics of Refusal _ _ _ _ _ _ _ _ _

PART ONE

1.

The challenge Langston Hughes presents is not that his work is obscure, his life operatic or achievements invisible—rather Hughes as person and poet presents too much, is far too accessible. His personal history seems clearer than Dickinson's, less tragic than Dunbar's; like Whitman's, his writing seems to need no explanation. Here, of course, lies the danger with Hughes, a writer who remains what I call "deceptively simple." Or, as a student of mine unwittingly, even intuitively, reversed, Hughes is "simply deceptive." For all his clear language, precise diction, and even his famous folk character Jesse B. Semple, Hughes is anything but.

The early life of the "Poet Laureate of the Negro Race"—a title Hughes wore with pride—speaks of the Great Migration of the early parts of the century. Born in Joplin, Missouri, he was uprooted and lived with his grandmother in Lawrence and Topeka, Kansas. Most people don't think of black folks when they think Kansas; fewer would dream of poetry.[1] As a fellow Topekan, however, I feel a special connection to Hughes, especially given this early and at times alienating portion of his life. Something in his poems' easygoing yet reserved tone feels forged from that Kansas background: what might be called a pragmatic skepticism has been an open heartland secret to anyone who has lived there; is what over the years has kept Kansans going through drought and locusts and floods; and is what ultimately kept Bob Dole from winning the 1996 presidential election. (Though this Kansas stoicism, steady on the plow, learned from his Kansas mother and grandparents, may be exactly what helped Barack Obama win the 2008 election.)

Kansans understand this skepticism verging on cynicism—and admit it to no one. We choose instead to export wheat and tornadoes and, oddly enough, black poets. Gwendolyn Brooks, the first African American Pulitzer Prize winner, was born in Topeka though she and her parents lit out for the greener pastures or at least taller skyline of Chicago by the time she was a few months old; this move to the big city also characterizes Kansans, including Hughes, who eventually settled and died in Harlem, U.S.A. Like Joyce's Ireland or Baptist Heaven, Kansas is a place defined by its absence, by distance. Not just the leagues that place contains, but the lengths from which we can see it well.

With this distance in mind, perhaps we can better understand Hughes's relation to his work and arguably his life—what I call his poetics of refusal. Perhaps Hughes's painful Kansas past, which he often describes as lonely, may help explain the "distance" sometimes found in his poems, as well as their underlying melancholy. In many ways, this ironic distance simply recasts a blues aesthetic that says

> But I ain't got
> Neither bullet nor gun—
> And I'm too blue
> To look for one.[2]

Du Bois's double consciousness becomes in Hughes's hands a double negative that for the blues author and audience adds up if not to a positive, then to a "dark" humor: *Laughing to Keep from Crying,* as Hughes named a collection of short stories; even more refusal is found in the title of his novel of the life of a boy in Kansas, *Not without Laughter.* For Hughes and us "blues people," survival means the small span between despair and laughter, between having and not, between buying a gun to off yourself and not being able to afford the bullets.

The difference between the blues figure and the hard-luck, absurdist stereotypes of minstrelsy so prominent in the early parts of the century is one of form—and audience. Both are things Hughes understood innately, and responded to—almost to a fault, in the case of audience, sometimes crossing the line he elsewhere drew between poetry and lighter verse. Of course, the innovations that Hughes achieved, in championing the folkways and form of the blues, seem obvious or easy now,

but when he published *The Weary Blues* (1926) and even more important, *Fine Clothes to the Jew* (1927), he caught hell. The black bourgeoisie
came down on Hughes the hardest, terming him the "Poet Low-rate
of Harlem" for writing about common folk, what today's tastemakers
might call "negative images": janitors, adulterers, juke jointers, bad
men, loose women, real people people people. And what advice he gave
them people! "Put on yo' red silk stockings, / Black gal. Go out and let
the white boys / Look at yo' legs." Even today such images get read as "literal advice" and not, as Hughes called it in *The Big Sea,* an "ironic poem."

"We know we are beautiful. And ugly too," Hughes wrote in his
groundbreaking manifesto "The Negro Artist and the Racial Mountain"
(1926), arguing either against whitewashing our images to make ourselves look better, or against (as he *signifies on* the unnamed "young
poet," likely Countee Cullen) wanting to be white. After climbing the
mountain, Hughes dug in, breaking first ground, trying to dig his way
back to the motherland by way of the Mississippi.

2.

Interestingly enough, for such a landlocked childhood, Hughes's first
famous poem was "The Negro Speaks of Rivers"—a classic-sounding,
long-lined, Whitmanesque reverie. In many ways the poem foreshadows
so-called literary Garveyism, a returning to African roots—and in taking the "white man" out of Whitman, Hughes taps into a larger zeitgeist, taking us through the rivers Congo, Nile, the "Euphrates when
dawns were young," and, ultimately, a river of the dead that, unlike the
mythical Lethe, refuses to forget. Or to ignore his blackness.

Listen to the reason Hughes gives for writing the poem on a journey
to see his expatriate father in Mexico: "All day on the train I had been
thinking about my father and his strange dislike of his own people. I
didn't understand it, because I was a Negro, and I liked Negroes very
much." This long memory and literary acceptance of his own blackness,
of the "motherland" as opposed to his "father's land," is part of his appeal, and a defining quality of Hughes's long literary life.

But in describing his early life in his stunning autobiography *The
Big Sea* (1940), Hughes leaves out plenty. Arnold Rampersad, Hughes's
biographer, literary executor, and champion, sums this up this way: "In

The Big Sea, deeper meaning is deliberately concealed within a seemingly disingenuous, apparently transparent, or even shallow narrative. In a genre defined in its modern mode by confession, Hughes appears to give virtually nothing away of a personal nature."[3] Rampersad links this reticence, let's call it, to a sort of racial code, "a gamble" by Hughes— "who depended almost desperately on the smiling surface he offered to the world"—to please white publishers while speaking to black readers who held decoder rings. Particularly when dealing with issues of his white patron (whom he had a terrible break with) or his sexuality (conveniently left undefined or defined as "unattached" by most biographers), Hughes is less than forward—we learn little of his Eastern European female roommate in Paris or, more to the point, his days on board (and below deck on) a merchant marine vessel.

For me, Hughes's reserve is less the smiling face of the slave than an elaborate, elegant storying technique found in Hughes's poetry and in much great art. To read *The Big Sea* is to learn dissembling as an art form—not as pop escapism but as a populist escape hatch—a refusal to give in, to give out, and especially to give away anything. To read his poetry or *The Big Sea* for traces of Hughes's life is to deny the doggedly unautobiographical nature of his work. As he himself wrote about his second book of poems, "I felt [it] was a better book than my first, because it was more impersonal, more about other people than myself, and because it made use of the Negro folk-song forms, and included poems about work and the problems of finding work, that are always so pressing with the Negro people."[4]

While certainly class figures here, I want to highlight Hughes's first given reason for the success of *Fine Clothes:* "It was more impersonal." In our current confessional climate where the memoir meets the talk show, it may be hard to read the impersonal as desirable, or even achievable. But if we let go of our preconceptions about poetry being "personal," or at least "autobiographical," we can see Hughes championing a poetry for all people that is not private—a verse that is truly "free" and open to the public. There is an anonymity to his poetry, or rather, a pseudonymity, that may startle us. "I have known rivers: / Ancient, dusky rivers." This "I" isn't, or isn't just, Hughes. Yet, if we look at his fellow modernists—the "extinguishing of personality" attempted

by Eliot, or even William Carlos Williams's lexicon of "thingness"—
Hughes stands, if not alone, then out, creating something new, vernacular, blues based, as American as lynching and apple pie.

This merging of the American promise and its pratfalls—a fragmented violence in one hand, a homemade wholeness and even whole-
someness in the other—Hughes negotiates most of his life. Just as his
grandmother's first husband, who fought alongside John Brown for
Bleeding Kansas (who Hughes was named "Langston" after), Hughes
adds his voice to our many Americas. Examining his long career from
the 1920s and the Harlem Renaissance to his death in 1967 during the
Black Arts movement, we discover many different Hugheses as well:
socialist, student, reporter, world traveler, novelist, sailor, dramatist,
busboy, dishwasher, poet. The *Langston Hughes Reader* (1958) contains
multitudes—poems, plays, blues, translations, autobiographies (plural),
songs, and, my favorite, "pageant." This short history of black people
in the Western world—straightforward, celebratory, funny, serious—
takes in all the ways Hughes saw we are. Only Hughes of his modernist
contemporaries—except perhaps Williams—would attempt such broad
American history.

Odd then, or perhaps fitting, that Hughes would come under fire
from the House Un-American Activities Committee in the 1950s. His
more overt political poems, especially of the 1930s when he went to
and wrote about the Spanish Civil War and Russia, came back to haunt
him—in particular "Goodbye Christ," which raises Marxism and not
the cross as deity. For decades the religious right dogged Hughes, even
though the poem had been published decades before in the rather obscure *Negro Worker* (and perhaps even without his knowledge).[5] Before the committee, Hughes recanted, and avoided the blacklist, so to
speak. (Here we might agree with Bob Kaufman when he asks, "Why
are all blacklists white?")

In contrast to Paul Robeson's standoff with HUAC and subsequent
troubles, Hughes's giving in seemed like a betrayal. He would go on to
repress most of the work from this period, excising if not excusing it—
to our great loss. Even if he was not blacklisted, black bars cover a great
amount of what we think we know about Hughes. Hughes's poetics of
refusal becomes a bit more understandable in this context—not just

as the black tradition of *signifyin'*, whether talking trash or "rhetorical understatement"—but as the kind of talk Othello used to win over Desdemona's father after he'd won her.

Such cagey talk did not serve him well in the straight-talking Black Arts movement of the 1960s. We were impatient, sick of rhetoric—action was called for—as Amiri Baraka (né LeRoi Jones) wrote, "We want 'poems that kill.'" This metaphoric murder, described as part of what the critic William J. Harris calls the "Jazz Aesthetic," involved offing the literary fathers, just as Baraka would say John Coltrane "murdered the popular song." Hughes took plenty of hits, yet few in the movement had read deeply enough to know of Hughes's radical work.[6]

But one wonders, even with the excised 1930s, what had folks read? Hughes had been speaking in a black idiom from *The Weary Blues* to his book-length *Montage of a Dream Deferred* (1951), and even in his latter work. Somebody should have told 'em Hughes was getting down all along. Caught between the Devil and the deep blue sea, Hughes, like Louis Armstrong, represented an earlier, seemingly bygone era—and though both artists responded to and even cleared space for radical changes such as bebop, both did so in such a way as to make their virtuosity simple. Deceptive.

What gets lost in most critiques is the depth of emotion Hughes expresses, despite or precisely because of the "impersonal" quality he possesses. He paints a community, a "Lenox Avenue Mural," not a self-portrait. This is why *The Big Sea,* a book that changed my life, looms large on the Hughes horizon. For like any picaresque tale—and this is largely how he constructs his life—Hughes's autobiography reveals much exactly by its gaps, by its discrete molecular leaps, by what he refuses to say.

Take *The Big Sea*'s opening paragraph when Hughes throws his books in the sea, as dramatic an opening of a writing life as any:

> [It] was like throwing a million bricks out of my heart when
> I threw the books into the water. I leaned over the rail of the
> S. S. *Malone* and threw the books as far as I could out into the
> sea—all the books I had had at Columbia, and all the books
> I had lately bought to read.

By this Hughes achieves a sort of wry anti–ars poetica, a refusal of the "inkellectual." In refusing book learnin' he accepts something else: people.

> It wasn't only the books that I wanted to throw away, but every-
> thing unpleasant and miserable out of my past: the memory of
> my father, the poverty and uncertainties of my mother's life, the
> stupidities of color-prejudice, black in a white world, the fear of
> not finding a job, the bewilderment of no one to talk to about
> things that trouble you, the feeling of always being controlled
> by others—by parents, by employers, by some outer necessity
> not your own. All those things I wanted to throw away. To
> be free of. To escape from. I wanted to be a man on my own,
> control my own life, and go my own way. I was twenty-one. So
> I threw the books in the sea.[7]

Here we see Hughes's emotion, in a confession, or at least a protest. Black, Africa bound, and twenty-one, Hughes does not burn books that offend but drowns books to defend. He also participates in the African American tradition of negation as affirmation—"Bad Is Good" one chapter is titled.[8] Such a powerful statement as Hughes jettisoning his books has gotten overlooked by many critics, largely because it flies into the headwind of current African American criticism, which emphasizes literacy.

By this I certainly do not mean to say literacy has not factored into black lives and, naturally, books; or that Hughes, the prolific author, advocated any sort of illiteracy. On the contrary, Hughes, in his poetry and in this and other symbolic acts in *The Big Sea*, embodies and embraces what I call *aliteracy*. By *aliteracy* I mean a trickster-style technique that questions not just Western dichotomies (bad/good, black/white) but provides a system beyond which one can be defined, even by writing, or by literacy or ill-.

In other words, Hughes prefers the ability to read situations and power structures more than books—what Houston Baker describes, in speaking of Caliban in *The Tempest*, as "supraliteracy."[9] For Hughes, *aliteracy* approaches more what we say when we say "she read him," as in figgered him for a fool. Not just Caliban but Prospero figures here, in that Prospero's rejection of his books, thrown similarly into the sea, recognizes shifting societal orders and their relation to the word. Often literate and literary authors, whether Prospero as character or Hughes as writer, may abandon their words in order to gain a new world. (This is something seen with the *fetish,* aliteracy's very embodiment.) Through it we take W. H. Auden and his "parable" of the poet existing in a dialogue between creative, beautiful Ariel and what Seamus Heaney calls "the countervailing presence of Prospero, whose covenant is with 'truth' rather than 'beauty,'"[10] we see how Hughes sidesteps such a truth/beauty dialogue altogether. Instead, Hughes sides with Caliban—reserving the right to curse, to cannibalize, to talk out both sides of his neck.

How significant, then, that Hughes, perched on a voyage back to Africa, Old World, motherland, throws his books into the sea! In a reversal of the Middle Passage, Hughes creates a rite of passage, turning around the paradigm of the slave stolen from Africa and taught (or, more likely, forbidden) to read English. He also turns inside out the idea of the ignorant, illiterate black who don't know no better, Massa—a figure that, despite their best intentions, African American critics seem to reinscribe when they write of literacy and the history of white authentication of black authors. Hughes rejects it all, booklearnin' both black and white. Often I wish I could do the same.

I am tired of ideas. Tonight I prefer lives, especially lies. I am sick of confession, thought, analysis. Throw the books into the sea and let them swim for it like Shine, the mythic black porter who refused to stay on the sinking *Titanic.*

PART TWO

Of course, the *Titanic* famously did not allow black passengers, including the heavyweight champion Jack Johnson, who, folk songs report, danced the Eagle Rock when he found out about his close call.[11] In drawing the color line, the ocean liner thought to be unsinkable proved an apt metaphor for the hubris of modernity versus a nature it cannot contain, as well as for the failure of racist pride. (Some might say these were one and the same.) The tale of the *Titanic* thus plays an important part in African American folk culture—not just with its rebellious porter who swam away from the sinking ship back to Africa (in a kind of bawdy Black Star Line of his own) but also with folk ballads like "Titanic" that took retribution as their theme, and other- and afterworldly justice as their means.

What for the folk songs is retribution, and rough cosmic justice, becomes in Hughes a poetics of refusal.[12] But like the archetypal Draft Dodger, whether in Ibsen's *Peer Gynt* or our own Muhammad Ali, it is what Hughes replaces this refusal with that startles most. "I do not have to be what you want me to be," Muhammad Ali said after becoming a heavyweight champ and converting to Islam, going against most wishes, white or black, and refusing on principle to serve in what could have been relatively easy duty during Vietnam. Through refusal, Ali expanded his assigned role as a boxer and a black individual and an American—elevating the everyday to the status, often literally, of poetry, both in and out of the ring. No wonder one of Ali's best poems may be what George Plimpton calls the shortest ever written in English: "Me. Whee!"[13]

Ali bobbed and weaved outside of the ring as well as inside. Such a rope-a-dope is strategic—not mere reticence, or worse, avoidance. In similar fashion, Hughes spends most of *The Big Sea* laying out shifting, seemingly contradictory points of view that refuse to be pinned down.

Hughes's two cabinmates on his voyage to Africa embody two *aliterate* storying techniques by which Hughes (and the blues he modeled on) maintains "impersonal" distance: storytelling and silence. "George had a thousand tales to tell about every town he'd ever been in. And several versions of each tale. No doubt, some of the stories were true—and some of them not true at all, but they sounded true." And, "Sometimes George said he had relatives down South. Then, again, he said he didn't have anybody in the whole world. Both versions concerning his relatives were probably correct." Hughes here is describing and owning up to dissembling, recognizing fiction, or better yet, the doubling truth of fiction in storying; George proves a foil to Hughes, our (supposedly reliable) storyteller. "Sounding true" is given more importance than being true, forgoing Prospero's "truth" again.[14] Hughes knows that stories can be simultaneously true and not true; that, as in a blues song, you can have a strong family down home and still have no one in the world; atoms can stay both particle and wave, particularly in Hughes's *Big Sea*.

Elsewhere in *The Big Sea* Hughes talks of "telling stories on one-self"—laughing, if not at a veiled self, then at the Negro's fictional life. But he is also enacting the self-reflexive (to the point of self-indulgent) qualities of the blues. Just as bluesman Robert Johnson will refer to himself in the third person, singing how sad "Mr. Johnson" is without his "Kindhearted Woman," Hughes casts emotion as "impersonal," objective even. We are both there with the blues and not, the protagonist's predicament thrown into relief by the third person. But as with Bo Diddley's song of self "Bo Diddley," the blues hero is also detached by his ability (and the blues form) to make myth from pain. No wonder then, as Hughes relates, "my best poems were all written when I felt the worst."

Between the sadness and the story falls the silence. This is a telling silence, similar to what Susan Sontag describes in "The Aesthetics of Silence" as occurring in a Warhol film. From what is left unsaid, even unsayable, we get insight. For in *The Big Sea,* alongside the quixotic Hughes and gregarious George, sits silent Ramon, a Puerto Rican sailor: "The only thing that came out of his mouth in six months that I remember is that he said he didn't care much for women, anyway. He preferred silk stockings—so halfway down the African coast, he bought a pair of silk stockings and slept with them under his pillow."[15] It takes little strain to hear behind these words the fetishized, silent African continent, and its totemlike *fetishes,* in opposition to Ramon's rather Freudian one—but in Ramon's literal silence and Hughes's literary one, can we also make out the distant echoes of undisclosed sexuality?

Our oblique answer may appear in a pun a couple of paragraphs later. Mess boy Hughes relates that "The lye made the washing easy because it took all of the dirt out quick."[16] The dirt here is out, so to speak—"the lye" is less "lie" than something removed, a "sin" omitted. In many ways, his is the discretion found in Elizabeth Bishop (though in few other poets of her "confessional" generation). Heaney gives some insight into Bishop, "this most reticent and mannerly of poets," who "was temperamentally inclined to believe in the government of the tongue—in the self-denying sense," holding her tongue "not based on subservience but on a respect for other people's shyness in the face of poetry's presumption."[17] And also, in a sexuality that neither author saw as defining their work.

However, I hesitate to let us think of this "lye" as a secret, or the secret as simply sexual: rather, "the lye" is mostly bleach, which is to say, it is about whiteness; or refers to the whiteness of blackness. "You see, unfortunately, I am not black," Hughes announces in the chapter called "Negro."[18] Here Hughes informs us that a Negro, which in America means one drop of Negro blood, in Africa means something "pure."

Hughes here is tripping, storying, riffing off some of his—and our—clearest convictions about hisself, declaring *he is not even black*. This of course not only relates to the shifting question of "the mulatto" or of passing—issues addressed elsewhere in Hughes's work—but also the seemingly settled question of blackness. Settled, that is, until Tiger Woods hits a white ball into a hole on a green, wins a green jacket, declares he is "Cablinasian" and then gets warned by a white man against serving up collard greens. (And do I hear "Caliban," itself a riff off "cannibal," in Woods's own portmanteau for Caucasian, black, Indian, and Asian?) Interestingly enough, Hughes quite often uses the term "black," far earlier than others did—with that in mind, his famous line "Night coming tenderly / Black like me" reads not just as musically riveting but as socially advanced.[19]

Significantly called "Dream Variation," the "like" in the poem's final simile represents the moment of linkage, of connecting to something wished for—the self—located in the improvisations of dream. It also questions the American dream, belied by the lie of race and the one-drop rule, or of the unrealized promise of equality between races, which will later become the background music of *Montage of a Dream Deferred*.

What bothers me so much about the book that borrows the last line of "Dream Variation" as its title, *Black Like Me,* is that no one is black like this white author who dyes his skin to "pass" as black. There's little "lye" here, just the lie that blackness is merely temporary, and worse, simply physical and skin deep: black is not a simile, nor metaphor, not something to be worn and then removed, despite how much white and sometimes even black folks may wish. Rather, what's more striking are the ways in which we as writers, Americans, black folks of all "hues," have taken Hughes's creed "I, too, am America" and written ourselves into America with it. In addition, generations of poets have written away from it: Baraka does obliquely when he declares "You are / as any other sad man here / american," lowercase and all. Or there's Bob

Kaufman, again the black Beat poet's assertion of self—delirious, divided, delightful—in "I, Too, Know What I Am Not." By the end of a series of denials—"No, I am not death wishes of sacred rapists, singing on candy gallows. / No, I am not spoor of Creole murderers hiding in crepe-paper bayous"—the self Kaufman creates is stitched not only out of what's left, as in a patchwork, but by a series of erasures, negatives that paint a clearer picture all the same.[20]

As with Kaufman, the refusal in Hughes's work is largely a rejection of the limitations of being, and an assertion of selfhood. In *The Big Sea,* the moments when his humanity is on the line, not just moments when he is on the other side of the color line, but the blurred moments when he could perhaps shift sides, Hughes refuses his father's self-denial and -hate. In one chapter, "Back Home," Hughes relates how in returning from his father and Mexico, he was mistaken for Mexican: "But I made no pretense of passing for a Mexican, or anything else, since there was no need for it—except in changing trains at San Antonio in Texas, where colored people had to use Jim Crow waiting rooms, and could not purchase a Pullman berth." After purchasing a berth (denied by his birth), Hughes relates two incidents integral to understanding how he views being "read": first, what he terms an "amusing" story in which a white man who sat across from him in the diner car began "staring at me intently, as if trying to puzzle out something. He stared at me a long time. Then suddenly, with a loud cry, the white man jumped up and shouted: 'You're a nigger, ain't you?' And rushed out of the car as if pursued by a plague."[21]

This white fear of the contagious black death leads Hughes to grin, declaring, "I didn't know until then that we frightened them that badly." But then, "Something rather less amusing happened at St. Louis," in the Show-Me State Hughes was born in. (The fact that Missourah was previously a slave state, and that Hughes was named after an ancestor involved in John Brown's and others' attempts to render Kansas free, should not be lost.) What he is shown is what he allows to be shown: the soda "jerk" in the train station asks if Hughes is a Mexican or a Negro, and when Hughes asks why, replies, "'Because if you're a Mexican, I'll serve you,' he said. 'If you're colored, I won't.'" When Hughes answers, "I'm colored," "The clerk turned to wait on some one else. I knew I was home in the U.S.A."[22]

Hughes details the life and lessons of an African American writer in direct contrast to conventions both black and white. Rather than presenting black life as oxymoronic, a walking contradiction, the very conundrums of the black self become its selfsame comforts. Hughes articulates both of these like a limb—one he went out on, one we have lost that, ghostlike, we still miss.

3.

Yet Hughes refuses to believe in ghosts, just as he refuses to fully "pass" as Mexican, as his father essentially did. The poetics of refusal violates stereotype, much like in *The Big Sea* his taking up a bet to spend the night alone on a haunted ship to prove to his white shipmates he is neither spooked nor a spook. I fear I have given the impression of monklike Hughes, stoically working without a care for material things or the world or sexuality, composing well-etched, impersonal lyrics. He is more Monk than that—Thelonious, that is—oddly phrased, famous, a musicians' musician till recently better known as a composer than as the skilled player he actually is.

It is as if we have been speaking of the blues as a 12-bar, flatted tone structure without discussing its radical content, its social commentary. We should not re-present Hughes as he can casually be read as: a good-hearted, chaste humanist who wishes to sit at the American table. Or someone who begins his life wanting to overturn the table, to refuse to eat "the leavings" of white folks, who then gets politically muzzled by McCarthyism and gradualism until he accepts scraps with a smile. Till he was merely, as James Baldwin pus it in the late St. Clair Bourne's documentary on Hughes, rehearsing the blues.[23] To counter this we need only to read "12 Moods for Jazz" from 1961, whose title sums up Hughes's and black folks' constant backtalk: *Ask Your Mama*.

For Hughes is not only including himself in America ("I am the darker brother") but also saying he is older than America ("My soul has grown deep like the rivers"), and far wiser. His poetics of refusal is one of protest in the end, the literary equivalent of a sit-in, and arguably its predecessor. He shall not be moved: his poems' heft and breadth (and breath) are not just part of Hughes's being that rare breed, a working writer, but also a critique of those who seek to limit or fail to understand black invention. His poems are speech acts made active, musical, and ultimately political in the manner of Coltrane's "My Favorite Things" or Hendrix's "Star-Spangled Banner"—not through talking on about the Man but by taking apart his forms. That both of these musical "covers" are wordless should not surprise us—they reach what lies beyond the limits of human speech, and for what's at the beating, tom-tom heart of jazz.

At his best Hughes achieves this same kind of jazz wordlessness, charting a refusal whose absence of direct reproach is in itself critique.[24] This poetics as refusal negotiates the refrain from *Montage of a Dream Deferred*—"Why should it be my dream deferred overlong?"—and the very idea of "refraining" as restraint. This refrain is also in the scat of the term "bebop" itself—which in *Montage* evolves to "re-bop," "mop," and even "Be-Bach." As with scat, what could be construed as silence, nonsense, or mere noise should instead be seen as emotion, expression, the dissonance of urban, American, and black lives.

This brings us full circle, to the same people Hughes spent his life defending and defining, and the question again of *aliteracy*—for besides "reading" people, there are also two other aspects of this idea. First, the *aliterate* notion of "writing"—or art in its forms, whether blues or Beethoven—as being essentially *nonliterary,* or beyond a rarefied realm usually reserved for scholars or other bigots. And second, and more telling, *aliteracy* embraces the *nonliteral,* recognizing in trickster fashion that things ain't always what they seem, that every shut eye ain't asleep, every good-bye ain't gone.

Hughes lets us know that literalness is often negative; that sticking to the letter of an unfair law can sure prove deadly. From Jim Crow to slavery this point may seem obvious, but in the right hands protest is exactly this—a combination of the obvious and the unsayable, an appeal beyond standard conventions to a greater, abstract—let's call it poetic—truth. "Besides the implicit mode of Negro-American culture is abstract, and this comes from the very nature of our relationship to this country."[25] Hughes in his wisdom realizes that this truth is deadly serious, yet often can get across better with humor, dark as it may be.

This irony pervades *Big Sea* and Hughes's work in general—Hughes gives us many examples of avoiding the literalness critics then and now have brought to bear on his work, instances where literalness works against those who insist on it. For one, George, the storyteller, has a landlord who has insisted that George get a job to pay his rent—George does as she says, and gets a job—the very one that, as he's relating this story, has taken him out of Harlem and literally back to Africa! He got a job alright, but one that ensures she'll not be getting any rent money soon. The landlord's insistence on literalness (recast as paranoia in *Montage*'s "Ballad of a Landlord") leads to its opposite, an escape hatch from "reality," a running away into metaphor.

Or, the fact that, quite simply, racism can literally save your life. In the chapter "Bad Luck is Good," a bigot who replaces the previous chief steward turns around and refuses to take an integrated crew, thereby stranding Hughes. "A day later, the boat sailed. And a month later it was at the bottom of the Black Sea!"[26] having been struck by a stray mine from the Great War. Thus the big sea is actually bad and black; life a series of near misses, much like Jack Johnson and the *Titanic*. Or refusals, if you prefer. I can see the ad now: *Segregation saves!*

The literalness and lack of humor that lead to the captain's insistence do not acknowledge the "black humor" of the situation, much less acknowledge the ways in which misreading allows "loopholes of retreat" in the letters of the natural or stated law. Such willful misreadings are the counterfeiter's comfort zone, and figure fruitfully in Hughes's work. As in his first famous poem, "The Negro Speaks of Rivers," with *The Big Sea* Hughes fords the Mississippi, not just the river, but the Deep South state with its famous joke "probably invented in vaudeville":

DARKIE, READ AND RUN!
IF YOU CAN'T READ, RUN ANYHOW!

all the while realizing the joke has a deadly punch line.

I have selected this last tale as another example of storying in order to indicate something of how Hughes keeps running away from the plantation of our expectations. Hughes's desire to throw his books in the sea is related to embracing oral, black, vernacular culture, but also a desire to read and run, to have books be active (even if his are, in part, secretive). We might think here of Hughes's job working for his father as rather staid "book-keeper" in contrast to his admiration for Harlem "numbers writers" who not only created a separate, autonomous financial system but in Hughes's view were often more forthright in their support of the black arts than the black bourgeoisie.[27] The numbers writer is a "runner" too—after all, to be a fugitive is in a very real sense to break the law, to go beyond what is written, prescribed, or proscribed. "Keep this nigger boy runnin'."

For Hughes the numbers writer serves as a hero much like Hurston's bootlegger—a kind of counterfeiter who may not fit but who provides a kind of outlaw identity that mirrors that of the writer and black folks alike. Violating his father's will (and his "fatherland's" laws), Hughes would rather be a *bookmaker* than bookkeeper, and it's no wonder—throughout *The Big Sea,* Hughes champions a life outside the law, and even outside this very land that insists on African Americans as fractions, whether three-fifths a person or one-sixteenth black. Hughes is, he's revealed, not black in some folks' eyes, and too black in others'. And when race and its racist numbers don't add up, forging a black identity outside such a system makes all the more sense.

In the end, what Hughes actually remembers about his trip to Mississippi "is a river front café with marvelously misspelled signs on the wall: ALL FIGHTIN MUS BE DID OUTSIDE; and another: IF YOU WANTS TO PLAY THE DOZENS GO HOME; and WHEN YOU EAT, PAY ER RUN / CAUSE MR. BOSS GOT HES GUN"[28] As with the art of Jean-Michel Basquiat, we should not take these misspellings as missteps, but rather as spells of another sort. The signs provide a surefooted procession, a pageant of the black vernacular Hughes champions: violent (yet somehow funny), trash talking, seeking flight. Hughes is running alright, refusing the whip, fleeing from convention, preserving the self as the artist must first and foremost—then sneaking back later under the cover of night to set us all free.

BOOK THREE
Heaven Is Negro

If you have any trouble, I would suggest that you check out your kitchen vibrations. *What kind of pots are you using?* Throw out all of them except the black ones. The cast-iron ones like your mother used to use. Can't no Teflon fry no fried chicken. I only use black pots and brown earthenware in the kitchen. White enamel is not what's happening.

I don't like fancy food. I like simple—plain—ordinary—call it what you choose. I like what is readily available. It is very easy to do special things. Like a cake you only make on your first cousin by your mother's second marriage's birthday. Or a ham you make for Sam's wedding anniversary every other February 29. I'm talking about being able to turn the daily ritual of cooking for your family into a beautiful everyday happening. Now, that's something else again.

—VERTAMAE SMART-GROSVENOR
Vibration Cooking; or, The Travel Notes
of a Geechee Girl

Chorus Three: Ugly Beauty
Postmodernism and All That Jazz _ _ _ _ _ _ _ _ _ _ _ _ _ _ _

Jazz is not just a noun but a verb. Not a destination alone but the journey; not the consensus but the chorus; not the meaning but the meandering: invention is jazz's hometown. Jazz takes what in other hands might be miscues, the ugly bits—soul food, you could say—and makes them swang. *It Don't Mean a Thing.*

Yet swing music itself moved "from verb to noun," as Amiri Baraka notes. "As it was formalized, and the term and the music taken further out of context, *swing* became a noun that meant a commercial popular music in cheap imitation of a kind of Afro-American music."[1] Such a movement, from vital form to fetishized object, from active agent to mere thingness, is what poet Nathaniel Mackey calls "othering"[2] and what black musicians, from Louis Armstrong to those who went on to invent bebop, hoped to avoid in their work and in their lives. Modernism too had a similar swing, moving from *verb*—modernism as a way of approaching a book or canvas, say, both in production and reading—to mere noun, a thing studied, dissected, and in that way dissolving before our eyes.

This initial swing in culture—the modernism that the blues predicted and jazz embodied—we can also see in terms of *verb.* Certainly, poet Stephen Spender does: "The imagination has been restored in modern literature to its position of Verb. The reinstating of imagination as primary, central, the verb, was perhaps the attitude responsible for the greatest modern achievements: works like the last novels of Henry James (particularly *The Golden Bowl*), *Finnegans Wake,* Yeats' Byzantium poems, the *Duineser Elegien,* put these writers in the God-like position of being isolated within their own creations, of having to reinvent the world and all its values within their art."[3]

Yet what to do now, after World War II, when modernism seemed to many a museum, for good or ill, and to others a mere mausoleum? When the author and even God seemed to some long dead? I'm not entirely sure, but I do know that the music on the way home from the funeral likely would be jazz.

NOW'S THE TIME

With the horrors of the Holocaust; with the dropping of the atom bomb; with simply having a war *after* "The War to End All Wars"; and now, faced with a Cold War and its looming possibility of a nuclear war to actually end All: human consciousness changed.

No wonder then, in November 1945, when Charlie Parker and his Reboppers stepped into a recording studio, they produced a sound that no one had quite heard before: *bebop*. The culmination of jazz artistry, parody, skill, irony, and cool, bebop represents the postmodern black aesthetic early and well, complete with sped-up solos and "klook mops" or "bombs" being dropped by drummer Max Roach. Bird and his cohorts entered the studio as jazz musicians playing "Cherokee" and emerging as beboppers with a tune called (and culled from, and made "collud") "Ko Ko." The new title's very onomatopoetic quality is reminiscent of bebop, both in sound and name—which the music insists are the same.

After the codifying of big bands, the swing back (and forward) to bebop—which, granted, occurred over time and not in just one after-hours jam or recording session—both predicts and parallels the new emphasis on personality and expression found in postmodern art more generally. Both bebop and postmodern poetry were to fight against commercialization, codification, and the impersonality championed by big bands and the New Criticism, which had taken Eliot's "objective correlative" and turned the poem into an object, if not a static icon. In particular, bebop and the many movements it spawned, from hot to cool to free jazz—just as the many postwar literary "schools," from New York to San Francisco, from Beat to Bohemian to Black Mountain—fought for personal, nonconforming expression.[4]

The transformation of music made by the beboppers is not just analogous to the postmodern change; it also inspired it. Whether in Charlie

Christian or Mary Lou Williams, bebop provided an avant-garde model, what Cornel West calls

> the grand break with American mainstream music, especially imitated and co-opted Afro-American popular music, by the so-called bebop jazz musicians—Charlie Parker, Theolonius [sic] Monk, Dizzy Gillespie and others. Their particular way of Africanizing Afro-American jazz—with the accent on contrasting polyrhythms, the deemphasis of melody and the increased vocalization of the saxophone—was not only a reaction to the white-dominated, melody-obsessed "swing jazz"'; it also was a creative musical response to the major shift in sensibilities and moods in Afro-America after World War II. Through their technical facility and musical virtuosity, bebop jazz musicians expressed the heightened tensions, frustrated aspirations and repressed emotions of an aggressive yet apprehensive Afro-America.[5]

Bebop also represented a departure for white youth who also found it, and saw it—along with the Negro, often imaginary—as a form of rebellion from white, bourgeois, and older European forms. Donald Allen, in his groundbreaking anthology *The New American Poetry* (1960), discerned this break in postwar music and art and explicitly linked it to the new poetry being written:

> As it has emerged in Berkeley and San Francisco, Boston, Black Mountain and New York City, it [the new poetry] has shown one common characteristic: a total rejection of all those qualities typical of academic verse. Following the practice and precepts of Ezra Pound and William Carlos Williams, it has built on their achievements and gone on to evolve new conceptions of the poem. These poets have already created their own tradition, their own press, and their public. They are our avant-garde, the true continuers of the modern movement in American poetry. Through their work many are closely allied to modern jazz and abstract expressionist painting, today recognized throughout the world to be America's greatest achievements in contemporary culture.[6]

To such achievement, Allen and his anthology add poetry as a vital part of postmodern culture. We can mark the transformation into the postmodern, and its rejection of what's been called the "museum of modernism,"[7] by any number of literary events: Charles Olson's "Projective Verse" manifesto (1950); the reading of Allen Ginsberg's "Howl" at the Six Gallery (1955); the publishing of Robert Lowell's *Life Studies* (1959); or, as I argue, the bebop brilliance of Hughes's *Montage of Dream Deferred,* which as early as 1951 suggested the connections between a shifting black urban community and the shifting form of bebop improvisation.

Such efforts inherently address Theodor Adorno's declaration, "To write poetry after Auschwitz is barbaric."[8] If all might agree that poetry as we once knew it cannot exist after such atrocity, some might suggest poetry must exist anyway: the desire for its comforts and conflicts are too great. In this way postmodernism is not so much a turning away from as a deepening of, reacting to, and in some ways embracing the modernism that preceded it, and the atrocity it witnessed (and which, some might say, abetted). The move from impersonal poetry to confessionalism, from *vers libre* to projective verse, from composition "as hardship" to composition by field, the completion of the movement toward the abstract in art, the very swing from Paris to New York as cultural center, are directly related to the war's upheavals, jazz's vitality, and postmodernism's beginnings.

PARKER'S MOOD

Emerging from Charlie Parker's horn was *plenty*—not just sped-up senses of the melody, not just playing above and below it, but also the notion of plenty itself. Parker's plenty riffs against the rationing of wartime America—felt all the more profoundly against the recording ban by the musicians' union in the early 1940s—not to mention against the rationality of the times. Parker's musical derangement of the senses predicted and even made possible the broader artistic trends of the 1950s and 1960s, even if at times his followers engaged him through imitating his drug use rather than his music and artistry.

There's something particularly African American about this plenty too, obliquely referenced in Hurston's visit to a Negro home in Mobile decorated with advertisements as a kind of art: "It was grotesque, yes.

But it indicated the desire for beauty. And decorating a decoration, as in the case of the doily on the gaudy wall pocket, did not seem out of place to the hostess. The feeling back of such an act is that there can never be enough of beauty, let alone too much."[9] Except for the "grotesque" comment, Hurston could be talking about my grandmothers' houses, the walls filled with well-placed calendars, funeral home fans, photo collages, and giveaways—or Parker's plenty, which took the seemingly commercial and ugly and made beauty from it. Beauty is not a state of being but a kind of belief, seeing past what is to what may be.

At its finest bop provided a crucial form of play, taking us, as the spirituals do, Elsewhere. Whether "The Land of Oo-Bla-Dee" or "St. Thomas," "A Night in Tunisia" or "April in Paris," even jazz's earthbound titles denote the breadth of its worldview and dedication to journeying. Fittingly, critic Brent Hayes Edwards has noted the ways Dizzy Gillespie and African and Latin jazz musicians even used jazz—or at least "that diasporic lingua franca, rhythm"—to communicate while in France.[10] Such connections are found not just in bop's musical brilliance, its sophisticated new grammar, but also in its own language and parlance—from the scatlike "Oo-Pop-A-Da" that mirrors the sounds of bebop itself, to the playful slang and speech of Dizzy Gillespie. Anyone who can turn "Salt Peanuts" into an evocation of both the music and the mood, then use it less as a chorus than as punctuation—a kind of controlled carnivalesque—bears the mark of genius.

Bebop's play on words, which became for the Beats a kind of "bop prosody," was preceded by Lester "Pres" Young, whose laid-back horn playing influenced Bird and whose famous vocabulary—including naming Billie Holiday "Lady"—influenced jazz slang, style, and history. Renaming is one of bebop's key strategies, remaking even the storying tradition in its own image.

Even years later, Pres is cool personified; or should we say, is cool as ultimate persona. After all, cool is the mask that insists it is a face. Or is cool a face striving to be a mask?

Cool has many components and proponents, and certainly there were other influences on bebop—namely, Charlie Christian, whose loose-limbed, seemingly effortless "hornlike" guitar invented jazz guitar, elevating the instrument and influencing rock and roll; and Coleman

Hawkins's horn, which is often seen as rather "hot" and thereby the opposite of Pres's.[11] But certainly Young's sense of poise, his cool in both playing and person, influenced the small-set combinations, cutting contests, and after-hours sessions that produced the music.

Cool, in fact, is not simply style but a strategy of living—"keeping cool" or "playing it cool" are all reactions to a volatile situation, especially to being black in a white world. Many have recently discussed "cool" in just this way, pointing to its African origins, and its African American inheritance and practice.[12]

The evolution of postwar jazz also centers on cool. One near-canonical version of the music's history recounts that bebop gave way to "cool jazz" such as Miles Davis's *Kind of Blue*—which in turn became what's thought of as "West Coast jazz," in contradistinction to hard bop. This supposed split between hard bop and cool jazz is often seen as racial, or cultural—or even coastal—with cool becoming something played and arguably appropriated as style (yet perhaps not strategy) by white California musicians, with the hard bop of musicians like Art Blakey evoking the blues origins and soul spirit of black culture.[13] More than any other artist, Miles Davis can be said to embody these shifting jazz styles and strategies—such a shifting, undeniably politically loaded terrain is well discussed in a study of *Kind of Blue* by Ashley Kahn, laying out as he does the various schools and fights over jazz that all too often seem more about recess than about playing.

But above it all, above even the times or Davis's chameleon qualities, is Miles's horn. Davis's distinctive tone and his growing confidence as a band leader provide an undeniable hold on jazz and its possibilities. As Davis says, he was trying to play fewer notes, countering—or should I say complementing—Bird's sense of plenty with an ethos of *spareness*. Such spareness makes Miles's playing more, not less, distinctive—and may prove a useful model for us as writers trying to look beyond simple notions of "voice" as a goal and method of artistic achievement. We do not need a distinctive "voice"—instead we need a tone that is our own.

We can easily see—or hear—the ways in which jazz inspires the writers and artists of our time exactly through its exactness and improvisation, whether through plenty or spareness. Think too of Billie Holiday's desire to make her voice sound like an instrument—in this way, the voice is functional, but not as an "instrument of change" in a simplistic way, but as a musical instrument. It is no surprise that the musicians I've named would go on to constitute the chief musical heroes in the roll call of the Black Arts movement. Or that black maverick Ted Joans reportedly started the graffito *Bird Lives.*

CHASING THE BIRD

Ironically, especially given its widespread influence, one of the important aspects of bop is the notion that in its expertise, its level of difficulty, the black musicians who invented it sought a music that couldn't be copied. The musicians, too often in the shadows, now stuck to them, refusing to record—as early New Orleans musicians had refused—in order to keep their work intimate and their own. This *uncopyable* aspect of bebop—or the desire to no longer be copied, the way that much of black music was and still is—throws its counterfeit into clearer relief. Bebop addresses counterfeit, playing above the theme of this book, relating to notions of originality and economics that are an implied part of the endeavor.

You could say that one of bebop's aims was to remove the white frame that had lain over black music for centuries—the same frame Mamie Smith and Langston Hughes stole away—returning it to a blues space both in tone and in freedom. The mistrust of technology, of the copy—or of being copied—had been with us since the white Original Dixieland Jazz Band had stepped instead into the studio black jazz innovators had assiduously avoided. The music, then, was itself a technology, providing its own system of preserving and recoding that sometimes surfaced as recordings—in classic and "Crazy Blues," say—or was sometimes captured, as it were, in field recordings.

But the transmission of the music itself, recorded or not, is made up of glimpses—which is to say, the black musical tradition was always a form of folk song, which conserved even as it evolved. The music's memory was again a form of technology pitted against and yet part of the recordings that preserved and at times oppressed it. Even if written, the music was played by ear—besides its creative pleasure and necessity, its transcription or rather its composed qualities emphasized anew by Gillespie and others meant just another way of converting that memory to a technology recognized by those in power as well as those who played the changes.

In the face of white cultural theft, however loving, in the face of the facelessness and invisibility that marked the times, no wonder then that bebop began as a kind of counterfeit, as storying filled with plenty.

Plenty, however, can easily give way to excess. And in the mix of cool and plenty, some find innovator Charlie Parker's life and art not so much resistant to exploitation as emblematic of it. Ellison speaks highly of Bird's playing in a memorial tribute, performing his own brand of ornithology by comparing Bird to a mockingbird: *"Mimus polyglottos."* In doing so, Ellison riffs off previous stereotypes of black culture as imitative, instead making "mocking" a compliment, something natural and even adaptive. Ellison's "On Bird, Bird-Watching, and Jazz" even quotes a Peterson's *Field Guide to Birds* that tells us that

> mockingbirds are "excellent mimics" who "adeptly imitate a score or more species found in the neighborhood," and that they frequently sing at night—a description which not only comes close to Parker's way with a saxophone but even hints at a trait of his character. For although he *usually* sang at night, his playing was characterized by velocity, by long-continued successions of notes and phrases, by swoops, bleats, echoes, rapidly repeated bebops—I mean rebopped bebops—by mocking mimicry of other jazzmen's styles, and by interpolations of motifs from extraneous melodies, all of which added up to a dazzling display of wit, satire, burlesque and pathos.[14]

Such burlesque makes clear the postmodernity and storying involved in Parker's very playing, if not Ellison's writing, noting "there was, without doubt, as irrepressible a mockery in his personal conduct as in his music."[15]

This mockery was part of a musical, metaphysical wit that, even as it recognizes the humor and play in jazz's roots, further attempts to remove itself from the music's perception as mere entertainment. Such a pressure to entertain is pervasive and is expressed by poet Philip Larkin in his introduction to *All What Jazz,* a gathering of over a decade of his jazz criticism. (Not enough or dare I say anything has been written about the credible influence of jazz on Larkin—if not on his prosody, then on his writing's postwar mood.) While Larkin likes jazz, and identifies its freedoms with his initial discovery of it, he regrets wartime jazz's link with what he sees as seriousness and difficulty of an earlier high modernism:

> How glibly I had talked of modern jazz, without realizing the force of the adjective: this was *modern* jazz, and Parker was a modern jazz player just as Picasso was a modern painter and Pound a modern poet. I hadn't realized that jazz had gone from Lascaux to Jackson Pollock in fifty years, but now I realized it relief came flooding in upon me after nearly two years' despondency [hearing bebop only after World War II]. I went back to my books: "After Parker, you had to be something of a musician to follow the best jazz of the day." Of course! After Picasso! After Pound! There could hardly have been a conciser summary of what I don't believe about art.
>
>   . . . All I am saying is that the term "modern," when applied to art, has a more than chronological meaning: it denotes a quality of irresponsibility peculiar to this century, known sometimes as modernism, and once I had classified modern jazz under this heading I knew where I was.[16]

For Larkin and countless others, jazz was symbolically and literally liberating, from the Jazz Age's "going wild" to the real rebellion provided for and by the jazz of "yellow music" in China and the Swing Kids in Hitler's Germany before the war. But while Larkin is terrific on jazz's freedoms—"This was something we had found for ourselves, that wasn't taught at school (what a prerequisite that is of nearly everything worthwhile!), and having found it, we made it bear all the enthusiasm usually directed at more established arts"[17]—he seems more focused on freedom for jazz's audience than for its performers.

For him, jazz remains best when hewing to its origins as entertainment, specifically as black entertainment for white audiences: "The tension between artist and audience in jazz slackened when the Negro stopped wanting to entertain the white man, and when the audience as a whole, with the end of the Japanese war and the beginning of television, didn't in any case particularly want to be entertained in that way any longer."[18] The thing Larkin cannot imagine is a *black* audience (or even any audience that is not him). In this way, the larger postwar desire for Dixieland wasn't just for the music but for its nonexistent nostalgic past.

Yet even entertainment is not the enemy of virtuosity; for innovators like Louis Armstrong who also saw themselves as showmen, entertainer is no less a mask than cool is for those who came later. "Certain older jazzmen possessed a clearer idea of the division between their identities as performers and as private individuals," Ellison reminds us. "Off stage and while playing in ensemble, they carried themselves like college professors or high church deacons; when soloing they donned the comic mask and went into frenzied pantomimes of hotness—even when playing 'cool'—and when done, dropped the mask and returned to their chairs with dignity."[19] This division between private and public, between persona and self, dignity and comedy might be said to be a marked one in the larger, earlier moment of modernity—indeed, the very presence of such clear divisions allowed for easy journey between the two. Shuttling between identities ain't the same as shufflin'.

Dizzy Gillespie, for one, played roles quite comfortably, clowning on the stand and off, serving as bebop's ambassador and embodiment of style, flair, and plenty, with a "savage eye for the incongruous," in Ellison's useful phrase. (We may be reminded of Hurston's describing the Negro's way with mimicry and love of asymmetry in her essential "Characteristics of Negro Expression.")[20] Gillespie's sense of irony, suggested by his sense of incongruity, may be what saves him from stereotype; but we should certainly not think Satchmo had no less a sense of incongruity, whether playing "West End Blues" or serving as King Zulu in the Mardi Gras parade in his native New Orleans, an honored role that outsiders mistook as a form of blackface by another name.[21] In fact, by avoiding the mask of comedy, Ellison argues, Bird faced something far more dangerous:

> No jazzman, not even Miles Davis, struggled harder to escape the entertainer's role than Charlie Parker. The pathos of his life lies in the ironic reversal through which his struggles to escape what in Armstrong is basically a *make-believe* role of clown— which the irreverent poetry and triumphant sound of his trum-

pet makes even the squarest of squares aware of—resulted in
Parker's becoming something far more "primitive": a sacrificial
figure whose struggles against personal chaos, on stage and
off, served as entertainment for a ravenous, sensation-starved,
culturally disoriented public which had but the slightest notion
of its real significance.[22]

Though Ellison overstates, he does point up how exchanging the mask
of comedy for one of tragedy might not mean one is better—or worth
more—than the other. There are sad clowns, after all, as Smokey
Robinson reminds us. And wearing the painted mask of King of the
Zulus is, at best, an honored highpoint of the Mardi Gras parade and, at
the very least, a complex relation to the unruly rule that is Fat Tuesday.
A day preceded, we might remember, by Blue Monday—the very name
hinting at the storying tradition of the carnivalesque in New Orleans
and in the insurrectionary blues, where down is up, if only for one day.[23]

Still, as with other postmodern art, the desire to overthrow the masks
and artifice of modernism often meant relying on the face to convey
large emotions for artist and audience. (Later, others would put on
more and more masks in response to the same thing.) In other words,
whether for confessional poets or performance artists or Charlie Parker,
the postmodern artist's abandoning the mask often led him or her to
rely on naked life as subject matter for art. And even *life* as a kind of art,
however destructive that life might be.
    That this was in pursuit of a kind of authenticity sought by those
who found the 1950s sterile (and later as an audience literally saw jazz
alongside "folk" music in various festivals) only heightens Bird's ironies. While I might argue with Ellison whether or not "Bird was indeed
a 'white' hero" or mainly a hero to "white hipsters," certainly "For the
postwar jazznik, Parker was Bird, a suffering, psychically wounded, law-
breaking, life-affirming hero."[24] Such heroism is all the more pointed
for being tragic—something that haunts those who feel it was the drugs
that helped Bird create, who romanticize pain, or who view black life as
inherently linked to suffering. As a kind of "picaresque saint," Bird "was
thrice alienated: as Negro, as addict, as exponent of a new and disturbing development in jazz—whose tortured and in many ways criminal

striving for personal and moral integration invokes a sense of tragic fellowship in those who saw in his agony a ritualization of their own fears, rebellions and hunger for creativity."[25]

The fact is that it is struggle, not mere survival, that characterizes the best of black life—struggle for meaning, pleasure, art, swing—much less suffering or sociology or suicide. Through the form of fiction, the burlesque of bebop, the force of the new face of jazz, in storying, in emboldened black style, such struggle shows its best or boldest face.

Bird is making a performance not just of pain but also of his resistance to it, however short lived. Such will to survive Ellison sees elsewhere as an inheritance that counters the view of the Negro merely as a set of symptoms or suffering: "there is also an American Negro tradition which teaches one to deflect racial provocation and to master and contain pain. It is a tradition which abhors as obscene any trading on one's own anguish for gain or sympathy; which springs not from a desire to deny the harshness of existence but from a will to deal with it as men at their best have always done." Ellison continues:

> For even as life toughens the Negro, even as it brutalizes him, sensitizes him, dulls him, goads him to anger, moves him to irony, sometimes fracturing and sometimes affirming his hopes; even as it shapes his attitudes toward family, sex, love, religion; even as it modulates his humor, tempers his joy—it *conditions* him to deal with his life and with himself. Because it is *his* life and no mere abstraction in someone's head. He must live it and try consciously to grasp its complexity until he can change it; must live it *as* he changes it. He is no mere product of his socio-political predicament. He is a product of the interaction between his racial predicament, his individual will and the broader American cultural freedom in which he finds his ambiguous existence. Thus he, too, in a limited way, is his own creation.[26]

Through Bird's many masks, we can see how he not only encapsulates the possibility of black artistry but insists on it. "Living it as you change it" seems an awfully accurate definition of the jazz aesthetic; the negotiation between individual will, cultural freedom, and the ambiguities of black existence may prove the best argument for the storying tradition of any.

So too Bird's own insistence on incongruity. An anecdote relates how Bird would go to a certain bar, followed by admirers and his fellow musicians. Once there, he would fill the jukebox with coins and pick endless rounds of country music, which his fellow jazzheads disliked but endured—this was Bird, after all. One day someone got up the courage to ask Parker why he liked country music. His answer: "For the stories, man, the stories." In country music's heartfelt fictions, Bird was able to discern common roots with jazz—descended from both the blues and the storying tradition.

HARD BOP

Playing the changes as you live them may not just describe the jazz aesthetic but also prove a useful gloss on one of the finest long poems of the twentieth century: Hughes's *Montage of a Dream Deferred*. Is it mere coincidence that, taking the hard-sought first edition of it off my shelf, I find Hughes has dedicated it "To Ralph and Fanny Ellison"?[27] The book itself serves as a community epic at the century's midpoint, taking bebop as its technique that is all the more remarkable in that it appears in 1951, only a few years after the very term *bebop* was coined. Luckily we don't need Ellison, who would go on to distance himself from Hughes—if not outright dis him—in order to describe Hughes's genius; we have Hughes's own headnote that inaugurates his book's music:

> In terms of current Afro-American popular music and the sources from which it has progressed—jazz, ragtime, swing, blues, boogie-woogie and be-bop—this poem on contemporary Harlem, like be-bop, is marked by conflicting changes, sudden nuances, sharp and impudent interjections, broken rhythms, and passages sometimes in the manner of the jam session, sometimes the popular song, punctuated by the riffs, runs, breaks, and disc-tortions of the music of a community in transition.[28]

I'm not sure anyone can put it better than that. Such "disc-tortions" course through the book and aptly sum up Hughes's technique and its relation to bebop's "conflicting changes"—as well as the changes in music and literature to come. That these changes mirror life in Hughes's beloved Harlem is made even more profound by his ability to do exactly what he claims: using "broken rhythms" much like Hopkins made his sprung, or seemingly "broken English" mining the ground first broken by Dunbar, Hughes forges poems that serve as popular and progressive song. Like bebop itself, Hughes's *Montage* is a mix of soloist and group, negotiating the community to make an "I" into "we"—a metaphor of transformation comparable to the community in transition.

For Hughes, however, it is important to note that such transformation not only occurs from the individual to the group but also with the group fracturing back to the individual. In other words, the "I" in *Montage*—and arguably in most postmodern productions, such as Bob Kaufman's—is one of restless fragment. While fragmentation may also be at work in modernism—think of Eliot's *The Waste Land* or the blues itself—the difference is in the postmodern era's acceptance of this fragmentation. However uneasy, such acceptance unites *Montage* and the community it invokes, whether through artistry, rugged authority, or a pleasure in its own plurality. You could even say that, in contrast to Du Bois's sense of double consciousness as "two warring ideals in one body," Hughes's opus provides not a corpse but a living, fighting, breathing body of work.

As with Gwendolyn Brooks's early books, *Montage*'s very arrangement provides an artful statement on community, with the individual poems playing off and talking back to each other, much like solos. Let's open the book at random—or just set the needle down, more like—finding "Sunday by the Combination":

> I feel like dancin', baby,
> till the sun goes down.
>
> But I wonder where
> the sunrise
> Monday morning's gonna be?

I feel like dancin'!
Baby, dance with me!

This poem is itself an evocation of the ecstasy and doubt found in bebop—and in the Sunday morning that serves as the Sabbath for the community, giving us a gospel-like redemption that also brings Monday one day closer. After "Sunday" we find "Casualty":

He was a soldier in the army,
But he doesn't walk like one.
He walks like his soldiering
Days are done.

Son! . . . Son![29]

In five lines, Hughes evokes the kind of pain, and challenge to pain, that Ellison speaks about and Bird embodied; he also taps into the postwar moment, the ways its promise was violated in the very faces of a dejected, presumably black, veteran—called a "casualty" not because he died but *because he survived.* Survival ironically means walking "like his soldiering / Days are done"—which they are, of course, but what's "done" for him is the presumed pride that "soldiering" once provided. Instead "he doesn't walk like one"—with no spring, or swing, or bop in his step, he seems to make physical both the pride bebop provided and the protest it waged against a postwar world where black folks returning from the front still had to sit in the back. In this, Hughes foregrounds his character's anger—rebutting the psychologizing of Lowell's "Mad Negro Soldier Confined at Munich," a few years later and anticipating a powerful poem like Yusef Komunyakaa's "To Have Danced with Death,"[30] about a black Vietnam vet returning to the States missing a leg. In *Montage* the vet is missing something metaphysical, far beyond the physical.

That would be poem enough—though perhaps stopping here we might overlook some of the poem's power without the last line: "Son! . . . Son!" This exclamation is spoken by whom? The narrator? The poet? The mother or father? By its very understated ambiguity—something found often, if ignored, in black life and in Hughes—the line, spoken, sung, pleaded, makes us part of that community, of that family. And, if not reaching for too high a C, even a sort of Christlike "son of God"—the audience or congregation is made up, after all, of "soldiers in God's army" as we used to sing in my church growing up.

With the next, slightly longer poem, "Night Funeral in Harlem," Hughes makes use of rhyme and his "broken rhythm" to give a sense of the questions of a boy's death. The boy is surrounded in the poem less by mourners—the "ten thousand standing round the burying ground"— than by insurance men, flowers, and observers who comment, *"Where did they get / Them two fine cars"* and who later ask:

> *Who preached that*
> *Black boy to his grave?*

> Old preacher-man
> Preached that boy away—
> Charged Five Dollars
> His girl friend had to pay.[31]

We may know that "preached to his grave" may simply mean who preached at the service, but having been to a few too many funerals lately (and of young black men), I for one can one fully feel the resentment, misdirected as it may be, toward the clergy member who appears to be taking the boy away. And for a fee, no less—one small enough to be insulting, but, you get the sense, big enough to hurt even more.

We are far from the ecstatic "Sunday by the Combination" or "Casualty," where lifelessness is a state of mind—but all of these poems take black bodies and put them in motion. "Night Funeral" ends with the form being broken like the rhythm, subtly altering the rhyme as the poem also alters its tone:

> That boy that they was mournin'
> Was so dear, so dear
> To them folks that brought the flowers,
> To that girl who paid the preacher man—
> It was all their tears that made
> > That poor boy's
> > Funeral grand.

The boy is only relatively speaking poor; he's rich in relatives, who the poem hints are poor themselves. As we've seen, "poor gal" and "poor boy" are versions of a blues identity that provides an implied critique of the conditions surrounding us; "poor boy" here is in fact a cause for celebration. Like a true counterfeit, value in the poem is something created out of whole cloth, and changed from the expected—in a word, reassigned—so that the boy himself is "so dear, so dear." But grandness too is relative, and like lifelessness in "Casualty," is as much a state of mind as anything—I am reminded of how my mom used to say folks were "classy," meaning that, like swing itself, class was an approach, a style, a working with what all you got, no matter how little.

If at times a mask—some folks just seem classy, and you imagine them inherently this way, however hard-earned—class, much like grace, can't be simply inherited, and only rarely realized. Most often, grace, class, even "grandness" is best embodied—even if it is, for the "poor boy" in Hughes's poem, only in death. This grandness is less grandiosity than something approaching glamour—though harder to fake than glamour, such "class" may prove easier to achieve.

As the title implies, *Montage* also relies on the technique of film, using the arrangement of images, juxtapositions in a way both bebop-inspired and cinematic—in fact, Hughes brilliantly recognizes the ways the two share an idiom. Cutting, jumps, takes: all these Hughes makes use of to get at his community's current condition.

"The dream deferred" in the book's title—and in the line of the most famous poem in the book, sometimes known as "Harlem"—is of course the American dream: a promise not just of equality but opportunity; of bootstraps, not bootblacks. Brooks writes of the dream from the perspective of a resident of a "kitchenette building" in Bronzeville, Chicago:

> We are things of dry hours and the involuntary plan.
> Grayed in, and gray. "Dream" makes a giddy sound, not strong
> Like "rent," "feeding a wife," "satisfying a man."[32]

Montage of a Dream Deferred's full title alone is enough to send us thinking of critic Jacques Derrida's notion of *différance*, with its notion of simultaneous "difference" and "deferral" that helped define postmodernism and post-structuralism—however, we don't need such a theory of the contrasts and delaying of meaning to know that in Hughes's Harlem or Brooks's Bronzeville the community's tenacity and tenor are measured by its poetic music, by its almost dreamlike evocation of a cast of characters, of shifting voice-overs and close-ups. Bebop tells us so.

It also tells us about violence. In a column based on his character Jesse B. Semple, full of folk wisdom, Hughes equates violence with bebop's very name:

> Every time a cop hits a Negro with his billy club, that old club
> says, "BOP! BOP! . . . BE-BOP! . . . MOP! . . . BOP!"
>   That Negro hollers, "Ooool-ya-koo! Ou-o-o!"
>   Old Cop just keeps on, "MOP! MOP! . . . BE-BOP! . . . MOP!"
> That's where Be-Bop came from, beaten right out of some
> Negro's head into them horns and saxophones and piano keys
> that plays it.[33]

Cutting up, Semple—known as Simple—shows us one underground meaning as if in a cutting session between musicians, his comical explanation hiding a real quality of hurt and musical violence as a symbol of a larger resistance. In (and like a) *Montage,* Hughes crosscuts, zooms, and then lowers the boom on violence, first giving us "Movies" and two poems later "Not a Movie," which contextualizes and historicizes such violence even further:

> Well, they rocked him with road-apples
> because he tried to vote
> and whipped his head with clubs
> and he crawled on his knees to his house
> and he got the midnight train
> and he crossed that Dixie line
> now he's livin'
> on a 133rd.
>
> He didn't stop in Washington
> and he didn't stop in Baltimore
> neither in Newark on his way.

Six knots was on his head
but, thank God, he wasn't dead!
And there ain't no Ku Klux
on a 133rd.

There's also this music, bebop, to chart these ironies and changes, offering a deferral that's also a refusal to settle.

THE LAND OF OO-BLA-DEE

Jazz risks chaos, constantly reinventing itself, storying as it goes. But
perhaps its biggest challenge to tradition is the way the music is also
willing to risk wordlessness: by this I don't mean an instrumental, but
a vocalization without words; in a word, *scat*. A technique of singing
like an instrument, scat embodies the wordless way jazz reaches the
Elsewhere of the spirituals, seeking an unspoken, often coded beauty.

Just in the way jazz is read as primitive, scat has wrongly been read
as a failure of language. "Scat begins with a fall, or so we are told,"
Brent Edwards begins his powerful essay on scat singing and Louis
Armstrong—going on to evoke scat's relation to excess and even excre-
tions.[34] Rather than recast Edwards's complex and brilliant argument,
I want to suggest that scat is in fact not about loss but, much like Bird's
bebop, about plenty.

Such plenty comes to full fruition in bebop, whose song titles and
refrains often imitated the instruments the musicians played. There has
long been an African-influenced tradition of instruments "talking"—
and an African American one of the "talking book"—but scat is not
about a voice behaving like an instrument. As in the case of scat in
jazz a generation earlier—say, Armstrong on "West End Blues"—we are
in the presence of a black intelligence not so much imitating an instrument as evoking an instrument's emotional pitch. Tonal and gestural,
scat stems from an impulse to express more fully than an instrument
possibly can; rather than a failure of language, scat is exactly a recognition that the voice can in fact fully express what an instrument cannot.

Even though wordless—or because it is—scat can express human
feeling better than little else can. (Scat finds its descendants not just in
pop music's *la la la* but in beatbox's unsteady rhythm.) Still, there is a

sense of incompleteness in scat; in songs, scat often proves a sign of desire itself, expressing the ways in which desire is always incomplete. Scat, early on at least, rarely starts a song—it is usually the exact moment in the song when the words can no longer contain the singer's longing. In this it is a bit like the gospel hum, described by Hurston: "As indefinite as hums sound, they also are formal and can be found unchanged all over the South. The Negroised white hymns are not exactly sung. They are converted into a barbaric chant that is not a chant. It is a sort of *liquefying of words.*"[35]

Take "Sleepy Time Down South," an Armstrong song that in other hands is nostalgic and even problematic in evoking a kind of pure plantation past, an Ole Virginny full of imaginary Negroes. With its scat virtuosity, Armstrong's version fights against the words, creating a tension between the South he is speaking of, and the South he is scatting from, and goes beyond. "Everyone has his south—it doesn't matter where it is—that is, his line of slope or flight."[36] Part babble, part "universal grammar," part speaking in tongues, scat suggests a language beyond language, a place both primal and full of utterance, both wordless and Esperanto—a symbolic place of one love and language, ever present and long lasting—a human ideal since Babylon fell. In the case of those descended from slaves, whether in Cuba or Cincinnati, the idea of scat as lingua franca becomes all the more telling.

If jazz is an Esperanto—an "artificial language invented for universal use" around the same time jazz was invented—then scat might resemble its rough contemporary Basic English, another invented system or "variety of the English language, comprising a select vocabulary . . . and intended for use as a medium of international communication."[37] The *Basic* in Basic English doesn't mean simple, but rather stands for "British American Scientific International Commercial"—an acronym that might describe some of bebop's ambitions. Maybe scat is not just an "un-English" but an "ur-English"?

After all, it is language, not scat, that is fallen; scat rises from the ashes and suggests you shake 'em.

Where Armstrong's singing voice approaches instrumentality in its phrasing, becoming evocative, even abstract, Armstrong's horn becomes verbal, active. A narrative without words, using words for emotional and sound content, rather than communication—storying—finds its form in scat. Sometimes scat does this through a blurring of actual words, bleeding over into the rest of the vocal itself. Much as scratching or dancing in the breaks of a hip-hop song, scat often serves as the literal bridge in a jazz song, especially an instrumental. Scat serves not just as break but as bridge between instruments and voice.

But also between music and the word. To Brent Edwards, scat itself is reproduced in the physical nature of Armstrong's own prolific writings, complete with diacritical marks that Edwards links to Hopkins, Dickinson, and Baraka's open parentheses.[38] For me, such inflections are also found in Armstrong's collages: part words, part photographic collage, often surreal, his artwork—meant as covers to his own home recordings—play interestingly against the aesthetics of his music. Here Armstrong is a recording artist, alright, combining press clippings, advertising, and photos of friends to craft collages that chart, like his horn does, the music of memory. Unlike in "Hello Dolly," Armstrong as writer and as collagist is unmediated: like his horn, this is modernism made physical, literal, musical, and even literary; like his home recordings, this is a way of representing the technology of memory; like scat, Armstrong's seemingly lazy river is actually a river of meaning.

Upriver from such meanings are those of Dizzy, and his compositions like "Ool-Ya-Koo," which take the music's sounds as their very lyrics, a kissing cousin to scat. In the composition "In the Land of Oo-Bla-Dee," written for Diz by former child prodigy Mary Lou Williams, the storying quality of his "Oop-Bop-Sh'bam" and "Ool-Ya-Koo"—which notably anticipate, or predict, the horn playing that will follow on the tracks—becomes narrativized. Complete with characters in a fairy tale of sorts, the "Land of Oo-Bla-Dee" is imaginary and necessary, an Elsewhere; it proves a place of possibility, a make-believe that enacts the journey the music itself intends. You could rename this land America.

Approaching and invoking scat, such bebop onomatopoeia is also *nommo,* the African attribute of naming. Clarence Major's important *Dictionary of Afro-American Slang* (1970) gives a revealing definition, found between *O* (meaning opium) and *ofay*:

O-bop-she-bam: an existential jazz phrase; perhaps a mystic effort to comment on the inscrutable in the black man's social,

moral, and spiritual condition in the United States, or simply a
way of talking *to* that "sense" of mystery often referred to as God.

African American and Afro-Cuban, tongue tripping, the music seeks a
beyond that's all the more paradise for its desire to have it also remain
earthbound, even earthy. In the words of another of Gillespie's compositions, "Oo-La-La."

DEEP DEUCE

You might also say scat provides an inflected language in English—an
ideal (or should I say form) of language long sought by Ezra Pound. My
feeling is that Pound was fascinated with Black English because it too
represents the kind of inflected language no longer found in English—
and that the Chinese language, for one, insists upon. Pound mourned
this lack of inflection—again, language as fallen, a sense of lack—and
Black English represented a kind of fullness he found otherwise missing.

This may help explain why Pound, "the inventor of Chinese poetry
in our time," chose a troubling black dialect to represent part of his
translation of the *Confucian Odes*. Commonly known as the "Classic
Anthology as Defined by Confucius," the *Odes* are a set of poetic wis-
doms dating from 5 BC.[39] Why turn to plantation-era dialect for such
a foundational text, especially given how far it was from the source of
dialect in terms of time and space? Pound's translation makes use of
black dialect in order to better indicate that meaning is not made just
from what is said but also from how. Despite the stereotypical speech he
used and his lack of facility in using it—the dialect is awful, and Pound
is awful at it—Pound here is not merely mocking the failures found in
dialect but marking English the best way he knows how.

A similar conflating—or should I say demeaning—of vernaculars between China and African America played out in bebop's founding. The
story goes that Dizzy, part of the trumpet section of Cab Calloway's big
band, would play what would soon be recognized as bebop riffs, either
during intermission or even while on the bandstand.

Though the band was good, Gillespie soon wearied of the act,
of popping up from the trumpet section to vamp "I'm Diz the

Whiz, a swingin' hip cat, a swingin' hip cat, swingin' hip cat,
I'm Diz the Whiz" three hundred nights a year. After he and
Parker hooked up and began pushing each other to experiment with flatted fifth chords and odd-ball harmonies, it was
inevitable that Gillespie and Calloway would clash. Finally,
one night, Calloway stopped the music suddenly and screamed
at Dizzy, "I don't want you playing that Chinese music in my
band!"[40]

That Chinese music: as in the common hip-hop verse "I'm harder than
Chinese arithmetic," Calloway's seeming insult renders what were avant-
garde yet traditional black techniques irrevocably and irredeemably
foreign and unintelligible, while inadvertently noting and even perhaps
praising the new music's difficulty. It is the abacus as accusation, bebop
a form of recalculation that challenges the big band's calcified sense of
numbers, sets, chord progressions, and progress. Such Chinese music
is a form of radical insurrection in "*my* band"; Calloway's big band is
understandably not a democracy, but neither is it communal, finding
itself far from the collective that began jazz.

In his insult I wonder whether Cab Calloway stumbled upon, quite
unintentionally, jazz's alignment with other traditions, the very "Afro-
Eurasian eclipse" later celebrated by Ellington. Such an eclipse wasn't
just figurative, as Ellington's recordings were in part responsible for the
rise of what scholar Andrew F. Jones calls the Chinese Jazz Age in the
1930s, chiefly through the "brisk trans-Pacific traffic in recorded music.
Gramophone records of the music of Duke Ellington and other artists
had already reached Chinese shores, spurring on a rage for black bands
in [Shanghai's] nightclubs and dance halls."[41] This transpacific traffic
suggests we might need to speak not just of the Black Atlantic but a
Black and Yellow Pacific too often unexplored.

Has Calloway foretold Bird's recording as Charlie Chan, his taking
on a stereotype as a form of pop commentary and possibly shared folk
wisdom? Or has he sensed the ways Dizzy and his fellow boppers sought
a new language, musical and actual, connecting to scat and bebop's
emergence as an international lingua franca? Were Dizzy's "odd-ball
harmonies" a way of getting even, of connecting—if not with just an
Asian presence, then with a nonwhite, non-American one?

Calloway's mistaking bebop as "Chinese music" may be exactly parallel to the ideogrammatic method Pound misread, if praised, in the Chinese language—both bebop and the ideogrammatic method moved by juxtaposition and instantaneousness. Certainly Gillespie's and Parker's search was for a new inflection, a new tone, and even new musical language that went beyond the pale. Strangeness was one of bebop's chief strategies. The music meant to be misunderstood.

Just as ancient and more recent Chinese poetry helped invent the concision and imagism of modernism, Pound too was drawn to the African American vernacular as early as Uncle Remus, but also in the cage at Pisa across the pond. We may choose for a start of postmodernism not just the symbolic (and cymbal-like) bombs dropped by bebop, but another moment of truth with the end of World War II: Ezra Pound, founding father of high modernism, facing treason charges for his wartime Italian radio broadcasts and breaking down—quite differently from Parker's breaking down a song—in the U.S. prison camp at Pisa. This experience did, however, break down Pound's art and forever separate the previous *Cantos* and the *Pisan Cantos,* dividing Pound's early personae from the self that now peered through. It is also the difference between the voice of History, and history lowercase—a distance modernism and Pound had often sought to maintain. For so long a devotee of the former, Pound now lingered in the more personal latter.

As others have before and since, Pound negotiates this personal, everyday, even fallen view of history through the black mask. He provides a way beyond the impersonality of New Criticism not just through his typical personae but also through a multiplicity of impersonations.[42] Consider the shifting voices of the *Pisan Cantos,* especially Canto 74 (charted in part by James Laughlin), the first of the cantos Pound wrote in the cage. Rereading the poem recently I was struck by its ambition—especially after the dull exercise of Henry Adams speaking in previous cantos, not to mention the excised Cantos 72 and 73, reportedly praises for the fascist regime in Italy and, until quite recently, exorcised from editions of *The Cantos.*[43]

Such silence breaks the desolation of the war, and the war of words Pound waged on the radio in speeches so filled with hate and gobbledygook that the Italians thought them somehow coded. "Oh my England / that free speech without free radio speech is as zero": Pound's fascist notions of freedom, to say what he wanted and to believe it was the will of everyone (and would somehow "save the Constitution"), brought him to prison. And broke his own constitution, amid the harsh conditions.

Now he was only a nigger.

Pound himself realized this, metaphoring the camp and the cage—reminiscent of nothing so much as Dunbar's caged bird—into a middle passage. Pound's famous lines about paradise are followed quickly by direct links to a slave ship:

> I don't know how humanity stands it
> > with a painted paradise at the end of it
> > without a painted paradise at the end of it
> the dwarf morning-glory twines round the grass blade
> magna NUX animae   with Barabbas and 2 thieves beside me,
> > the wards like a slave ship,
> > > Mr Edwards, Hudson, Henry   *comes miserae*
> > > > Comites Kernes, Green and Tom Wilson
> > > God's messenger Whiteside

> and the guards op/of the . . .
> > was lower than that of the prisoners
> "all of them g.d. m.f. generals c.s. all of 'em fascists"
> "fer a bag o' Dukes"
> > > "the things I say an' dooo"
> > ac ego in harum
> so lay men in Circe's swine-sty;
> > ivi in harum *ego* ac vidi   animae
> > > "c'mon small fry" sd/ the little coon to the big black;
> of the slaver as seen between decks
> > and all the presidents
> Washington Adams Monroe Polk Tyler

> > > > > > (CANTO 74/436)

These presidents, of course, are actually the black prisoners alongside Pound, the "2 thieves beside me"—Pound feels crucified, but seems to realize the irony of "all the presidents" being black and thieves, "surrounded by herds and by cohorts looked on Mt. Taishan" (74/432). Perhaps not entirely consciously, by identifying with them (and even in identifying them), Pound indicts the bigger thieves who stole and named them thus (including his beloved Jefferson). He indicts by juxtaposition, by allowing the fellow prisoners to speak; by calling them (and perhaps himself) generals; by giving the men a poetry even among the cursing; by realizing that it is Caliban's lot to curse; by recording their speech in contrast to "His Master's Voice." Pound doesn't just give the prisoners poetry, but recognizes the poetry of their own mouths: listen to the lines of presumed speech where we have the abbreviated insult "c.s." rhyming with "fascists," "Dukes" (a pun on Il Duce?) rhyming with the song of "dooo," and in the end, an elevated comparison with warriors and the *Odyssey*, "so lay men in Circe's swine-sty," the doo-doo of history.

Black folks are the hidden heroes of Canto 74. They are "God's messengers" even—much like the men lying in wait in the swine sty, in view "of the slaver as seen between decks / and all the presidents." The suggestions of the small thievery that landed them there is contrasted not just in their presidential names but even in the name "Green":

> niggers scaling the obstacle fence
>   in the middle distance
> and Mr Edwards superb green and brown
>   in ward No 4 a jacent benignity,
> of the Baluba mask: "doan you tell no one
>   I made you that table"
>   methenamine eases the urine
> and the greatest is charity
> to be found among those who have not observed
>   regulations
>   not of course that we advocate—
> and yet petty larceny
> in a regime based on grand larceny
> might rank as conformity nient' altro
> with justice shall be redeemed[44]

While certainly Pound's "every bank of discount is downright iniquity / robbing the public for private individual's gain" (74/437) might make us uneasy given his anti-Semitic views and paranoia about money, it is interesting how Pound's take on "petty larceny" is tied to the kindnesses of the other black prisoners and his Allied guards. The will to survive and escape we can see in lines like "niggers scaling the obstacle fence / in the middle distance"—a distance we now know as a middle passage. And while Pound might be reduced to this only by circumstance, while he refers to one prisoner's lying "on his back like an ape" and refers to most all his fellow prisoners by the n-word, his identifying, however fleetingly, with the blacks "below board" proves enlightening. If only for a moment, just a moment, Pound is, if not in the hell of slavery, then a fellow traveler in Purgatory, trapped "between the decks," awaiting his black fate.

Many critics, such as Aldon Nielsen and Michael North in *Reading Race* and *The Dialect of Modernism,* respectively, see Pisa's Pound as merely racist. Racist he may be, but I feel it important to see the ways even a black reader might find something smuggled within the lines worth preserving, just as others found in Pound's poetics a radical form that fought his own fascism.

Where Pound's earlier work has the sense about it of an achievable, modernist purity—and its opposite, in the Hell Cantos, impurity—here in Pisa purity is long gone, and not even desirable. This, interestingly, does not so much reduce as redeem: "in short shall we look for a deeper or is this the bottom?" (74/438). Like the tradition of calling the black neighborhood "The Bottom," there is something black about this depth, a place so down it looks like up. *Every tub on its own black bottom.* Descent as ascent; "down" as a place to find up again: this is the journey that the spirituals took not that long ago.

The variety of poets who visited the "bullheaded father" in the hospital—William Carlos Williams, Louis Zukofsky, Charles Olson, Caresse Crosby, Allen Ginsberg, to name a few—were often Jewish, and all were outraged by and often outspoken about Pound's abhorrent views. Yet many found in his poetics something necessary to "howl" from, or against. We too might participate in a metaphoric visiting

St. Elizabeths, re-creating the ways many writers, despite their unquestioned outrage at Pound's unforgivable anti-Semitism and casual racism, have found in Pound's fascist or freeing form a radical model—one that undermines even his own view of history.

Robert Lowell, whose *Notebook* contains a version of his encounter with Pound at St. Elizabeths, describes the visit this way:

> You showed me your blotched, bent hands, saying, "Worms.
> When I talked that about Jews on the Rome
> wireless, Olga knew it was shit, and still loved me."
> And I, "Who else has been in Purgatory?"
> You, "I began with a swelled head and end with swelled feet."

In the middle of this swelling and swill was Pound's passage through a privileged version of the black experience: imprisoned, stripped of his sacred texts, exiled, threatened with death or dubbed insane.

CARELESS LOVE

Robert Lowell could be said to be Pound's postmodern progeny. Not only was Lowell one of the judges responsible for awarding Pound the controversial Bollingen Prize for the *Pisan Cantos* in 1949, reigniting the age-old discussion of whether art can be separated from the artist, Lowell in his own work was interested in turning the personal into myth. The connections between public history and personal history may be de rigueur now, but still should be counted as a significant part of his confessional poems' achievements. One of the breakthroughs of Lowell's *Life Studies* is not just the rhythms, or the peeling back of public (and in his case ornate stylistic and family) masks, but also the merging of public and private history—one that doesn't so much expose his family's background as it finds in it a metaphor for society as a crossroads. As the title implies, Lowell "paints" not from the studio but from life itself, examining human nature in his own mirror.

In his *Notebook* Lowell moved back and forth between personal myth and history: he revised this volume several times, and then to death, into two, even three, books. Lowell renamed the personal one *For Lizzie and Harriet,* and the other, longer book, simply *History.* Lowell's now seemed an attempt to sunder again, a mix of memory and history that Pound had, in the *Pisan Cantos,* managed to put together.

I've always been fascinated by Lowell's use of the black prisoner as metaphor: where Pound's black prisoners were facts, Lowell's seems a hollow black mask. While Pound's quotation as composition is reminiscent of jazz or the elegant collage of the "floating verses" of the blues, Lowell's "A Mad Negro Soldier Confined at Munich" speaks entirely in quotes in *Life Studies*—marking and framing its elaborate, if thin, fiction. With just a simple device, "Mad Negro" reifies the paradox of black strangeness (or strange blackness) found in dialect: language as both artificial and never spoken; and language as *only* spoken, exotic, unaffected by experience. The "tin ear" Roethke accused Lowell of seems supported by lines that clunk and clang as the soldier, another Othello really, discusses his *"Fräulein"*

> stitching outing shirts
> in the black forest of the colored wards—
> lieutenants squawked like chickens in her skirts:
>
> Her German language made my arteries harden—
> I've no annuity from the pay we blew.
> I chartered an aluminum canoe,
> I had her six times in the English Garden.[45]

The desire here, unconfined, is another symptom of the nameless soldier's madness. We almost feel his ladyfriend is just another part of his delusion.

Rather than named after a president, or actually unnamed, Lowell's prisoner is overnamed: "A Mad Negro Soldier" describes a thrice-cursed identity, much like Bird's; his is less double consciousness than a lack of any particular one. Helpless, the soldier is merely one of the "slaves of habit" in the colored wards for whom blackness is binding and confining.

The poem ends, "It's time for feeding. Each subnormal boot- / black heart is pulsing to its ant-egg dole."[46] What Lowell doles out is the curse of being less than human, and also foreign in both tongue and color. His soldier is not just a German exile but a grotesque—a gargoyle that allows Lowell his own madness, which he evokes far more movingly in "Skunk Hour" with its blues of "Love, O careless Love." (Or elsewhere in the beautiful ambivalence of "For the Union Dead," one of the most introspective poems on race of the last century, particularly by a white writer.) In "Skunk Hour" Lowell includes Bessie's blues to echo his own. He reveals, invoking *Paradise Lost,* "I myself am hell—" yet Lowell's hell is mild compared to the soldier's, where any sense of history is missing, not to speak of justice. However noble, Lowell's own actual confinement for being a conscientious objector in World War II, as found in poems like "Memories of West Street and Lepke," seems mild by comparison.

Still, it is with Lowell, via Pound, that the postmodern replaced the notion of the poet as "exile"—an extension of the romantic notion of the poet as wanderer—with a new paradigm of *madness.* Even Pound's very madness quickly became metaphor and more in the hands of the postmodernists; confessional poets in particular took madness as symbolic of a more general cultural malaise. Or even cure—we all are hell; hell is other people. Needless to say, confessional work performed best, however, when this madness did not resort to the ritual "becoming a Jew" that found its way into Plath's "Daddy" or to the blackface that sometimes swirls through Berryman's latter-day Daddy Rice two-step. But blackface persists in the poets of the day, becoming less an exorcism for slavery than an elaborate ritual that allowed them to speak to the soul in crisis, mirroring a society at war with itself and with the demons of racial injustice.

Is madness, like the blackface it often cloaked itself in, actually a form of hiding? Langston Hughes (who, turns out, kept up a correspondence with Pound over the years) put it this way in 1966: "A poet may try to hide in the bosom of Ezra Pound as long as he wishes, but the realities of conflict are inescapable. The color problem is a drag on the whole world, not just on Negro poetry."[47] Hughes here insists on a poetry that takes race into account; for if the epic is a poem containing history, as Pound argued, how in the world (and in America) can it *not* include race?

While Pound's captivity ended, returning him home, as it were, to Italy, others were not so lucky. Speaking of one of his fellow prisoners,

"'St. Louis Till' as Green called him" (77/473), Pound notes "Till was hung yesterday / for murder and rape with trimmings." Though Pound attempts to make myth (and a bit of gallows humor, "with trimmings") of Till's hanging, Pound's poem may best be thought of as testimony, inadvertent or backhanded though it may be.[48] You could say that for the African Americans in prison, Pound—whom Gertrude Stein called "a village explainer: nice if you're a village, if not, not"—was a distributor of "race records," a vessel to get *down* history, theirs, that might otherwise remain overlooked. The phantom opponent in tennis that Pound played in the cage—a staving off yet symptom of madness—may have been just this shadow book.

For the *Pisan Cantos* record the fate of another important father of history—the Louis Till in question was the father of Emmett Till, whose own death from lynching in 1955 would inspire nonviolence, further testifying, and seasons of change that were centuries in the making.

MISS BROWN TO YOU

"Strange Fruit," Billie Holiday's signature tune from 1939, bears not just fruit but witness. The song offers up testimony against lynching such as Emmett Till's; it does so in large part not by embracing, but by abandoning the "self."

Throughout the song, the first-person narrator is notably absent, the verses relying instead on the power of description, reportage even— showing us a symbolic lynching photograph whose horrors cannot be avoided. Doing the blues one better, "Strange Fruit" is the ultimate anti-pastoral, associating the harvest not with plenty but with the reaper and seeing the lynching bee as a white spectator sport. No wonder when confronted with the crime of looking, a guilt by association, "Strange Fruit" resorts not so much to the abandoning of the frame as to the abandoning of a self altogether.

Who, then, is speaking in the song? With Holiday's powerful rendition—at times whispering, and times a haunting near whine—the song pushes what might remain reportage into testimony. The voice becomes omniscient but decidedly not omnipotent: there's no Lord to lean on here. For without an "I," the song doesn't just ignore the "we" of the spirituals but also avoids a "you." Even a glance over Holiday's song titles indicates the ways she often sings of *you* as ennobling force—this *you*, even if absent, is tied integrally to the "I" who covers the waterfront, who'll be seeing you, the I who is "yours." In these other songs, Holiday creates a "we" much like the jazz combo or the expansive "I" of Whitman does.

Yet in "Strange Fruit" neither the "I" nor this intimate "you" is anywhere to be found; there's not even a God to Bless the Child. Instead, there's just us: witness and bystander, active recorder and, for just a moment, helpless victim. The landscape the song calls forth is a haunted, ghosted place. *Look away, Dixieland.* Such a realm is only partly glimpsed in the lynching photos and postcards of the time, themselves a form of capture, the ultimate contraband: missives from a guilty, suffering, seemingly nonchalant psyche.[49]

Holiday herself participates in a long tradition of popular song turned populist—as with Paul Robeson's "Old Man River," which he would frequently turn into an explicitly political song, the river becoming the power of the worker or whatever other inevitable force he made it be. As with the spirituals, both Holiday and Robeson took songs not written by them, but in fact by whites—one intently political, one less so—and made them their own. Their signature songs are vehicles for expression, but also one these singers—and at times, only they—can make mean. Such transformations are part of the storying tradition, and an important continuum with the remapping of American landscape, of shifting the river of song.

An examplar of pain and its performance, Lady Day embodies a strategy of silence. "Strange Fruit" itself is surrounded by silence: not only talking back to the silence of lynching, which you can almost see in a lynching photograph, but to Pound's blasé recording of Till's death. The song was also performed amidst silence: there was never applause when Holiday ended her sets with it at Café Society. Such silence indicates the audience's respect for the song but also reverence for Holiday's stark rendering, spareness as a form of survival.

Spareness is a virtue and strategy Holiday linked, even in the horrors of "Strange Fruit," to glamour. Like silence, the gardenia Holiday wore was itself a kind of fragile blooming, glamourous and somehow telling. Her trademark flower spoke, in that moment of singing "Strange

Fruit," against the magnolia that appears in the song as a moment of beauty—if only as an ironic counter to cover the ugliness of the "scent of burning flesh."

Black glamour has taken a hit in recent years, stripped away by the post-soul insistence on realness, as well as falling victim to the devastation of AIDS and illness on glamour's fast friend, sexuality, in all its forbidden and freed forms. One small example: pro basketball, once the forefront of black male glamour in the 1970s, has given way to endorsement, corporation, and the kinds of excess Bird only dreamed of, yet all married to a sleek sterility. Glamour remains far more unique than even a stockpiled episode of MTV *Cribs* might suggest. Flashier than "class," tamer than, strictly speaking, "bling," glamour is the flowering of expression mixed with restraint: *I am unknowable,* it says, *yet desirable;* elusive and visual, silent but welcoming; beyond even beauty, or the ugly beauty of the postmodern, glamour is all about lighting, about transformation in a sense as radical and rescuing as jazz.

Glamour's allure can also prove fatal. Glamour is the tragic in soft focus, an illusion no less powerful for its being removed—if only because glamour occurs at a remove. To call glamour phony is like saying stage sets aren't real; both seek not reality, or realism, but illusion so complete as to be believed. In the wrong hands it becomes camp, or worse, mere cliché.

Though certainly diminished since the 1970s, glamour has just now undergone something of a comeback. Its most recent incarnation is "ghetto fabulousness," in which you "front" like you got money. Part performance, part pain, the phrase "ghetto fabulousness" itself denotes both sides of the coin—heads and tails, your best face forward—choosing to save your hard-earned money for fabulous accessories (often at a discount) and extravagantly spending money you don't got just to show "how good I got it." Or, better yet, cobbling together a look as designed as it is designer, an aesthetic no less fabulous by being ersatz or on layaway. After all, glamour likes to shine in the most unlikely spots. Fur, gators, silk: glamour insists on the animal, recognizing its own primal, preening nature. As well as its reliance on artifice, or artfulness, if at times in a once-natural way. In Billie Holiday, ghetto fabulousness takes its first form. Holiday's melancholy voice is glamourous, elusive, and illusory, much like "the ghetto" in the public imagination.

Following in Louis Armstrong's footsteps, Holiday changed the concept of vocal singing, and not only for jazz; where Armstrong and scat did not seek to sound like an instrument, Holiday somehow manages to. This is part of her very phrasing, the samizdat book she was writing by her performances. In her study of Holiday, *If You Can't Be Free, Be a Mystery* (2001), Farah Jasmine Griffin quotes Count Basie on Lady Day's artistry: "She had her own style, and it was to remain that way. Sometimes she would bring in new things and she would dictate the way she'd like them done. That's how she got her book with us. She never left her own style. Nobody sounded like her."[50]

The *book* Basie mentions is not literal but no less real, a songbook revised, reworked, memorized, and made Holiday's own. This book, a kind of counterfeit, is the one I am most interested in, is the sound at the back of Holiday's phrasing, her storying.

For Holiday, such storying is intimately tied to a notion of telling a story beyond the song itself, in part "recomposing" it herself:

> Billie Holiday sang lyrics with impeccable diction and clarity. Musical historian Eileen Southern notes early travelers' observations of black American women who mesmerized white children and adults with their story-telling. Holiday was a twentieth-century version of these women. She painted pictures and told stories through the songs she sang, spellbinding her audiences. . . . Even during the final years of her life, when her voice was practically gone, Holiday was still capable of rendering a lyric with profound meaning and drama. Shirley Horn says, "Billie Holiday helped to show me that lyrics have got to mean something, have got to paint a picture, tell a story."[51]

The *book,* then, is part of this "spellbinding" and "story-telling," both Holiday's own innovation and participation in a long, black, female tradition. The binding of the imaginary book is an active, participatory process, that, like any true spell—which is also said to bind—goes beyond the grave. The notion of "spellbinding" we may take seriously: there's a sense of that outlaw identity, the rootworker, around Holiday's mesmerizing. The very notion of spells also returns us to glamour, which originally meant "enchantment" or a literal "magic."

Holiday's songbook is a kind of fakebook for the ages, different from her autobiography, which was a fakebook of another sort. Like most performers, Holiday's recomposing extended to the self, starting with her renaming herself Billie Holiday (before being renamed again by Pres). Griffin fascinatingly dissects the truths, half-truths, and what's more, the function of Holiday's autobiography, *Lady Sings the Blues* (1956), noting that though the book's chapters are titled after songs, the songs aren't autobiographical either: "In many ways, this *[Lady Sings the Blues]* is not the life story of Eleanora Fagan, or maybe not even the story of Billie Holiday, but it is the story of Lady Day. And that story is filled with subtle allusions to the life stories of the other two. Just as her improvisations were subtle, so too are the glimpses of truth that peep through the gaps, silences and allusions. If one reads *Lady Sings the Blues* in this way, one finds new dimensions of 'truth-telling.' Where subsequent biographers claim embellishment or falsity, in fact, the book provides us a way of reading it that reveals something much closer to the 'truth.'"[52] An apt description of storying.

It is in the silences that Lady Day's songbook and "autobiography" of songs tell loudest, urging us, "Don't explain." Holiday implies or implicates rather than reveals—which is not the absence of artistry, but instead its height. This in many ways is because of the jazz definition of "fake": "in music, to make the best of a lean situation; to sing or play without other musical backing."[53] I don't mean to make Holiday emblematic of victimhood, or martyr to a sacrificial god. Rather, victimhood is what Billie Holiday sang about, and against.

MEDITATION (FOR A PAIR OF WIRE CUTTERS)

"Bitter Crop," the last phrase of "Strange Fruit," was Holiday's preferred title for *Lady Sings,* Griffin informs us. Holiday's alternate title would have tied her to the blues tone of other jazz autobiographies, anticipating Mingus's own "fakebook" *Beneath the Underdog.* Holiday's unwritten—or at least unused—title "Bitter Crop" forms a shadow book no less powerful for being not fully there. "By calling her life story 'Bitter Crop,' she linked it to centuries of dispossession, oppression and terrorism experienced by black Americans. She made her story part of that larger historical narrative."[54] This narrative, while silent, still speaks through her and her songs.

In Holiday's rendition of "Strange Fruit," the last line, *This is a cruel and bitter crop,* actually feels cropped—its clipped nature remains part of its power. Where for black Beat poet Bob Kaufman—like Holiday, an occasional detainee—silence proves refuge, for Holiday silence is a sign of her being a refugee of sorts, without a home, in her case often literally. The refugee is displaced, sure, but unlike the exile, the refugee usually seeks to return—yearning is the refugee's tongue, itself always exiled, not in use. *I'll Be Seeing You:* is jazz the music of the refugee?

Certainly song, and storying, are the refugee's claim; the refugee too, is not alone (as the exile may be) but decidedly of a group, however threatened, fragmented, dispersed. *Wherever You Are:* the refugee, disembodied, is Elsewhere incarnate.

The refugee of course seeks refuge, even as she yearns for home. In turn, "refuge" means shelter—and often, "an institution providing safe accommodations for women who have suffered abuse at the hands of a husband or partner."[55] Is refuge gendered? Does Holiday's voice itself provide a refuge?

To be a refugee after all originally meant "fleeing back" but also implies refusal—offering up a resistance similar to that found in glamour (though there's undoubtedly nothing glamorous in being a refugee). Asylum is what the refugee seeks, with that word's dual echoes of madness and safe haven. In Billie Holiday's rendition, "Strange Fruit" shelters and smuggles meaning beyond the borders of what is acceptable—or even seen. Still, even here Holiday cautions us about the dangers not just of glamour, but our heretofore halcyon notion of Elsewhere. Both may merely be way stations to worse.

Is silence another name for restraint? Restraint is glamour's god, or at least its sacrificial rite, earned by the "I" becoming both more and less than it can be. This is not Bird's plenty, or Miles's less is more, but a kind of reworking of both—Holiday's enunciation and clarity and phrasing replace their blurring and vibrato.

Perhaps you could say that it's not just restraint but silence as a sign of absence, and abstaining, that are at work in Holiday's glamour. But hers is not just a rephrasing of the possibilities of song, instead using the unexpected, unspoken qualities of song—some of them instrumental—to sing for her, and us.

Is glamour just *cool* in its female guise? It ain't necessarily so—but cool itself has elements of restraint in it, found in in part in Holiday's performance. Clarence Major's indispensable later edition of his dictionary of African American slang, *Juba to Jive,* helpfully traces the origins of cool to Africa, and specifically to a Mandingo notion of "gone out" and fast, being "gone man, gone."[56] And while many studies of cool seem to focus on maleness, at least in origin, this doesn't seem quite right; nor does it seem right to equate cool with glamour, though the two are related. In more contemporary terms, if to be cool is to be "chill," then to be glamorous is to be "fly"—which gives a sense of glamour's very elusiveness. No wonder Major indicates that "fly" was "originally a Gullah term; to be fast and ecstatic; brash; good or great," meanings stemming from as early as the 1880s.

Part surreal, part spectacle, glamour's power is its embodiment of time-lessness even as it is helpless to time—it is fashionable yet permanent, the angel with a whiff of death. Its preferred medium is the "touched up" photograph (after once being the art deco etching). Its enemy, the document of distress (such as the lynching photograph). Glamour fades quickly, like a dream described in the light of day. Or a gardenia. While it defies description, glamour is also defiant—not in begging us to look but in insisting without asking, daring us not to.

Glamour is not physical but an aura achieved far beyond the body. The fetish inside out, glamour is more than female "cool" because it can also be male; it also is not gendered in that, as in its original usage, it is often performed by otherworldly beings beyond gender: faeries and Ariel. It is sexy and at times sexless; magic. To glamour's original meaning of enchantment, we must add an even earlier one: glamour shares a root, or should we say rootwork, with *grammar*—not just in terms of language but also with a "grammatica" or an occult kind of learning.

Holiday's song and storying provide a new kind of grammar after all, not just reworking or "recomposing" a tune but also rewriting the notion of how we sing.

Broken Giraffe
Bob Kaufman, the Song, and the Silence _ _ _ _ _ _ _ _ _ _

It's hard to know how to begin talking about Bob Kaufman, Poet—
should we talk about his beginnings in New Orleans and his connection to a blues and jazz tradition? His time in the Merchant Marine,
which, as he spoke of it, began his vocation as a poet through his reading upon the high seas? Kaufman's wanting to be "anonymous" and
forgotten? Or, his stance as an oral poet, as a poet who reportedly rarely
wrote down his work, which survives as much from others writing it
down and rescuing it as from his composing it?

Perhaps I should begin with my poetic relation to Bob Kaufman,
which began at least in part with the Dark Room Collective, the Boston-
based black writers' collective I was a member of, starting in the early
1990s. (Once in, you're in forever.) Founded in 1989, the collective was
interested in black culture and history, and the preservation of both,
hosting readings and recording interviews with established and emerging black writers (before "emerging" became just another stick without
much of a carrot). For us, Bob Kaufman was an avatar of sorts—an
incarnation of poetry in what may be called its purest form, or perhaps, most accurately, its most useful, impure form, complete with a
sense of music and line that can be hard to find. Rare, but not rarefied.
(I have a T-shirt somewhere, hand-drawn, that reads "The Dark Room"
with Kaufman's "Golden Sardine" inked in yellow, swimming below
it.) Kaufman's sense of poetry's immediacy, its performative qualities, his mix of speech and surrealism, appealed to us; he was one of
the few people I know who could append the phrase "Poet" after his
name, which is what he did in a poem-letter reprinted at the end of his
second book, and have it stick. He was so dedicated to poetry that he
didn't write it down; he was so much a poet that he committed a vow

of silence for over ten years, from Kennedy's assassination to the end of the Vietnam War. While others were out in the street protesting, or in a VW van "dropping out" and dropping acid, Kaufman was silent, which is one kind of crucial protest. Perhaps the most crucial.

For now, let's stick with what Bob Kaufman meant to me as a young poet, which was plenty. Thinking back on it, my internalized sense of what the important themes should be comes in part from Kaufman. "Music, silence, and noise" was my recent answer to an interviewer asking what I thought my own themes were,[1] and in rereading Kaufman I see the presence of all three in his multiple, musical selves.

I should say that I've tried writing on Kaufman before, even getting a small grant while in college in the summer of 1991 to consider his legacy. With its five hundred dollars I went to San Francisco—where Kaufman spent most of his adult life—with the full intent of interviewing folks who knew him. After crashing with friends in Oakland—most of whom are fairly well known today—rotating off the futon in a Berkeley apartment with four other guys while staying with the generous house sitter for a pot dealer for the Bay Area who was off making some deals, I ended up with an August sublet shared with four stinky cats and two guys I didn't know. (One nice, one something of a racist: when I once complained about the rats that would sometimes scratch below the floorboards all night, he mentioned they might nest in my dreads, implying they did already.) I lived in what was called the Lower Haight, but used to be the Fillmore—the lively black neighborhood and street that stretched north from Haight Street (and below and east of what became Haight-Asbury) and that had been urban-renewed mostly out of existence by the 1970s. A highway running through the neighborhood meant replacing black businesses with housing projects, and the working poor with crack.

By the time I got there, there were some divey, reincarnated bars and a few artists, or more accurately slackers, though it was still dangerous enough that one night I was nearly mugged on my corner, and strange enough that sitting in one of our favorite hangouts, Hotel Casa Loma, a place with a bar below, you could see more than your share of fights and car crashes. (A few years ago during the dot-com boom I went back to Lower Haight and there were SUVs parked on a curb in the neighborhood, and some young lawyer house party that left the door to her apartment wide open. I couldn't bear it, so stood outside pretending to be a bouncer and asked the young esquires for IDs.)

That summer I enjoyed living in a traditionally, though not necessarily traditional, black neighborhood—no matter how different Lower Haight had grown. In feeling, if not fact, it seemed not so different from the Mattapan my aunt and uncle had lived in since the 1960s, and that was a refuge from ivy towers come holidays or whenever I needed one. That was the summer of MC Breed & DFC's "Ain't No Future in Yo' Frontin'," a forgotten hip-hop classic, whose Middle Eastern sample proved a rather regular, if welcome, alarm clock ringing from passing cars.

If I had to name the somewhere I lived, it was that roving neighborhood Bohemia. This I suppose I shared, albeit superficially, with Kaufman, and later, with Basquiat, whom I began to write about soon after. But I didn't think of it that way then: I was simply living the life I hoped might lead me to a life of writing. It was enough to share the same air Kaufman had once breathed. Black Bohemia, like black surrealism, is a topic that deserves more and mo betta written about it— race I suppose is what some think isn't discussed in bohemia, though that was exactly not my experience.

One reason black bohemia is rarely discussed, or discussed well—as it is, say, in *How I Became Hettie Jones* by Hettie Jones—is that it gets into questions that have more traditionally been addressed by the black expatriate. Perhaps expatriate life is where thinking about black bohemia begins—with literary exiles like Baldwin, Wright, and Du Bois, not to mention jazz musicians from Ada "Bricktop" Smith to Dexter Gordon. Bohemia may be the solution for a younger self, expatriatism for the older: bohemia is often what is being rejected by black folks as they progress toward self-imposed exile, whether moving Uptown as Baraka did; or abroad to Paris and then, literally, Timbuktu, like Ted Joans.

We might remember here that Joans used to be a beatnik for hire—a brilliant spoof on the artificiality of identity, and the commodification of both blackness and the Beat generation. It also earned him a few bucks. In this it is the counterfeit made flesh, his Rent-a-Beatnik providing partygoers both a laugh and a bit of frisson; the fiction of his belonging, of his being not invited (as was sometimes chic to do) but hired, makes him more than "help," while also parodying it.

But returning to expatriatism, self-exile may seem redundant for the black writer—or perhaps it's a case of rejecting bohemia before it rejects you, whether from the natural limits of artistic community or the painful limits of a perceived America. Yet as Langston Hughes or any other number of artists point out, black community and bohemian community overlap, confront, complement, distract, ignore, and often are no different from, each other—the life of the jazz musician is just one example of a life without labels but not without race.

Certainly, it seems, bohemia never meant the absence of blackness for Kaufman, as Kaufman's work is infused with blackness—which is to say, music and silence and noise.

A brief bio: Kaufman, like jazz, was born in New Orleans. The year was 1925. Kaufman often claimed to have been half-black and half-Jewish, but his brother has said that that's not true, that his distinctive last name came from a Jewish grandfather, or recent ancestor. In any case, Kaufman often identifies with Jewishness, I think to highlight his stance in an America that regards both Jewishness and blackness, especially in postwar America, as outsider identities. (In this, you could say his origin resembles the ways early writers saw jazz as an unholy hybrid made up of black and Jewish elements.)[2] I'd also say that Kaufman is participating in the imaginary notions of identity discussed by the late Leslie Fiedler, who wrote that we're all imaginary Americans. (Fiedler also wrote that all Americans spend their childhoods as Imaginary Indians, and their adolescence as Imaginary Negroes, an apt summary of the desires in our Imaginary America.)

After a stint in the Merchant Marine, Kaufman settled in San Francisco, living mostly in North Beach, an Italian neighborhood famous for City Lights bookstore and also the Condor, the first topless club in the States, and later the first bottomless one. The Condor's full-figured neon sign was still quite a landmark when I was living there; last I was there it had turned into an open-air fern bar. (Though Kaufman never left bohemia, it left him.) As I mentioned, Kaufman reportedly chiefly recited or declaimed his work, making a name for himself locally and publishing in magazines including *Beatitude,* which he helped to found with his wife, Eileen, as well as in important broadsides like *Second April* and the *Abomunist Manifesto,* all published with City Lights in the late 1950s. Kaufman then took Harvard, New York, and even

France—where he was called "the Black Rimbaud"—by storm. He published only three full-length books in his lifetime: *Solitudes Crowded with Loneliness* (1964) and *Golden Sardine* (City Lights Pocket Poets no. 21, 1967) appeared in quick succession the 1960s, then nothing till the 1980s. Kennedy's assassination aside, it seems no accident, or a fascinating coincidence, that Kaufman's vow of silence in essence began with his first book publication.

The last book Kaufman saw into print was *Ancient Rain,* published in 1981—he died in 1986, survived by his wife and son. In an interview in the *New York Times Magazine,* even his son spoke of being unsure of his legacy, frustrated by folks telling him his dad was a genius when he didn't have always pleasant memories of the poverty and instability of life as a poet's son. Kaufman is often credited with inventing the term "Beat"—at the least, he best embodied it, not as what Norman Mailer called a "White Negro" but instead as a "Black Negro and Imaginary Jew," exiled even from the Beat movement he helped name. He often falls out of black and Beat anthologies alike; he is rarely mentioned in either experimental anthologies or the recent spoken word revival though he was "spoken word" before it was a sales category, and experimental when it meant something musical, not just for its own sake. Surely Kaufman experienced Ginsberg's lowercase "negro streets" quite differently, not seeking out madness or its cure, but instead suffering police harassment, frequent arrests for vagrancy, and on several occasions involuntary electroshock treatment while in custody.

Kaufman's three lone volumes were like bibles to me, and the means by which I learned to love him—though now there's *Cranial Guitar,* which contains uncollected poems and reprints the hard-to-find volume *Golden Sardine.* When I was looking for *Sardine* back in the day, the book's elusiveness was part of its appeal, not to mention indicative of something of Kaufman's character. The third edition from 1976 I eventually found contains photographs of him that show him young, clean shaven, and devastatingly handsome, long before the scruffy beard of later years. From the cover of my coffee-stained copy he stares, a kind of Bedouin in a scarf and hat. The pictures seem to capture both beauty and bitterness, as do the poems.

One of the most powerful pieces in *Solitudes Crowded with Loneliness*—one of those titles only Kaufman could get away with, and that, upon further reflection, renders a nice series of reversals and revisions, getting us to think of the difference between a crowd and solitude, between a voluntary aloneness and the isolation found even in a crowd—is "Jail Poems." A sequence of thirty-four sections, or shorter poems, it begins:

> I am sitting in a cell with a view of evil parallels,
> Waiting thunder to splinter me into a thousand me's.
> It is not enough to be in one cage with one self;
> I want to sit opposite every prisoner in every hole.

In what feels like solitary confinement, Kaufman's loneliness is clear—made all the clearer by his desire for expansiveness, to be many selves, to "sit opposite every prisoner in every hole." He is writing to be heard, literally saying later on, "Here—me—now—hear—me—now—always here somehow." As the poem shifts between being "heard" and being "here," meaning both in jail and being alive—a shift that occurs differently on the page from simply being heard aloud—Kaufman makes his presence known while facing the absence of justice.

The end of the poem lets us know it was *"Written in San Francisco City Prison / Cell 3, 1959,"* answering the "here" only partially. Or, only literally. Each section of the poem seems a day, or an hour, or an eternity; no wonder the sections get shorter as they proceed, as if losing hope or its expression. Here's all of part 3:

> In a universe of cells—who is not in jail? Jailers.
> In a world of hospitals—who is not sick? Doctors.
> A golden sardine is swimming in my head.
> Oh we know some things, man, about some things
> Like jazz and jails and God.
> Saturday is a good day to go to jail.

The poem ends with sections that read in full:

> 26
>
> I sit here writing, not daring to stop,
> For fear of seeing what's outside my head.

27

There, Jesus, didn't hurt a bit, did it?

and finally

34

Come, help flatten a raindrop.[3]

The whole has the feeling not just of being written but of the urgency of speech—it is the utterance of the prisoner, furtive and filled with a wish for freedom and survival. I am reminded of the *Amistad* rebels' letters from jail; or George Jackson, or Jean Genet, or even Ezra Pound; I recall too South African poet Breyten Breytenbach's years in jail and his daily writing, which each night was removed by the guards. He called it pure writing, for survival—he had no notion he would see any of it again, if and when he got out.

On the outside, of course, there are other kinds of guards, often unseeable, who remove writing not necessarily from our shelves but from our cultural memory. Kaufman's every book is a shadow book. Kaufman himself dares us to forget him—as an introduction to *Ancient Rain* says, he told the editor he wants us to. "'I want to be anonymous,'" the editor's note quotes Kaufman as saying. Kaufman's poetry expresses much the same wish; consider "Unholy Missions":

I want to be buried in an anonymous crater inside the moon.

I want to build miniature golf courses on all the stars.

I want to prove that Atlantis was a summer resort for cave men.

I want to prove that Los Angeles is a practical joke played on us
    by superior beings on a humorous planet.

I want to expose Heaven as an exclusive sanitarium filled with
    rich psychopaths who think they can fly.

I want to show that the Bible was serialized in a Roman
  children's magazine.

I want to prove that the sun was born when God fell asleep with
  a lit cigarette, tired after a hard night of judging.

I want to prove once and for all that I am not crazy.[4]

Kaufman's desire to be anonymous is both ironic and sincere, as is his
wish to prove Heaven false, or himself "not crazy." In wanting to expose
Heaven, his is a blues irony, fingering the jagged grain between desire
and its fulfillment, between tragedy and comedy. Only in this way is
he "unholy"—crazy in the blues and bad man sense—and in sending up
our assumptions in a way that Countee Cullen would also, a generation
before.

A word about anonymity. Many have written on the importance of
naming in the African American tradition, including this very study.
Having been "called out our name" for centuries—being renamed, unnamed, invisible—African Americans view the act of naming oneself,
whether Malcolm X or Frederick Douglass or Billie Holiday, herself
further renamed "Lady," as a powerful, symbolic act. (Hell, look how
many names Diddy has had in the relatively short time he's been on the
scene—Sean "Puffy" Combs, Sean John, Puff Daddy, Puffy, P. Diddy,
Diddy—all these are reclamations and rebirths, or at least marketing re-
launches.) With this in mind, what does it mean to wish to be nameless?
  Namelessness is not necessarily a symptom of being without a name,
or between names, though it can be—Baldwin's early works *No Name
in the Street* and *Nobody Knows My Name* both make this unnaming
trope visible. Nobodyness for Baldwin is a kind of resistance, related but
somewhat different from Malcolm X's—whose *X* stood for indeterminacy, for both his ancient, unknown African name, and for the one he
was to take, El-Hajj Malik El-Shabazz, when spiritually reborn. There's
also the nobodyness of Dunbar, Bert Williams, and even Dickinson.
  In Kaufman's case anonymity is not indeterminacy, but rather, namelessness as a state of grace, an acceptance of being part of the unnameable
universe. You could say it is *satori,* the Zen concept of "enlightenment"
fellow Beat Jack Kerouac adopted for his own 1966 novel *Satori in Paris.*

But Kaufman's desire to remain nameless in a crater on the moon proves a form of "acceptance" older than Beat, though perhaps not Buddhism; is the state of waiting to be named, as in Eden; or discovered and dubbed, like craters on the moon itself. It is also a desire for a secret name, one unknown to others, but not the self—a kind of protection sometimes offered in African societies, where one's "real" name is never told to strangers. Anonymity is also Kaufman's recognition of his being a "stranger at the gates," to quote Baldwin—a recognition of blackness as strangeness—which then takes comfort in the vast blackness of outer space.

"For most of history, Anonymous was a woman," Virgina Woolf wrote, recognizing the ways in which anonymity is a symptom of not being valued or recognized by one's culture. If so, *Pseudonymous* has always been black.

The pseudonym, the act of renaming, is a particular African American theme—but also a means of survival, of coding not just behavior, or art forms, but *one's own name,* so that it can have many valences. Part of this is a nickname, which most all my kin have—I can tell a genealogy program I use to input my family tree wasn't written by a black person because it has no space labeled "nickname" or better yet, "nicknames" plural. A sign of intimacy, history, respect, or just language sounding good, a nickname is something you can't give to yourself, hard as you try—just as it can be hard to shake a nickname you may have grown out of or dislike. A nickname's usually a sign of home. And *home* itself can mean a name for a person. Even Anatole Broyard, passing as white, was still "Bud" to his black Creole family that he rarely, if ever, acknowledged.

But the other aspect of the pseudonym is as a hiding place, or state, a means to go in secret, to move beyond the bounds either of external name or internal limits. This is not simply an alias but a "basket name":

> Most of the Gullah people use two kinds of given names. One is English, and they call it their real or true name and use it at school, in their correspondence, and in their dealings with strangers. The other is the nickname, known also as the pet name or basket name. In their homes and among their friends and acquaintances they use the nickname almost exclusively. In fact, so general is its use that many of the Gullahs have

difficulty in recalling the English given-name. The nickname is
nearly always a word of African origin.[5]

Kaufman embodies this self-naming, becoming "Bomkauf" in author-
ing the *Abomunist Manifesto,* the title even a kind of anagramming
of his first and last name. Documents in the full manifesto, first published as a broadside and then sadly missing from *Cranial Guitar*'s re-
print, ensure that it is a "mock" manifesto, much like Frank O'Hara's
"Personism"—but while Personism is a movement of one, Kaufman's
is a movement of none, of only Abominable Snowmen or other mythic
creatures, like Bomkauf himself.

The manifesto has "Craxioms," letters, "Notes Dis- and Re- Garding
Abomunism," an Election Manifesto and a "Rational Anthem," "Boms"
and "Excerpts from the Lexicon Abomunon." One of my favorite words
in the lexicon is Kaufman's new verb, *frink,* which like "crunk" in recent
hip-hop or the idea of "mingering," seems a catchall term to describe
whatever it is that the protagonist does, a sensual satori. *Frink* might be
closest to "funk"—it too can be a stand-in for sex, but also remains an
attitude, an activity so positive as to at times be troubling, frightening
even. Kaufman's lexicon defines *frink* this way:

> *Frink:* v. To (censored). n. (censored) and (censored).

Silence indeed! The delight Kaufman takes in parodying dictionaries,
censorship, Dead Sea Scrolls (found around the time of the manifesto's creation), and the manifesto form, not to mention elections and
lexicons, is infectious. It is also found in his various pseudonyms, not
just Bomkauf but the lexicon's being "compiled by Bimgo." These se-
rial names—who says you need just one pseudonym?—also parody
the pseudoscience of the manifesto and manifestos alone, gathering
evidence Bomkauf merely manufactures. Forges and stories. They are
kinds of "boms" or "bombs" in the bebop sense: intense forms of percussion and punctuation, whose pleasure is in their sounds making a
new kind of meaning.

I'm also interested in the form of "Unholy Missions": Kaufman's long
lines reveal a kind of blues line, and influence on the wannabe bad-boy

jazz prosody of Ginsberg and many of the other Beats. If Kaufman's strophes don't always predate or upstage "Howl," they don't copy it either: like the discovery of the double helix, the long lines seem to stem from some of the same sources as Ginsberg's even as they are interested in something different. You could say that where Ginsberg's is a "howl," Kaufman's work is a "shout"—not in the obvious sense, but in the gospel one. (Which would become R & B soon enough.) Kaufman's line echoes Kamau Brathwaite's sense of "nation language," which "may be in English: but often it is in an English which is like a howl, or a shout or a machine-gun or the wind or a wave. It is also like the blues. And sometimes it is English and African at the same time."[6]

Such *shouting* is as physical, and even silent, as it is vocal. As Hurston reminds us, "There can be little doubt that shouting is a survival of the African 'possession' by the gods. In Africa it is sacred to the priesthood or acolytes, in America it has become generalised. The implication is the same, however. It is a sign of special favor from the spirit that it chooses to drive out the individual consciousness temporarily and use the body for its expression. . . . There are two main kinds of shouters: (1) Silent; (2) Vocal."[7] The anonymity and silence Kaufman sought are as physical as they are vocal, as holy as they are unholy—an erasing of individuality in order to reach the cosmic.

Where Ginsberg's line measures breath, the body's pace ("I saw the best minds of my generation destroyed by madness, starving, hysterical, naked, / dragging themselves through the negro streets at dawn looking for an angry fix"), Kaufman's line parses a kind of turning often found in the blues—a line not of breath but music.

The blues turn, between its repeated lines and the kicker, happens *within* Kaufman's line, or right after, so each line becomes a series of leaps and reversals. (In this he reminds me of the caesura in the middle of the blues line, which I usually hear—and Langston Hughes represents in his poems—as a separate line.) There are several examples from all his books; one of my favorites is "Heavy Water Blues":

> The radio is teaching my goldfish Jujutsu
> I am in love with a skindiver who sleeps underwater,
> My neighbors are drunken linguists, & I speak butterfly,
> Consolidated Edison is threatening to cut off my brain,

The postman keeps putting sex in my mailbox,
My mirror died, & can't tell if i still reflect,
I put my eyes on a diet, my tears are gaining too much weight.

Skipping ahead, the second half broadens as the blues often do, speaking of submerged histories:

It is perfectly all right to cast the first stone,
if you have some more in your pocket.

Television, america's ultimate relief, from the indian
    disturbance.

I hope that when machines finally take over,
they won't build men that break down,
as soon as they're paid for.
. . .

Why don't they stop throwing symbols,
the air is cluttered enough with echoes.

Just when i cleaned the manger for the wisemen,
the shrews from across the street showed up.

The voice of the radio shouted, get up
do something to someone, but me & my son
laughed in our furnished room.[8]

What makes this a blues is the mix of emotions throughout, of humor and despair, with the strange transcendence of the ending. That this ending calls its attention to the music, or its delivery ("the radio") proves interesting—and so is the final response, laughter. The room is not bare but furnished with pleasure, family, and ultimately a kind of resistance to cavemen extinctions, manmade scripts, machine-made men, shrews, symbols, or fruitless searching for the end of the circle. I suppose this resistance (or speaking "butterfly") could seem passive or apolitical, as the Beats sometimes are seen, but when there's a "cater-pillar industry down in Washington D.C." and television is "america's ultimate relief, / from the indian disturbance," deciding not to "do something to someone" might be a useful refusal. Another name for "nonviolence" is "passive resistance," after all, a strategy that can, and does, overthrow empires.

To see how this strange hope carries through Kaufman's other work, consider the end of "Fragment" from *Solitudes:*

> Our Lady of Nicotine, madonna without child,
> Releases her pale balloon, snatched from the folding year,
> All the daring young headhunters, traumatic in inflammatory
>   bathing suits
> Shriek grim fairy tales, while convenient needles fall out of
>   haystacks.
> Charlie Parker was a great electrician who went around
>   wiring people.[9]

Nearly every line consists of a reversal, shifting back and back, both revising and rewiring, often in a single phrase—"madonna without child" or "grim fairy tales," rather than Grimm's. Instead of double en-tendre, the poem seeks double meanings—a doubled agency—invoking and violating clichés. In this it is a blues both in spirit and form, its form fighting the feeling of the blues, gone electric, "wiring people."

As the last line of the poem indicates, not just blues but jazz—par-ticularly bebop—influences Kaufman. He even named his son Parker and reportedly carried him in a clarinet case. Raymond Foye, in his editor's note to *Ancient Rain,* says by "adapting the harmonic com-plexities and spontaneous invention of be-bop to poetic euphony and meter, he became the quintessential jazz poet."[10] Kaufman's line could also be thought of as the series of riffs, of repetition with variation, that mark a jazz line. Kaufman riffs off Ginsberg himself in a poem called "Ginsberg," beginning "Ginsberg won't stop tossing lions to the mar-tyrs." And, "The Church is becoming alarmed by the number of people defecting to God." But I am most interested in his line "I am not not an I, secret wick, I do nothing, light myself, burn."[11]

In this, he is not just the great electrician Charlie Parker is, but a "secret wick" both unknown and glowing. What I want to call our attention to is the line's negation of a negation—or negation as affirmation—which others, like Keith Byerman, have pointed out is a crucial aspect of African American culture. *Not bad meaning bad but bad meaning good.*

Likewise, Kaufman often reverses not just our expectations but our very terms: defecting from church (or draft dodging) as heroism, anonymity as beatitude, defining jail by who is not there (jailers). Even the term black, of course, is a reversal, adopting a previously negative term to turn it beautiful. Kaufman reveals blackness as Beat, and turns it into a beat, a rhythm that stretches in lines like those that end "To My Son Parker" or in "Walking Parker Home," or in the literal beat (versus the cop's "beat" and "beatings") discussed in "Bagel Shop Jazz."

Besides meaning a beating, "bop" is also the name of a black poetic form begun by Afaa Weaver at Cave Canem, the writers' workshop and community of black poets. Weaver describes the form this way:

> "The Bop" draws on the several connotative meanings of the
> word bop, first of which is a Black man's manner of walk-
> ing, that distinctive manner that was his signature in the East
> Baltimore of my youth where young brothers worked diligently
> to have a walk that was singular and sharp. As a word, bop
> also draws on its application to BeBop, inasmuch as there was
> a certain cloaking involved in this musical form where Parker
> and others endeavored to encode jazz from the white artists
> who were imitating and thus stealing it for their own desires.
> Therefore, resistance is the very spirit of the bop as poetic form,
> which properly contextualizes the essential purpose of this
> particular poem, which is to realize a constructive and creative
> response to anger, whether the source be a broken heart or the
> soul aching from the dehumanization of racial oppression. . . .
> The procedural stages of the process of the Bop's efficacy as
> form are thus—locate, work, resolve.[12]

Like the blues, like Kaufman's blues line, the Bop's tripartite form (whose "line lengths are to be determined by the pitch of emotions") does not just evoke the music it circles but a strut, a sound, and a reference to the violence of those selfsame "guilty police" who arrive at the end of "Bagel Shop Jazz."

Often Kaufman's poems tell a sort of story ("Grandfather was Queer, Too"), but they are just as content to be just a fragment, a figment, "Results of a Lie Detector Test," a fractured fairy tale (such as "Song of the Broken Giraffe," which ends, "Yes, beyond a shadow of a doubt, Rumplestiltskin was emotionally disturbed"), or, as one of my favorite titles has it, "Novels from a Fragment in Progress." He keeps jazz phrasing—not in the dated "bop prosody" of the Beats (consider Kerouac's slight *Book of Blues*), but in the blues tone that bebop restored to jazz. Perhaps these aren't so much "solitudes crowded with loneliness" as solos? Think of the last part of Kaufman's "Battle Report":

> One hundred drummers, each a stick in each hand,
> The delicate rumble of pianos, moving in.
>
> The secret agent, an innocent bystander,
> Drops a note in the wail box.
>
> Five generals, gathered in the gallery,
> Blowing plans.
>
> At last, the secret code is flashed:
> Now is the time, now is the time.
>
> Attack: The sound of jazz.
>
> The city falls.[13]

We see here the coding of destruction as creation, the ultimate negation as affirmation. If we take the term "Black Rimbaud" seriously, we also note that surrealism or a derangement of the senses is at the heart of much of Kaufman, that the destruction he invokes is much like destroying the song to see it new again, flashing its secret code.

We also see in a similar poem, "War Memoir," the parenthetical notion that "(Jazz is an African traitor)," which I think beautifully and simultaneously invokes the African roots of jazz and its blooming in American soil. Even the phrase's parenthetical quality echoes jazz as a secret name or language.

"War Memoir" also indicates the oral nature of Kaufman's work, those qualities of repetition jazz and blues share and the "floating verses" passed around by the black and blues community. Such phrases provided a different sense of origin and originality based on making your own distinctive version, using the familiar to tell your own story. Such call and response is at the heart of African American culture: you could say that, in a larger sense, the blues singer represents a response to the call of the floating verse. Culture is the call; the black singer, or poet, or soloist of any form, the response. The very idea of a solo, after all, only gains power in a culture of recurring collective artistic endeavor.

In a song—or over time—the response quickly becomes another kind of call; the solo aspects of the blues are in turn answered by the collective creation of jazz. You could say that jazz returns us to the "we" of the spirituals. This germinal, collective aspect of African American experience cannot be overstated, just as it cannot be reduced to consensus. Of course, pseudonymous or not, the "I" of the blues is an "I" that is actually a "we," gaining power by how it speaks to the group.

With jazz, however, it may be easier than with the blues to see just how the "I" (soloist) negotiates with the "we" (the jazz combo, the congregation). Singular and shared, this communal self represents a significant development from the "we" of the spirituals, the itinerant blues of freed slaves, and the traveling notes of the soloist who must, in the journey of the song, match and challenge the group. This group "I" provides a significant contrast to the denuded, deracinated "I" of the modern era, even while it serves as a vast parallel.

Though art, even jazz, is not democratic, it does provide an essential freedom—in the case of jazz, one based on "chops," a vital form of meritocracy and excellence. *You can't join the throng till you got your own song.* The contribution of the soloist to the whole can be seen as a quintessential part of the American experiment.

Kaufman himself is a collective and an "I," a soloist and a small combo— Bomkauf, Boms, and Bimgo, all in one. A "cincophrenicpoet" as a short poem claims.[14] Kaufman often riffs off himself, changing his own tune: "Jazz—listen to it at your own risk" appears in "War Memoir"; this line reemerges in *Golden Sardine,* rewritten as the title "O-JAZZ-O War Memoir: Don't listen to it at your own risk." Yet again, in *Ancient Rain* Kaufman has a poem "War Memoir: Jazz, Don't Listen to It at Your Own Risk," whose chief difference from "O-JAZZ-O" is that it ends with "And we listen / And feel / And live" instead of "& die." A big difference—but one that Kaufman seems to say is all in how you look at it, such reversals being natural, or at least inevitable.

Let's take a look at another poem, "I Too, Know What I Am Not," ending with a catalog of everything the poet isn't:

> No, I am not the eyes of the infant owls hatching the roofless night.
> No, I am not the whistle of Havana whores with cribs
>   of Cuban death.
> No, I am not the shriek of Bantu children, bent under
>   pennywhistle whips.
> No, I am not whisper of the African trees, leafy Congo telephones.
> No, I am not Leadbelly of blues, escaped from guitar jails.
> No, I am not anything that is anything I am not.[15]

This poem has always reminded me of Langston Hughes—both "The Negro Speaks of Rivers" and "I, Too, Sing America," with their respective bids for inclusion in history (and prehistory), and the present day. If Bomkauf the pseudonym seeks multiple selves, Kaufman's riff off Hughes includes by exclusion, creating a self through rejecting "leafy Congo telephones," "Cuban death," and even Lead Belly, his fellow Louisiana native. Of course, even in rejecting Lead Belly, he must invoke him, if only for a moment: there's a sense in the case of Lead Belly that the "cincophrenicpoet" is not negating the musician but one view of him—say, the same one that wanted, as Lead Belly's white "discoverer," John Lomax did, to keep him performing in prison stripes, preserving him in a "guitar jail" even after he'd been freed from an actual one. Kaufman proceeds by paradox, as does the blues—and even as Hughes does in singing praise for an America that might not value him.

Such negations and reversals, happening as they do in language, are even more dangerous than those of jazz, which Kaufman well knows, can silence a city. To be, or not to be; "Jazz—listen to it at your own risk"; "Jazz, don't listen to it at your own risk": even risk, or its realization in jazz, can be reversed.

These reversals also happen in terms of race. *Golden Sardine* ends with a 1963 poem-letter to the *San Francisco Chronicle* after his return to the city only "to find a blacklist," asking, "Why are all blacklists white?" Notably, this is written right before his Buddhist vow of silence—which I once asked one of his fellow Beats about, and as he said, Kaufman kept silent alright, except to ask for drugs.[16] Drugs of course can be just another kind of silence—"buddha" means grass, after all.

In *Ancient Rain,* Kaufman's poems find fruition in titles like "Bonsai Poems" and "All Those Ships That Never Sailed." Kaufman broke his silence in 1975 by reciting the speech from "Murder in the Cathedral" mashed-up with his own "All Those Ships," a mix of modernism, martyrdom, and what I take to be a take on the Middle Passage. *Ancient Rain* also includes "Oregon," one of my favorite works by Kaufman. In it, the word "Oregon" is repeated till it becomes not so much a place as a word, and not so much a word as a sound he fills with meaning:

> You are with me, Oregon,
> Day and night, I feel you, Oregon,
> I am Negro. I am Oregon.
> Oregon is me, the planet
> Oregon, the State Oregon, Oregon.
> In the night, you come with bicycle wheels,
> Oregon you come
> With stars of fire. You come green.
> Green eyes, hair, arms,
> Head, face, legs, feet, toes
> Green, nose green, your
> Breast green, your cross
> Green, your blood green.
> Oregon winds blow around
> Oregon. I am green, Oregon.
> You are mine, Oregon. I am yours,
> Oregon. I live in Oregon.
> Oregon lives in me,
> Oregon, you come and make
> Me into a bird and fly me
> To secret places day and night.

The secret places in Oregon,
I am standing the steps
Of the holy church of Crispus
Attucks St. John the Baptist,
The holy brother of Christ,
I am talking to Lorca. We
Decide the Hart Crane trip, home to Oregon
Heaven flight from Gulf of
Mexico, the bridge is
Crossed, and the florid black found.

It is tempting to unpack the many meanings the poem incorporates: the references to St. John the Baptist, Revolutionary War martyr Crispus Attucks, and two great modernists who died young, Hart Crane and Federico García Lorca. The poem rephrases Lorca's "Sleepwalking Ballad," which has a line translatable as "Green how I want you green"; here green becomes "Negro," becomes Oregon, with all becoming a verdant place of possibility based in language. "Oregon is me, the planet / Oregon, the State Oregon, Oregon": once again simply a word, the state is also now more than that, a state of mind, and self. A Cosmos. "The florid black," a riff off a contemporaneous translation of Lorca's ballad, means both the space and destination the word and poem "Oregon" eventually achieves.

We might also find the fertile, florid black in the poem, "Untitled," that follows; it always seemed to me a rereading of the poem "Oregon" facing it. In full "Untitled" reads:

THE SUN IS A NEGRO.
THE MOTHER OF THE SUN IS A NEGRO.
THE DISCIPLES OF THE
SUN ARE NEGRO.
THE SAINTS OF THE
SUN ARE NEGRO
HEAVEN IS NEGRO.[17]

By rewriting even heaven, Kaufman manages to make it not just a place disproved but improved, a place where he is included and not anonymous, the stars not so much named as nicknamed and Negro. Which

I take to mean both culture and color. In this, he follows in the re-mapping of heaven found in the spirituals, which saw the afterlife as an empowering Elsewhere (not to mention the rendering of outer space as the black haven to come). As critic James H. Cone puts it:

> In the black spirituals, the image of heaven served functionally to liberate the black mind from the existing values of white so-ciety, enabling black slaves to think their own thoughts and do their own things. For Tubman and Douglass, heaven meant the risk of escape to the North and Canada; for Nat Turner, it was a vision from above that broke into the minds of believers, giving them the courage and the power to take up arms against slave masters and mistresses. And for others, heaven was a perspec-tive on the present, a spiritual, a song about "another world . . . not made with hands." It was a black life-style, a movement and a beat to the rhythm of freedom in the souls and bodies of black slaves. It was a hum, a moan, and a hope for freedom. Blacks were able, through song, to transcend the enslavement of the present and to live as if the future had already come.[18]

Besides siding with the spirituals, "Untitled" also sides with Countee Cullen's ironic epitaph "For a Lady I Know":

> She even thinks that up in heaven
>   Her class lies late and snores,
> While poor black cherubs rise at seven
>   To do celestial chores.[19]

The lady's dream of heaven is a white one, of course, Cullen indicting not just a segregated afterlife but a daily life of injustice. Cullen's poem is also quite funny, skewering the selfsame "rich psychopaths who think they can fly" as Kaufman's "Unholy Missions." In his nameless "Untitled" Kaufman manages to transform the notion of heaven from a place filled with ladies who know less than they think, into an all-black one, a kind of Oregon above, and within, less a place than a state of being. As Kaufman seems to suggest blackness is.

Of course, in his dance between the self and the society, Kaufman invokes Whitman (and not the self, or soul, *as* a society that is found in Dickinson). He too is larger than life, one of the roughs; like the Rimbaud he was sometimes nicknamed, he gave up writing in a world more surreal than he could possibly make it. Kaufman also manages, in *Golden Sardine,* a language beyond words—or jazz, if you prefer.

DERRAT SLEGELATIONS, FLO GOOF BABER,
SCRASH SHO DUBIES, WAGO WAILO WAILO.
GEED BOP NAVA GLIED, NAVA GLIED NAVA,
SPLEERIEDER, HUYEDIST, HEDACAZ, AX—, O, O.

DEEREDITION, BOOMEDITION, SQUOM, SQUOM, SQUOM.
DEE BEETSTRAWIST, WAPAGO, LOCOEST, LOCORO, LO.
WOOMETEYEREEPETIOP, BOP, BOP, BOP, WHIPOLAT.

DEGET, SKLOKO, KURRITIF, PLOG, MANGI, PLOG MANGI,
CLOPO JAGO BREE, BREE, ASLOOPERED, AKINGO LABY.
ENGPOP, ENGPOP, BOP, PLOLO, PLOLO, BOP, BOP.[20]

That this poem appears, only slightly adjusted, in *The Abomunist Manifesto* is one of its pleasures. (There, it is credited as written by "Schroeder.") Here, it is a separate poem called "Crootey Songo": the word "songo" both "bop" and suggestively African, ancient and modern, a hum and a moan, spoken and unstated, a scat sung. Part of the wordlessness that goes beyond silence and beyond words themselves.

As for me and the grant, I never did compile the Kaufman bibliography I said I would—I fear, even now, it would have proved quite short. I did manage to write some of the poems that made up my first book—trying to get down the music of my family, my ancestors, in our shared Louisiana origins. Mostly, I drank the money away at local watering holes, listening to a lot of live underground jazz. Bomkauf would have been proud.

Photo Display by Jim Bland

THE SUPREMES

SMOKEY ROBINSON & THE MIRACLES

JR. WALKER and the ALL STARS
Soul Recording Artists

ARTHUR PRYSOCK

CHUCK JACKSON

JEE WARWICK

JACKIE WILSON

TOMMY HUNT

JAMES BROWN

SAM & DAVE

ARETHA FRANKLIN

TEMPTATIONS

Chorus Four: Moanin'
Soul Music and the Power of Pleasure _ _ _ _ _ _ _ _ _ _ _

Growing up, I wanted to be a Pip. Not in the sense of something small or insignificant, but rather one of *the* Pips, spinning and singing behind Gladys Knight while she sang *He's leavin'—on that midnight train to Georgia.* Even at the time it was clear to me I wanted some of what soul music provides: a sense of praise even among the heartbreak; to hold your head up high and bow only when dancing; or, as *pip* can mean, "to break through in hatching."

Choreographed yet spontaneous-seeming, stylish and sating, soul learnt me that blackness could mean an afro in a tuxedo. To riff off one of the other definitions of a *pip,* soul turns what might otherwise be tragedy into a "minor, unspecified human ailment." Taking its cue from the blues, seeing beauty among the bittersweet, soul can make even heartbreak look good.

Could the Pips be short for "pippin," which can mean both "apple" and "something admired"? I admired the Pips in large part because of my sense early on that they were family—Knight's brother and cousin and, if I recall correctly, a family friend who might as well have been kin. Soul music insists on community, one filled with calls that you could respond to. *Whoo-whoo.*

Drylongso, when Knight takes her own "Midnight Train," singing *I'd rather live in his world*—the Pips behind her echoing *(live in his world)—than live without him* (long pause for effect) *in mine,* we know full well where she's been and where she's headed. This living in two worlds is also a condition we've seen before, whether in Du Bois's double consciousness or in the spirituals' claiming an otherworldly future: the midnight train journeys between here and there, the midnight special between there and Elsewhere. *People get ready, there's a train a-comin'.*

There are always "two trains a-running." In soul music the dueling trains of heaven and hell become the Love Train or Friendship Train. (They will go on in hip-hop to be "bombed" subway cars and then "Trans-Europe Express" retrofitted to reach "Planet Rock," a funk steam punk.) In "Midnight Train," capitalize the "His" in the phrase *I'd rather live in* his *world, than live without* him *in mine* and you can see how close we are to the holy roll. In Knight's song—indeed, in her very singing—we see up close the ever-present tension between the spiritual and the secular, not just as two competing parts of culture, but within each of us.

"Midnight Train to Georgia" conveys us not just with its *chug-chug* rhythm, but also, like so many blues and folk songs before, with train imagery; its blues correlative is surely part of the song's persistent popularity. Of course all the correlative in the world would mean little without Gladys Knight's emotional delivery, touched with restraint—yet, in the eternal battle between emotion and restraint, restraint here is chiefly performed by the Pips themselves, who serve as a chorus commenting on the first-person action, the wrenching decision that Knight enacts and helps us to know. Their Black Greek chorus not only echoes but predicts the action: *All aboard,* they sing, and soon Knight is singing it too, saying *I got to go—I got to go*—and, boy, do we believe her. We realize suddenly we have been listening to someone convincing herself to leave all along—in this case, to find her way to what must feel like home. This is all the more powerful because it appears the singer is not coaxing forth the song, but that the song itself is convincing the singer. Knight ain't singing; the song is singing her.

Such singing is hard to do—at least without having the song overwhelm you, as many lesser singers might. I recall a too-young singer on television's *American Idol* doing just that, taking the song as a lighthearted romp, an upbeat number more reminiscent of "Boogie-Woogie Bugle Boy." The other risk is there too: many a "good" singer, from Whitney Houston to Mariah Carey, faced with such a song, rather than trusting it—*take your time now*—will overpower the thing, oversing it, blow it out. You can hardly blame them: it is scary to let the song sing you.

But soul insists not so much on perfect pitch as a perfect ear to find the heart of the song in all senses. This is what I call *inner form*. You could call it a song's *soul*.

PEOPLE GET READY

The blues had a baby and they called it rock and roll. Gospel had a child and nicknamed it Soul.

Soul music is to gospel what the blues were to the spirituals: a secular, earthbound, and earthy expression of an older religious counterpart. While suffused with transcendence, soul music's emphasis on rhythm and expression—as in jazz or early blues—marks a recognition of the rhythms and realities of daily life. Such daily livin' is not contradictory to spiritual life: for soul musicians such as Sam Cooke, Ray Charles, Aretha Franklin, Al Green, and Curtis Mayfield forward, the church is just a short drive or long Saturday night away. It is a *midnight* train after all. The willingness of—or the call for—the soul artist to travel between soul music and saving one's own soul is crucial to understanding the role of spirituality and duality in black art, not to mention continuing the extended argument over existence found in the blues.

Soul music don't mean pleading, or preening, as too many singers seem to think today given their whiny delivery: instead it is that churchy mix of restraint and overwhelming emotion. One requires the other. It isn't what you say but how you say it, soul knows, seeking the song within the song. It charts another kind of Elsewhere, one as internal as it is eternal.

Where jazz is double-voiced in its playing, whether Louis Armstrong or Albert Ayler, soul requires a doubleness in our listening to fully understand its expression. You might say that because of the nature of seemingly dominant culture, black expression requires this "veiling"; I would say that this underground meaning is part culture and part condition of the African American desire to mask not just defensively but ritualistically. Through veiling, African American music is multivalent, its meanings many, inveighing against those massed against black culture.

Yet too often soul gets read as a "pure" form of black expression, an essentialism that obscures its roots—even if we properly see in these roots the black ones of gospel, early rhythm and blues, or its combination with country music by Chuck Berry and others to make rock and roll (a black phrase, after all). In fact, soul represents two unified yet seemingly contradictory impulses that soon would contribute to the Black Arts movement it helped give rise to: the rough secularization and improvisation of soul (and bebop) on one hand; and the polish and integrationism of Motown (and what became cool jazz) on the other. I want to stress that this is a false distinction—in our experience of the music and of life we are not divided, but whole. Even Amiri Baraka, early on highly suspect and critical of things deemed assimilationist, knew this. "Baraka interpreted the popular preference [for R & B] as part of a dialectical process that would help create the new black world," Craig Werner notes in discussing Baraka's "The Changing Same (R&B and New Black Music)." "The gospel moans and blues cries, Baraka wrote, carried a musical energy that transcended their capitalist and Christian origins. He praised Motown, the Impressions, and James Brown for providing 'a core of legitimate social feeling, though mainly metaphorical and allegorical.' Soul music represented a stage in a larger revolutionary process: 'the song and the people is the same. . . . the songs, the music, changed, as the people did.'"[1] No wonder Werner's book is called *A Change Is Gonna Come,* named after the sublime Cooke composition.

This "change" gets complicated by the Black Arts movement's emphasis on overt politics, instead of the often-subtle rebellion found in the music they grooved to. Record companies wouldn't release Cooke's "Change," after all. While James Brown sang "Say It Loud (I'm Black and I'm Proud)," others, like Mayfield and Franklin, said "Keep on pushin'" or demanded "respect," politicizing the popular. If Coltrane "murdered the popular song," as Baraka had it, deconstructing "My Favorite Things" until it is one of Baraka's and our favorites, then soul insists we need not murder to transform. Such symbolic murder courses throughout the work of Baraka and Black Arts, from *Dutchman* on. Yet despite the macho claims of gangsta rap and agitprop, soul knows that to find freedom we need only claim it—*reach out, I'll be there*—which, soul insists, ain't the same as begging.

Soul is not necessarily an "all-black" production but a black means of transforming material, whether traditional or "white." In this way, soul's genius is related to jazz and to bebop's return to the blues tone of the music. Listen to the late Isaac Hayes covering "Walk on By" by Burt Bacharach or Mayfield singing The Carpenters' vanilla-seeming "We've Only Just Begun," and you realize soul's insistence on transformation: Mayfield in particular makes the song not just about love but the start of revolution. You might even argue, as soul does, that these are one and the same.

In his recorded, onstage introduction to the Carpenters' cover on his essential *Curtis Live!,* Mayfield puts it this way: "A lot of folks think this particular lyric is not appropriate for what might be considered underground. But I think underground is whatever your mood or your feelings might be at the time so long as it's the truth."[2] Just as we understand Mayfield means a kind of soul music when he says "underground," listeners must grasp how soul always seeks and sends its meanings underground like a railroad—"so long as it's the truth."

RESPECT

The dominant mode of the soul era is *metonymy,* a word or phrase standing in for something else. "Metonymy moves attention from thing to thing; its principle is combination rather than selection," Language poet Lyn Hejinian reminds us. "Compared to metaphor, which depends on code, metonym preserves context, foregrounds interrelationship."[3] *You are the sunshine of my life.* The word, from the Greek, means "name change."[4] In the case of soul, from Mayfield to Franklin, sexual and romantic freedom stands in for a broader one; relationships and situations, while seemingly those of love, are actually bigger. If we don't understand this, we cannot fully comprehend that while Cooke, inarguably the first soul singer, croons "Wonderful World," he is talking not just about personal love but political possibility.

Let's take Aretha's "Respect," a definitive soul song. *Just give me my propers when you come home.* Most any listener rightly intuits that the "respect" spoken of is not just personal—a lover demanding respect and "propers"—but more broadly political. Like the term *propers* itself, Franklin's demands are a metonym understood by the audience, a stand-in for black political demands of and for respect from the nation; they also are also a demand for gender equality. The song's continued popularity is a sign of its timeliness, and the ways in which its struggle is neither simple nor complete.

"Respect," of course, was penned by Otis Redding. In his version, the song does have its double and even multiple meanings, though arguably not as many as Rea-Rea's,[5] whose cover could be said to be definitive. This transformation of seemingly simple material, the personal into the political, is one aspect of soul—even if it is an aspect often provided by the listener. The audience for "Dancing in the Street" (1964), as Craig Werner reminds us, understood that it was a song that captured and coded the unrest at home in those same streets.[6] Those who heard "Tracks of My Tears" (1965) grasped that the lover addressed might as well be the country that didn't dare look in the collective black face, unable to face the despair that might be written there. *Oh yes, I'm the great pretender.* In instance after instance, from Smokey Robinson and the Miracles' "Tears of a Clown" (1967) or "I've Been Good to You" (1961), soul singers were speaking for a feeling behind the veil no less powerful than Dunbar's "We Wear the Mask."

Take Redding's version of the Rolling Stones' "(I Can't Get No) Satisfaction": in the Stones' original, called by many the best rock-and-roll song of all time,[7] "Satisfaction" speaks to a generation's dissatisfaction, the hedonist, ironic, even angry side of the hopefulness found in the time's protest songs. Yet, famously, Keith Richards said that in Redding's version he heard the song like it sounded in Richards's head, how he meant it to sound.

In seeking and finding the soul of the song, Redding's version of "Satisfaction" is an original of a kind only possible in the postmodern world of multiple versions, and the postwar world of the *cover*—a concept charged with race, if only because it typically meant the absence of race. (Race here being ascribed only to blacks—not "raceless" whites. This "race" designation is not always unequal, though always segregated, as in "race records" being synonymous with black records sold to black audiences.) Covering black records held a multiple purpose for the white artist (or for Pat Boone, hardly an artist): most obviously, making money with a proven original; and, secondly and more subtly, also implying that the black original is merely raw material best consumed when premasticated for the masses. Whether copied (as in the Stones) or covered over (as in Boone), both actions imply black culture is an unfinished original: for the former this "rawness" is its best quality; for the latter, rawness is exactly why we need a white version.

For the Rolling Stones or the millions whom they stand in for who have at least taken black culture seriously in taking *from* it,[8] the cover provides a way of providing authenticity—a case of not whitewashing an original, but blacking up the copy. In this, the cover operates much like blackface, providing the same freedoms as the black mask; more important, it also reverses the all-too-typical view, found in even our best critics, of authenticity only sought or required by blacks from white sources that allowed them to speak (or confirmed they *could* write). The cover song reveals the ways white folks quite often require black originality and authenticity, ironically through their "white" copy. *Brown sugar, how come you taste so good?* Not just much of their music, but the Rolling Stones' very name is part love, part theft, taken—like the name of both the magazine and the Bob Dylan hit—from a Muddy Waters song.[9]

DISSATISFACTION

Just as anxiety over slavery required the exorcism of blackface, the cover song reenacted and reacted to the schism of segregation. *Love and Theft,* Eric Lott's tremendous study of blackface minstrelsy—whose title Bob Dylan borrowed for his record by that same name—describes the ways "minstrelsy is claimed as the *completion* of black culture, its professional emergence." Minstrelsy comes about in two ways: through "absorption (in both senses)" or "a transfer of ownership, through theft (or occasional payment). . . . Both paradigms, it is safe to say, share an anxiety over the fact of cultural 'borrowing,'" Lott says. Further, both paradigms "have as their purpose the resolution of some intractable social contradiction or problem that the issue of expropriation represents. That of the first is miscegenation; that of the second slavery itself."[10]

The white cover, in turn, represents an anxiety over the inequality that threatened white and black alike (if also unequally); and a sinking suspicion that black culture was richer and more varied than its counterpart, and, while hemmed in on all sides, represented a form of freedom. *A rolling stone.*

The postwar fascination with the "White Negro" is nothing less than this, a dissatisfaction with America expressed through black culture. Never mind that this fascination often mistakes black culture for blackface, confusing fun for the funhouse mirror where black people were distorted, mimicked, and often outright mocked.

Redding's "Satisfaction" reverses this process, stealing back an original from the band who, especially in their origins, copied black music and its irrepressible style. Redding's version becomes about "satisfaction" in the broadest sense, a sense not just "underground" but foregrounded in soul music: in a word, *yearning*. It would be a mistake to see this yearning as less ironic than in the Stones' version—instead, the song's irony comes from Redding's larger desire for social change, hinted at in the Stones but brought front and center by his delivery.

The difference between the two is the difference between indirect complaint and direct protest: both versions walk the line between the two, tightroped in part by the famous guitar riff. But it is in Redding's own "No no no" that we see the full feeling of soul—and a recognition that soul is not simply a feeling, or a form, but an idiom uniting the two.

Or does it explode? Redding's repeated *Nos*—as in his famous whistle in "Sittin' on the Dock of the Bay," as in Franklin's *Re-Re-Re-Re*'s, riffing off her name and "Respect"—are a way to speak beyond even speech, a poetics of refusal to rival that of Langston Hughes.

From struggle, style. Like its kissing cousin black talk, black style proves a crucial if subtle kind of resistance. Some have even suggested that the black strut is a holdover from the walk of slaves wounded by the lash, or recaptured runaways hobbled to prevent further escape. Black style is itself a form of escape.

It is for this reason, apart from its economic and colonizing questions, that the borrowing and debasing of black style have proved so troubling. Whether homage or covers, love or theft, these white borrowings are fraught not just with the history of black folks literally being *stolen themselves* but also with the failure on the part of certain whites to acknowledge the struggle behind style, mistaking nonchalance or cool or a seeming effortlessness—letting the song sing you—for a lack of mastery.

If the classic mistake with the blues is confusing the music with the feeling it fights—mistaking pain's performance for unmediated rawness and despair—and the misconception with bebop is that it is merely expressionistic improvisation, with soul the misapprehension is that the music is all-out emotion. While both bebop and soul certainly depended on or deepened feeling—a standard of emotion depicted and shared by the musician—both were so dependent on coolness and seeming effortlessness, however ecstatic, that many never saw soul's formal qualities. No matter how understated or overblown, soul's strict expressionism depends less on raw emotion than on restraint, woodshedding, and tradition. *Only the strong survive,* singeth the Iceman, Jerry Butler.

What for jazz was going to the woodshed becomes in soul music "going to church"—not just as a place to learn how to sing but the moment in the soul song where the singer lets go, and loose, the song overtaking you, and not vice versa. *I got to go, I got to go* is not so much a departure as an arrival.

It may help to see soul not as style but *idiom,* a crucial vernacular that provides a counterpart and counterpoint to bebop. For even as it is about transformation, soul remains untranslatable. "Soul music is more than either secularized gospel or funkified jazz," Cornel West reminds us. "Rather, it is a particular Africanization of Afro-American music with intent to appeal to the black masses, especially geared to the black ritual of attending parties and dances. Soul music is the populist application of bebop's aim: racial self-conscious assertion among black people in light of their rich musical heritage."[11]

Such "Africanization" is also at work in Redding's taking black culture back from the Stones, making "Satisfaction" *his* original; or in Mayfield's turning the Carpenters' song "We've Only Just Begun" into an undeniable statement about the larger promise of black liberation. The transformative "we" of soul is almost always larger than the *you* or *I,* the moan or falsetto that it may use to say so. With it we see not the metaphoric "we" of the blues or the allegorical "us" of the spirituals but the metonym of the postmodern moment.

Yet why don't folks know how to sing soul music no more? Where all the soul singers gone?

Where storying enters is by defining excellence not as borrowing or even elusive originality but "telling your own story." Pleasure in soul does not deny, but combats, pain. For at its best soul is not simply style, or struggle, but strategy.

SHOUT (YOU MAKE ME WANNA)

The very origin of soul as a secular version of gospel speaks to transformation—gospel music could accurately be said to be soul's true original, as the very name *soul* implies.

In the noteworthy case of Ray Charles's "I Got a Woman" (1954), soul's transformation is literal, with Charles changing the lyrics from gospel ones to secular (and sexual) ones, rendering the distance non-existent—or more accurately, harking back to the secular blues music that influenced gospel in the first place. The career of Thomas A. Dorsey, the father of gospel music, is indicative of the porousness of the barrier between the musics: a former player with Bessie Smith and others in the tent shows, Dorsey wrote "Take My Hand, Precious Lord" after the death of his wife and child in childbirth, converting his blues experience into gospel expression and initiating a new sacred form.

In soul, the conflict lies not so much in the tension between the worldly and the otherworldly—in the blues and the spirituals, respectively—as in the conflations and tensions between romantic love and a religious One. In this, soul music ain't too far from Dante. We can practically hear this conflict in the music, and it is at stake in the lives of the soul musicians themselves—most all, from Green to Franklin, have been conflicted over their religious origins, often abandoning the worldly world for the sacred one. And usually back again. *This is my lover's prayer.*

To hear soul music fully, we must listen for this almost-religious longing, and its relation to romantic yearning. Listening to Sam Cooke sing *That's the sound of the men / Working on the chain ga-ang,* who doesn't hear the yearning of the black prisoners and their work songs? "Chain Gang" merges the folk tradition of work song—as recorded by Lead Belly and Sterling A. Brown, Bessie Smith and Zora Neale Hurston—with a popular one. In the process, Cooke does not demean the "sound of the men / working on the chain ga-ang" but returns them to the realm of pleasure, linking our pleasure in hearing the music to their struggle. This in fact mirrors the folk tradition, descended from African song, wherein African Americans turned their struggle (on the gang, say) into some small yet significant, even pleasurable, form of self-expression (the work song). One of soul music's key pleasures is how easy it makes our difficulties look.

The fact that there is a distance between the actual sounds of a work or gospel song and their transformation into soul is exactly the point. By recontextualizing the black oral tradition of work or the Word, by emphasizing pleasure in the midst of pain, by making sure folks dance in the street or juke or blue-light basement, soul music announces "people get ready" or "(don't worry) if there's a hell below we're all going to go" or "it's all right (to have a good time)."

Pleasure is a revolutionary act in the face of pain.

Soul's acknowledgment of the pain of the everyday retains a power that participates in the blues tradition, frequently locating its concerns with a "lover," or in "love," the Beloved serving as a stand-in for a larger yearning. *Don't know much about history / Don't know much biology:* when Cooke sings these lines, he evokes (and revokes) the very things that might limit a black man in the South or in the States, his history and biology being overdetermined; the song can be read as an ironic comment on exactly what a black man, particularly at midcentury, knows all too well.[12] In denying history and biology, time and the natural world, Cooke takes pleasure where some would see only struggle. This pleasure, in the end, is one found not just in the listener—even as the soul artist is describing pain—but in the performance, which in its virtuosity, emotional accuracy, its *soul,* achieves a secular transcendence.

We see such transcendence most clearly in soul's wordlessness. Following in the tradition of the field holler, the blues moan, and jazz scat, the soul shout expresses the inexpressible. No wonder such "going to church" is often found at the edges of 45s, or the end of soul records. In an interview, Cornel West discusses this riffing in terms of the margins of the music providing, despite the strictures of radio formats and the recording industry, a place for gospel-based improvisation; he also registers his dislike for radio DJs who cut such songs off too early. *(Amen.)* Imagine hearing James Brown's "Please Please Please" without the final hollers, or worse, "Let's Get It On" without Marvin Gaye's final plea, almost an aside, *Make me feel sanctified.* This sanctifying of the sensual (or the sensuality of sanctifying) is at the heart of soul music and is missing, for instance, in comedian Jack Black's otherwise faithful version of "Let's Get It On" from the movie (or should I say "cover") version of *High Fidelity.* Black sings *Something like summertime* instead, making the yearning for a time and place, instead of a space beyond the worldly, an Elsewhere.

Soul isn't just transformation, but transport.

As with other kinds of storying, soul seeks the transport of the self through worldly means, yet with otherworldly implications. This is a universal desire in a secular form—and arguably involves the increasingly postmodern problem of *how*. Redding's solution, found in "Fa-Fa-Fa-Fa-Fa (Sad Song)" or "The Happy Song (Dum-Dum)" or the whistle in "Dock of the Bay," is to foreground the inexpressible, to verbalize it through means other than words. The consistency of Redding's use of the wordless soul riff—even found in the "no no no" of his "Satisfaction," bringing to mind the king's "O" at the end of *Lear*—gives the lie to those who insist the whistle in "Dock of the Bay" occurred only because he forgot the words. As with scat or the gospel shout, this wordlessness is not merely a lack of words (though sometimes it is that), but an improvisation of, and persistent need for, a sound just beyond reach. Found in postwar black culture from bebop to late Coltrane, this often-wordless yearning takes many different forms, from the broken rhythm of Hughes, the bold, half-bitten form of black concrete poet N. H. Pritchard, to the blues haiku of Sonia Sanchez, and the blues sonnets of Gwendolyn Brooks.

Suffice it to say, even if we believe that Redding forgot the words, such a story chiefly ignores the power and proficiency of his solution: his whistle while "sittin' on the dock of the bay" forlornly and momentously embodies what the entire song attempts to name, a storying sound that tells us all we need to know about yearning and waiting, the loneliness that won't leave him alone. Or us.

TIRED OF BEING ALONE

Soul music reminds us that the voice is not always natural, but often artificial. You could say that black folks' very yearning is a kind of technology—a conveyance, if you will, that like the soul shout or moan is meant to usher us beyond the beyond. *Falsetto* in soul music, where it occurs with notable frequency, is such a chariot, partly earthbound, with claims on a sound beyond nature—a reaching for the supernatural. *Sometimes I just fold my arms and say—aaaaah.* This is in part a secular solution to the ways "nature" has been corrupted, made, like biology and history, to serve racist ends. Especially when running away from bondage was seen as a medical disease, the so-called natural inferiority of blacks (and racist cures for such) would be enough to make nature, not to mention "naturalism," suspect. *Sometimes I wonder.*

The African American emphasis on Elsewhere also insists that all we see ain't all there is. Falsetto is the supernatural made vocal, Ariel for the airwaves: simultaneously hypermasculine and lovingly feminine, sexy yet chaste, falsetto in soul music is a sign of vulnerability that emerges from strength. It is the deepest voice, after all, that often creates the highest.[13] As falsetto reveals, soul embodies a set of opposites, even contradictions: "Love and happiness" Al Green sings, and helps us to know these may be two different things. *Something that'll make you do wrong, will make you do right.* These contradictions are found in the song's instrumentation, the organ playing and the horn section providing a sorrowful undertow and a hopeful Negro heaven all at once. The attempt is as important as the result, soul says, taking the tragicomedy of the blues to heart in ways pop songs rarely did before. Like the woman talking on the phone late at night, the song is trying not just to make it new but *make it right.*

Falsetto is also a "machining of the voice" whose descendants—from "Computer Love" to Autotune, from the strange modified voice found in the funk of "Don't Call Me Nigger, Whitey" to the electric spankings of P-Funk—will crowd the radio soon enough.

Such a falsetto can also be found in *mingering*—that elusive word found in the folk art of Mingering Mike. Recently discovered, "Mingering Mike" was a best-selling musical artist for years, starting in the late 1960s and early '70s—at least in his imagination. Mike would craft records and whole record companies by hand, making folk art in the form of album covers that feature a rotating and increasing roster of performers, usually his friends and family members in different guises. (In this he is not necessarily different from actual record companies, from Stax to Motown.)

Mingering Mike's grasp of the conventions of the soul singer and the soul label—with its staple of stars and lesser stars who'd guest on their records, its various imprints and spinoffs, the girl singer and girl group, bands named "The _____," much like the Temptations or the Supremes (or any other of the recent white "The" bands for that matter), the offshoot comedy records, the hard-hitting later antidrug and/or antiwar record by their major recording artist—proves the ways in which soul is an idiom to be mastered, and can provide a vision beyond the expected.

It also reveals how the soul artist is a chorus of one—if not a record label. Turning pop into hand-drawn folk art, and turning folk art of his albums into pop, if not popular, masterpieces—so much so that Mike often slipped his handmade records into the flimsy cellophane wrappers of real records, price stickers and all, even occasionally placing them in the bins of real record stores—Mingering Mike doesn't just have soul artist but post-soul artist written all over him. The result, his mingering, asks questions of the real and the imaginary and the ways that storying disrupts the universe by making its own world, leading us out of our constrictions, beyond the groove.

Part lingering, part "meandering" and "thriving on a riff," all imagination, mingering might best describe the elusive black art of escape. Maybe then *mingering* is not just an adjective but a verb—like blackness itself.

Soul takes the analog both as its method of transmission and as a metaphor. It is exacting inexactness, its improvisations demanding. Soul also proves analogous to the movements in black writing that it in part spurred: the search for a written, black-based, oral aesthetic in contrast to a "white" one (which could be said to belong to Black Arts); or, in a search for an equally black, transformative aesthetic that takes from either folk material or white material, but that knows that blackness is never just style but an improvisatory process whereby material is made "black."

What's become of the brokenhearted? Black culture does not worry the gap between the black origin and destination; in fact, it remakes the gap into its own image. It shares the tradition of reinvention found in the spirituals, which not only invented new material but sometimes transformed white hymns; the African American preservation and transformation of the once-British ballad; and the remapping first performed by the spirituals of the American landscape. As Amiri Baraka would argue in his groundbreaking *Blues People,* it is exactly this moment of transformation of musics whereby the African first became the African American.

I want to reiterate here, and dissent a bit too, that unlike Baraka in *Blues People,* I don't believe there is a pure, prelapsarian blackness that once it becomes "American" evaporates. Instead, I believe it is black culture (which is distinct) that transforms American culture (making it more black, and thereby more distinct). Baraka himself has come to see the ways his groundbreaking book hadn't quite realized this: "When I talked (in *Blues People*) about surviving Africanisms in Afro-American culture I did not take into consideration that *American culture itself* is historically partially constructed of continuing and thematic Africanisms!"[14] *This is my country.* American culture is black culture—and it is this unique African American culture that in large part makes American culture popular the world over.

My sermon tonight is on the blackness of blackness: the question is no longer the influence of black culture on American culture but the influence of blackness on black culture itself.

GET ON THE GOOD FOOT

Soul is exacting where the blues blurs; both meet in the moan, where form and content collapse. This *moan* may be traced through the music. I have come to articulate the tradition as a kind of pyramid, centered on the blues, built on the moan, and reaching for the North Star. A heritage of transformation extends not just from soul music but from the many idioms that inform and surround the music itself—soul, after all, charts not black essence but artfulness.

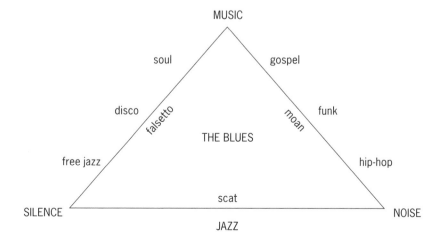

The distinction between the two is best maintained, even though soul came to be synonymous with black identity, so much so that folks identified their shops as being owned by a "Soul Brother" during the 1965 riots in Watts to spare them from destruction. A way of saying "black-owned," *soul brother* also implied identifying with the struggle in those streets, and with the not-insignificant purpose of protecting one's property.[15] Sam Cooke too embodied this by being one of the first black artists to start his own publishing company, realizing the real money in the music industry came from writing, not singing. Retaining and even creating your rights—and writing—is part of soul's aim. Soul may be best thought of as a totem, a kind of conjure or fetish, to be carried like a badge of courage or worn like a marker; soul brother or sister meant you were "down" with the cause, which could be said to be blackness itself.

Soul is not a color but a culture; not innate so much as an ethos. Internal, but signified by external qualities, soul is international, cosmopolitan, generative. It's remarkable how many soul songs are named "Think." But don't take my word for it, let's consult Mr. Dynamite, the Godfather of Soul, the Funky President, Soul Brother Number One: James Brown. In his 1971 evaluation "The Lyrics of James Brown: Ain't It Funky Now; or, Money Won't Change Your Licking Stick," Mel Watkins defines soul in a manner that complicates any reductive view of soul as merely "the essence of blackness," making it instead the height of artistry—and ecstasy.

> If the truth be told, the artistry of James Brown is epitomized by the guttural grunt (uh, uh) or the equally familiar cry of "oo-wee" that punctuates practically every song he has recorded. In those simple, primal utterances Brown comes nearer his poetic goal than in any of his more elaborate lyrics. For there, he is not singing *about* black life—he *is* black life. The object is subject and vice versa, distance is eradicated and the lyric is snatched from abstraction to reality. Form and content converge as one. Thereby Brown expressively simulates one of the essential qualities of the black life style: its straight-out, direct nature and insistence upon commitment to life, not reflection upon it.[16]

As with Redding's nonverbal acuity, Franklin's riffs, and Mayfield's falsetto, James Brown's moan manages to achieve a wordlessness that borders on brilliance.

This doesn't mean that the Godfather of Soul's shouts—channeling the shouts and hollers, the sacred and secular songs of slavery—aren't self-conscious, any more than his negotiation of "both the arrogant, swaggering quality" characteristic of soul along with "the qualitative need to challenge and reaffirm (with, of course, the awareness of the possibility of loss) that underlines that posture."[17] The authority and reaffirmation that Watkins identifies as James Brown's "ethos of immediacy" are notably theatrical. Storying and counterfeit can help us better position and maintain in our sights the very "real poses" in soul that Watkins goes on to mention. And also to understand the way authority is achieved—not through simple authenticity but by means of an ironically genuine reaction from a black audience based on the effectiveness of Brown's "act."

The posture of soul—even if a measure of the distance traveling from abstraction to reality—is found in James Brown's very titles, and Watkins's use of them in his own title. "Licking Stick" or "Papa's Got a Brand New Bag" or "Mama Popcorn" all take nostalgic concepts of a black past, however recent, and make them present—in other words, a tradition.

For Brown, soul is ritual, as in the famous putting on of his robe when, after his performance, he is spent from hours of "begging" *Please Please Please,* or from "rapping" to the crowd about the dangers of heroin—two aspects of his performance integral to his themes. Brown's finale, Watkins reminds us, "is perhaps the most obvious example of his intent": "The act is repeated several times, each time with a more sumptuous and ornate robe and with more dramatics, until finally the curtains close. It is a ritualistic act, performed at every show. And despite critics, who find its obvious theatricalism boring, few black viewers object. The reason is simple: Symbolically, it cements the performer-audience rapport; it is a put-on, a parody of posturing and an act in affirmation of the acceptance of absurdity, the adhesive which binds James Brown to blackness and to his audience. From this core attitude, his lyrics flow effortlessly, like good pot-liquor from fatback."[18] The very qualities found in the downhome metaphor of pot liquor make up soul:

Brown's "good foot" may be the selfsame "putting your foot in it" folks say when the food tastes expecially good.

Where the blues make mention of food in order to make hay, or to roll in it—cookin' as a metaphor for lovemaking—soul uses food as a metonym for memory.

A CHANGE IS GONNA COME

Don't know much about history: rather than depend on the official record, black folks have used memory as a new means of transmission; a shadow book of ear music, coded complaint, and burrowed belief.

We could call this transmission, this memory as history, this changing same, *the groove.* Much like a record, machined yet handheld, musical and vocal, delicate yet hardy, even damaged the groove can still be heard. Like the ring shout, it goes round and round, cyclical but progressing—and even progressive. No wonder the storying tradition looks like a circle, wheel within a wheel, the record a talisman carried like those sacred objects that made up a slave's hidden cosmology. So too the slave's sacred, Africanized songs became the secular, spiritualized ones a century later, their shouts and hollers now bought and sold instead of their bodies. But never, even in slavery, their selves.

With the advent of "race records"—the earliest recording of black folks on wax, from "Crazy Blues" to "West End"—black audiences could hear their own culture talking back to them from the machine itself. It must have been remarkable, a response for a call that had been a long time coming. Much like when black folks were first beginning to be on television in numbers—appearances were notable enough to make *Jet* magazine in a one-page listing—and the literal call would go round saying *Tune in.* That was soul. Each transmission an insurrection. Each tuning-in a turning of the culture.

Each groove the needle found was an actual sound wave made physical; each record was the transmission of a knowledge we always knew we had and had held dear but hadn't heard coming out of a phonograph or squawk box before. *His Slave's Voice*—a voice of mastery.

The moan and falsetto are a particular technology and form of this transmission—seeking both the higher and the lower frequencies to make meaning beyond words. Though these words too changed: the slave's assertion that *Before I'd be a slave, I'd be buried in my grave* became Muddy Waters singing

> I don't want you to be no slave
> I don't want you to work all day
> I don't want you to be true
> I just want to make love to you—

as well as Sam Cooke's *You know I'll always be your slave till I'll be buried, buried in my grave* in "Bring It on Home to Me." In the song, background singer Lou Rawls literally echoes the feelings and phrases Cooke is singing of; the line not so much repeats as shadows Cooke, often changed slightly, sometimes just behind the beat, and in that way both blues and gospel. The song shadows two voices as one, enacting the relation of the voice to the tradition that also predicts it. It is a mix of memory and ecstasy, which is to say, soul.

HARRIET TUBMAN RAGOUT

Like singing, cooking was one of the few resources and means of invention openly available to the slave. Alongside the other, often secret inventions of the storying tradition, soul food does stand out (and up): we can see in the often-shared palate of the Southerner the ways in which black influence, reportedly hard to trace, is both undeniable and remarkable. The naming of soul food as a category is a recognition of this influence while also a reclamation of black inventiveness by and for black folks themselves.

In the classic foodways narrative *Vibration Cooking* by Vertamae Smart-Grosvenor (1970), the first section is called Home; others include "Away from Home," "Madness," "Love," and "Mixed Bag." Subtitled *Travel Notes of a Geechee Girl*, the book conjures travelog, notation, genealogy, and that African American form, the Geechee, reclaimed from a sometime slur. "It's a possibility that it's the same tribe in the south now. Some people say Gullahs, some say Geechees and some refer to us as maroons."[19] In *Vibration Cooking*, Verta Mae (the name she originally published under) crafts an update to Hurston's *Mules and Men,* both narrators insisting on becoming part of the narrative. By combining recipes and stories, she declares both as forms of memory as history.

Much of the book is about naming, as well as "name-calling." Verta Mae remedies these misnomers even with "so-called okra," which she calls not by its slave name but by its African name, *gombo.* She often refers to people not mentioned before by their first names, as if we already know them; doing so calls and recalls us into her widening circle, familiarity being more important than narrative, storying over chronology. Even by not using her last name in her early publications, Verta Mae gets familiar and down-home with her readers.

The relation of the recipes to the narrative is quite a counterpoint, or riff, more like the jazz of the Sun Ra Arkestra she performed with—or even like the crosshatch paintings of her "homeboy" Jasper Johns, who hails from the same South Carolina town. Throughout, Verta Mae connects self to soul, soul food to story, and story to a slave past and presence, and telling stories on yourself:

> I had an uncle named Costen. They say that education run him fool. They say that he knew more than anybody in Allendale County including white folks. . . .
>
> He could recite poems and add up as many numbers as you could throw at him. All in his head, too. He didn't need to write nothing down. Uncle Costen used to tell us stories about slavery. How it was and how it wasn't. One story that he told was about the Underground Railroad. He said that sometimes they would be in the middle of their dinner when the stops (homes that hid slaves en route to freedom) got word that a slave or slaves were coming through that night. They might even have some neighbors or even members of the family there who were not cool. Everybody wasn't in it all together like the Browns (John & sons) so they had to have signals to let each other know that tonight it would happen. Uncle Costen said they had a special dish they would serve called
>
> HARRIET TUBMAN RAGOUT[20]

Foodways are an essential part of the community's coding and escape. Such escape is also part of not just Verta Mae's family but her birth: we are told she was born a three-pound baby, one of twins; her six-pound brother did not survive and she was not supposed to. Placed in a shoe-box on an open stove, she is tended to by her Aunt Rose, who fed her with an eyedropper and goat's milk, her mother having "the childbirth fever." Soul is that nurturing in the face of nothing; it's the close call amid the fever of childbirth; it is the homemade incubator cooking up more than just food.

Soul is also the escape of Smart-Grosvenor's family from and during slavery: her great-uncle, "Uncle Willis' father could read and write so he made up free issue passes and had what they called a 'bootleg pass ring.' He sold the passes for sacks of flour, sacks of corn, bacon, hogs, etc., and *comme ça* he managed to feed his family."[21] The counterfeit is both the "bootleg pass ring" and the food provided as currency, buying a broader liberty.

Soul food is a form of exile. If not the food of the refugee, soul food provides the makings of a migrant meal—filled with connotations not just of place and locality but also of foods first carried by Africans imported into the slave states, then later brought north as part of the Great Migration, and onward to Paris and beyond. Soul food meant a foodstuff carried on the person as well as a form of personhood, whether "black rice" or *gombo,* root vegetables or Douglass's *root.* Verta Mae's descriptions all bear this out, whether writing about Philly, Paree, or a transatlantic voyage in which the talk is less of food than a fellow passenger's racism (at a children's party and meal) and Verta Mae's setting her straight by bringing sewing on deck and pretending to make a "voodoo doll" (in a chapter called "I Love . . . Bon Voyage Parties"). What all this has to do with food is the shared presence of the fetish, of Africanisms and African American ritual—forms of sustenance that are equally nonverbal, powerful, and even playful.

There is, however, often omen: Verta Mae in the midst of other recipes mentions peacocks and how they "are too beautiful to be eaten and I don't think the Creator meant for people to have peacock feathers sitting in vases on window sills. If I was Jimi Hendrix I'd get rid of that vest. It is said that peacock feathers bring bad luck and I believe it."[22] (The call was apparently not heeded.) This don't mean that Verta Mae is not interested in the put-on of soul—the "put-on" just might mean "putting on" a pot of greens. All are alchemy.

In her reading of Hurston's *Their Eyes Were Watching God,* British biracial writer Zadie Smith touches on the ways soul provides a kind of transatlantic sustenance:

> I always thought I was a colorblind reader—until I read this novel, and that ultimate cliché of black life that is inscribed in the word *soulful* took on new weight and sense for me. But what does *soulful* even mean? The dictionary has it this way: "expressing or appearing to express deep and often sorrowful feeling." The culturally black meaning adds several more shades of color. First shade: *soulfulness* is sorrowful feeling transformed into something beautiful, creative and self-renewing, and—as it reaches a pitch—ecstatic. It is an alchemy of pain. In *Their Eyes Were Watching God,* when the townsfolk sing for the death of the mule, this is an example of *soulfulness.* Another shade: to be soulful is to follow and *fall in line* with a feeling, to go where it takes you and not to go against its grain. . . . A final shade: the word *soulful,* like its Jewish cousin, *schmaltz,* has its roots in the digestive tract. "Soul food" is simple, flavorsome, hearty, unfussy, with spice.[23]

Soulfulness, then, is the way black folks can, like Hurston, make "'culture'—that slow and particular and artificial accretion of habit and circumstance—seem as natural and organic and beautiful as the sunrise."[24] Cooking soul food is a direct example of what Smith calls "an alchemy of pain," culture as ongoing and transformative as yeast.

We may not like soul food as a term (my father liked to say when he was young, he and his just called it "food") and we don't have to eat it (though I cannot imagine why not), but if we cannot see the ways soul food's ethos of reclamation and reuse—making more than making do, of taking leftovers and leavings and making them not only palatable but desirable, *making it right*—if we cannot see this desire as not mere survival but a heroic act of reinvention—then we're missing out on a large part of the storying tradition of black culture.

It is soul food that first brought the current buzzwords of organic, sustainability, and recycling to bear in the culture. Like storying, soul food was born out of necessity, but now is a form of pleasure. Once the territory of those who couldn't afford to let any part of, say, the hog go to waste—from the rooter to the tooter—now offal is no longer awful. If black folks aren't always sharing in the profits or the prophecy of returning to the soil, or soul, we mustn't mistake the lack of a label of "certified organic" for a lack of influence—instead it is the very presence of influence. What we helped make, we can't always taste.

NO WOMAN NO CRY

Food in soul music represents a desire for radical renewal. When James Brown hollers *grits and gravy* and *cracklin bread* at the end of the record, he is not simply performing a kind of praise or roll call or naming, though he is doing that too. His is a kind of radical nostalgia: something too often ignored in Black Arts, which sought a new, black future, understandably; however, in their desire to make it new, artists of the period too often tossed out the greens with the pot liquor. Some soul's memory is both aware of, and pitched against, history, just as the falsetto is pitched against a notion of nature: both ideas have, over the years, at times proved oppressive to black folks.

The kinds of food may have been different, but even reggae, soul's Caribbean kin, shares not just the notion of food as fellowship but the crucial kinds of freedom celebrated and reified, even deified, by soul. Bob Marley would take soul's transformations, as well as his initial failing to make it as a soul singer in the States, and synthesize them into reggae—just as he took Mayfield's "People Get Ready" and turned it into "One Love." *Everything's gonna be all right* he sang, a refrain found in several of his songs—whether sung in a concrete jungle or sung by three little birds outside his window—but that might as well describe a politics carved from a hard-won hope. As much as the sound system or the dub mix, it is this scrappy, syncretic spirit that would make its way north to the South Bronx and form one of the wellsprings of hip-hop—alongside James Brown's moan and his funky drummer's persistent perscussion.

How many white musicians give shout-outs to foodstuffs in their songs? From "Salt Peanuts" to Brown's *smothered steak* (two times) holler at the end of a song, black performers make food a staple of their performance in ways rarely seen elsewhere. (Only punk music comes to mind, where the Ramones or Descendants declare the straightahead pleasures of a cheeseburger or chicken vindaloo, fast as their music.)[25] The cornmeal porridge Marley sang of in "No Woman No Cry" might just be another name for grits, in the end; or, polenta, if you're feeling fancy.

Soul and reggae also know what it means to go hungry: *A hungry man is an angry man.* Such hunger is not just literal, but lyrical; hunger is yearning made physical. We want more, it says; we want our sweet potato pie and to sing about it too. Soul marries this yearning to music, whether as struggle or ritual, sustenance or the shout.

This in part is because all these foods can mean *home*—which in black talk is not just a place but the nickname of a person who reminds you of it. Nostalgia, after all, means homesickness.

TALKIN' LOUD AND SAYIN'

Soul means the performance and its perspiration, a ritual and riff, a fancy robe and its being discarded in a mix of power and pretense. Like any good drama or falsetto, the perennial coronation of Mr. Dynamite, his making and remaking each night, is an act or even affect crafted in order to get at something real, actual, earned. The robe ritual, like the rituals of Southern black life that James Brown sings of and transforms, are aspects that approach something of our sense of the fetish: a symbol of black power, made visual or at least nonverbal, flirting with that "oowee" at the edge of words.

Such power is familiar to those in the black church, where, Hurston reminds us, "Shouting is a community thing. It thrives in concert," so to speak. And yet, as she says in nearly the next breath, "It is absolutely individualistic. While there are general types of shouting, the shouter may mix the different styles to his liking, or he may express himself in some fashion never seen before."[26] This fruitful tension between the group and the individual makes its way through the culture and finds its avatar in James Brown. Where the shout, chant, and hum are ways church folk express devotion, Brown's use of the same might be said to be in service of self-determination: *please, please, please.*

What the Godfather's hollers articulate—and they do articulate—is exactly the fetish's sense of power and sexuality. Not to mention glamour. Just as Frederick Douglass's *root* provided a measure of physical and psychic freedom, James Brown's rootworked and conked-root glamour does much the same. If the ritualistic and performative nature of soul—its function as fetish—originates in the field holler, then soul's postmodern aspects are found in the Godfather's self-conscious and self-referential discussing with his band what's next: *D, down D, funky D, sweet D.* By incorporating stage directions into the playing itself, Brown brilliantly anticipates and parallels the post-soul incorporating of everything into one "brand new bag."

That this bag is down-home and ritualistic, soulful and smart, African American talk and Africanized rhythms, also tells us a lot about blackness and postmodernity—where they meet and how each makes the other possible. You could even say this bag is the selfsame "brown bag of miscellany" that Zora Neale Hurston describes herself as in "How It Feels to Be Colored Me." Ralph Ellison sums up soul and its struggle this way: "It is this ability to articulate this tragic-comic attitude toward life that explains much of the mysterious power and attractiveness of that quality of Negro American style known as 'soul.' An expression of American diversity within unity, of blackness with whiteness, soul announces the presence of a creative struggle against the realities of existence."[27] Such border crossings—the "expression of American diversity within unity"—and synthesis in dissonance and everyday ecstasy are the postmodern point.

And, soul asks, if you can look good doing it, why not?

BOOK FOUR

Cosmic Slop _

I too wanted to be possessed by language, to have poetry swoop down upon me from outer space, and perhaps take me with it when it returned there.

—REGINALD SHEPHERD
Orpheus in the Bronx

"I VOTE TO SEND THIS EXCITING ARTIST TO RUSSIA AS OUR ANSWER TO THE SPUTNIK"--KAY

"THE GOOD LORD HAS SPRINKLED THIS PERFORMER WITH STARDUST"--MILTON

"THIS BIG TALENT RANKS WITH MAHALIA, PRESLEY, BOJANGLES, YARDBIRD, JOLSON AND BERLE."--BLAND

Interstellar Space
Toward a Post-Soul Poetics _ _ _ _ _ _ _ _ _ _ _ _ _ _ _ _ _ _

When he stepped onstage to close the Woodstock Festival in August 1969, one lunar cycle after American Neil Armstrong was the first human to walk on the moon, Jimi Hendrix and his newly formed band could not have known they were launching something even bigger. Some would say that the "3 Days of Peace & Music" was the flowering of the 1960s, the height of flower power and protest against injustice. Yet even cloaked now in nostalgia and boomer revisionism, even without the high-priced reunions and the violence of the third and seemingly last Woodstock, the first Woodstock (a strange, anachronistic phrase) also marked an end. Though it took awhile for the memo about the apocalypse to trickle down.

Hendrix—who had journeyed through the chitlin circuit, and rhythm and blues, playing for Little Richard and the Isley Brothers, and through his own blues in songs like "Hey Joe"; who had traveled through folk music, both black and white, that had been made electric by Bob Dylan (himself elliptical and apocalyptic), and then made static by Hendrix's cover of Dylan's "All Along the Watchtower"—took the stage and famously tore through his set. He did not make his guitar a fiery sacrifice, as he had in Monterey two years before, but, recognizing the sacrifice demanded by a Vietnam-era America, his distorted, stretched, feedback-fed rendition of "The Star-Spangled Banner" was less a reformulation of our national anthem than a recognition of the song's inner life and country's mounting casualties abroad and at home. Without seeking soul music's synthesis, his was a new thing, not so much a thesis as an antithesis, at first unrecognizable—part inversion, part homage, all antidote—simultaneously natural and artificial—a benediction, but into what kind of world, his rendition seems to ask—a riot of sound, a series of questions, a quest, a survival of an original, a misquoting—a fierce copy that is itself totally original—a counterfeit.

Hendrix's "Banner" makes it hard to hear the original without thinking of its offspring, forever changing the original in the way all good works of art do. With Hendrix we are not just in the presence of history—and of a performance that changes our sense of history—but the ever-present. Hendrix's performance replaces a sense of history with Right Now—something found in the postmodern playing of bebop, blowing "Now's the Time," but also in the ancient African concept of Great Time—all of which Hendrix makes into a sign of our turbulent times.

While Hendrix's "Purple Haze" has become shorthand, even cliché, as the soundtrack for any montage of the 1960s, his far less known (and less user friendly) "Machine Gun" may not only better describe the Vietnam era but also speak louder to its concerns. "Machine Gun" was a kind of boiling down of his previous work, a condensed and arguably more direct protest. In its elliptic electricity, "Machine Gun" furthers Hendrix's sense of *feedback*—a form that may in some ways govern this new era. Static as ecstatic.

In live performances, former soldier Hendrix would dedicate the song to "all the soldiers fighting in Chicago" as well as Vietnam. Playing with Band of Gypsys, his second, mainly black band, Hendrix automates the soul song "Shotgun" by Junior Walker and the All Stars (who he once played behind), hijacks the high-pitched riffs learned behind Little Richard, and makes them all the more rapid-fire and dangerous. Like the rest of us, "in mid-1968 all Hendrix needed was *space*."[1]

Here, behind his back, on fire, in Hendrix's southpaw playing, we can hear the last great shift up to now: from R & B to rock and roll to post-soul.

I'LL TAKE YOU THERE

Eras of course are never as neat as we pretend they are: the 1960s as we popularly misremember them did not end until the mid-1970s; it is only with the end of the Vietnam War era that 1960s optimism, however hard-won, was replaced by national cynicism. Certainly with Watergate—even after a decade of assassinations, protests, and general civil strife, includ-

ing those in the vital year before Woodstock—the resigning of a president for deceit and lies marked something of a sea change in American
character. An even bigger resignation, you could say.

For now we find ourselves in an era that critic Nelson George has
termed "post-soul." Black nationalism gave way to Blaxploitation films,
the righteous soul of Curtis Mayfield to funk, free jazz to Miles Davis's
fusion—nothing is safe, or at least stable, in such a consumer, crossover society. This was the society Motown had made, and mastered—
Marvin Gaye for one, had transformed from the gospel-infused pop of
"Can I Get a Witness" through the spiritual contemplation of "What's
Going On" and outrage of "Makes Me Wanna Holler" into the sensual,
secular, yet transcendent vision of "Let's Get It On."

This new post-soul era is one of social change—marked by everything from feminism to black power—though in many ways, it marks
the beginning of the end of that change. The King of Love was dead,
and the Kennedys, not to mention the men and women of Vietnam
(on both sides). Certainly it meant the end of the full flowering of the
Black Arts movement, an end that could be datable to the publishing
of Baraka's *Hard Facts* (1972), and his disavowing the strict national-
ist terms of the movement he had helped found a few years before—a
movement he had, to many, come to symbolize.

Such was the microcosm of transformations and tensions between
the sacred and the secular, between what once was high and low. And
after even presidents, especially presidents, were no longer sacred, certainly the boundaries of language and what could be said—pushed by
postmodernism in its proper and popular forms—were expanded to
the point that they seemed not boundaries at all. In post-soul's own remapping, our nation's capital and its commander in chief were replaced
by Chocolate Cities and the Funky President, James Brown.

I don't know karate, but I know ka-razy. This line from the Godfather's
"The Payback" (1973) reveals the anger behind the drama, the protest
implied in the ritual now made front and center. Funk and foment are
right around the corner. Or you could say, are right there in the pocket
of the song. Soon we'd need it, *funk* a metaphor—and funk music the
cure—for what ails us.

My patience ends, I want revenge! This repeated riff replaces the
sanctity of soul with the outrage, if not the outrageousness, soon found

in funk. In such an explosion of bass and bothersomeness, nostalgia is nowhere in sight. Or at least easily seen. Forget memory, revenge instead: the vendetta Brown sings of may be unspecified but is no less understood by the listener, and may prove all the more ominous. We get the feeling that the "I" is telling us his personal history, yet one that we share. It is almost as if Brown is recounting a narrative we can't quite see—storying—and we'd be literally right: the album *The Payback* was originally meant as a Blaxploitation soundtrack. But even as he was making it, the film—like *Superfly* or *Black Caesar* or *Trouble Man*—must have paled beside the depths of the sonic shadow book the musicians made. The music was less a score than a reckoning far more sophisticated than the films ever could be.

Soon, not just his beats, but James Brown's own contradictions would power hip-hop, his moan made abstract. Too soon for some, DJs and MCs would craft soundtracks to movies only they could see—some filled with horror, others comedy, others gangsters or love or exploitation or even memories of other movies—turning Brown into a Black Godfather. Soon not just his music but Brown's declarations of independence and his dance moves would become breaks to move a crowd, b-boys and b-girls spinning like his records. He on his feet, they on their backs. Brown's work wouldn't just go international but intergalactic; soon Papa's Mess would mean not just a mess of greens but Cosmic Slop.

For some, this lack of boundaries seemed freeing, for others horrifying—more to the point might be an acknowledgment that these boundaries were artificial in the first place. The boundary between black influence and American culture was thin at best—and imposed and segregated at worst. Post-soul as a term describes these new cultural forms, applying as well to the range of responses to that change and conducting a remapping that is part of the storied African American tradition.

Much as with the term *postfeminism,*[2] I fear that post-soul could start to be seen, fallaciously, as antisoul. (At a hip-hop summit—a post-soul event if ever there was one—aired on television, an NAACP youth organizer used *post-soul* in exactly this way, indicating that soul, along with church and heart, has been lost.) This wasn't the point, I take it, when George coined *post-soul* to describe the shift in black and popular culture, which he dates from the release of filmmaker Melvin Van Peebles's *Sweet Sweetback's Baadasssss Song* (1971). If anything, given George's cultural reference to the start of political, if confused, black guerrilla cinema (and not simply the start of the often-cynical Blaxploitation that followed), post-soul is meant to underscore the complexities of independence and popularity that started by the early 1970s.

But I also understand how some might not want soul to be over in any sense. Witness Thomas Sayers Ellis's discussion of soul and every other "post" out there:

> Somebody said the other day that so-and-so was a post-language writer. Like they stopped writing or something. Like all the deconstructionists, after deconstruction, they wrote memoirs. "I think it's time to talk about me now." All the black people are talking about post-soul. I don't want post anything. I don't want to be post-anything.[3]

Sayers, I think, is right here in his impulse—certainly I can relate to it, as I feel much the same way about the term *post-black*[4] that often floats around (and has resurfaced again after Obama's "painting the White House black"). Blackness is not something I wish to be beyond or past; it is still ever-present and remains unavoidable, and more important, pleasurable. More than post-blackness, I am concerned with pre-blackness—what made and makes up blackness.

By using the term post-soul I mean to indicate the many changes that have occurred in black culture since the 1960s—many of them because of the 1960s—indicated by the full range of black music in the Americas, from funk to hip-hop, from disco to Fishbone, from reggae to folk. But this shift is not just musical but social, as indicated by Hendrix's desire for freedom onstage and off-. But there was a more nefarious feeling: the King of Love was dead; Sam Cooke, one-time sacred singer, inventor of soul, would be shot dead too, shot near-naked in a fleabag motel after fighting with a prostitute. Did soul music's contradictions, which helped power it, now threaten to overpower it? Certainly for soul, asserting "this is my country," was no longer quite enough: "Curtis Mayfield, who had once sung 'Keep on Pushing' for Martin Luther King Jr. and other freedom marchers, now warned of the 'Pusherman.'"[5] Hendrix's very history with the circuit indicates that post-soul is a mood and a moment, as well as a music.

Post-soul well knows black is not just a color or a state of mind but also a state of being; and that black art is whatever art is made by black folks. We should not want to place any limitations on such an aesthetic, whether using white or black standards. After all, it was strictures on what black folks could write about, or how, that Black Arts sought to overturn, and did, following the example of the Harlem Renaissance—but after discarding limitations on what black art can be, it proves difficult, however well meaning, to impose new, albeit "blacker," ones. Once achieved, freedom is difficult to relinquish.

So, post-soul it is. It's our Punky Reggae Party, and we can define how we want to.

Is post-soul a feeling too? For good or bad, post-soul is filled with nostalgia—doubled even from the radical nostalgia we see in soul's origins. As with questions of black vernacular, a comparison with Irish literature and language may help us understand how, as Seamus Deane's *Strange Country* discusses, nostalgia and its accompanying ruin can be rather intoxicating:

> [F]rom an Irish point of view, the renovation of tradition
> remained more closely attached to the notion that the renova-
> tion could only be desired, the more so because there was no
> state, no social or political apparatus to support it. It was a
> romanticism that needed the spectacle of ruin to stimulate it
> to an imaginative intensity that would be the more impressive
> precisely because it derived from a history that had been lost,
> displaced, a history that had no narrative but the narrative of
> nostalgia. Nostalgia was the dynamic that impelled the search
> for the future.
>
>   . . . It is not merely a nostalgic lament for the traditional
> pieties and the values that they produce. It is a lament for
> an idea of the traditional in which nostalgia is a constitutive
> element. This is a social and political vision that has potency
> precisely because it is a lost cause; lostness is central to its
> meaning, not just an emotive aspect of its appeal.[6]

And if soul music meant a kind of secular spiritualism, an earthy romanticism, a powerful, personal postmodernism, part of that romance was its distance from the Beloved. Quite often, in soul music this Beloved was America. Why you wanna make me feel so bad?

In post-soul, the Beloved became soul itself. The country, not to mention the countryside, that African America had long remapped, the nascent Black American Nation, after 1968 seemed further away than ever—the freedom that had long seemed achievable grew all the more nostalgic for having been nearly achieved. Post-soul is concerned with freedom all the more exactly because it proved so fleeting.

> We were born insurance salesmen and secretaries,
> Housewives and short order cooks,
> Stockroom boys and repairmen,
> And it wouldn't be a bad life, they promised,
> In a tone of voice that would force some of us
> To reach in self-defense for wigs,
> Lipstick,
>
> Sequins.[7]

(CORNELIUS EADY, "THE SUPREMES")

Whatever we call it, the post-soul era is certainly obsessed with its soul origins. Not just soul but post-soul is engaged in nostalgia for a simpler time that wasn't all that simple. But when post-soul looks romantically to soul's unity, it isn't wishful thinking but forethought, a yearning to provide a way back to a bright future—which is to say a black one. It is a second sight blinded by the light. No wonder some of us reach "for wigs, / Lipstick, // Sequins": it's a way, before bling, of both hiding and being seen.

In post-soul, the future is here and it ain't exactly what we was promised. To quote Rita Dove:

> Sometimes
>
> a word is found so right it trembles
> at the slightest explanation. You start out with one thing, end

up with another, and nothing's
like it used to be, not even the future.[8]

IN THE WHOLE

After Black Arts' crucial emphasis on purging of seemingly European
forms in literature—and celebration of black ones—not only could black
forms be sought out, but rather ironically, white forms, newly "freed,"
could now be taken back by black writers as needed. In other words,
writing in a seemingly "white" form, while discouraged in some quarters, in others could prove a form, as it were, of rebellion. For what, after
all, in a world of rediscovered black identity, was a whites-only form?

There were plenty of powerful black artists maligned by the Black
Arts movement for being retrograde (such as Robert Hayden) or made
marginal by the movement, often for violating sexual taboos (such as
Audre Lorde) or both (James Baldwin), all of whom had powerful roles
in creating a broad, black aesthetic that represents the range of attitudes
and visions found in black culture.

For many, the revolution worked from within, countering Lorde's
declaration that "the master's tools will never dismantle the master's
house."[9] We are in the presence of demolishing walls, boundaries, the
whole structure of power; we need not simply march on Washington,
D.C., but also on Washington State (right next to Bob Kaufman's
"Oregon"); we may find there, again, the example of Jimi Hendrix, Seattle
native, former parachutist, kissing the sky. Such sorties often meant the
destruction not just of the master's house but of the tools—or musical
instruments—in question. Or crafting a new anthem out of an old one.

We might also look toward Melvin Van Peebles's musical cum
novel—we could just call it a counterfeit—called *Ain't Supposed to Die
a Natural Death* (1973). The play in fact opens with "The Star-Spangled
Banner"; in the book version, Van Peebles's stage directions riff off the
anthem in a way that may be the reverbalization of Hendrix's instrumentation, Van Peebles's strung-along syntax and sometime lack of
punctuation a kind of verbal feedback:

> [T]he national anthem is perfect because it lays out to people
> where their heads are at nationwise, at least where they want
> other folks to think their heads are—besides, when the old

notes start and the old knees start stiffening in a reflex action, folks get to remember how conditioned they are, maybe
even start wondering about what else they are conditioned to
besides the Star Spangled Banner. The song is played straight,
not jazzed up or solemned down, and the house lights stay
up full so folks can make their statement and be seen and dig
other people making theirs. Decisions, decisions, decisions.
Does standing mean you want crackers on the Supreme Court?
Does it mean you have forgotten the Vietnam casualty lists,
or does it mean you are remembering the guys who got it at
the Alamo or the Battle of the Bulge? . . . Does sitting mean
praising Malcolm . . . does it mean betraying the Kennedys . . .
is it showing solidarity with Kent State or is it showing solidarity with Fred Hampton? . . . What means what? . . . Stand? . . .
Sit? . . . Bob up and down? . . . Go blind? . . . Stoop? . . . Shit? . . .
The stage doesn't have curtains and the set hulks there, a multi-
leveled composite of all the urban black reservations. It is
scarred and comic, dangerous and tender, with things blending
and shifting back and forth in an instant the way they do in
reality, there's a car carcass and there are light bulbs, lampposts,
signs, dark rooms, stoops, steps, corners, concrete crotches,
whiskey bars and prison bars. It's that place black folks mean
when they talk about the Block.[10]

The Block is dominated by what Van Peebles calls a "perch": "like the
platform politicians make promises from or the thing they spot whales
from in the movies on Saturdays or hang patriots from on late late
shows or string gunslingers or niggers from. Breen ribbons hang down
from over the railing of the perch like some immense vine trailing and
spreading over the front of the set and into the street below. The ribbons
give the set the air of a prison, or a gigantic present." The "gigantic present" is also the ever-present expressed in both Hendrix's rendering and
in Van Peebles's prose prologue, the stoop both a place and an action
beneath the "perch" of belief—a place of American dreams and African
American reality, "scarred and comic, dangerous and tender" as the
blues. The Block becomes both "black urban reservation"—a kind of
twisted reality—and the kind of Elsewhere the slaves dreamed of. Van
Peebles's is the kind of yearning also expressed in Hendrix's vision,

which isn't so much political as questioning ("What means what? . . . Stand? . . . Sit?") and questing. *We Gotta Live Together.*

The number of innovations found in Hendrix is indicative of his strong place in the storying tradition. These include feedback and any number of the other techniques guitarist and writer John Perry catalogs in his informative study *Electric Ladyland*—including "de-tuning" (an old R & B guitar trick) and "associative" guitar playing where "he [Hendrix] used his guitar to imitate everyday sounds (from non-musical sources) heard around him," evoking everything from a "convincing seascape" to babies' crying to even talking. In Hendrix's electrified hands, the guitar itself became a microphone, and, as bebop before did, used "disc-tortions" as a means to music.

What's more, Hendrix, starting with the self-produced *Ladyland* in 1968, viewed the studio as a large-scale instrument, and the new 12-track technology as a way of expression akin to his feedback; on the album, Hendrix matched his polyphonic guitar playing with a multi-tudes of tracks, using 12-tracks I would argue much as the blues art-ists had used 12-bars before. "To an extent never before possible, the mixing desk could now be played almost like an instrument—and Jimi wanted to get his hands on the faders."[11] Sounds like the first hip-hop artist to me.

But we do not need hip-hop's own innovations, or to even know all his technical innovations, to hear the future in Hendrix's "Star-Spangled Banner." We could also just listen to Gaye's soul rendition of the an-them at the 1983 NBA All-Star Game to hear post-soul at work, and the linked ways in which bending notes and making the possible impossible has long been part of the fabric, and fabrication, of black expression.

Other writers of course, through innovation and free expression of the kind demanded by the Black Arts (but not always put into practice by its proponents), were also pushing the envelope of what was acceptable and changing our notions of literature and Americanness. In fiction, Clarence Major, Gayl Jones, John Edgar Wideman, and Ishmael Reed, and in poetry Audre Lorde, Michael S. Harper, Jay Wright, and Sherley Anne Williams, to name a few, wrote with a new vigor, an eye to his-tory and interrelations—whether between black and white (Harper), black and Indian and Latin and white (Wright), or between black and woman and lesbian (Lorde). It is oversimplifying to say these writers sought to write themselves into the American; to do so denies a larger point of this study, namely, recognizing the role of blackness in the making of Americans. As Jay Wright indicates, both in his speaking of his poetic project and in his poetry's illuminating the connections between cultures in the Americas, he's not so much weaving these elements together as uncovering the weave that already exists.

In its early brilliance and sustained shine, the fiction of Toni Morrison also recognized this blending of boundaries, looking at connections between and within black people, particularly communities. You could say the era of social protest and critique of society gave way in literature to considering and creating communities—it is through such writers and editors as Morrison that this became possible and necessary.

But what these diverse writers have in common is the ways they saw and see blackness as a given, both as a subject matter and a subjectivity. The what and how any such writer would choose to write, from epic to blues to both, are not so obvious. Or proscribed.

It is here that the post-soul artist enters, with the whole of history not streaming like an angel with debris at its back but as a devil's music that moves you, made up of a million sounds and temptations—but that don't mean you can't come to church the next day and sing of redemption. Post-soul culture is exactly this tension between sacred and secular, between past and future, between degradation and redemption—realizing degradation can be just what leads to redemption. Or, remapping the world in your own image. To be a black artist today is to stand at the crossroads of culture at which the black artist bargains, trades, borrows, makes, steals, and stories in a world of his or her own making—and naming.

WE NEED THE FUNK

Yet we must never fail to recognize that the blending of sources to create black style makes it neither less black—just think of that black form, rock and roll—nor less American. Though of course it is exactly this Americanness, seen as synonymous with whiteness, that Black Arts writers such as Larry Neal, sought to eliminate. We can see why, given the times and their terror; but we must also admit, as a friend of mine wisely pointed out, the desire to escape America is as American as you can get. And if exile is the dominant mode of postmodernism, particularly self-exile, then this Black Arts desire to de-Americanize harks back to an earlier, modern, and dare I say American one.

Black artists respond to the post-soul shift—one we could call a late stage of postmodernism—in a variety of ways. In the case of Amiri Baraka this meant moving from a critical yet relatively mild discussion of popular culture nostalgia (in "Memory of Radio") to the rejection and exploration of popular culture stereotype (in "A Poem for Willie Best") to praising John Coltrane's "murdering of the popular," which to him meant "white" forms. Extremely popular himself, Baraka would go on to recently note the distinction between the popular and the commercial, a useful distinction.

The post-soul black writer realizes that so-called popular culture had harmed the black body and mind and culture. For the black artist the popular has remained both a dream and a nightmare, a thing to aspire to and to rebel against—at least since Paul Laurence Dunbar. While also realizing that just as often as pop culture takes black folks for granted, post-soul saw the ways American popular culture takes them as inspiration and appropriation—whether in white "covers" or white stereotypes of black people—noting that the two were connected. Black popular culture sustained black folks even while some sought to dismantle it. *They don't know like I know.* This full, free range of blackness we can see post-soul writers sharing with the music around them—namely, funk, fusion, and free jazz.

This could be one way of reading Morrison's *The Bluest Eye* (1970), a groundbreaking work that traces the difficulties of black life in a world bound by the white popular image, whether Shirley Temple or "Dick and Jane," viewing both as primers on behavior, beauty, and the undesirability of blackness. But Morrison goes further, helping us see how blackness was often undesired *even by black folks,* showing us both the black body and the black community in pain. Community can be complicated, and in the book's best parts, Morrison evokes the shame of a past that leads to present and future pain.

Without repeating Morrison's many achievements here, let's consider one aspect of her work: *funk.* The nature of funk in Morrison is eloquently discussed by Susan Willis in *Specifying,* who sees it as a celebration of the black and female body, often by contrasting "stifled womanhood with girlhood sensuality." The discomfort one character in *Bluest Eye* expresses about "funk" is a sign of her limited self-acceptance, related in this case to bourgeois pretensions or strivings; in contrast, the narrator's pleasure in her own body is a sign of her self-satisfaction. Willis sums up: "'Funk' is really nothing more than the intrusion of the past into the present. It is most oppositional when it juxtaposes a not-so-distant social mode to those evolved under bourgeois society."[12]

What for Willis may mean Morrison's use of magical realism, I see instead the kind of familiar, fierce nostalgia that surrounds funk music, juxtaposing a folkloric blues past with its futuristic strivings and instrumentation. Just as the blues inform her title, Morrison's *Bluest Eye* provides a useful definition of funk, if only by defining what it's not; the novel describes the strivings of certain kind of bourgeois, or bougie-pretending, women who "straighten their hair with Dixie peach, and part it on the side":

> They go to land-grant colleges, normal schools, and learn how to do the white man's work with refinement. . . . Here they learn the rest of the lesson begun in those soft houses with porch swings and pots of bleeding heart: how to behave. The careful development of thrift, patience, high morals, and good manners. In short, how to get rid of the funkiness. The dreadful funkiness of passion, the funkiness of nature, the funkiness of the wide range of human emotions.
>
> Wherever it erupts, this Funk, they wipe it away; where it crusts, they dissolve it; wherever it drips, flowers, or clings, they find it and fight it until it dies. They fight this battle all the way to the grave. The laugh that is a little too loud; the enunciation a little too round; the gesture a little too generous. They hold their behind in for fear of a sway too free; when they wear lipstick, they never cover the entire mouth for fear of lips too thick, and they worry, worry, worry about the edges of their hair.[13]

The bourgeois or striver's fear of funk—of the black self and its physicality—is not shared by the book's protagonist, who loves her body and her sister's and mother's awareness of it, even if such awareness at times is harsh. Her celebration of her own funk is both natural for a little kid—try and get one to bathe after a certain age—but also, in Morrison's work, a sense of being comfortable in a black, emergent self.

For Morrison, this "dreadful funkiness" contrasts both with bourgeois propriety and with a deadly wish for whitened self.

The Negress, the Lady, "the poor girl," black glamour, even womanism: all are an attempt to move beyond stereotype, strategies of resistance to gender oppression. Related to other outlaw identities, these strategies—often female, sometimes gay male or "queer"—rework what Farah Jasmine Griffin calls "the politics of respectability" in a way similarly exploded in *The Bluest Eye*. Funk goes even further, a fourth world and term that plays with both respectability and being outré, if only by reveling in the body and black being. Funk also can be added to most anything, from food to feeling. No wonder that, where I'm from, good cooking's called "putting your foot in it"—a sign of funk's appeal and physical nature.

Let's go on down the road a bit farther, however, and tie Morrison's use of funk to the contemporary rise of *funk music*. Generous, swaying, lipstuck, and loud, this funk, this electrified gospel, this amping up of the blues, relies on several techniques that serve as a vital model for the post-soul era's many triumphs. You can hear these in the difference between the Jimi Hendrix Experience and his Band of Gypsys. Such funk, the past intruding on the present, provides an apt metaphor for the post-soul artist's stance.

HEAVENLY BODIES

If soul is to gospel music what the blues are to the spirituals, then funk concerns itself with what I call the *holy body*. This is both the body politick ("One Nation Under a Groove") and the physical body (often booty) celebrated, under God or the Groove, in Blackness we trust. The music, like the secular musics before it, is meant to make us move: *funk,* named for the "stank" of dance and sex and work, emphasizes the moment's journey beyond even the body, a physicality that mirrors spiritual motion. *I woke up—in a cold sweat.* Often the word *funk* is a code, not just for fun but also for the more impolite "fuck"—after all, you can say funk on the radio, where it serves as double agent. Recall too that a funk is another, Africanized word for the mood we call having the blues.

In funk the physical makes the spiritual possible. What makes funk music unique is that the connection found in gospel, for instance, is all the more explicit than in the other musics that have gone before it; the sexuality double-entendred in the blues is taken further too. The "holy body" leads us, as the Bar-Kays' song has it, to "The Holy Ghost"—though funk is in itself enough. Just take James Brown's "Sex Machine," which started this whole funky mess through a celebration of the presumptive black body and its power. In funk the body itself is a prayer.

This body is often female—and not just on the covers of Ohio Players' albums, their gatefolds more like centerfolds—but also fulfilling of the womanism of Alice Walker and others, with its recognition of black female power and the limits of male-based (black, as well as white) traditions. Such fulfillment finds renewed emphasis on the body—even as a site of renewal—reclaiming a black female self and even ancestry. As with Zora Neale Hurston's "How It Feels to Be Colored Me," funk recognizes the permutations of the black self, which did not always "feel colored at all."

Despite its favorite hairstyles, funk ain't always natural. For funk—which Cornel West interestingly refers to as "technofunk"—was always aware of the artificiality of such things as voice. Or at least, in its use of synthesized voices and sounds, emphasized that even voice is distorted. In this it is reminiscent of Hughes's attempt in *Montage of a Dream Deferred* to examine the "disc-tortions" of bebop and as he put it, a "community in transition"; funk realizes that the community might be, if not artificial, then constantly constructed, reconstructed, and taken apart. And that, depending on our stance, this reconstituting community is liberating or threatening. Or both.

Think of Stevie Wonder's "Ghetto Paradise" or "Living for the City,"[14] which both consider the black body in relation to place and community in a way fresh, new, and vital. Or Richard Pryor's recasting of "Living for the City" by presenting it as a preacher's sermon, the ultimate story. All are efforts to negotiate the city's physical life, and its spiritual death for the black individual and even community. This is funk's specific cultural strength and may be distinguished from soul's emphasis on the "I"—or on an "I" speaking to the other (usually absent) half of a romantic "we." (Though, as we've seen, this "we" often resonates with a larger social desire, either for "respect" or a world made wonderful.) While desire is discussed in funk, for the most part it is physical in its start and often ends with a general "we," a call out to the crowd, representing funk's orgiastic sense of community. *We want the funk.*

Just as often, this desire approaches wordlessness in a way evolved from jazz, whether in an evocation of physicality (think P-Funk's nasty/natty instrumental "Nappy Dugout") or a seemingly simple, mostly instrumental evocation of communal nostalgia (*Pass the peas like they used to say,* reminiscent of nothing so much as Dizzy Gillespie's "Salt Peanuts"). The instrumentation of funk is choral, plural, African; the conga drum becomes an important part of the music. Even the large size of the funk band (not to mention the ubiquitous white guy in an afro) suggests a sense of community, a striving toward a sense of plenty.

COSMIC SLOP

We could see the funk of our post-soul era as simply a return to community, were it not for its need for the mothership—and an escape. In the hands of such practitioners and innovators as Parliament-Funkadelic, funk represents another form of gospel transcendence, "the creative encounter of the Afro-American spiritual-blues impulse with highly sophisticated technological instruments, strategies and effects. Parliament invited its listeners, especially the dwellers of 'Chocolate cities' and to a lesser extent those in the 'Vanilla suburbs,' to enter the 'Fourth World,' the world of black funk and star wars, of black orality, bodily sensuality, technical virtuosity and electronic adroitness."[15] The Elsewhere funk sought was a space as outer as it was inner.

Artist Adrian Piper, who conducted a series of fascinating performances called *Funk Lessons* in the early 1980s, calls this funk's "desire for self-transcendence: to 'become one' with the music, one's lover, other people, the universe."[16] Much like the notion of plenty performed in bebop, outer space represents a frontier beyond the West, the collapsing of the holy body into black wholes. Outer space has been seized on as beneficent by the post-soul artist in what's lately called Afrofuturism—not to mention by the black avant-garde, from Sun Ra to Bomkauf to P-Funk, who reached the heavens first. And who declared not exile in the Americas but a home in the heavens.

But we also may see in funk a broader notion of *space*—what critic Fredric Jameson views as one of the postmodern era's dominant features. Just as Jameson sees space as taking over from a previous paradigm of time, let's stick with space here too—but we need not see it as simply a negative aspect of late capitalism. For the black artist, from Hendrix to OutKast, painter David Huffman to poet Tracy K. Smith, sees *space* in all senses not so much as negative as negative capability—a new resource to be played with. Such play is freeing, fun, funky, and sees any artificiality of voice not so much as cold or technical as technological—it is certainly not some postmodern simulacrum or degraded pastiche (what Jameson calls a "blank parody"). Our awareness of the counterfeit tradition can provide a useful way for discussing such artifice—and provide a sense of space—within a post-soul paradigm.

It is within this paradigm we may consider Robert Hayden's *American Journal*. After the modernist mastery of "The Middle Passage," Hayden's great late book embodies a range of "blacknesses," dealing with everything from poems in the voice of Phillis Wheatley to the voice of Matthew Henson, the first person, black or white, to reach the North Pole. The sense of avant-garde blackness, of discovery, of other cultures—in Henson's case, Eskimo or Inuit—of New Norths and even of other tongues other than "American," dominates the post-soul era. The book ends with the title poem "[American Journal]" in which a space alien discusses his estrangement from, yet love of, this country and "this baffling / multi people   extremes and variegations   their / noise   restlessness their almost frightening / energy" in a report back home. It is we earthlings who are alien, strange—the outer space visitor here, the ultimate exile, provides both a sign of race and something far beyond it. It is American talk that he must master, must understand, in order to not give himself away:

> must be more careful   item   learn to use okay
> their pass word   okay[17]

which, some say, is an African word.

This fuller sense of storying may be easily contrasted with one found in white culture's metaphors of space as negative blackness, as mere absence. Think of Stanley Kubrick's *2001,* in which space is rebirth, eventually, but along the way necessitates a kind of havoc in the process of evolution—caused by a black monolith—just as it does in the "dawn of man" at the film's start. Or, more sharply, space is the troubled realm of David Bowie's brilliant "Space Oddity," with Major Tom's trip to outer space as a metaphor for his alienation from family and "ground control." *You're feeling very strange:* such strangeness Bowie would take further in the figure of Ziggy Stardust, his onstage, extraterrestrial, androgynous persona, and his band the Spiders of Mars. *Ziggy played guitar,* embodying a kind of "beyond" that is beyond gender and even self. Bowie's sophisticated sense of persona—the kind that eventually erased even itself, announcing as he did that he would no longer perform (but like a prizefighter, unable to remain outside the ring)—stands in stark contrast to a notion of performance or art as "natural" and of the self.

This strangeness it seems was also black, plastic soul using soul's idioms but not its yearning. Maybe white folks are post-soul too? Certainly the culture at large experienced great changes, traveling beyond even the postmodern that Fiedler had helped name: "The passage into Indian Territory, the flight into Outer Space, the ecstatic release into the fantasy world of the orgy: all these are analogues for what has traditionally been described as a Journey or Pilgrimage (recently we have been more likely to say 'Trip' without altering the significance) toward a transcendent goal, a moment of Vision."[18] As Fiedler goes on to tell us, the basic images of "Pop forms like the western, Science Fiction and Pornography"—the latter two at least at play in Bowie's stage show—"suggest mythological as well as political or metapolitical meanings." The pop journey is the contemporary version of a religious pilgrimage—witnessed in the case of glam-era Bowie or P-Funk by their cult followings.

We can also look to Elton John, Bowie's poppier counterpart and contemporary, for such transcendent uses of space. Both were engaged in a theater of pop culture—each costumed and "outrageous," one ambisexual as Ziggy, the other asexual, dressed as Donald Duck—but both managing spectacle tied in some way to sexuality or its absence as a kind of chaotic freedom. (Or a Philadelphia one.) Elton John, even in his more recent, tamer, knighted (and benighted) persona, still is a persona and a stage name that share some strategies with funk.

And where Elton John may not always reach the heights of "art" that Bowie does, that also is the profound pleasure of his music. One tires of art, particularly artists—sometimes you want an old-fashioned or new-fangled show. If John, more than Bowie, sat at the center of the so-called mainstream culture, what's surprising looking at, say, "Rocket Man" are its similarities with Bowie's "Space Oddity." Even John's subtitle—"(I Think It's Going to Be a Long Long Time)"—is indicative of the alienation and separation space means for the eponymous, anonymous speaker. He'll miss his family, he'll miss his wife—he's also not "the man they think I am at home," space throwing his identity in doubt, as well as of that earthbound home. For if home don't get us, who and where does?

Of course, there is a clever gay subtext here, one it could be said Elton John played out in his personal life, toying with straight married life, then leaving that "home." (Unlike in the song, in real life the wife was presumably not missed.) But home is something larger than the normative, straight white world, as African Americans in their exile well knew—it wasn't just society that was destabilized by the 1960s but an entire planet that seemed perched on the edge of destruction. Ours was a world seeing itself for the first time—only with the rocket men of the Apollo missions did we first glimpse earth as the blue-green globe we now cannot imagine any other way. Along with such knowledge came a sense of us humans as space oddities, improbably alone in a universe, or a crowd, or a crowded universe.

For the practitioners of post-soul, space generally is not a place to feel "odd" or alienated—even if it is a place, as in Bowie's fertile imagination, to free oneself or one's persona from these feelings. In its black conception, from Sun Ra to P-Funk, ESG to Kanye West, space represents both a start and an end:

> I've been working this graveshift
> And I ain't made shit
> I wish I could buy me a spaceship
> And fly . . . past the sky

The Fourth World. Freedom. New North. The Ultimate Elsewhere. *Mother Earth is pregnant for the third time.*

For Parliament-Funkadelic, space is a place of play and of simultaneous origin and destination. Space isn't, like it becomes for Bowie's Major Tom, the place where he becomes denatured—*Ashes to ashes, funk to funky / We know Major Tom's a junkie*—starting the descent to an all-time low. For the "Afronaut," outer space (or its companion, underwater) becomes a kind of home, not this planet darker than blue. Like Negro heaven before it, the blackness of space, its vastness and unexplored quality, represents a powerful and intuitive critique of the earthbound, blues-based lives we live. Not to mention "Whitey on the Moon."

At the age of five, I was abducted by aliens, starts P-Funk's "Electric Spanking of War Babies" in a dialogue, Socratic of sorts, between an artificially low and high (and high-pitched) voice. Falsetto can be a weapon: this high voice—far beyond even falsetto—is the one that in the P-Funk pantheon aligns with the no-good "Sir Nose D'Void offunk"; the deep one tells us that he has long since been programmed to transmit the message, *When you learn to dance / You won't forget it.* This dance is both earthbound and beyond—as the chorus has it, *You can walk a mile, in my shoes / But you can't dance a step in my feet.* The War Babies are the Vietnam-era children, both the boomers and the being-born Gen Xers; they are the community around us, but also those who can walk a mile, or shoot the moon, yet can't dance a step in our feet. *Here's our chance to dance our way out of our constrictions.* We got a lot more dancing to do.

Space, that endless series of speculations and origins—of rebirths and electric spankings—is here not so much a metaphor as it is a series of fragmented selves, a place of possibilities and debris and explorations and atmosphere.[19] "A moment of Vision." This is why we can say that the dominant mode of this post-soul era is *fragment:* pieces that don't so much stand in for others (as in postmodern metonymy), or as mere metaphor (as in modern blues and Waste Lands), but that serve as a series of synonyms, equivalences as a form of equality.

In a post-soul world, the pieces may not unite, and may not need to—at least yet—but we can dance under the flag of funk, under the groove, united for now, finding not so much ideology as funkology, a place where biology and spirituality meet. Like in *Star Trek,* the search is all. This ain't "Four Quartets" but "Cosmic Slop," the holy body seeking both praise and defiance, as the song has it, in a world that literally prostitutes the singer's mother, that also praises the mess we're in and her fortitude, her sheer survival, her calling out:

> Father, Father, it's for the kids
> Each and every thing I did

Please don't judge me too strong
Lord knows I meant no wrong.

THESE ARE THE BREAKS

Both jazz and hip-hop seek the song within the song. That is, they often take older songs—and indeed, song itself—and bend, stretch, and riff it till it almost rips at the seams. In jazz, however free, the desire is to see how far the song can go without breaking; in hip-hop, the wish is to find the breaks, to break on it, to divide and conquer and reconfigure. In our own image.

It don't take a historian to know that both jazz and hip-hop take their impulses from the blues, which takes its name in part from the blue notes, those blurred scales in the music. Turn the blues from the voice into an instrument, and from the instrument into a recording that you then manipulate with your hands, and you can see the evolution from blue note to Blue Note to funk to hip-hop antidote.

When jazz bends the song, making instruments sing and singers sound like horns, the sound is human—if at times superhuman. High Cs. In free jazz, or late Coltrane, the sound is divine—or seeks to be. This is done by parsing the place where harmony and cacophony co-exist, a place inner but perhaps stellar, less of nature than of all existence itself. Divinity is integral to the spirituals, they are not songs of doubt; on John Coltrane's *A Love Supreme* the spirituality is one of seeking and sometimes, even if for only a moment, finding. Both jazz and the spirituals record struggle, as found in their tone. But beyond the wondrous chant of *a love supreme, a love supreme* that returns Coltrane's music to the status of hymn, the most poignant part of his masterpiece is the notes he can't quite hit—the moments where human yearning, the blues' consolation, and the future's uncertainty meet, transcendently, in Trane's horn. The farthest reaches—as if Trane is trying to transcend the notes themselves.

Inner space seeks an inner form innate in all things, simultaneously atomic and celestial.

"Who stole the soul?" asked Public Enemy in a song from 1990, a rhetorical question, but also one answered quite differently over the years—in

the nineteenth century, the answer might best be "No one," because no one could touch the slave whose soul was satisfied. "I keep a mind just for me": satisfaction a form of rebellion in and of itself. In the twenty-first century, when P.E. asks "How Do you Sell Soul to a Soulless People Who Sold their Soul," the best answer may be another question: who is prepared to steal it back? *Who's gonna save my soul now?*

Here is where *storying* comes in—for there is a crucial way in which remaking a song is both avant-garde and traditional, is based both on current technology and on ancient impulse. Today's ease of sampling music, hijacking beats, biting—for even in hip-hop, especially in hip-hop, there are standards of originality—does not mean that remaking hasn't been a constant figure of culture for centuries. And of course, the story of the twentieth century in music isn't just the color line but the dotted line and the bottom one. The large-scale theft of African American music, the cover song, should prove far more troubling than a kid in his basement somewhere making it new, mixing the Beatles with Jay-Z. Or, as Eady reminds us in the epigraphs to his selected poems, James Brown's directive "Make it funky" proves just as important as Pound's dictum "Make it new" to the post-soul artist—and you find your funk wherever you can. This is integral to the hip-hop aesthetic.

One of the most important things to remember is that, especially early on, hip-hop found its funk in the least likely places. Hell, if a cow-bell can become funky—or if its funk can be recognized and recorded—why not Billy Joel? *Don't go changing to try and please me.* Elton John already was kinda funky, a fact recognized (that word again) by his having hits on the black charts back when they were called "R & B/Soul"—an achievement that meant much to him, as did his appearance on Soul Train, where he performed "Benny and the Jets." *It ain't easy.*

But you haven't lived till you've heard Biz Markie cover "Benny and the Jets" as I did in the 40 Watt Club in Athens, Georgia (he was perhaps persuaded by our screaming for it at the end of every other song). Those of you not lucky enough to hear him live can still enjoy it off the Beastie Boys collection *The Sounds of Science,* where it's one of my favorite things: not only does Biz make the music with his mouth, he makes an art of *not* being able to sing; when he actually gets to the verses, he mumbles-sings them so that not only is it a perfect pastiche of how Elton John sang it originally but also a re-creation of *how we heard the original.* That is, when Elton first belted them, you couldn't quite make out the words, and Biz Markie parrots, parodies, *stories* this. Both funny and triumphant, the now-new song dares you not to sing along. Or to dance.

Can't we think and dance at the same time?

All good music, black music, insists upon this double duty, means to make you move, whether in your church pew or the front row, in the aisles or the juke joint's tore-up dance floor. Even if now regarded from the safety of a classroom or car, our music originally was dangerous in this way—after all, slavery banned not just drums but also dancing, defined as crossing the feet. Putting off for a moment the terrifying thought of hip-hop being played only in a classroom a hundred years from now and young black students feeling as distant from it as they sometimes do from the blues, hip-hop at its zenith insists on thinking and dancing simultaneously. In fact, it sees them as synonymous.

The play in hip-hop suggests not only the power of words but their powerlessness. Just as the music of jazz flirts with silence—for in an improvisatory (and storying) art, reaching for the next note to find only silence is always the risk—hip-hop also befriends silence. It does so mostly by battling silence at every turn.

Case in point: the reason for the proliferation of sketches (or intros and outros) on hip-hop albums is both to unify them (say, under a theme of "Miseducation" or being "AmeriKKKa's most wanted") and to make sure there are no gaps at all. Following in the footsteps of De La Soul's debut, these bits are both interruption and continuation, often at odds with the actual songs—take Common's emotional love song that's followed by a skit parodying his being praised by a female fan for his righteousness, when shortly after, an aside suggests he's literally a pimp! If at times less dramatically, the breaks in hip-hop are always played with and filled in.

The unifying impulse in hip-hop doesn't stop there. While funk celebrates the holy body, at its best hip-hop celebrates the whole being, body and mind. *Body and Soul.* At its worst, which might as well be now, these two are as divided as ever—exploiting its unique potential for embodiment by being merely bawdy. *My Neck, My Back.* While sometimes enjoyable, such crass sexuality is not ultimately as pleasurable as the depths or brassy doublings of meaning in Bessie Smith or any other rounder. Beats are bought not made—if souls are not sold, soul music might be. Nothing wrong with getting busy—and one can see the impulses in accepting the bawdy over the body, but also the all-too-real downfall. Sometimes literally, in the case of booty-shaking music videos. Who's going to step up and unify us, to gather us together under one banner for the sake of the Party?

PARTY FOR YOUR RIGHT TO FIGHT

The Party I mean is not a political one—though in this way, it is. This Party is no mere panacea, but is filled with possibility. Just ask those who made hip-hop in the South Bronx; or Lester Bangs, whose manifesto-like essay "James Taylor Marked for Death" (1971) is one long riff about the Party:

> The Party is one answer to how to manage leisure in a society cannibalized by it, but it's not bread and circuses either because you can't co-opt jive because jive is the true folk music that liberals can never appropriate or master and only an urban aborigine will understand. And far from being anti-intellectual, the Party is *a*-intellectual; it doesn't make any promises or ask for any field workers. As an answer to the kind of mysteries of life it's a Bronx cheer, and not a dada one either but the kind your uncle Louie used to razz the quarterback with from behind a Schlitz on a Saturday afternoon, but as a *way of life* it's a humdinger.[20]

So the Party is in the end political; a vote for it is a vote for a way of life, and even for Life itself. *The one thing that can solve our problems is dancing*, to quote James Brown.

And every few years, let's call it four, someone comes along promising to make us whole. Lauryn Hill, Tricky, Dave Chappelle, OutKast: these are only some of the elect whose abilities to make us move and to move us will not let us forget them, despite their rejecting, in whole or in part, their medium. They might think they are rejecting the media, but it is the audience they turn from—and their role as *mediums* for our feelings. A more Romantic view might say that it is the pressure to unify that drives these groups apart—or their own selves. Lauryn Hill, for one, was for years as missing as the roll call that starts her first solo album.

OutKast still holds out the most promise, despite Andre 3000 changing his name back to Benjamin and apparently preferring acting to performing; he has decided as of this writing not to perform music in public anymore. Such a desire is both understandable and unforgivable and all too familiar. My daddy always used to bemoan, thinking of Al Green or Aretha Franklin, why do these folks give up singing? For God? Can't they have both?

Can't we dance and be divine at the same time?

A further, Romantic reading might note that the only other option for these folks, besides repudiation, is death. Charlie Parker, Basquiat, Richard Pryor, Billie Holiday: the martyrs to the cause of black genius are many, and all far too young. *Only the good die young*—my uncle the preacher said he used to hear that saying as a child, and sit around waiting to go. The sainting of Tupac after his murder is an attempt to reconcile his best songs with his worst rhetoric. And the only way we can reconcile this is by declaring him still alive, because death would mean the rhetoric is real, and living by the word may mean dying by the sword.

But I want to believe instead that the good go long—no matter how short their time might be. And that just as death is part of life, good isn't the absence of bad—as our ancestors well knew—but maintaining faith among the bad, seeing the bad among the good. *Not bad meaning bad, but bad meaning good.*

Bob Marley. John Coltrane. Arthur Ashe. Nina Simone. All these didn't embrace the Party because of escapism but as an escape route. When Simone sang "Feeling Good," the feeling was the most important thing. *Sun in the sky you know how I feel. It's a new dawn it's a new day it's a new life for me.*

Now Is the Time. A Love Supreme. One Love. The World Is Yours.

Ride with me—not into the after, but into the future. Which, jazz and funk and hip-hop insist, is now.

TRANSMITTING LIVE FROM MARS B/W EYE KNOW

Or, *I know I love you better.* That's what De La Soul promised on their debut, *3 Feet High and Rising.* They of course weren't the first to say this, either in the history of love or of recording: the song samples Steely Dan for part of its chorus, transformed not just through spelling into "Eye Know."

But if we backspin to 1988, we can see how by sampling everyone from Johnny Cash (in the title song) to P-Funk (on "Me, Myself and I") to French language lessons to Hall and Oates, *3 Feet High* reimagined not just hip-hop but all music, ruling nothing out. De La Soul's debut felt both earthbound and psychedelic, a country unto itself. In the process, De La Soul became one of the first groups sued for sampling without authorization, specifically for using a few seconds of a 1960s song on their short interlude "Transmitting Live from Mars." De La Soul, who actually had cleared most of the samples, lost the suit along with their record company.[21] This in turn signaled a sea change in hip-hop, which soon would move from late-'80s layered collage to far less interesting '90s hooks. If you're paying, such thinking goes—if you can call it thinking—you might as well make it a smash hit with little risk.

What's at stake now and in danger of being lost is an expansive view of culture—as a set of crucial, and common, freedoms—replaced by one based on mere consumption, or co-opting, on samples going to those who can afford it and not to the most inventive. While certainly I am happy James Brown now can get paid for beats he and his "Funky Drummer" made with their own holy bodies, I do miss some of the shared, floating verses, the common culture of backbeats and shared samples that governed hip-hop at its earliest and finest.

There was a strangeness to hip-hop before the lawsuits—hip-hop artists would sample not just the obvious, and not even use one sample, or giant hook, but use a multitude of sounds layered over each other in a commanding collage of cultures. (In this they followed in the feedback loop started by Hendrix as early as *Electric Ladyland*, where Hendrix layered vocals, and his own instrumentation, the solo artist as a band.) If other, new school rappers began to craft a worldview, *3 Feet High and Rising* held a world.

Take the opening song, "Magic Number," with a chorus that references Schoolhouse Rock's "Three Is a Magic Number" from the 1970s— for those who don't remember, like I do, staring too close to the TV to watch *Schoolhouse Rock,* these were educational animated shorts between cartoons on Saturday mornings. To hear such references, themselves a form of reverence, years later at a dance party, is to be filled with nostalgia—and possibility. This is in part because a "reminiscence," as critic Louis Menand reminds us, "was a late-nineteenth-century term for a poetic borrowing."[22] Such allusions and borrowings are forms of memory, the song seems to say, and may prove just as interesting as Dante was to Eliot.

The other various layers and songs carry the song along, recontextualized, funky, and new. And at the end of the record where the soul singer would "go to church," riffing and singing full-out emotionally, where the funk band would call out to a racially mixed crowd, De La Soul gives us a choir of samples: first, a church-worth of "What does it all mean?" in an electronic voice above the refrain of "No more no less"; then the preacher-like call and response of what turns out to be Eddie Murphy asking, "Anybody in the audience ever been hit by a car?"; and ending with Johnny Cash's not so much singing as calling and questioning "How high's the water, Mama?" Deep.

In just three minutes and sixteen seconds, De La Soul can invoke music history—dare I say recorded history—as a manifesto of their very being, signifying on being a three-person group, not to mention the trinity of meanings that have governed Western culture. Their rising is an uprising—an elevation of sonic possibilities. And that's just the first song.

Soon we're in the realm of "Buddy," whose 12-inch remix is one of the highlights of the era and that much-mourned Native Tongues collective of artists (that included Tribe Called Quest, Jungle Brothers, Queen Latifah, Black Sheep, and Monie Love).[23] On the remix, Queen Latifah sings and also puts on a fake voice, here suggestive of a native Spanish-speaker speaking English: desire is always a voice beyond this one; and there is always another voice waiting. "Buddy" is the holy body as someone else's, "buddy" becoming a catchall term, much like "jelly roll" in the blues, for the beloved and his or her body and its parts; part obscene, part loving, black-owned. By the time we reach the track "Eye Know" we find a swinging chorus from Otis Redding whistling "(Sittin' on) The Dock of the Bay"—a fact I've never really seen discussed. (Now, when you mention it at a party, you have to give me credit for your own sampling.) Just as Redding reached for whistling, not as a failure of language but to say wordlessly what words could not, De La Soul reaches for Redding to provide a beat, and pleasure that no other sound could.

So what if it wasn't made from scratch?

Hip-hop is not so much canned as uses the best ingredients you happen to find in the pantry, some of which you happened not to grow yourself. A good cook—or DJ or post-soul artist—puts his or her foot in it, can make most anything sing.

ATLIENS B/W THE WHOLE WORLD

The hip-hop group OutKast, De La's eclectic inheritors, know tragicomic history, but are committed to the future. In a song like "Rosa Parks," OutKast summons the spirit of the civil rights struggle and also reverses the curse of the "back of the bus." Instead, they claim the fuss at the back of the bus is far more fun, a place of possibility—one visited by post-soul writers, such as Rita Dove in her book *On the Bus with Rosa Parks*—a metaphysical place that helps the club "get crunk." The Southern notion of *crunk* takes funk and makes it cryptic, internal—combining what some claim is a mixed drink of "crazy" and "drunk" in a way that jazz-hound Mamie Smith might admire. The journey that OutKast takes in their songs is from a shifting exterior to an interior filled with possibility, where knickers and silk kneesocks on men can become fashionable again—and, as in the video to "Ms. Jackson," a Confederate flag can even become a belt buckle on a black man. An accessory, without the crime.

OutKast's name indicates their relation to place, and the imagination. And to the much-missed *weirdness* of early hip-hop, a legacy of its folk foundations. The group's very titles, from *ATLiens* to *Aquemini* to "The Whole World," indicate their relation to outer space—or the underwater as ultimate underground. Yet OutKast's chief locale is as Southern as it is internal—perhaps it is best to say their staking a claim on Stankonia, renaming ATL, is not just a search for an interior place, but for the origins of Elsewhere? Originality is a circular motion, a cipher, something not made but found. OutKast seems to subscribe to poet Lyrae Van Clief-Stefanon's compelling definition: "The South is an imaginary place where real things happen."[24]

OutKast's song "Rosa Parks" itself is about originality, critiquing the way a favorite group *ain't coming with it,* and that *you're only as funky as your last cut.* Listen to the moment in the song essential to understanding post-soul, when a harmonica solo both breaks and joins the song in two—"the bridge," both musically and symbolically—the mouth harp and accompanying claps taking us not so much to church as to the Saturday night before—and not just to last night, but a dusty, dusky night umpteen years ago. The sound of the break is that of history: chaotic, and filled with possibility, the song less a tribute to than an embodiment of Rosa Parks's own studied determination. The sound and song are not just about post-soul, they *are* post-soul speaking straight at us. For the first time in a long while, Miss Parks is not mere symbol but sustaining force, a music we can hear.

That this wasn't recognized by Parks or her crew (who sued OutKast for using her name) shows the range of responses to post-soul, and the ways in which it may not be for everyone. And especially the ways in which it violates the notion of the Lady that, as critic Farah Griffin reminds us, was one key form of a previous generation's resistance to oppression. But the possibilities of a post-soul aesthetic may be best represented by a classic album like Lauryn Hill's *The Miseducation*—part soul, part rap, all hip-hop, her album even manages to channel "doo-wop" and the blues. Anyone who refers to "that thing" knows her Bessie and Mamie Smith. Hill's music is many musics at once, containing the whole history of music—or the music of history—within it.

Yet the limits of a post-soul aesthetic may be found in Hill's follow-up album, *Unplugged 2.0*. Of course, the very idea of "unplugged" (not to mention 2.0) is strangely postmodern, post-soul even—it requires such an undoing of history, such untangling, turning off the amplification that helped the blues give birth to rock and roll. One height of the unplugged form can be found in Nirvana's *Unplugged* album taped shortly before Kurt Cobain's death; the album amounts to Cobain's version, inverted, not only of his band's history but also of the history of music as he sees it, taking in everyone from the Meat Puppets and David Bowie to Cobain's stated favorite, Lead Belly. The other pinnacle of the unplugged form is found in LL Cool J's amazing performance of "Mama Said Knock You Out," complete with strange, ragtime redux piano that brings hip-hop back to its roots, and to an alternate future it has never really fulfilled.

For Hill, going unplugged is more a chance to be unformed—her overemphasis on process, both in the songs and in the talk between them, undermines her performance. Hill fails to recognize the need of the performative; she makes the classic mistake that soul is the full expression of emotion, when it is actually its rehearsal, relying on the tension between release and restraint that provides art its power and soul its artfulness. "I used to be a performer—and I really don't consider myself a performer anymore," she declares. Songs are overlong, underdeveloped yet somehow overwrought. It is less a performance or even an unmasking—which might make it interesting—than the undoing of all that made her previous effort a masterpiece. In short, from its techno and in-progress title on, Hill's *Unplugged 2.0* fails because it does not invoke the useful fictions, the art of storying, that made her other work resonate. "I used to get dressed for y'all—I don't do that no more, I'm sorry. It's a new day," she laughs at the record's start. But the result is less nude than naked, less undressed than undone—erasing all glamour—and while raw has come to be a flavor favored by the post-soul nation, raw can quickly become not so rare, less special than expected. Truth ain't always naked, but it is often cloaked—something James Brown knew well.

I am not saying rawness does not have its place—I find Hill's album fascinating, if flawed—but rawness too is a performance, which to work at all requires reveling, not wallowing, in emotion.

Here we've found the dilemma of soul, post-soul, and of art, writ large: How to contend with forces that are in many ways, beyond our control? How to maintain control over subjects, from love to God to war, so inherently filled with a lack of control? Amidst such a dilemma, not to mention in the face of personal crisis, the desire to undo—perhaps a predecessor to redo—might make more sense.

This desire *not* to perform, this poetry of refusal, has its place and is actually integral to African American culture. It is why Miles Davis turns his back on the audience; it is why once big bands held sway, black musicians sought out spaces small, intimate, and after hours, in order to swing in their own way; it is a tradition that Dave Chappelle, in his flight to Africa at the height of his fame, reenacts. But there's an important counter to this, the African American tradition and impulse to resist pain, to survive and even transcend it. There is of course the pain of performing, of having to, but forgive me if I echo my father, who would often wonder aloud: Why do all soul singers reject their songs, and go gospel? Why silence the self in all its flowerings? *We need the funk*—why be afraid of it?

The answer, the millennial and perennial tension between saying and the unsayable, between the self and society, between gospel and being good, between the holy book and the holy body, is what makes post-soul move, and what makes African American culture multiple and meaningful—and ours. The dance goes on. *We can dance underwater and not get wet.* And dancing, funk reminds us, is a form of listening.

Final Chorus: Planet Rock
*The End of the Record*_____

PART ONE: THE THIRD COMING

For African Americans, life is not an open book but a talking one. Not in the sense of being "books on tape," nor even the African slave's powerful idea of the "talking book," but rather, a mixtape: something homemade yet public; fragile and formidable; personal yet meant to be heard (or at least unignorable); loud as hell yet clandestine, whether passed around like love notes or sold from the trunk of a car. Two tapes, ten dollars; one for five.

It is tempting to say that this inexorable energy only moves forward as a tape might and an 8-track must—"how to move / forward like a shark / or 8-track"—but that would forget that the tape has another side too. My old cassette player, which I still have, would flip automatically if you let it. *Chunk, chunk, hiss*—the sound was that of another world revealing itself. Like the ends of a record, the sound wasn't just static and certainly wasn't silence—in the analog era there was no such thing.

In our digital age, we only pretend there's silence. Things are louder than ever; you need headphones just so you don't hear the constant barrage of squawking televisions and cell phone conversations. Analog knew better, knows the pleasures of sotto voce, inexactness, and chance; the idea of recording not everything, but getting down all you can: completeness may be an analog goal, but analog knows true pleasure comes from the hunt. Cut to: me in my bedroom, tape on REC-PAUSE waiting for a song to come on the Top 9 at 9, futzing about, though not idly, then running over in anticipation at the end of an ad, pressing PLAY in hopes the recording caught the start of the latest cut. If it didn't, oh well—from then on, the song always started a little off-cue.

If it was harder to be *professional*, DIY was often easier in them mixtape days. I think of all the purposeful editing I did on mixtapes—songs cut off, noises and jarring transitions added—trying to get the songs to start almost on top of each other, or allowing "radio silence" between tracks to beg someone to fall in love with you. Semisilence as a prayer to what couldn't be said. What I miss in the digital age is the way a mixtape once wasn't just what the original recording artist wanted, even song to song, but meant *reordering,* a collage of sound and even sense; meant my own fade-outs and connections between songs that weren't theoretical or instantaneous as they often are these days, but audible, choppy, and done in real time. Certain songs from a tape made years ago and unheard of since still make me anticipate the next one—because I placed it there once, it is there for me forever. The mixtape means anticipation.

Memory itself is a technology—our common metaphors for memory may change, but have included "the tape" and even "the record," whose very name indicates its relation to the archive. Reproduction or memory, live or Memorex: all these are ways black folks have upended the status quo, shattering the glass—using quotation, sampling, storying, and saving the scraps of things to stitch together something altogether more powerful. The gumbo aesthetic was hip-hop long before anyone knew to say so. No wonder when my Louisiana father first saw "breakdancing" on TV, he simply said, *That's just what we used to call alligator dancing.*

It is from my audiophile father I learned mixtapes: how to preserve my favorite LPs by taping them and then listening to the tape instead of the original. The tape's other side may be a collection of hard-to-find B-sides or 12-inch mixes; mixtapes taught me how to see the whole of a thing, and also let me know you cannot glimpse everything all at once. *Content is a glimpse—it's very tiny, very tiny, content.* It was hard to skip ahead unless you had that technology that did so on your boombox, pressing FF while PLAY was going; I still miss the sounds of human voices, their own music, blurring as the tape sped. Such comprehension or comprehensiveness wasn't always easy, but again, getting close, or closer—not necessarily the getting there—was much of the thrill.

Analog always knows that there's a ghost in the machine, and that sometimes that ghost is you. And sometimes, when you play a tape too much, you can hear the other side bleeding through.

The number of African American songs about this other side—Elsewhere—are staggering. *I'll Take You There; (I'm Doing Fine Up Here On) Cloud Nine; Up on the Roof; A Place in the Sun; Higher Ground; I Want to Take You Higher; Groovin' High; I Will Move On Up a Little Higher; I Want to Get High; Ezekiel Saw De Wheel.* Not all these are paradisaical. Most are paradoxical as Cloud Nine is, the stark contrast of paradise and what is often a wrecked reality providing its profound sense of possibility. A "Pastime Paradise."

This Elsewhere extends to an earthbound place that parrots and in some ways promises paradise: *Come On in My Kitchen. Meet Me at Mary's Place. Erotic City. I'll live a lush life in some small dive. . . .* Sometimes this originating tension we might call pleasure; other times oppression, or the loneliness "of those who feel lonely too." Whatever the source, it sends us into the ether alongside it, out of the either-or and into the And.

The tape, like the record—like the story itself—has at least two sides.

There's something in hip-hop that, despite its protests to the contrary, wants to be misheard, and even unheard. It is a music of the lower frequencies, after all. The storying tradition is rife with coding and incompleteness as a set of strategies—hip-hop's slang alone, like the black vernacular more generally, seeks to draw distinctions and circles, some more inner than others. With hip-hop, it's speak locally, dream globally.

This is why it is perhaps not surprising that *The Anthology of Rap* (2010) has come under fire for its incorrect transcriptions of a number, however small, of lyrics. As with blues lyrics, it's tricky to get down a mainly musical form—no matter how frequently the songs start out as written down in "books of rhymes." The transcriber's challenge is much like the modern translator's: to render the original, but to make enough subtle, studied choices—of line length, of stanzaic form—that we have a new version that evokes and does not mock the work's first form. This is hard enough with the blues—I've done it, I know—but with hip-hop it may seem impossible.

What the controversy over the lyrics illuminates is less the anthology's failure than the extent to which hip-hop remains an oral and aural form. Not to mention a form based on allusion and ultimately elusiveness, that quality Hurston calls "asymmetry" that we see at work in all African American forms based on improvisation. These misunderstandings are not mistakes. Rather, as in soul food and bebop, making do is a way of making it new. And funky.

Even the passionate, partisan discussion surrounding the anthology mirrors the multitude of voices found within a rap song. It is no wonder that some of the best accounts of hip-hop's tradition are oral histories, such as Brian Coleman's *Check the Technique,* providing liner notes for a form that doesn't have them; or are merely just lists upon lists, like *Ego Trip's Book of Rap Lists.* The idea that a book of rap might not include some material "borrowed"—in the case of the antholology, transcriptions alleged from a wiki sourcebook of rap lyrics online—doesn't take into account the music's origins. Hip-hop was *wiki* before wiki was, just listen to that scratching sound: *wiki-wiki-wiki-wiki.*

It's not just the storying tradition on view in the missed words, the missing music, the wordless wishes, in the gaps in the groove. As had been the case with the blues and jazz that helped birth it, hip-hop is a music of the ever-present.

But more than any other music, hip-hop is in love with lostness. It is always looking for a haystack in a needle.

Delight

"Rapper's Delight," the very song that named hip-hop, remains fascinating, necessary, and at times great—especially when you want to fill the dance floor. At fourteen minutes and thirty-eight seconds, the long version contains a cohort of black speech acts. Not only does it rely on play for play's sake (as in the very phrase "hip hop hippity-hop"), the song makes use of old-fashioned storytelling; braggadocio and its opposite, ritual dissing à la the dozens; folk rhymes and folktales; talking blues; pure sound and wordplay; chant; the whole host of storying. Such folk forms get embodied in the famous refrain

> *Hotel, motel, Holiday Inn*
> *(You say) If your girl starts actin' up,*
> *Then you take her friends.*

The theft suggested here applies not just to the song's recasting of the beat from Chic's "Good Times" but also to the lyrics, which borrow so wildly and wholesale from both folk culture and from other rappers—namely, Cold Crush Brothers' Grandmaster Caz—that the song doesn't even bother to change Caz's name. Hank the rapper uses Caz's rhyme (*I'm the C-A-S-A-N-O-V-A and the rest is F-L-Y*) apparently verbatim. Even the song's braggadocio is borrowed.

This isn't a problem only, but a strength signaling that the song emerges from deep within black culture, one of those collaborations of familiar phrase and unique sound that mark all leaps in pop culture. From Nirvana's "Smells Like Teen Spirit" to Bob Dylan's "Like a Rolling Stone," in pop music, deep familiarity—sounding both strange and familiar—is an asset and part of the form. These kinds of pop songs sound distinct, but like something somehow there all along. Very few songs that sound like "nothing nobody's ever heard before" tend to go to the top of the charts—Prince's "When Doves Cry" comes to mind as an exception. In such exceptional moments, the "weird, old America" that Greil Marcus speaks of comes to light for a brief, fateful, flickering instant—before being quickly subsumed by the cannibalistic, capitalistic one.

Hip-hop's focus on both its poor roots and its inevitable rich future knows this: one raps of being rich in order to become rich. Such an alchemy—gesturing toward Elsewhere, here a counterfeit thin as the bills it promises to earn—if still sometimes troubling, should by now be familiar. (Most rides in hip-hop videos are rented.) At its best, however, the folk and epic qualities of hip-hop, found in nascent form in "Rapper's Delight," coexist comfortably in ways last seen in jazz. Where the two qualities meet, we welcome what might best be called "lyricism" at its finest—storying by another name, this lyricism is the same that Ellison spoke of in the blues, a tradition we have been tracing through the centuries.

Even "Rapper's Delight" knows that hip-hop was born live. Turns out the beats on "Delight" weren't actually sampled but were re-created by Sugar Hill Records' house band in the studio. (The rhythm would be re-created further by Queen on "Another One Bites the Dust," borrowing not just the beat from "Good Times" but rap's makeshift machismo.) You can't fake that kind of funk.

The synthesis of a long, varied tradition of African American music and folk forms, rap is a migrant music, midwifed in the South Bronx by Jamaican immigrants like DJ Kool Herc who brought with them traditions of toasting and sound systems at parties—and, as Jeff Chang records in his history of the hip-hop generation, *Can't Stop Won't Stop,* something of the politics of their Caribbean homeland's ongoing upheaval. The gang warfare of the South Bronx, *the South South Bronx,* had its mirror in Trenchtown; so too its desire to unite and triumph through the alchemy of music.

Enter Afrika Bambaataa, former gang member, who founded the Zulu Nation as an alternative to the Bronx gangs' violent ways, forging a group as worldly as his name. Like Sun Ra—and to a lesser though noteworthy degree, poet Countee Cullen—Bambaataa renamed himself in order to craft something interplanetary, his earlier identity erased so effectively few if any know it. Where Cullen looked to Africa as a form of questioning, and Sun Ra and his Arkestra to outer space as a form of prayer, Bambaataa journeyed to both the heavens and the homeland. His "Zulu Nation Throwdown" wasn't all male either, featuring a strong female MC on his black ark. You could say that he erased his birth name to be reborn as a nation, or even a continent, to claim as his birthright "Afrika" in an America that some would spell with three Ks.

Like Ellington, Bambaataa saw all music, especially his own, as collaboration. His defining of the four elements of hip-hop—rap, b-boying and b-girling, graffiti, and DJing—only helps to point up its quintessence of style and spirit. Swing. Groove. Eclectic to the core, Bambaataa's musical tastes are certainly catholic and might even be said to be ecumenical. As such, the church he crafted was a secular, international, peace-based one. His genius as seen in the music is to see the funk in things seemingly far from it, such as Kraftwerk or Public Image Ltd (PiL), Johnny Rotten's group after the Sex Pistols. Where the Pistols' 1977 tour was one long good-bye—"fuck you" as farewell—PiL's first song, "Public Image," (1978) started with *Hello Hello Hello.* A new beginning: *Two sides to every story,* Johnny, no longer Rotten, now Lydon again, sang. *My grand finale my good-bye.*

Planet Rock b/w Zulu Nation Throwdown

Sampling Kraftwerk's "Trans-Europe Express," the hopefulness of Bambaataa's "Planet Rock" didn't just imagine "One Love" but one universe—

the same thing perhaps—couching its revolution in terms of the orbiting black cosmos. *I've got a home in dat rock, don't you see:* the song's "rock" was both Planet Earth and the songs African America had crafted from it. *We didn't land on Plymouth Rock, Plymouth Rock landed on us.* Bambaataa then recolonized this forbidding planet, seeing past the bounds of the Bronx and its buildings bombed-out from slumlords and decades of Nixonian "benign neglect." It was the invisible church of slavery made visible, and required second sight to see. A "loop" isn't just a circle after all, but a "loupe," something used to view a jewel or a watch up close, flaws and fortunes and all.

Bambaataa looked beyond the subway cars: much like the graffiti writers who "bombed" trains to carry their messages from the underground, now sent above and beyond; much in the same manner that the civil rights movement had turned public transportation into what Robin D. G. Kelley calls "moving theaters." Jeff Chang reminds us:

> Graffiti writers had claimed a modern symbol of efficiency and progress and made it into a moving violation. As their mini-riots spilled all-city all day every day, authorities took their work as a guerilla war on civility. They were right. Ivor Miller has written that northbound trains had once been a symbol of freedom, and in decaying postindustrial cities, subway trains were merely the beginning of the daily circuit of alienating labor. [Graffiti writer Lee] Quiñones told Miller, "Subways are corporate America's way of getting its people to work. It's used as an object of transporting corporate clones. And the trains were clones themselves, they were all supposed to be silver blue, a form of imperialism and control, and we took that and completely changed it." The writers replaced the circular logic of trains with their own.[1]

Bambaataa didn't just imbue the train with freedom—the railroad already and always had meant that in the blues correlative—but hijacked its silver blue, a symbolic Brotherhood of Sleeping Car Porters marching not just on Washington, D.C., but on the airwaves. In sampling the robotic chant of "Trans-Europe Express" Bambaataa repurposed it like only a genius could, both derailing it and doing a "youie" or U-turn sending it skyward, defying even gravity like some Hot Wheels race-track constructed on the apartment stairs.

Colson Whitehead describes Bambaataa's achievement in much this way in his novel *Sag Harbor,* set in an all-black enclave on Long Island in 1985:

> Funk, free jazz, disco, cartoons, German synthesizer music— it didn't matter where it came from, the art was in converting it to new use. Manipulating what you had at your disposal for your own purposes, jerry-rigging your new creation. But before sampling became an art form with a philosophy, biting off somebody was a major crime, thuggery on an atrocious scale. Your style, your vibe, was all you had. It was toiled on, worried over, your latest tweak presented to the world each day for approval. Pull your pockets out so that they hung out of your pants in a classic broke-ass pose, and you still had your style. If someone was stealing your style, they were steal-ing your soul.
>
> . . . I liked what Afrika did with Kraftwerk. Across the ocean right there, the Germans banged out tunes on state-of-the-art synthesizers. Soulsonic Force, they had the reverb up so high it sounded like they were playing that "Trans-Europe Express" melody on some floor-model Casio job from Radio Shack, the dying C batteries croaking out through broken speakers. I pictured the beat box covered in electrical tape, only work-ing if you kept it propped at a forty-five-degree angle due to a loose wire inside, envisioned them recording the song in a janitor's closet deep in the bowels of some uptown high-rise. They dismantled this piece of white culture and produced this freakish and sustaining thing, reconfiguring the chilly original into a communal artifact. They yelled, "Everybody say, 'Rock it, don't stop it,'" and the crowd yelled back "Rock it, don't stop it" in dutiful assent. How could they not? Probably it was up on Planet Rock where I wanted to be half the time, where they transported us unlikely chosen, *Close Encounters*–style. There were other places besides this, the song said.[2]

His *Rock it* was a rocket; and quite a racket. Colson told me once that he almost followed his novel's amazing riff with another on Bambaataa's collaboration with PiL as the group Time Zone on 1984's "World Destruction." In the spirit of the shadow book, or the mixtape, insert your own riff on it here:

Hard Times

The journey between an infinite loop that "don't stop"—something hip-hop regularly reasserts—and not just self- but world destruction, is a trip hip-hop takes daily. Even old school wasn't all apocalypse as rapture; often hip-hop's four elements proved more the Four Horsemen heralding Armageddon. To some, hip-hop must have sounded like the end of the world. Or at least music.

Even for those, like my father, who thought as much, "The Message" proved oddly welcome. He used to borrow my copy on vinyl to test his stereo, the eerie, echoing synth swirling out of the Grandmaster Flash and the Furious Five song, its bass booming from his speakers. The song revisits a verse by Melle Mel from the group's older song "Super Rappin'," where his bars were only a cautionary tale among other riffs about partying or boasting—just one tale among many. Here the lines become "*The* Message" as a whole, unique and isolated as the famous line, *It's like a jungle sometimes it makes me wonder how I keep from going under.* The jungle always threatened to spread—especially now that it was concrete.

This "going under" was, in a sense, far removed from the man who lived underground, or the Moses who led her people through the Underground Railroad into Canaan. But if "Planet Rock" celebrated freedom, "The Message" declared desperation as a temporary hideout to find emancipation from, knowing full well that even after winning freedom you might still feel, as Harriet Tubman did, "a stranger in a strange land." "The Message" was brave enough to make art from the streets, "close to the edge" where such music was born—out of knowledge, which is to say, darkness.

To achieve freedom, it would seem you must first experience visions as Nat Turner and Tubman did, her spells brought about after a violent attack from an overseer. Such was the high price of prophecy and freedom, the two inextricably linked in the African American imagination. "Apocalypse means revelation, and when art becomes apocalyptic, it reveals," says critic Northrop Frye. "But it reveals only on its own terms, and in its own forms."[3] Frye could be talking about hip-hop after "The Message"—ever since, revelation has seemed an urgent possibility.

"The Message" begins with *Broken glass, everywhere* as a sign of chaos, even providing a sound effect of glass breaking in case we don't get it. *There's a riot going on.* It is as if Satchmo's trumpet at the start of "West End Blues" now became the shattered herald of the postindustrial End of Everything, the undertow of tragedy. As if the broken glass Baldwin saw after his father's funeral was not just a visual wilderness but a sonic one. A jungle.

Pioneering DJ Grandmaster Flash would help solidify the breaks. These "breaks" in songs were first mined by Kool Herc at the live parties he'd throw—then made metaphoric by Kurtis Blow, the first rap artist signed to a major label, in his classic "The Breaks"—but it was Flash who perfected the break, linking them with two turntables to craft whole songs. Not only did such repetition propel the "break-boys" and "b-girls" and other dancers, it gave Flash a chance to "speak with his hands." In his "Adventures on the Wheels of Steel" Flash found the linkages, the "wheel within a wheel" first seen by Ezekiel and the slave singers who sang of it, now made almost literal. Composed of breaks, the music was the message—a dissonance you could dance to. And now, with "The Message," a slow-motion apocalypse that, if you couldn't dance to, you could at least bob your head to in assent. If not ascent.

The apocalypse had been a long time coming. Hip-hop, like the blues before it, was good-time music born out of hard times. As Kurtis Blow rapped:

> Hard times spreading just like the flu
> You know I caught it just like you.

These same times in fact spread to Hollis, Queens, where Run-DMC would record a cover of "Hard Times" on their eponymous debut. Is this the first hip-hop cover? It is certainly one of the most notable in an art form that made its art not by covers, as white rock and roll had from Elvis to the Beatles, but of uncovering what lurked in a song's inner form.

"The future shock" both Blow and Run-DMC rapped about hinted at the art's "shock of the new" and the shock of the decidedly every-day. One used African drumming and a scat-style beatbox, the other what sounds like an electronic, percussive breathing to heighten the unspoken urgency of the message. Is "future shock" praise or portent? It seems both; which is to say, prophecy. The opposite of the ominous future shock is the "sure shot," providing a couplet whose off-rhyme belies its mixed meaning. Though it might seem otherwise, "the sure shot" is pure praise. Its sound is that of glass breaking, a noise that mirrors the break.

Bring the Noise

One of Flash's crew, Grand Wizzard Theodore, is credited with discovering *scratching*, that way of not just rewinding the song, as Flash did to preserve the breaks, but turning the turntables into a percussive instrument—much as the African slave had turned the body and Thelonious Monk the piano. Such scratching sought an itch also found in scat and the gospel hum, that liquefying of words, as well as in falsetto, with its machining of the voice.

Scratching meant a *machining of words*, a realization that the voice can be physical, and that speech isn't just spoken but uttered by a body language—or by black wax. Scratching made music from noise—declaring with a gesture that the marred world could be manipulated, or disfigured even further, in order to preserve and protect against the future shock that threatened the end of the break and the record. Scratching, like the gospel hum, suggests infinity.

Wherever white Christian culture (and the secular culture that stemmed from and circulated around it) took the biblical imperative to "make a joyful noise," it tended to emphasize the "joyful" part. Black culture tries rendering the *noise* part, not just by saying it loud, but by rescuing all that seeming racket and even equating it with joy. Given static, make something ecstatic. No wonder one of the first important studies of hip-hop is called *Black Noise.*

Too often black folks are the noise in the culture seen as sonorous without us. If only they'd keep it down! Paradoxically and simultaneously, black incursions into noise are often not registered either by art rock or by "noise band" enthusiasts, much less in terms of minimalism or the "white cube" of the contemporary art space. "Indeed, throughout its whole history as a dispositif, from the 1920s to the present, a period that also coincides with the history of recorded black sound, the white cube has been curiously reluctant to open up to black sound. As artist Jennie C. Jones puts it, there are endless historical junctures where black sound and art were talking about the same thing, but were kept completely separate from one another in discourse."[4] At the same time that punk declared DIY a key value downtown, just as appropriation was seen as the height of visual art, folks uptown were dancing to the very same sounds and ideas, getting down.

It wouldn't be till the early 1980s that Fab 5 Freddy and others brought the worlds together, symbolized not just by the classic film *Wild Style* but by Blondie's video for "Rapture"—where Basquiat shows up awkwardly as a DJ and Fab 5 Freddy is name-checked and sprays graffiti in the background. The song's "Man from Mars" appears black as his sunglasses, wearing an all-white top hat and tuxedo in a future shock of Flavor Flav a few years later. (I always did think Marvin the Martian in Warner Bros. cartoons was black too, a stranger in a strange

land with a stranger "falsetto" voice.) Blondie's mention of outer space
didn't mean that downtown trains bombed with Campbell's Soup Cans
in homage to Warhol by Fab 5 Freddy, or subway walls stained with
SAMO© seeking entrée into the art world, hadn't journeyed Elsewhere
already.

From the start, hip-hop was on a mission to "take the A train" and
rig it into a rocket, or a World War II bomber ceremonially decorated,
painted like the bombs themselves, before going into battle. The Ca-
dillacs and Lincolns too that the Man from Mars eats, the cars and
then the bars, might that be the hunger of hip-hop itself? *Now he only
eats guitars.* Certainly, outer space was somewhere black folks had long
sought to inhabit, even felt more at home in: a planet called Up.

And you don't stop, to the punk rock.

PLANET ROCK

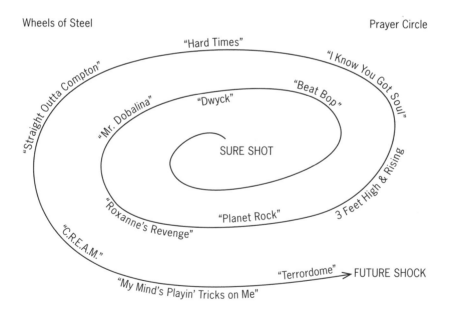

Blank Generation b/w Black Generation

The future shock was also a blast from the past. The rhymes of "Hard Times" were just the latest synthesis of the black secular protest song, or better yet, the street sayings and rhymes that filled the stoops much as doo-wop had. It ain't just that hard times are as contagious as the flu, rhymes about it are too. I for one first heard Run-DMC's "Hard Times" on a mixtape a cousin of mine passed me in Louisiana. That Groove is going round.

Even the urban decay of the South Bronx was cosmopolitan and communicable, occurring both miles and seemingly worlds away, both downtown and across an Atlantic that from the air looks mostly black. Punk's birth in lower Manhattan in the early 1970s, as charted by such books as Legs McNeil and Gillian McCain's *Please Kill Me,* sometimes suffers in favor of accounts of the white riot of British punk. McNeil too saw punk as a righteous whiteness, purposefully eschewing any black sound. Either way, punk's parentage in the blues still seems a dirty secret that needs to be told—while critic Dick Hebdige saw its connections to reggae in Britain, Lester Bangs was one of the few who directly drew the connection between the blues and punk (and who railed against the almost reflexive racism too often found in the latter's "white noise supremacists").[5] The Blank Generation was also black.

Like most British invasions before and since, Lydon and the Pistol's 1977 U.S. tour was the return of African American music to the shores of its founding mothers and fathers. Years before, the Beatles and Stones had brought back home the blues and R & B that had inspired their bands; the Who sang on "Substitute," *I look all white but my dad was black* in both an admission and wish fulfillment of their cultural origins. Years later, on "Rise" from 1986, Lydon would sing *I could be black, I could be white,* racial ambiguity a continued sign of cultural outsiderness. Johnny Lydon would also, as PiL, write "Death Disco," which seemed to embrace the latter in defiance of the former. *Anger is an energy.*

The Blank Generation, reacting against the broken promises of the 1960s, had no metaphor in place for such a sorry state of betweenness. No wonder they turned to blackness for such—this in-between state was one the African American generative tradition had long since named. In the storying tradition, every Zion had its Babylon; every Canaan a Gomorrah; every Negro heaven was a protest against a hell not of our own making. (The secular songs also rang out that the white man's heaven was the black man's hell.) *It's Dark and Hell Is Hot,* DMX would name his first album—the dark wasn't exactly hell, but the dark was all around us, synonymous with but not identical to the inferno. Hell, if here on earth, might instead prove instructive: "You're dealing with heaven while you're walking through hell," Rakim said. "When I say heaven, I don't mean up in the clouds, because heaven is no higher than your head, and hell is no lower than your feet."[6]

Between hell and Elsewhere flowed that river: sometimes Jordan, sometimes Styx, ofttimes the Ohio, and not quite Lethe. Forgetting was never the point of Negro heaven, which pointed to the future while keeping an eye on the sparrow and the past. *I've got many rivers to cross.*

What were we doing here on this stony shore? While making heaven our home, we still spoke and sang of hell's part in it—death meant a crossing, a journey undertaken, and didn't always mean death. This wasn't just Christian (or ancient Egyptian) imagery of death as rebirth, but also death as passing over into a Canaan that meant literal freedom. Storied in all senses, this Elsewhere is never far, the songs insist; if it required travel it was a trip as internal as anything else: *Can you send me an angel? I know you got soul. You don't need no ticket, you just get on board. We are not the same, I am a Martian.* The music, whether "Swing Low" or "I'll Take You There" or "Planet Rock," seeks transport.

While British punk, from "London Calling" to "God Save the Queen," would issue a bare-bones blues wail against Britain and Britishness, in hip-hop the *boom-bap* and the briar patch meant home. The blues sang of trouble in order to court it, and hip-hop held no different. Even old-school hip-hop artists, accused of merely seeking to party, did so because the Party was both a means and an end, balm and remedy— something hip-hop shared with its closest kin, disco.

Both hip-hop and disco were repetitive dance music made at the fringes that revealed themselves to be mainstream. Both were dance music made by self-defined "freaks" in love with the edges and innards of records. Old-school acts rapped not just over but about "the disco beat," suggesting a disco flow that spoke to the fluidity and continuity not just of genre but also of attitude, in which the Party meant freedom itself. If disco was dead, the news hadn't reached the South Bronx— either that or they were throwing one hell of a wake.

Death Mix Live b/w Death Disco

Death is often transformative in hip-hop—it always is in disco. In his book *Tea,* poet D. A. Powell, who has written of his taking influence not just from disco but from Black Arts poets, quotes from what he sources as his "personal 'book of lists'":

> Eleven Disco Songs That Equate Sex and Death
> Through an Elaborate Metaphor called "Heaven":
>
> 1. "Paradise" [Change]
> 2. "Heaven Must Be Missing an Angel" [Tavares]
> 3. "Angel Eyes" [Lime]
> 4. "Heaven Must Have Sent You" [Bonnie Pointer]
> 5. "Take Me to Heaven" [Sylvester]
> 6. "So Close to Heaven" [Trix]
> 7. "Be with You" [Sylvester]
> 8. "Tripping on the Moon" [Cerrone]
> 9. "Earth Can Be Just like Heaven" [The Weather Girls]
> 10. "Lift Off" [Patrick Cowley]
> 11. "Heaven's Where My Heart Is" [Marsha Raven][7]

Paradise is what disco promised, often in the form of a garage—and later a "house," which, whatever the origins of the music by that name, seems also to reference the African American concept of home.

Early hip-hop turned the end of disco and what Chang calls the "Necropolis" of the Bronx into a necromancy that brought the party back to life as Bambaataa's "Death Mix." The fact that his "Death Mix" had a "live" version is enough to indicate hip-hop was interested in being "all the way live" no matter how poorly it was recorded. From the

Netherworld, turned into Elsewhere; from Necropolis to the Promised Land. Only hip-hop could imagine the place where punk and disco might intersect, where heavy metal and lite FM met for a drink. Better make it quick.

The word "punk" itself has many meanings, and is a term some have called intentionally slippery.[8] Might the black vernacular meanings of "punk," somewhere between a curse word and worse—a word some have equated with "sissy," but may best approximate "queer"—yet be redeemed to incorporate the "I'm Against It" ethos of CBGB with the partying potentiality of Paradise Garage? Some have sought such redemption already, including in the "punk'd theory" of Tavia Nyong'o and in the fierce, self-possessed strut of "sissy bounce," however poor the name.[9]

For white bands, claiming to be a "punk" at times provided the same defiance, and others the very "put on," also found in black gay culture. (And before that, both traits appeared in jazz—though punk music, like disco, didn't go for jazz's exact kind of cool.) Both glam rock and punk borrowed gay culture's defiant style and its lipstick, often literally— outlandishness as a form of outrage. Early hip-hop artists also borrowed disco's glamour and funk's costumes—a way of promoting not just a party but the Party. The Stonewall Uprising was not the last straw but the first echo of Little Richard's choir-director holler, those defiant colored queens refusing to eat cake or crow in ways that soon would reverberate from the Bronx to Queens.

Might the homophobia found in hip-hop in particular (as opposed to its presence in the many other facets of our broader knee-jerk culture) be the pronounced nervousness of its origins in disco? Certainly any declaration of "I ain't no punk" swirls deliriously between saying "I'm not a chump" and a more nervous denial of—well, not homosexuality, necessarily—for while fucked-up and homophobic certainly, the black (and turns out older British) meanings of "punk" aren't exactly gay but specifically a fear of getting "fucked" in all senses. No accident that often the most homophobic of rap disses—see *The Chronic*'s "Dre Day" if you must—turn on a homoerotics that can neither be redeemed nor fully explained. Except, perhaps, to say, "If you're going to fuck me,

I'm going to fuck you first." Such doublethink is a Babylon of our own making no rhyming can redeem.

Though early recorded hip-hop saw itself as not so separate from disco, the Disco 3 would soon become the Fat Boys, renamed after their first hit song. Better to be fat than disco, apparently.

Still, leave it to disco to fully embrace the body first made holy by funk. In no other music would a group call itself Two Tons of Fun, except maybe hip-hop, whose embrace of corpulent MCs and names looms large. The Fat Boys, Chubb Rock, Large Professor, RIP B.I.G., Heavy D, Big Pun: the largesse African American (and Caribbean and Nuyorican) culture feels for largeness is recorded in the very names of many of its "biggest" stars. It took hip-hop to make "phat" a compliment. This bodiness is not just a rebuke of European standards of beauty—you can't be too rich, but you can be too thin—but maximalism made literal. Living large, more is more: this embrace, even to excess, first found its falsetto voice in disco, after its instrumental innovation in Bird's horn. It is a celebration of plenty.

So too the emphasis on "realness," albeit of a quite different sort. For a time there, disco and hip-hop each reveled in the artificialness of existence, the body inside out. Donna Summer's "I Feel Love" was not an earthy, soulful vocal but rather a high-pitched android sound reemphasized by her trancelike movements in concert. Realness was merely a stance, or a dance. The Human Beatbox, the Robot, popping and locking, "The Show": all were ways of self-consciously going beyond to a place that admitted the body might be just another gadget. One that, on occasion, breaks.

A gadget is a funky machine. Human-scaled, smaller than a machine can be, a gadget is something you can hold in your hands. A gadget is James Bond's pen that turns into something else; an Inspector whose theme song can become a hip-hop classic. Like the song in hip-hop, the b-boy or b-girl body is always becoming something else. If we were Deleuze and Guattari we might say that breakin' was the becoming-body, just as the duo spoke of "becoming-black" and "becoming-woman" as a state of being, and the desirability of a "body without organs." William Carlos

Williams called the poem "a machine made of words"; the break-dancer is a machine made of wordlessness—which is to say, a body.

Body body rock body body rock: the movement is the message, the body constantly becoming something more—even artificial, or unknown. No wonder another word for *gadget* is *contrivance.* Or, "Any unspecified or unspecifiable usu. small object; something one does not know the name of or does not wish to name."[10] It is the ineffable.

Too soon "keeping it real" went wrong—hip-hop lost sight as disco never did that "realness" was not a way of reaching reality, but was in fact reality's main adversary. Consider Elizabeth Alexander's evocation of "Queer real, diva real, affirmation":

> "You make me feel mighty real," the late, great Sylvester sang; and realness was the pinnacle of fulfilled existence, the most desirable state. Realness is also the ultimate litmus test that progress-minded black people place on one another, with often narrow definitions of how that realness might be embodied or enacted, or what it actually means to "keep it real." "Got to be Real," Cheryl Lynn wails, and her "Real real real real real" repeats and careens and keens and becomes its own thing, the anthem of a generation, a call to arms, a call to each other and our newfound communal freedom-in-racial-and-sexual realness. The verb "to be" becomes a new verb, "to be-real." In that disco-era hit, "realness" as sound has become abstract and therefore leaves room for invention and redefinition, a realness that goes so far as to be emptied of meaning and reclaimed as possibility.[11]

Disco's anthemic possibilities found fruition in its offspring hip-hop (and its "outside child," house music). Hip-hop got most the glory, electronica got to keep the house: but for a while there, all were under one large roof where the Party raged. *We don't need no water, let the motherfucker burn.* And Paradise reigned.

The Golden Chain

After paradise, the Golden Age. As most heads know, the Golden Age of rap started with Run-DMC, who reinvented the form with the brilliance of their lyrics and flow—not to mention record sales. The rap group from Hollis, Queens, also asserted its place in history: in songs like "King of Rock," Run-DMC boldly and self-consciously evoked being new school, rapping, *It's all brand-new, never ever old school.*

The group's "Sucker MCs" is arguably their most important record and certainly the one that changed hip-hop forever, forging it as a form based not on stories but rhymes that were "def and then went this way"; not on my-turn-then-your-turn MCing but MCing as a series of overlaps and interruptions; rhymes and similes based not on expectation but surprise; and sparse, fat beats. Such starkness also extended to their dress: Lee jeans and Adidas, black and white, "Don't want nobody's name on my behind."

From its title forward, "Sucker MCs" asserted the role of the MC (master of ceremonies) over the DJ, who had reigned over hip-hop from the get-go (as *grand*master). Though there were great MCs in the old school, such as Melle Mel or Roxanne Shanté, Run-DMC dared to crown themselves not just "king" but "king of rock," to reclaim the genre Bo Diddley and Chuck Berry had made and the title Elvis had taken to his grave. This self-consciousness extended to their name, cloaked in plainness: Run-DMC wouldn't dub themselves Fabulous or Cold or use adjectives at all. No ideas but in things; their name was simply noun, proper or not. Even what *DMC* stands for kept changing in their lyrics—I'm partial to "devastating mic control"—but may in the end just stand for Darryl McDaniel's initials turned inside out. *Boom-bap.*

My own Golden Age of rap also started with Run-DMC. The first record I bought with my own money was *King of Rock* on vinyl. What I found was a "kingdom" that didn't merely mean status but a state of mind, shifting and ambitious. Most all the rappers of what we now call the Golden Age seemed self-aware, and even self-important, in ways that later would seem forced. While aware of being part of a burgeoning culture, theirs was an urgency of the moment, as artistic as economic: *I can't live without my radio.*

The giant radio, portable and loud, was much like the music—it was meant to be unignorable. The holder of a boombox was a one-person broadcast booth. Annoying it might be, but memorable certainly. *Memorex:* the tapes such gadgets played were a form of anticipation and memory rolled into one; a sonic *boom-bap* that could even break glass, as Ella Fitzgerald's recorded voice did in the 1970s Memorex commercial.

When they invented the rap single, Sugarhill Gang's true innovation was not that "Rapper's Delight" clocked in at fifteen minutes, though that remains rather amazing, especially given its extensive radio play. Rather, as Chuck D, who before leading Public Enemy used to rap over "Good Times," says, "the ironic twist is not how long that record was, but how short it was." Chuck D still marvels at how the Sugarhill Gang (and record label) had managed to condense a whole party into a mere fifteen minutes: "It was a miracle."[12] Like other black innovators committed to live music, such as early jazz pioneers, for the DJ the live gig remained the thing; hip-hop pioneers such as Grandmaster Flash and Kool Herc saw recording as both unnecessary and impossible: they were famous in their neighborhoods, known on the streets, got paid for parties, what was the point? You couldn't capture the party on wax anyway.

While they had come up in clubs, Run-DMC helped make the studio just as important as the parties, not to mention the streets where their music ultimately got heard. Run-DMC reinvented the rap single, making the radio not just a thing to carry but a place to conquer. Radio play was both sought by the "new school" and rendered irrelevant—in the end, a boom box or a passing car bumping your tune might be a far more enormous radio:

> One time, in probably 1983, I was in the park in Brooklyn. I was getting beat up by about eight kids, I don't even remember why. But as it was happening, this dude was walkin' by with one of those *big* boom boxes. And as he's walking by, we hear [imitates the unmistakable intro drum pattern from Run-DMC's "Sucker MCs," loudly]. They all stopped beating me, and we all just stood there, listening to this phenomenon. I could have run, but I didn't, I was just so entranced by what I heard. Then the dude with the box passed by and the kids continued to beat me up. But it didn't matter. I felt good.[13]

Rapper Pras's memory of hearing the transfixing "Sucker MCs" beat while getting beaten up reveals how the song's Pied Piperness made folks press PAUSE to hear.

In condensing the hip-hop song, Run-DMC emphasized its poetry over its Party. Where the old-school song's length was a holdover from disco and its presence as club music, the group's first single was so relatively short that it was an innovation as important as the notion that the Ramones didn't play short songs but regular-length songs really fast. Run-DMC made drum machines stand in for drums, and made the *boom-bap* stand in for the bass line entirely. *Jay cut the record down to the bone.* Like many of the leaps forward in any art form, "Sucker MCs" amounted to a stripping back to the roots.

These roots revealed not metonym, as soul music did—in which another name for a thing stands in for something else—but synecdoche, one part standing in for the whole. The very names "soul" and "hip-hop" are forms of metonym and synecdoche, respectively: *soul* is another name for a music that means far more; and *hip-hop* is literally part of one song that signifies an entire culture.

A typical example of synecdoche might be the phrase *All hands on deck.* We know that "hands" is one part of a person referring to an entire person (even if the term is "deckhands," itself a synecdoche). So when an MC says, *Just throw your hands in the air, and wave 'em like you just don't care,* what is the whole being evoked? In many ways it is the very community, the collective, reaching out toward the unreachable. That this unreachability is rendered as "not caring" makes it all the more interesting.

Take Run-DMC's "My Adidas" from 1986: The "Adidas" in question aren't symbolic, they don't mean lots of complex things; they are one part standing for a whole being, at least we hope. When it works— "My Adidas," "Miuzi Weighs a Ton," "My 98," *Just like a test, I cram to understand you*—such synecdoche is more than the sum of its parts. It's a way of going big by way of the smallest things. When it don't work, well, it's just gold chains and bling for bling's sake, reducing a world filled with fullness and yes, even symbol, to being full of it and "Life ain't nothing but bitches and money."[14]

Hip-hop too takes the smallest bits, the breaks, and makes them bigger: the *boom-bap* is itself synecdoche. Scraps don't stay that way, but are sampled, sung, looped, riffed, ripped, and plain ripped off.[15] This looping, existential always, is the most radical version of nostalgia—

repetition as a kind of recognition. Or desire. Or maybe it's just déjà vu, a glitch in the Matrix. Sometimes back in the day you'd find an old tape unwinding in the wind, a message no one would ever hear again.

In the often over-the-top *Signifying Rappers,* David Foster Wallace has an interesting riff on synecdoche and hip-hop's difference from (and superiority to) punk music:

> Confession: D.'s first sampler draft, of which this brief digressive riff is a grim fossil, began as more about rap-as-synecdoche than about rap *esse.* For rap *presents* itself as synecdochic: its dual identity as both head and limb, speaking both to and for its audience, is a huge part of the authority it claims in every cut.
>
> Too, the rhetorical relation of Part to Whole symbolizes (and so captures!) all too well rap's multileveled superiority to late-70s Punk. A synecdoche is a Part so powerful symbolically as to be eligible for the conceptual absorption, containment, and representation of what it's Part of. A stereotype—immigrant Irish are butt-ugly dumb drunks; poor urban blacks are vulgar and lawless—is just a false synecdoche, a token of the conceptualizer's ignorance or laziness, not of some certain distorted features' representative power. See, though, that, ideologically, genuine Punk was really no different from outside listeners, *stereotype* of Punk. "Alienated" from everyone and everything, especially itself, Punk couldn't "speak for" anyone, because Punk couldn't aspire even to the role of Part—"Part" of *what?* There was no Whole to be Part of in Punk's fashioned, fragmented nihilism, its studied alienation from all "Wholes" (they even found sex nauseous). The Punks "Whole" was themselves, but not as a unit, or even a sum; it was just each of them, individually; together they composed more a sick body's symptom than a functioning digit or limb.
>
> Synecdoche's potency in art depends on a community as backdrop and context, audience, and referent: a definable world for the powerful, dual-functioning Part both to belong to and to transcend.[16]

Where the old school spoke to a specific audience, a community that often broadened to all those within earshot, Run-DMC had the gall to speak to and for everyone. They were kings, they were rock, they said their patch of earth was the entire world, and that, for their part, being black, they felt whole.

Two Tears in a Bucket

One of the pleasures of hip-hop—and sometimes one of its frustrations—is the way it veers between folk and epic. Such a reach is not in and of itself unusual: the blues too are a folk form that regularly reaches the heights of epic. The river, the train, the mountain, the valley: these four elements form a spiritual geography African Americans regularly riff off of and remap. But the blues and their correlative do this so regularly as to be an epic form disguised as a folk one, or an epic impulse found among the folk. "Indeed the improvisation on the break, which is required of blues-idiom musicians and dancers alike," Albert Murray reminds us, "is precisely what epic heroism is based on. In all events, such blues-idiom dance gesture is in effect an exercise in heroic action, and each selection on a dance program is, in a sense, a rehearsal for another of a never-ending sequence of escapades."[17] You could just call them escape routes.

With hip-hop, however, this veering between folk and epic is instantaneous, from line to line—even within a single line. This is why we can find the heights of the form, a wordplay previously unimaginable, right alongside something so f-ed up that it can be hard to reconcile if you aren't in the right mind-set (or the wrong crowd). A song like Jay-Z's "Empire State of Mind" makes you move not despite its strange forays into what some might call nonsense but because of them:

> Mommy took a bus trip, now she got her bust out
> Everybody ride her just like a bus route
> Hail Mary to the city you're a virgin
> And Jesus can't save you, life starts when the church ends

All forms have some contradictions, but in hip-hop they are pronounced, persistent, and so ever-present that one can only say contradiction is an integral part of the form. Jay-Z speaks of these contradictions himself in describing "Empire" in his *Decoded,* and the way he crafted his lyrics to fight against the smooth, hitlike track he'd been given.[18] Don't think, however, that the disturbing parts of hip-hop are the folk parts, as epic often needs to be troubling too. Just now the "Scenario" remix came on, for instance, and in a song I've heard a trillion times I heard again that great folk phrase "two tears in a bucket," which seems to have been expressly invented to allow a rhyme with "mother mother fuckit."

The distance in such a couplet is often the dizzying dance between "Good Times," written by Niles Rogers of Chic, and the group's other smash hit "Le Freak," written originally because Rogers couldn't get into Studio 54: instead of "Freak Out," the chorus originally said *Fuck you.* The journey from "fuck you" to "Le Freak," from "Le Freak" to "Good Times," from "Good Times" to "Delight" to "Hard Times," from delight back to fuck you again, is one that hip-hop recounts, and sometimes reenacts, from line to line.

As a folk invocation, *two tears in a bucket* does what "Krik? Krak!" does in Haitian folktales: it lets us know that a story has begun, will begin, so listen good. It is speech calling attention to itself, for itself, and thus, is to be beloved (if not believed). The couplet's obscenity is both incidental and purposeful, as in Method Man's "Bring the Pain"; or, in Ice Cube and Flavor Flav's "I'm Only Out for One Thang," where the floating verse is recast as "two peas in a bucket": it is a way, understood by its original audience, of bringing us into the fold. Much like *just wave your hands in the air (and wave 'em like you just don't care),* it is a call whose response is both expected and understood.

With hip-hop, the folk form may be the call; the epic the response.

The response is always a form of revision, however subtle. Yet subtlety was not quite at the start of that celebrated set of answer records, the Roxanne Cycle. Kicked off by UTFO's "Roxanne Roxanne," the original song was about a "crab," an imaginary girl who then became real: first in the form of Roxanne Shanté (with Marley Marl) who rapped "Roxanne's Revenge"; then by yet another Roxanne who called herself "The Real Roxanne." (Even "Roxanne's Doctor" would eventually get into the mix.) Realness was of course a strange concept to introduce in taking one's theme, if not name, from a song about a fictional girl none of the MCs could win over. But the whole was rather ambiguous, even contradictory—UTFO sounded both proud and wounded at not getting the girl in the first place. *Calling her a crab is just a figure of speech, 'cause she's a apple, a pear, a plum and a peach.* Shanté sought her "Revenge" by calling the Untouchable Force Organization out for their self-described roles, which were overdetermined in an old-school way—Kangol, Doctor, Educated Rapper—and then assaulting their masculinity. That she did so in a tough, not-stereotypically feminine manner, and was just a young teenager, was all to the better. If she could be unexpected, and violate the roles some would seek to establish, why couldn't they?

By jump-starting the answer song, and the dis as a creative act on wax, Roxanne Shanté realized that hip-hop, especially over the long haul, was ultimately a dialogue. It was the final form of "talking back"— backtalk as powerful and empowering revision of whatever we're given. *My mike sounds nice; My cow is fine I don't need your bull.* In many ways, this is why a male rapper's casual yet caustic dissing—say, calling a woman a "ho"—is rarely seen as the last word by those in the hip-hop game. This revisionary view is more sophisticated than merely seeing oneself as an exception—saying "oh, he doesn't mean me when he says 'ho'"—instead, these two women take on the role or at least the name of Roxanne on their own, identifying only in order to deny.

While in some way trying to cash in on the original's popularity, both Roxannes take on the role of "Roxanne" without taking it merely at face value. Rather, the women of the Roxanne Cycle recognize the ways UTFO's song relied on a form of mask, as signaled by their very characters, from doctor to "Mr. Sophisticator"; and that to declare the rappers phony or corny or impotent was just the start of getting revenge on their own terms. The goal was to do it better than even the original could; even to make a new original; to claim the heights of epic as one's own. Not to mention the depths of the dis.

Just like Run-DMC's austerity, the Roxanne Cycle marked the change over from old-school flash, costumes, and characters to the more sophisticated personae of hip-hop's Golden Age. *Everybody knows it's me the R-O-X-A-N-N-E.* Roxanne Shanté had answered the culture's call first.

"Roxanne's Revenge," "The Message," "Rebel without a Pause," "I

Cram to Understand You," "My Mind's Playing Tricks on Me," "Passing Me By," "Ex Factor"; "Today Was a Good Day," "Paid in Full," "Top Billin'": all these achieve lyricism bordering on epic. That they do it without using every tool in the folk or epic toolbox is a sign of their confidence—or single-mindedness—in selecting among many possible idioms. They are not songs of synthesis, or expansiveness, but deep feeling and individual achievement, ultimately getting that honor that some might call classic, and we call golden or old school. Schoolin', after all, is what such culture seeks to do.

Two tears in a bucket is one person's definition of tragedy, another's of comedy. It might be best to say it is the tragicomic impulse behind the blues, expressed lyrically by those individuals for whom life is an everyday epic they seek on their own terms. *This dance is on and on and on—Dance until your breath is gone!*

PART TWO: 100 GUNS

Rap and I grew up together, if it could be said to have grown up; we are almost exactly the same age. It also just so happens that I was a DJ on our college radio station during rap's Golden Age. (Funnily enough, other DJs there included the two founders of the hip-hop magazine the *Source*.) At WHRB, I spun records and pressed play on CDs, not mixing certainly—though I did get to broadcast the mixtape I had in my head to whoever was listening on my late (or early) overnight shifts given to newbies.

Once called "The Dark Side," the program I worked on didn't start till 10 p.m. anyway: by then it was known as "AR&B," short for "alternative R & B." While not the best term, "AR&B" did describe something of how hip-hop was just one music of many—and justified, say, my starting a set with King of Go-Go Chuck Brown or all of James Brown's "Funky Drummer" before segueing into a more proper hip-hop cut that sampled it. The mental mix became the sonic one: some tapes of my friend Philippe Wamba and me spinning, sometimes with another, proper mixmaster DJ, still exist as both relic and proof. Others were lost to the mixtape gods, and my play-uncle's car, shadow books that talk to no one.

At the risk of romanticizing the role of the DJ further, it seemed that the DJ was a more useful metaphor for the work the culture and we consumers of it did. We weren't trying just to rhyme in the culture but rhyme with it—to find connections, especially where there seemingly were none. Whether to call it rap or hip-hop (or AR&B); whether to listen or to dance; whether KRS-One or Rakim were better: the answer to all our open-ended arguments seemed *Yes.*

Too soon the gangsta would come to replace the DJ as the "man" to be, and hardness won over truth. I still miss the way a DJ might hint at what's next, then never show you, would mix two songs so perfectly you couldn't tell till it was too late. To not just make but predict the action. If the mixtape meant anticipation, the DJ meant infinity and possibility—in other words, prophecy. These days DJs turn down one song before bringing up another, abandoning flow to the rappers and history to the textbooks, not the dance floor where it belongs.

People don't dance no mo', all they do is dis.

People Don't Dance No Mo'

If Reaganomics provided an unlikely muse for "The Message" of the old school, then the commodification and abrupt discrediting of "breakin'" (and, in the art world, graffiti art) had taught hip-hop another message about navigating the rough waters of the so-called mainstream. To those who weren't in the game, hip-hop meant rap and rap meant hip-hop's lowest common denominators, with beatboxing/tagging/scratching/ *Breakin'* the movie as lesser forms of the four elements. This wasn't a permanent effect, but as with tap dancing before it, what was once a percussive form of protest threatened to become bland, backspins taught in strip malls alongside jazzercise and tap dancing to "Tea for Two."

Rap had to regroup, and while it was never merely a novelty as some thought—just as beatboxing or scratching was never simply silly noise—by the mid-1980s hip-hop had left the radio airwaves only to gather its strengths not around fads but flow, not singles but records and remixes. As a result, the Golden Age of hip-hop is the age of the rap concept album, kicked off by Run-DMC's eponymous first record and *King of Rock,* and culminating in now-classics like *Three Feet High and Rising* (1989), *It Takes a Nation of Millions to Hold Us Back* (1988), *All Hail the Queen* (1989), *To the East, Blackwards* (1990), and *People's*

Instinctive Travels and the Paths of Rhythm (1990). Even the album titles were more ambitious then.

With 1988's *Straight Outta Compton*, NWA made good on the concept album as a hip-hop form by exploding it with their badness. Taking its cues from predecessors like Boogie Down Production's *Criminal Minded* and Schoolly D's *Saturday Night!*, the album's opening lines declared: *You're now about to witness the strength of street knowledge.* NWA's songs, such as "Straight Outta Compton," "Fuck tha Police," and "Gangsta Gangsta," penned chiefly by Ice Cube, were death ballads in choral form—announced by Cube, carried by MC Ren or Yella, then culminating in Eazy-E, whose high-pitched whine made him less terrifying and far more. The sound was of a whirlwind in our midst, saying the unsayable and saying it loud, making the listener as deliriously uneasy as the unrest that NWA hinted was the music's real source. This was the sound of a genre being born: where the Sex Pistols chanted "no future," gangsta rap said there wasn't even a present. NWA simultaneously protested, diagnosed, and dismissed consequences of any sort: *I don't give a fuck, that's the problem.*

The seeming topicality of gangsta rap, and its apolitical politics, masks its origins in storying rituals of tall tales, the dozens, and toasts both Jamaican and African American—bragging and hyperbole as a form of critique. The genius of NWA wasn't just in their name, "Niggaz With Attitude," which itself was defiant and even a dare, but rather in the way that their songs veered from and fit a black narrative begun with bad man Stagolee, the black folk hero who shot a man just to see him die. NWA had the smarts to call this quicksand home. Home as a foundational concept courses through African American thought, and by both celebrating and cursing theirs (often literally), NWA made Compton something that was both representative of America and far from its promise.

Where Public Enemy perfected the rap group as a lead "singer" and a "hype man" in Flavor Flav, NWA reinvented the rap group as a sort of jazz combo, circling a theme improvised on—only where jazz provided a heroism of the expressive artist, NWA now gave us the antiheroism of the gangster, something as American, to paraphrase H. Rap Brown, as violence and cherry pie. For despite hip-hop being, as Chuck D declared, "CNN for black people," we also listen to hip-hop not just to hear the "news" about, say, police brutality, but to enact broad fantasies of our triumph over it. This is as true for white listeners as for black— the power of gangsta rap was not to let white listeners become black, but to espy one kind of blackness from afar or a-near. It helped that it was marketed as truth rarely found elsewhere. "The Nigga Ya Love to Hate"—Ice Cube's ironic title, indicting and empowering himself— could have been describing the ambiguity and ambition of such hip-hop itself, daring you not to like it.

As Nasty As They Wanna Be

Those who saw the image of "gangsta rap" as negative weren't wrong inasmuch that negation was its chief strategy. What the would-be censors, from Parents Advisory Council to DeLores Tucker to the FBI, failed to see were the ways that such negation, while at times nihilistic and even opportunistic, wasn't ever just those things either.

This is in part because gangsta rap's negation is a form of affirmation— related to, but quite different from, the blues' long-standing use of the same. Gangsta rap formed such a poetics of refusal from an unlikely nexus of disco affirmation and punk negation, something different from mere nihilism. Greil Marcus spends the early part of his *Lipstick Traces* defining such an artful negation versus a weaker nihilism:

> "'Anarchy in the U.K.' is a statement of self-rule, of ultimate independence, of do-it-yourself," said Sex Pistols manager Malcolm McLaren, and whatever that meant (do what yourself?), it wasn't nihilism. Nihilism is the belief in nothing and the wish to become nothing: oblivion is its ruling passion. . . .
>
> Nihilism means to close the world around its own self-consuming impulse; negation is the act that would make it self-evident to everyone that the world is not as it seems—but only when the act is so implicitly complete it leaves open the possibility that the world may be nothing, that nihilism as well as creation may occupy the suddenly cleared ground. The nihilist, no matter how many people he or she might kill, is always a solipsist: no one exists but the actor, and only the actor's motives are *real*. When the nihilist pulls the trigger, turns on the gas,

sets the fire, hits the vein, the world ends. Negation is always political: it assumes the existence of other people, calls them into being. Still, the tools the negationist seems forced to use— real or symbolic violence, blasphemy, dissipation, contempt, ridiculousness—change hands with those of the nihilist.[19]

Gangsta rap's blasphemy was homemade, a Molotov cocktail—or an 8-Ball—thrown from a cruising car. But it was hardly ever solo—if it was a drive-by, there was always a carful doing the shooting. As NWA said, sampling PE: *Too much posse*. Gangsta rap put the gangs back into hip-hop, less in the form of "real violence" than in the heightened crews that rolled deep, especially on the records.

You could define the Golden Age of rap—like the golden age of modernism before it—by the censorship it encountered. While some have valid points that can be hard to defend against, rap's detractors align too readily with rap's censors, not to mention those racists who sought to obliterate the music as one of the few remaining ways they could attempt to kill the culture entirely.

Even after the precedent-setting obscenity trials of *Ulysses* and *Howl*, the courts and the court of public opinion weren't content to damn rap music, say it wasn't music at all—they also sought to prevent anyone else from hearing it. Its obscenity needed to be destroyed: 2 Live Crew's bad taste (if obvious humor) on their "Me So Horny" quite literally warranted arrest of its performers. The court case that ensued went all the way to the Supreme Court (which, in not hearing the case, upheld the overturning of the case against the group at the state level). Ice-T's album *Freedom of Speech . . . Just Watch What You Say* seemed to be less a provocation than a prediction, the First Amendment apparently not applying to rappers.

The fact that the FBI wrote to NWA threatening them with dire consequences if they performed only proved that "Fuck Tha Police" wasn't art to be understood, but a document to be redacted. Blacked out. Police forces nationwide mobilized and sought to arrest NWA for performing the song, and threatened worse, earning Compton's finest the name of "The World's Most Dangerous Band." They too became an institution whose name stood for something else.

NWA could hardly be called victims—this singling out by the feds only upped the group's outlaw status, while also connecting them to the host of civil rights and black power workers before them unfairly targeted, often literally, by their own government. (NWA had already anticipated such censoring by naming one of their songs "Parental Discretion Iz Advised.") Still, the Golden Age's metaphors of "Public Enemy" and "Menace to Society" were not accidental, but all too real. Artists of every avant-garde who sought danger as their muse must have been red, black, and green with envy not to be so hunted.

The radio too became an enemy to be kept close. "How To Kill a Radio Consultant," "Turn off the Radio": the very song titles of hard-core hip-hop dared stations *not* to play them. What's more, when Ice Cube and others would later find radio play for a song like "It Was a Good Day," the so-called clean version contained bits, or should I say lots, of code. Lines like *I had the booze she had the chronic,* [inhaling sound], *the Lakers beat the Supersonics* or *I pulled out the jammy and killed the pootenany* were naughty and sometimes absurdly funny, an inside joke. The fact that radio couldn't catch such lines, or saw them as innocuous, was proof of the rappers' ingenuity and their lyrics' storying qualities—the lyrics' meaning changed whether you were inside or outside the music.[20]

The absurd apotheosis of this coding, some native, some imposed by censors, is found in the radio edit of Snoop Dogg's "Gin and Juice," whose chorus sounds like this: *Rolling down the street, smoking* [bleep], *sipping on gin and juice.* Last I checked, drunk driving was just as illegal as smoking indo, but somehow the word "indo" is a problem but smoking it is not. Radio (and MTV) is not bleeping an idea but a word that contains it. Such is the bullshit doubletalk of our prudish, public-face culture, one that "doesn't inhale" and would rather pretend not to enjoy what it regularly consumes.

The flip side of the radio censors is the way the radio often would not bleep out the word "nigger"—a far more shocking word than indo, and arguably far more obscene. Such paradox found its way in rap that used the word "nigger" while trying to diagnose racism. Luckily, sometimes the clean version of a song wasn't just bleeps but the savvy electronic slurring or "un-English" reversing of a curse word—or the "izay" talk Snoop brought back, hearable in old-school classics like "Roxanne Roxanne." All are interesting solutions to the idea of safe speech. Perhaps the best example of a "clean" version is Ol' Dirty's "Brooklyn Zoo," which replaces curse words with the sounds of shotguns loading; noise as music, wordlessness more telling than any word might hope to be. There are things worse than a curse. Ominous and omnipresent, "Zoo" is but one example of the radio version as not just a single but practically a remix. Whether on a 45 rpm single or a 12-inch, such a remix was for all practical purposes another song; its relation to the original is much like in jazz, expansive and exploratory.

Sometimes a song's clean version has new lyrics entirely: here it can become most troubling, as when a clean version of "Straight Outta Compton"—if you can imagine such a thing—substitutes "brother" for "nigger." Such a change only highlights what I learned in high school, and from Black English itself—what those who bowdlerize *Huck Finn*, changing "nigger" to "slave" haven't figgered—there ain't no such thing as a synonym.

Cut Creator

Hip-hop has fulfilled a view of the black artist as collagist begun in the blues, now reappropriating materials from musics that originated in African American culture. *What's my DJ's name? Cut Creator!* The music sought to show and prove that it ain't a question of using the master's tools to dismantle the master's house, but of what you do with your skills, taking your beats and rhythms from anywhere—the street, mainstream culture, dirt roads, obscure records, seemingly incongruous cultures, and ultimately, from your own flow—and rhyming over them. *It ain't where you're from, it's where you're at.*

With hip-hop, we have a full sense of the fragment, of meaning produced by juxtapositions of disparate elements.[21] The mash-up may be the post-soul artist's chief method of madness—not just combining things that heretofore we didn't know went together, but also making things masquerading as other things. In the post-soul lexicon, *mad*, after all, is a compliment. To perform; to render; to riff; to plunder: these are the post-soul artist's chief means.

Where Eliot's *Waste Land* owed some of its "riddims" to jazz (and St. Louis), and Pound's ideogrammatic method the grammar of black soldiers imprisoned in Pisa (not to mention the written Chinese language, however misread), hip-hop took such juxtapositions as its very base. "We think of the key, each in his prison / Thinking of the key, each confirms a prison." Reading Eliot's and Pound's long poems now in a hip-hop fashion may help us hear them less as echoes of other texts than as new originals, a pleasing, if jarring, sonic patchwork. As in hip-hop, we need not get every reference or sample. Rather, even the footnotes to *The Waste Land* become another poetic form, realized later by Langston Hughes's own *Ask Your Mama*, whose "Liner Notes for the Unhep" are prose poems of a sort that do not actually annotate but extend the long poem—to the very edges of the record.

Structured around the "Hesitation Blues," *Ask Your Mama* is the first poem of the break, anticipating hip-hop by a decade or more. Its music is of the time, but ahead of it—just as Lester Young entered always just a bit behind the beat. Like Satchel Paige's hesitation pitch, it can fool you, most every time—but leave you swinging.

How does hip-hop collage differ from the riffing montages found in the jazz aesthetic, or the transformative aesthetic found in soul? Hip-hop takes these fragments in their original, found form; the fragments in hip-hop are not necessarily shored up against the ruins, but left as representative of it. Often these breaks never unify, remaining comfortably or uncomfortably discrete, distant, and difficult to discern. It's not where the fragments are from, but where they now are at.

The freeze, pop-lock, the backspin, the stratch: these innovations were ways of testing and extending the tradition, of highlighting the here and now and the new kinds of hearing hip-hop sought, building its melody around the break.

If funk is indeed the intrusion of the past upon the present, no wonder what we might call the gangsta or "G-funk Era" used funk music to define a certain "O.G." or "original gangsta" quality. But gangsta rap took funk's groove for its own also to provide the feel (or better, the illusion) of smoothness—which made its nihilism more terrifying, not less. Through such a patchwork, hip-hop reenacted not only its own history but the history of modern music—which is to say black music—only in reverse. First disco, then funk, then heavy metal, reggae, and soul: all were sampled in their turn. But this ignores the many ways and means hip-hop moved sideways and roundabout through the past, looping as a form of longing.

You could say that the sound of the break was the search for history. I say it is the sound of history itself.

This longing is nostalgia, certainly, but also recovery—remembrance as totem, as fetish—not just repetition but repast, the meal after sending off who or what's gone. There are mournful turns and tones behind the music that aren't just the blues but that live in hip-hop's very structure. The blues fight the feeling of the blues; their descendant hip-hop mourns that feeling: and even that is missing. In hip-hop something, or someone, is always missing.

The Third Coming

The hip-hop DJ constantly contends with two seemingly competing forces: extending the groove versus maintaining the break. This proves a difficult dance to do, hip-hop insists—proving it by spinning the world on its head. Or by *piecing,* a form of graffiti writing (short for "masterpiece") in which connections between letters are maintained while also keeping their separation. Like names on the side of a train, this motion isn't just circular but cyclical; not just cyclical but cyclonic: in a word, a *cipher.*

The term for a hip-hop circle, particularly a rap gathering in which one freestyles and flows, a cipher might be an apt metaphor for the tradition: audience and artist are interchangeable, and might be "tagged" in at any time; anyone can join the circle, but you will become required to prove your worth within it once you're here. The cipher is both taut and loose, physical and a "mental state," a circle to "spit" or smoke in, a record and its backspin—which itself describes both Flash's innovation of keeping the break going, and the b-boy and b-girl's floorwork within the groove.

Hip-hop is fractal and molecular: look for one aspect of the culture and you find it somewhere else. Is it the observing that makes it move? Or is motion hip-hop's very essence? A *cipher,* after all, means a circle and a zero, a symbol of nothing—or, rather, of something not to be (easily) understood. Like "cleave," *cipher* is a self-antonym, a word that can mean two opposite things; *cipher* paradoxically means both a code and the key to that code. Like the Navajo code talkers during World War II, the cipher's native tongue cannot be easily discovered nor decoded. It cannot be broken, only spoken.

Hip-hop cannot be broken because it is broken already—it takes the "broken tongues" (and "broken giraffes") of the tradition as representative of the whole. Sometimes in doing so it seeks "unity" as previous generations had, whether in a disco or at Woodstock, through Paradise or the Party. This was the "We" generation's goal, as articulated by Leslie Fiedler: to be done with pretenses, to Close the Gap between there and here. If seeking such a "moment of Vision" required drugs, all the more fitting: whether man-made or homegrown, built or bought, such drugs suggested you used a technology to combat the gap technology had first produced between "Man" and "Nature"; or you clung to nature in order to get back to nature.

It is tempting to see this "we" also at work in hip-hop. But as the "We" Generation gave way to the "Me" Generation of the 1970s, the illusions (and some of the aspirations) of Woodstock rang hollow: the Great Funk grew. Soon it wasn't pot or LSD but cocaine—the unholy mix of natural and denatured—that held sway. In such a context, closing the gap and bridging the break became all the more important. Paradise stepped in as it often does, as balm and promise of Elsewhere, of being one with the universe—or at least with whomever you were dancing with. As Tricia Rose's *Black Noise* suggests, "In the mid-1970s, dancing to disco music was a seamless and fluid affair." Affair, indeed: the 1970s' real one-night stand was with the idea of unity itself.

Where "disco dances, such as the Hustle, emphasized the continuity and circularity of the beat and worked to mask the breaks between steps,"[22] hip-hop foregrounded the breaks as a way to toss away the mask. It sought a different kind of hustle. *Face* became not just a noun, nor a verb, but an interjection: as in, *In your.* The ultimate metonym.

Even "unity"—as in the title of that song by Afrika Bambaataa and James Brown, not to mention Queen Latifah's antisexism song by the same name—always stands for something else. It is, for Bambaataa, as his collaboration's subtitle suggests, "The Third Coming," backspin as rebirth. Bambaataa and Brown's duet is a song not just about peace and unity but about what those ideas are not: the song chants "anti" as much as it does "unity." *Anti-you and anti-me, are we really facing reality?* It is not vision but revision that the graffiti writer, the DJ, and break-boy or b-girl seek. How to do it not just well but again? How do we get back to now?

Prophets of Rage

Like few other musical forms before it, hip-hop is almost painfully aware of its own history. More like baseball, or boxing, hip-hop believes that its history, filled with struggle, early triumph, and exploitation, is also the history of America; and as in the national pastime or the sweet science, hip-hop insists that any view of history must include race in the mix. History in hip-hop is always in flux—circling back or talking back, the point is to find the breaks, looking for the perfect beat.

To step into the ring, or the cipher—the park, either ball or public—is to engage a history whether you know it or not—and not knowing might mean your undoing. The literal presence of earlier voices in the music haunts hip-hop in the form of samples. Just as the presence of the repeated party-starting phrases echoes about, there's always something slightly missing, untold in the hip-hop song. *Somebody, anybody, everybody: Scream.*

Public Enemy may be the last case of hip-hop seeking not just history but prophecy. If De La Soul invented the whole "skit" theme that unites hip-hop, then Public Enemy's *It Takes a Nation of Millions to Hold Us Back* was unified above and beyond the skits. *It Takes a Nation* sought not just nationalism but a worldview that suffused the entire record. From its title forward the record lied up a nation, insisting on an "us" defined by using negative space—or negative capability—outlining, or better yet piecing, another "nation of millions" that sought to hold "us" back. It was in all senses historic.

Structured like a concert complete with introductions by a British emcee (not an MC), *It Takes a Nation* greets the listener with sirens. These prove the backbeat of the album: in fact, with PE, I always loved that their instrumentals like "Show 'Em Whatcha Got" are made up of sampled vocals; their vocals are made of screeches and instruments; and their instruments are actually sirens, strangled beats, accelerated rhythms, and DJ Terminator X "speaking with his hands." A talking book.

It Takes a Nation was the first time I heard what postmodernism sounded like. Loud, layered, filled with longing and language—not just self-conscious but self-referential—the songs as produced by the Bomb Squad contained bits and even samples of songs by other people (such as Queen's "Flash Gordon" in "Terminator X to the Edge of Panic") as well as samples of other songs on the album itself. Like the nation, it suggested, the whole was the sum of its parts. Like DNA, or some good gumbo, each part could conjure the whole.

A few things sampled in Public Enemy's "Night of the Living Baseheads": sirens; "Sucker MCs"; "I Can't Get Next to You" by the Temptations *(Hold it, listen);* "UFO" by No Wave group ESG; Jesse Jackson introducing the Soul Children at Wattstax with the phrase "Brothers and Sisters, I Don't Know What This World Is Coming To"; "The Grunt" by the JBs, the source of those horns that sound like sirens; "Scorpio" off Dennis Coffey's *Evolution* (Coffey being a hip-hop favorite); "Fame" by Bowie; "Rappin Ain't No Thing" by the Boogie Boys with Disco Dave, Kid Delight, and Kool Ski; *Yo, Herb!* shouted by Salt-N-Pepa on "My Mike Sounds Nice"; Rufus Thomas performing "Do the Funky Chicken" live at Wattstax *(Wa-it a minute!);* and PE's own "Bring the Noise." This does not count the title's riffing off George Romero's classic movie *Night of the Living Dead,* which has a black protagonist fighting off zombies alternatively read as conformity or the status quo or a general cultural malaise—all of which ultimately prove less dangerous to him than an armed posse of white men with dogs à la Birmingham.

Some samples are used for just a second, others, like "The Grunt," form the basis of the song; it seems noteworthy that most if not all samples are from another, previous golden era, of soul and funk. This sampling also includes several white artists whose work crossed over to the R & B charts in the 1970s, including Coffey and Bowie. The result, or shall I say, the mix is that we are hearing not other people's music but how another era sounded; the listener as well as the original artists call up the plastic soul black folks chose to claim as their own, twice now. It is a sonic nostalgia almost doubled, brought to the fore and yet fought against by the fragmented form. Hip-hop is not just the past made present but an attempt to capture and re-create the music of one's parents and one's childhood, of soul and all it stood for. In many ways, Jay-Z suggests, it is an invocation, or literal connecting with, the albums a father may have left behind—music as an inheritance filled with loss.[23]

Now here's what I want you all to do for me, Rufus Thomas says at the end of "Funky Chicken," which in turn becomes part of the intro for PE's "Don't Believe the Hype." Wattstax, a celebration of black music and independence through soul music (and the Stax soul label run by whites and made famous by Isaac Hayes and others) was a form of re-building after the Watts riots; in sampling the concert so heavily, PE is connecting to if not channeling the earlier, live event (not to mention the riot going on). The Wattstax concert's asides, like James Brown's breaks, have become PE's centering force; PE has even borrowed the conceit of a concert to unify (yet break up) their album as a way of honoring the shared origins of hip-hop and funk.

The savvy of both Public Enemy and NWA may now be seen as two sides of the same counterfeit coin—not that they were fake in any way, but rather a recognition that both groups remained conscious of the ways outrage might sell and yet was the proper, if not the only, response to having the crazy blues. The downpressor may not have been news, but it could be best combated by making the thing new. If not right.

Called the greatest hip-hop song of all time, the PE song "Fight the Power" starts with *1989! a number, another summer.* Looking back, despite PE's attempts to make it the herald of a new era, 1989 seems a nadir for race relations, embodied in the names of two divergent New York locales: Bensonhurst and Central Park. We might agree with Jeff Chang that "Welcome to the Terrordome," Chuck D's musical response to his group's implosion, was the real sound of 1989—rather than the promise and empowerment of PE's "Fight the Power" a few months earlier.[24] As a haunting underscore of the time's troubles, the year would end with Charles Stuart killing his wife and unborn son in Boston and blaming a fictional black man, when Stuart was in fact the murderer.

With the case of the Central Park Jogger—when five black youths were accused of raping a white Wall Street banker in April 1989—the horrific event and subsequent arrests replayed old tapes in the national imagination. In many ways it was the era's own Scottsboro Boys case, though certainly the two incidents had key differences: not least of which that the jogger (only sometimes identified by name) was undoubtedly the survivor of horrific sexual violence that nearly killed her.

But the five teenagers were also the victims of a search for perpetrators and rough justice that led to a media frenzy despite or because of a lack of evidence; and ultimately to false confessions by some of them, later recanted, that led to their convictions despite lack of evidence. Several recent reexaminations of the case note how across the board the media coverage at the time appears overwhelmingly sensational, racist, and in search if not of a "monster" or predator—headlines called the boys a "Wolf Pack"—then a scapegoat.[25]

None other than Donald Trump called for the death penalty in full-page newspaper ads in all the four New York dailies.[26] Even acclaimed journalists sensationalized aspects of the case: "In his April 23, 1989, piece in the *Post*, A SAVAGE DISEASE, Pete Hamill, the celebrated city columnist, painted a menacing backdrop that would color the coverage to come: 'They were coming downtown from a world of crack, welfare, guns, knives, indifference and ignorance. They were coming from a land with no fathers. . . . They were coming from the anarchic province of the poor.'"[27] As many have pointed out, such media treatment (or "coloring") was not given to the perpetrators of the murder of Yusef Hawkins, killed for simply being black in the wrong Bensonhurst neighborhood later that summer.

Years later, after the Central Park Five served hard time, the real assailant and rapist came forward, DNA linking him and him alone to the crime scene. In 2003, even the original tough prosecutor asked for and received vacated sentences for the five young men. If they were now proved innocent of the crime, innocence seemed long lost.

Stories abounded that the Central Park Five sang Tone Lōc's "Wild Thing" while in jail—at the time seen as proof of their presumed guilt—giving us the word "wildin" as a verb. Like the recently disproven phenomenon of "crack babies," or the false accusations of Charles Stuart and later Susan Smith, these media-abetted falsehoods, however short- or long-lived, reflect real and largely racial fissures in the culture.[28] They are synecdoches as stereotype.

False accusations yielding false confessions: these all become forms of contraband. Their impact is no less troubling, or with real-world implications, than the use of "spectral evidence" to convict witches in Salem—foremost among these being Tituba, the black slave who offered her own false confession in the witch trials. Such a swirl of history—of spectral evidence and false confession, wildin' and witchhunts—can prove overwhelming for any but the most savvy to sort. Sometimes I wonder if those like Stuart, or the woman who recently falsely claimed that a black woman threw acid in her face—she had actually defaced herself—are some of our most insightful, if troubled, cultural critics. Racism is the actual perpetrator of these real crimes with false black faces; racism leads white people to deface or hurt themselves, their spouses, or children, rather than admit its prima facie wounding of their souls.

"Wildin'" would enter the lexicon, sounding, like "nigger" does, quite differently in black and nonblack mouths. The term was not of origin unknown (meaning black) but, like the recent fakeout term "flash mob," of dubious (meaning racist) origin. (Flash mob when whites do it = fascinating performance-art prank. When black kids are involved, it's seen as less flash than mob.)[29] As LynNell Hancock notes, wildin' was "a term that came to define the inhumanity of these kids. But it was never clear where it came from—the kids, the police, or the media ozone." I for one doubt any teenager would be singing a song as corny as Tone Lōc's "Wild Thing"; the song was in fact a huge crossover hit most popular with white frat boys. "'Wilding' was defined by the *Post* writers as a phenomenon not unlike the violent raves in *A Clockwork Orange*—'packs of bloodthirsty teens from the tenements, bursting with boredom and rage, roam the streets getting kicks from an evening of ultra-violence.'"[30] It is odd that it takes a famous fiction, like *Clockwork Orange*, and a highly moralizing parable at that, to describe another fiction—though in this case, one with real-world implications.

The gap between 1989's promise and its powerlessness is a duality of the kind literally held in the hands of that summer's *Do the Right Thing*, the Spike Lee film that "Fight the Power" provided the soundtrack to. "Power" was also the theme song of the character Radio Raheem, who wore large four-fingered rings that read LOVE and HATE. Raheem's death at the hands of police was far less fictional than it should have been, its real-life antecedents like graffiti writer Michael Stewart too many to name.

As with *Clockwork Orange,* many sought to censor the film, rather than agitate against the violence it indicted—not least of which was black critic Juan Williams who I won't forget declaring on *Oprah* that the film was dangerous and would cause riots. (More flash mobs, I suppose.) I myself saw a preview in Kansas City where our opinions were sought after the screening—should this movie be shown? My mother and I, with our strong favorable views, weren't exactly the test audience the company sought. Thanks anyway. What no one seemed to understand was the way *Do the Right Thing* was not interested in reality per se but prophecy. Soon enough, the uprisings in Los Angeles would speak louder than any cinematic riot.

Welcome to the Thunderdome

"Welcome to the Terrordome" describes the other side of "Power" and protest: pain. Chuck D raps, *I don't smile in the line of fire, I go wildin*[31]—a line that never was literal, but knew that to mistake a fear of "wildin" for the real thing was a place far beyond Babylon, a full-blown Terrordome no speech could survey. Much less redeem.

Utopian "Planet Rock" had given way to a fear of a black planet. On the PE album by that name, the Watts chant "Burn, baby, burn" would become "Burn, Hollywood, Burn" (after having first become a "Disco Inferno" and Wattstax's guiding flame). Soon, gangsta rap would transform what once was disco even further: PE's anthemic "Bring the Noise" would become Wu-Tang Clan's "Bring da Ruckus" before ending up as Method Man's "Bring the Pain." But as early as "Terrordome," noise and pain had begun to become one and the same. *Come on down.*

"Terrordome" remains the angriest, loudest, and most forceful song hip-hop ever produced—and that's saying something. Its ire elemental, its vitriol sparing neither Jew nor Gentile nor Black Muslim *(Every brother ain't a brother cause a black hand squeezed on Malcolm X the man),* "Terrordome" was a two-man apocalypse, "an intellectual Vietnam." The song takes in not just Chuck's fury at the position he was in—edging over into an anti-Semitism that Professor Griff's dumb-ass comments had gotten the group into trouble for in the first place—but a broader cultural moment, from Bensonhurst to the shooting of Black

Panther Huey Newton. What *isn't* in the song? Listening now, it sounds less like a polemic than a plea, a series of references without a center: this is not London calling, but the Terrordome talking.

Jazz's wordlessness became Chuck D's words, some of which were alarms, and all of which prove as much a howl as Ginsberg's decades before. *Writers treat me like Coltrane, insane.* The song was cyclonic, a spiraling down—and out—in a way reminiscent of Coltrane's late sax solos and also of what poet June Jordan terms "vertical rhythm":

> In traditional Western poetry, the rhythmical organization of words has been measured in relationship to the horizontal line. . . . In the 1960s, we, black poets, developed a different kind of rhythmical structure for poetry. I call it vertical rhythm. Rather than depending only upon a distribution of stressed and unstressed syllables in a line, the rhythmical structure of black poetry depends upon the exploitation of musical qualities inherent to each word, and existing between and among words as well. Assonance or alliteration, for example, can produce a smooth movement from one word to another, from one line to another, and can even propel a listener or reader from one word or one line *without possible escape.* Conversely, exploitation of musical devices such as dissonance inherent to, and discoverable between and among, words can slow or stop the movement from one word to the next or from one line to the next.[32]

We might expand Jordan's "vertical rhythm" to encompass a swirling poetics that takes in everything, from topicality to personal grief.

This poetic wildin resembles *wildstyle,* the technique graffiti writers used to express their own vertical rhythm on the sides of trains. A "complicated construction of interlocking letters,"[33] as defined by the classic book *Subway Art,* wildstyle is made up of connections and arrows, of three-dimensional naming and color. Often unreadable, or shall we say hard to decipher at one glance, wildstyle is a tangle that while visual also symbolizes the writer's skill and name, and provides a metaphor for a world being pictured—and conquered—around the graffiti writer.

In poetry, this form's exemplar is Jordan's own "Poem about My Rights," which swirls around a series of meanings connecting the author's emotional state with the news of the world. At its best—say, in Ntozake Shange's "choreopoem" *for colored girls who have considered suicide/when the rainbow is enuf* or Jordan's "Poem for Buddy"—such a poetics sees the political as deeply personal, which is to say made up not just of autobiography (as it is conflated with too often) but testimony, of people and events linked in, and sometimes only by, the poet's imagination. "I am not wrong: Wrong is not my name." Such a poetics went *wildin'*, linking the dissonance not just between words but between ideas.

At its worst, this has devolved into the all-tragedy-is-the-same poem, often unaware of its own bias, mired in what passes for history but managing in its buzzwords and arm's-length outrage to remain highly ahistorical. Centuries-old conflicts and whole countries—and continents—are reduced to less than headlines. Politics as platitude rather than protest. The result is a poem of equivalences and preagreement, not discovery but the party line.

It is in such a context, poetic and impossibly political, that the sirens of "Welcome to the Terrordome" announced not just an emergency but its being ignored. Echoing the Thunderdome found in the third Mad Max movie, the Terrordome is a place not just of negation but nihilism. Where the Thunderdome was actually a site of feudal justice crafted by Tina Turner's character in the postapocalyptic world of the film—a cipher where blacks are blond and "two men enter, one man leaves"—the Terrordome is both singular and all-encompassing, like the song. No justice, no peace. *My home is your home.* The method to PE's madness is often a recasting of James Brown's asides, the edges of the record, its soul moans and hollers, here forming the center of the song and transformed into one long wail. Chuck D's riffs aren't exactly autobiographical, or even sensible, words themselves almost reduced to their atomic level: *What I got, gotta get some, get on up, Hustler of Culture.* From the fissures, fusion of a near-nuclear sort.

Beside Chuck D's rap, the song's other principal vocal effect comes from Flavor Flav reciting lines from the end of Al Pacino's *Scarface:* these quotations, unattributed, serve as an alternative to a chorus; or rather, render the chorus not as a break, but a breakdown taken from Brian De Palma's exploitation film. Especially as an early reference to *Scarface* in hip-hop, for which the film has taken on the status of myth, the song doesn't seek to contextualize anything. Flavor Flav isn't speaking, as others would go on to do, *about* the movie; instead Calvin Broadus raps as Flav *as* Scarface, saying, *Who I trust? Who I trust? Me.* The potent, paranoid, coke- and dialect-addled drug lord—who, recall, dies in a hail of bullets and incestuous hubris—becomes here a chilling expression of fury as well as its critique. (Such is the vector of the exploitation film, which shows us the money before moralizing it as blood money not worth the price.) Flav's *So long now, have a good trip* would prove a sayonara as ominous as the Sex Pistol's *Destroy!*

Though I at first misremembered "Terrordome" as the final track on *Fear of a Black Planet*, "Fight the Power" actually has that honor. First released as a single well before the album, here at the edge of the record "Power" sounds a near-final note not of nihilism but negation: *Ah Beloved, let's get down to business, mental self-defense and fitness.* "Power" sounds hopeful and almost sweet after "Terrordome." Hearing its negation may put us in mind of Lester Bangs writing about punk and free jazz:

> For me, I'll stake ten years of writing about this shit on *Blank Generation* and *The Metal Box*. And *On the Corner* and *Get Up with It* by Miles Davis, which got kudos from jazz critics who never listened to them again and were rejected by the fans. The reason is the same: this is negative music, in all cases this is bleak music, this is music from the other side of something I feel but *I* don't want to cross, but if you feel the same then perhaps at least you can affirm this music, which knows that there is nothing that can be affirmed till almost (and that's my word, not theirs) everything has been denied. Or you can laugh hysterically at it.[34]

Such laughter would have to be provided by Flavor Flav. Speaking as Pacino's cracked-out character only heightens the gallows humor. *Come on down,* Flavor would chant, part game show host, part armchair colored-commentator broadcasting Armaggedon.

"Terrordome" seems especially poignant when listening to it now because you can practically hear how the Prophets of Rage had been almost innocent up till then, even as they demanded that we all "fight the power." *Scarface* then becomes an even more interesting matrix for the song: especially given that De Palma's film is a remake (at least at the title level), the movie is principally about the fall from innocence for someone who hardly had a claim to the term. Likewise, Chuck D sounds actually hurt on "Terrordome" in a manner that hard-core, even his own, rarely cops to.

Or is it exactly this hurt that we hear again and again on display in gangsta rap? Are the breaks in hip-hop actually a wound? The song's sirens, whether police or ambulance, signal no help is on the way: after all, as another song on the album declares, *911 is a joke.*

PART THREE: 36 CHAMBERS

You could say that if the so-called black condition now had many diagnoses, it still didn't have a cure. Enter Dr. Dre's *The Chronic,* its name standing for the "dis-ease" of the black nation made unignorable by the 1992 Los Angeles uprisings as well as its herbal palliative. Released later that year, *The Chronic* was both root cause and remedy, a smooth musical cure that went down rough—administered, after all, by a doctor.

Though the editors of *The Anthology of Rap* indicate that rap's Golden Age ended with *The Chronic,* they do not say why—nor do they include Dre at all. Instead, the editors file his huge hit "Nuthin' but a 'G' Thang" under Snoop Dogg, who appeared on the track—a bold move, it would seem, to indicate they are most interested in MC skills, not influence. (They could have credited many of the album's writers instead, such as the DOC.) But *The Chronic* ended the Golden Age because its real concept ain't cheeba after all, but replacing the MC—*to me, MC means to move the crowd*—with the producer who can rap and who crafts and sells beats to the highest bidder.

By the midnineties, many of the best rap lyrics aren't whole songs but guest appearances such as Busta Rhymes's life-changing star turn—and I mean life-changing for the listener—on A Tribe Called Quest's "Scenario." While a sign of rap's popularity, and in some way its love of apprenticeship, the guest appearance revealed the ways in which rap was no longer about getting there together, but about getting yours. *Doing for delf*—a distinction from self, which is both more expansive and less. *Delf* is the self as autonomous agent in the world—even a hostile one—going for broke, which isn't always the same as a self, which can and must contain others, even rivals, as other incarnations of one's own consciousness. Delf is also, like "def," a version of "death" as a good thing. It is speaking of the self in third person, *singular*.

That the choral quality of the Golden Age (an age, ultimately, of the MC) would from now on be replaced by the guest star (such as Snoop Dogg on *The Chronic*) reaffirmed the ways that any such appearance was ultimately a duet with the producer. Enter Puff Daddy (and Mase); exit Chuck D (and Flavor Flav). I started to feel that Dr. Dre is left out of *The Anthology of Rap* less because of possible permissions or aesthetic reasons but so that the editors can maintain the fiction that the MC's lyrics still reign supreme.

The Chronic

Around this time rap went mainstream due to two divergent, if not diametrically opposed, developments: its embrace by other musics on the radio; and its pilgrimage underground, where gangsta rap took over exactly because it couldn't often be played on the airwaves. (Ironically, the two seemed to meet most often in music videos.) Rap was once one music of many—soul, funk, reggae, even disco—all of which it would eventually come to devour and even replace. Back in the day, rap was the kind of music that had its time and place; party music, you played it to get down, not to get busy. Soon, my cousins would listen only to rap if they could—and given the increasing privatization of the musical experience, through headphones and vehicles, it was easier to do so.

Because halfway hidden, hip-hop spread, underground: listening to hip-hop was a sign of being with it; the farther you were from its seeming urban center, its hard core, the more crucial it became that you knew the real deal. Soon even pop music sought producers—often the same as hip-hop ones—to unsettle the surface of pop music, or realize the unsettling that had already long ago occurred with hip-hop's advent. Hell, even Prince had to learn to rap when he had practically perfected what used to be called "rap"—that talking at the end (or middle) of the track designed either to make it plain or make a play for a lover.

The rise of the guest appearance also meant the resurrection of the crew. Crews were to the 1990s what the gangs first were in the 1970s, before their allegiances became community organizations that then gave way to local and then upstart record labels, from Sugar Hill to Def Jam to Ruthless. These label years, from 1979 to the mid-'90s, were important ones; you could easily tell the story of rap using just labels as a bellwether. "Label" too seems the exact right word, as groups often identified with a label almost as much as their hometowns. "Def Jam, tells you who I am"; "Ruthless, is the way you to go, they know"; "You're rollin' with Da Lench Mob." (Chris Rock parodied this, hilariously saying you never heard the Jacksons give a shout-out to Epic Records.)

From at least *The Chronic* on, the dissolving and reforming of crews, from NWA to the Dungeon Family, would come to define this era as much as its commercial success. Any solo artist, whether Eve or Jay-Z or 50 Cent, would have to be part of a crew (often associated with a record label) to blow up; or would use solo success to blow up the rest of their crew. That these alliances shifted radically was a sign of their necessity in ways that the Golden Age's loose affiliations never could amount to: before, Native Tongues collective; after, D12 crew. One made records, the other sought to make it. For the crew is not a communal group—or an expansive American self—but a postapocalyptic one, tribal and tightfisted, ride or die, Death Row, Da Lench Mob. While diverse, the crew was by necessity united in ways that demanded a "we" but denied an "I."

Bring da Ruckus

Enter the Wu-Tang and their *36 Chambers,* managing far better than any other group to disperse and reconstitute, to continue to be Wu-Tang no matter the name on the record. Theirs was a last chance for the crew as collective: Wu-Tang took the form of not so much a supergroup as a group of superheroes; like the Avengers, they could reunite and do battle against all others, could visit and make guest appearances, and remain, above all, a "clan." They even referred to themselves with superhero aliases on top of their rap names: though he took his name from a villain in the kung-fu film *The Mystery of Chess Boxing,* Wu-Tang's

Ghostface Killah is "AKA Iron Man, Tony Starks, Sun God, Wally Champ, Tony Starks [again], General Tony Starks, Starkey Love, Pretty Toney."[35] *Ghostface Killah, knowumsayin', he on some now you see me now you don't.*

Like DNA the members of the clan recombinate. Speaking of GZA, Raekwon says, "He the backbone." "He the head," Method Man continues: "We form like Voltron, and GZA happens to be the head."[36] The RZA, Abbot of the Clan, not only was Bobby Digital, a superhero on wax (and in a movie of the same name), but RZA says, "Bobby Digital is about what molded me: comic books, video games, the arcade scene, breakdancing, hip-hop clothes, MCing, DJing, human beatboxing, graffiti plus Mathematics and the gods. That's hip-hop to me."

But Bobby Digital wasn't just an alias: the RZA sought to take it one step further, and become a superhero "for real":

> I had the car and I had the suit I was getting ready to go out
> at nighttime and right some wrongs. That was my plan—like
> on some Green Hornet shit. I had this suit built for me that's
> literally invulnerable to AK fire. The car was a black Suburban
> that I had made bulletproof and bombproof up to government-
> security-level standards. I called it the Black Tank. I still have
> it—it stays at the Bat Cave. I even had a good butler almost
> ready to go. He was going to be like my Kato, but he wasn't old
> enough yet. I was really on a mission, I really felt compelled.
> I spent hundreds of thousands of dollars. To get Bobby Digital
> up and online. To keep it real.[37]

What was once "suburban" now turned black and bulletproof: what could be more hip-hop and surreal than that?

Can It Be All So Simple

Hip-hop had gone from underground to outer space, from Boogie Down Bronx to Planet Rock to a Black Planet to Apocalypse, from "Midnight Train to Georgia" to Shaolin, an island of rescue, inaccessible by subway. Wu-Tang Clan sampled Gladys Knight's version of "The Way We Were," first grafted by her in concert onto the show tune "Try to Remember" as a spoken word piece that serves as a manifesto on memory: *As bad as we think they are, these will become the good old days for our children.* Nostalgic even for now, Wu-Tang had Knight's sample ask again and again, *Can it be that it was all so simple then?* If not tied to where we were from, then where we were at was intimately tied to how far we'd come.

The nostalgia Wu-Tang expressed was for a Far East fantasy, a place as real as Chinatown and as near as ancient China, as familiar as kung-fu movies and as urgent as the Blaxploitation flicks that balanced the B-movie double feature. Wu-Tang's love of the Japanese toy Voltron was a form of solidarity with the Black-Brown-Yellow Pacific, whether that meant the Asiatic-Black man and or what Ellington called the "Afro-Eurasian Eclipse." No surprise the Shogun Warrior toy I had as a kid (and still have) can raise his fist in a Black Power salute.

So what if the history or myth Wu-Tang echoed was not strictly their own? In their hands, this seems to me exactly the point, providing the highest fidelity. While Chinatown, as historian Ronald Takaki notes, had for some remained a site of fantasy, Wu-Tang took this fantasy not as gospel but as the basis of a shared hybrid philosophy—combined with a nostalgia for the old country, and their present island homes as Elsewhere. "Chinatowns in San Francisco and New York and across the country were *cultural islands,* cut off from the mainland of American society, perceived by whites as strange places to visit as tourists," Takaki writes, but "viewed from within, Chinatown was not a quaint ghetto, an attraction for tourists. For the people living there, the colony was their home and community—a place where they could live 'a warmer, freer, and more human life among their relatives and friends than among strangers.'"[38] As PE before them had dubbed Long Island "Strong Island," Wu-Tang would rename Staten Island "Shaolin," simultaneously meaning a series of trials and a temple. Theirs was a mythic and mystic geography, the ghetto a cultural island born out of exploitation and a shared plantation and inner-city past, raised on Chinese food, and grown into a place symbolic and sustaining. "A nine-man hip-hop crew based on Mathematics, chess, comics, and kung-fu flicks wasn't springing up in the middle of a Manhattan art scene. Only on a remote island can something like King Kong grow to his full capacity."[39] Shaolin is an Elsewhere descended from, and no less real than, the African slave's.

Remember '79? '87? *Everything was lovely.* You could say that while trying to sound new, hip-hop always had its own form of nostalgia. A nostalgia for things that never happened, for a "back in the day" that, if not strictly speaking myth, was ever expanding—or re-forming like Voltron. It was a past made of soul music and Saturday morning cartoons, the sacred (for them) meeting the profane of the present.

Hip-hop's longing is not for a past that never existed—as was the point of Dixie—but for a future that may never be. What hip-hop yearns for is *the past's view of the future*—sometimes soulful, others technological—a time when the future was filled with promise, with brotherhood and jetpacks, Voltron new in a box looking like nothing so much as a boombox unfolding. Back in the day, when a regular guy could be a superhero, not just a superstar.

Quite regularly, in songs from "Can It Be All So Simple" to "C.R.E.A.M.," Wu-Tang expresses less a nostalgia for a soft-focus childhood than a yearning for a childhood at all. Even if the childhood was difficult, or especially if. A song like Ghostface Killah's "All That I Got" both remembers and romanticizes childhood in a way familiar to African American culture—survival requires a bit of humor, even gallows humor, as well as self-reliance, that American mainstay. *Four in a bed, two at the foot, two at the head*: having had to sleep that way myself with my cousins in Louisiana, I and other folks—and with sufficient distance—remember it not simply as hardship. Rather, it is struggle as a form of sustenance.

Hard times aren't just protested in hip-hop. Now that they are moved past, hard times are revisited and held in solution, if not resolved. Hard times have totemic, even fetishistic power: "C.R.E.A.M." recounts the "bad old days" not to protest them, but to protest the present. "Cash Rules Everything Around Me" as a chorus does not describe a wish but is a statement of fact. The wish is hidden in the lyrics themselves, which describe the high cost of C.R.E.A.M. and imply the wish that it were otherwise.

From "C.R.E.A.M" to Notorious BIG's "Juicy," the first hit single of a hard-core group usually recasts the American dream: describing its limits through a "ghetto" past; but in describing it, putting it in the past. Such songs describe how once "It was all a dream," describing the illusions of the American dream while mourning its disappearance.

Hip-hop nostalgia is a form of conjure, conjure being one response to a history found in fragments. A remix.[40]

The spirituals beg the Lord to "trouble me," singing of the future as a protest against the present; resolutely present tense, the blues sing of trouble in order to sing a way past it; to rap about trouble is to insist you're no longer in it. *Rhyme pays.* Hip-hop raps of and samples the past as a corrective to the present, protesting past troubles even while missing them dearly.

What hip-hop longs for was long ago lost and is not quite innocence. What hip-hop longs for is longing itself.

Amen Break

Hip-hop courts ruin, which is the form of history it knows best. This does not, as some listeners fear, signal doom or threaten the end of the record. Sometimes this longing means rebuilding, other times declarations of "Triumph"—though even those triumphs are never as complete as hip-hop's boasts may suggest.

There's that mournful tone even in Wu-Tang Clan's own "Triumph," perhaps the best group song ever: though when Ghostface Killah says, *Yo, that's amazing* in a handoff from the previous MC, he immediately turns to a very different story view of "Triumph" from all that went before. It is a triumph too familiar with tragedy—or at least with its techniques, which hip-hop itself mirrors, shattering if not the self then societal norms—to ignore the break.

The break meant modernism itself. As Louis Menand says, "Insofar as readers of Eliot's early poetry experience a sense of thinginess, feel that this is the way the city really is for a particular consciousness at a certain pitch of *aboulie,* it is perhaps the consequence not of the creation of a new form but of the shattering of an old one, and, if so, it is important to the effect that the damaged vessel not be mistaken for a new and more adequate container—just as it is important for poems that break cultural artifacts into bits such as *The Waste Land* and Pound's *Cantos* that some of the shards be too small to identify."[41]

When folks sample something, they borrow not just the outside of the thing, the sound, but also a bit of its inner form, its meaning and history. While inner form is usually found by the blues or soul artist in a layered search for meaning and history, the hip-hop artist begins on the other side, making meaning from history and meanings already established, moving from inner form to an outer one.

It was ever thus. As Menand points out in *Discovering Modernism,* when Eliot stole a form, he also borrowed some of its sincerity.[42] Eliot did this seamlessly, however (which isn't to say it isn't brazen or ostentatious). But in hip-hop, as in certain African textiles, the seams are meant to show. The past keeps poking—or breaking—through.

For instance, NWA's "Straight Outta Compton" samples what's now known as the "Amen break." Dr. Dre borrowed not just its beat but also what was in back of it—the Amen break is the moment of excellence, ecstasy in the middle of a wordless prayer recorded in a cover of Curtis Mayfield and the Impressions. (Aren't all prayers wordless in some crucial way?) Mayfield's "Amen" itself is a form of storying, a version of a church saying arranged by Mayfield till it was both his own and all of ours—we sang it in my church and I assure you I had no idea it was something recorded anywhere. As with much of Mayfield's music, it was the tradition singing, it seemed.[43]

Hip-hop is not just a patchwork but an abstraction—like those quilted by the women of Gee's Bend. The quilters' tradition of reinventing, say, a husband's jeans into a pattern, or reworking bicentennial flag fabric, reconstitutes an America even better in memory, rivaling any other abstract expressionists of the twentieth century.

Forget history: too often it forgot them. Many members of the Gee's Bend community, it turns out, were left as "unidentified" in photographs made by white photographers in the 1930s for Roosevelt's Resettlement Administration; however well-meaning, photograph titles like "Home of the Pettways, Now Inhabited by Negroes" erase the people currently living in the house in favor of the former "owners," in all senses. This is especially true because Gee's Bend was filled with Pettways who were African American descendants of the plantation system.[44] The naming of the photos tells a larger story of history that named black folks after their "owners" and a reinforced forgetting that leaves them yet unnamed.

Against such forms of forgetting masked as preservation—or worse, sociology—the quilters of Gee's Bend crafted quilts, community, and gospel songs, putting these forms to both "ordinary" and extraordinary use. The quilts and even three-dimensional assemblages—reminiscent of nothing so much as the work of black contemporary artists like David Hammons or Leonardo Drew—that the residents have traditionally made were forms of storying, and counterfeit:

> The found-object assemblage and the quilt are two sides of the same coin; a quilt is simply a two-dimensional assemblage pieced together with the same philosophies and techniques as the three-dimensional one. As means of encoding information, both media can hide absolutely private meanings within often public manifestations. As a result, these "vernacular" arts that developed among blacks in the South were highly personal expressions, indecipherable by the general population of whites and many blacks, and easily overlooked or dismissed as meaningless by potential adversaries. . . .
>
> These found-object assemblages and quilts are deeply rooted in the philosophy of improvisation. In music, we hear it as variations on a theme; we see it in variations on a theme in African American cooking, dance, speech, and dress; and we see it in quiltmaking. Improvisation is so endemic to African American culture that children often learn it unconsciously by simply watching their families. Improvisation does not imply postponing decisions or basing them on impulses that arrive with a moment's notice. Rather, it represents an entire way of life in which predictability has been systematically, purposefully altered.[45]

But the key here—*I turn the key, and get this chorus* (Kraftwerk)—is that where jazz fusion or other ideas of improvisation implied mixing or maxing out harmony, hip-hop—that "found-object assemblage"—insists on fission, going down to the atomic level and splitting even that apart. Break beats. Divide and conquer. Dissembling as much as assembling. Survive, then thrive.

When done right, this splitting yields an explosive, near-nuclear reaction; when the mash-up works, it is an atomic collider that helps create a new form, forging an alloy and ally. It is history as unsaid, recording an undersong we might call prophecy if not concerned as it is with unpredictability.

Bring the Pain

While "Rapper's Delight" had borrowed braggadocio, by the 1990s the layers would be beyond any form of masking, the permutations of persona dizzying in their depth. For his part, Ice Cube stars in a movie called *Boyz N the Hood,* named after a song he wrote in the first person but that was rapped by Eazy-E; in the film, Cube played Doughboy, an alias playing yet another nickname: all this claimed to be real. I'm not sure why, given the coded continuity of African American expression, some thought that just because the words were more direct the message was too. If for a while the words of gangsta rap seemed no longer masked, the personae were all the more so. One might say that the two were in an inverse relationship.

It isn't just that the music industry or capitalism changed rap but that rap changed society—its desire for "realness" matched our own. Rap was first to declare the war on illusion that David Shields named in his book *Reality Hunger;* you could say that while responding to actual, ongoing problems—inspired, like the blues, by the often-devastating social conditions around it—rap's persistent personae, its aliases insisting they were just keepin' it real, found in realness *the* metaphor for our time. Realness, whether rap or "executive," is now found everywhere in our culture, from television to—well, is there any fiction left us? As one writer sampled by Shields puts it, "Realness is not reality, something that can be defined or identified. Reality is what is imposed on you; realness is what you impose back."[46]

Realness, then, is defined by what it's not. In this, realness is very much a descendant of the negationist strategies of the punk and the gangsta—as well as the pomo (I first mistyped "porno") artist. All have their own forms of hard core. To quote John Austin, as does visual artist Keith Arnett in his *Thousand Word Piece:*

> It is usually thought, and I dare say usually rightly thought, that one might call the affirmative use of a term is basic—that, to understand "x," we need to know what is it to be x, or to be an x, and that knowing this apprises us of what it is *not* to be x, not to be an x. But with "real" . . . it is the *negative* that wears the trousers. That is, a definite sense attaches to the assertion that

something is real, a real such-and-such, only in the light of a
specific way in which it might be, or might have been, *not* real.[47]

In African American culture, X represented the unknown necessary for
understanding, Malcolm's X. The result is a poetics of refusal—*by any
means necessary*—taken to the end of the record.

Is it any accident that the rise of hip-hop realness precedes and parallels
that of "reality television"? Or that so many rappers, male and female,
easily slipped into the role of onscreen actor? The very term "reality
show" is a paradox of the highest order, but does describe the mix of
mask, role-playing, and personae found on these forms of television—
complete with literal and societal scripts—and in far more subtle form
in hip-hop. Nor is it a coincidence that participants in both rap and
reality TV—even when it is seemingly for love—refer to their respective
genres as the Game? If for rap it's called that because of the business (as
well as its symbolic relationship to the "drug game" or the "fight game"),
both genres are highly aware of the parameters (which are few) implied
by the idea of a game, and refer to realness and gaming in nearly the
same breath, without irony (which is otherwise rampant).

Gangsta rap aliases would give way to multiple personalities, aliases
whose very tongue-tying length signaled their playfulness and prolific
quality: Ol' Dirty Bastard had perhaps the most names (the best being
Big Baby Jesus); not to be undone, Bushwick Bill would become Dr.
Wolfgang von Bushwickin the Barbarian Mother-Funky Stay High
Dollar Billster, "the longest alias ever."[48] More recently, Nicki Minaj has
taken up (and on) Lil' Kim's status as Queen Bee, if only by borrowing
her wigs. A figure like Kool Keith is the Fernando Pessoa of the rap
game, taking on not just other names but heteronyms complete with
unique characteristics and backstories. *The Doctor Is In.*

In contrast, the foibles of just two of those without rap aliases—
Kanye and Lauryn Hill—indicate not just the difficulties of being an
artist but the special challenges of the game for those who do not create
a distinct persona who says them things, who acts in them movies,
and who refuses to perform. (Even Tupac recorded as 2Pac.) Once un-
adorned as her nonnickname, Hill's recent adding of the prefix "Ms."
indicates the way a pseudonym offers not just realness but real protec-

tive powers—whether as an honorific or the kinds of protection offered by "basket names" in certain Gullah and African societies.

Fernando Pessoa may provide a further comparison here, not just for his love of disquiet, but for his poem "Autopsychography":

> The poet is a faker. He
> Fakes it so completely,
> He even fakes he's suffering
> The pain he's really feeling.[49]

It is as "autospsychography," as real pain masked by pretend pain, that hip-hop is poetry.

Torture

Hip-hop now took what first were old-school characters, then new-school personae, and replaced them with heteronyms—one person with different names, each with distinct if shared stories. Realism and reality had never been further away from each other, the artifice of what passes for "realism" never starker. No wonder the G-funk Era would lead to bling—showing more than proving.

In *The Theater and Its Double*, Antonin Artaud discusses theater in terms that quite often and surprisingly apply to hip-hop—especially when he discusses theater in terms of plague. "In theater as in the plague there is something both victorious and vengeful," Artaud writes, and we might recall that the Golden Age (and the gangsta era) also were plague years; years of disease and of epidemics, both real and imaginary, from crack cocaine to black extinction to the hype of the "crack baby":

> Between the victim of the plague who runs in shrieking pursuit
> of his visions and the actor in pursuit of his feelings; between
> *the man who invents for himself personages he could never*
> *have imagined without the plague,* creating them in the midst
> of an audience of corpses and delirious lunatics and the poet
> who inopportunely invents characters, entrusting them to
> a public equally inert or delirious, there are other analogies
> which confirm the only truths that count and locate the action

of the theater like that of the plague on the level of a veritable epidemic. . . .

Compared with the murderer's fury which exhausts itself, that of the tragic actor remains enclosed within a perfect circle. The murderer's fury has accomplished an act, discharges itself, and loses contact with the force that inspired it but can no longer sustain it. That of the actor has taken a form that negates itself to just the degree it frees itself and dissolves into universality.[50]

The sound of smoking and hits from the bong in Snoop and Biggie, not to mention the sounds of oral sex or other fluids, were ways of hard-core rap's further declaring its verisimilitude—often literally pissing on its territory. This is real, the songs insisted, and realness was, just like the broken glass in "The Message," everywhere.

But perhaps the verisimilitude of the rapper's body fluids has another purpose: not to reinforce realness, but a realization—or symptom—of an epidemic? "Extending this spiritual image of the plague, we can comprehend the troubled body fluids of the victim as the material aspect of a disorder, which, in other contexts, is equivalent to the conflicts, struggles, cataclysms and debacles our lives afford us."[51] You might call this epidemic *reality*. The hard-core rapper, the "tragic actor" enclosed within a cipher, seeks to free the self, dissolving into universality—any reluctance to do so is belied by the desire to be seen. Hip-hop is its own double.

The artistic overturning found in gangsta rap was a refusal of representation. Which is why it is so odd that it sought the illusion of transparency, of a clear view of life, rather than of art or at least artfulness. Such overturning was also inaugurated by NWA:

Time was, rappers were eager to tell you what they did for a living, and how well they did it. In fact, that seemed to be the only thing they wanted to talk about. Like generations of three-card monte men before them, they rapped about rapping, explaining how the trick worked even as they pulled it off. You can hear this on virtually any earlier hip-hop record. . . . Things changed with NWA. They were riveting storytellers, and they realized, long before many of their peers, that hip-hop storytelling was built on a paradox. How could any rapper be convincing if he kept reminding his audience that he was merely a rapper? How could he draw listeners into his narratives if he refused to stay in character?[52]

As critic Kelefa Sanneh indicates, by constantly referring to the art of rapping, early hip-hop had let the fact of its performance overshadow a necessary suspension of disbelief. Gangsta rap replaced this form of self-consciousness for another—it didn't so much drop the mask as re-establish the fourth wall between audience and those onstage.

In lieu of a theater of cruelty, hard-core rap would insist on a music of pain.

Is it real son is it really real son let me know it's real son if it's really real: in these lines from "Bring the Pain," Method Man issues less a chorus than a chant, less a question than a demand. The song ends with another example of "torture," the skit that starts "Method Man," his eponymous theme song from *36 Chambers.* "Torture" is the dozens on steroids—or better yet, skunk weed—the skit consisting of a series of traded permutations of imagined torture with fellow Wu-Tang Clan member Raekwon. Method Man wins, it would seem, if only by getting the last word—*I'll sew your asshole closed and keep feedin you, and feedin you, and feedin you, and feedin you*—and his namesake song begins.

Though many disses start out "Yo mama's so . . ." and end only when the mama invoked is actually too close for comfort, "Torture" starts there instead: with absence and without "Yo mama." Such displacement is as notable and symbolic as the dislocation expressed by the "mother-less child" of the Negro spirituals. When does such a ritual end?

Witnessing the presumed black body under stress in this skit only tells us the ways in which hip-hop provides a form of role-play, cultural work, and ritual. Some would say this ritual bears witness to the black body's assault from other precincts—but ritual also points to the ways realness is tied intimately to fantasy. However cold-blooded it may seem, Wu-Tang's torture is imaginary—and is as much a test of what we can stand to hear—and, occasionally, in its elaborateness and ironies, not just hyperbole but hyperreal, slightly funny.

Feeding and feeding, real and realer: all speak to the omnivorous qualities of realness, which can swallow almost anything. *I'm the dark side of the force.* The dangerous glamour, part performance, all spell, is no less effective for being conjured by mere words. *Come inside my astral plane:* realness is a mind-set, an astral and aesthetic one, the psychic posed as physical. *I'll fuckin cut your eyelids off and feed you nothin but sleeping pills.* However violent, what realness seeks is wakefulness: it is both the clamps keeping the eyes open in *Clockwork Orange* and the eye makeup the droogs don before committing ultraviolence.

The violence isn't just the way of keeping it real, but in insisting on being imaginary, "Bring the Pain" evokes this form of nihilism while also emitting a cry of consciousness. The cannibalism being evoked is also reminiscent of the hunger evoked decades earlier in Will Marion Cook's account of creating the first black opera on Broadway; it is less carnage than the cravings of imagination. The effect is reminiscent of a zombie movie, where the zombies' hunger is the only humanity left them. Not being conscientious about one's cravings is the point—and may prove far less harmful than actual torture justified in the name of governments and gods.

All this devouring and dismembering is synecdoche incarnate. Not just the song but the soul too is in pieces, masquerading as the body. Recall "The Message," where the lines

> They pushed that girl in front of the train
> Took her to the doctor sewed her arm on again

appear as if from out of nowhere. Yet this train has been circulating both in the blues *(I'm going to lay my head / On that lonesome railroad track, / But when I hear the whistle, / Lord I'm going to pull it back)* and in "The Message" itself, which declares, *I think I may highjack a train!* Part subway, part Trans-Europe Express, this train may actually be the "Black Diamond Express to Hell" sermonized by Rev. A. W. Nix. The couplet's disconnection from the rest of the lyrics is a way of enacting, and not just describing, profound loss.

As such, our discomfort with "Torture" may be directly related to the comfort Method Man seems to feel with the same. But like Eliot before him, it is the cultural fragment—if not a fragmented culture— that finds its way to a whole, or at least an audience. But this particular Method may make you dance.

It is at the end of the record—where Marvin Gaye goes to church, sanging, *Makes me feel sanctified,* where Otis Redding whistles—that the song "Method Man" starts, inverting both sanctity and destruction, denying one and welcoming the other. "Bring the Pain" would end with torture, inverting the inversion, declaring not eternal sleep as sanctuary, but eternal sleeplessness as a state of pain made permanent.

Just because the truth hurts don't mean all pain is truth.

PART FOUR: 99 PROBLEMS

Some had always taken the Golden Age literally, wearing it as chains around their necks. Soon, we'd need a new word to describe both the new flash and the high price of what followed: *bling.* Coined by Lil Wayne, bling was the synecdoche turned symptom—and was so catchy that it is now a word almost always used in invisible quotation marks.

In such a world, any distinctions between personhood, personae, and character—in all senses—begin to blur. In his 2010 book *Decoded,* rap superstar (and mogul) Jay-Z writes interestingly about the relation of realness and the game:

> Rappers refer to themselves a lot. What the rapper is doing is creating a character that, if you're lucky, you find out about more and more from song to song. The rapper's character is essentially a conceit, a first-person literary creation. The core of that character has to match the core of the rapper himself. But then that core gets amplified by the rapper's creativity and imagination. You can be anybody in the booth. It's like wearing a mask. It's an amazing freedom but also a temptation. The temptation is to go too far, to pretend the mask is real and try to convince people that you're something that you're not.[53]

I would say the process of wearing that mask *requires* saying what you're not—over and over again. From gangsta rap on, this has meant saying I'm not this, I'm not that—or you're this, I'm that—less negation as a form of transformation than as mere denial. *You can get with this, or you can get with that.* The recording booth becomes Clark Kent's phone booth from which the rapper emerges as Superman. Or Jigga Man. Or Hova.

This renaming began as reclaiming—NWA claimed Compton as a symbolic not just a geographic area, similarly ambiguous and terrifying as Chinatown was to those outside its bounds; Eazy-E was the little man (played by auteur Roman Polanski) in the film *Chinatown* who cuts Jack Nicholson's character Jake's nose open. Both Eazy and Polanski charted a city within a city—a Los Angeles some would call underbelly, others home.

Eazy-E was also the little man in Chehaw Station, who, Ellison wrote, knew more than we might about the tradition—or at least its end. If Eazy-E helped open the door to the gangsta era, his death in 1995 from AIDS-related illness closed another. Is it once-invincible Eazy's passing from a too often silent disease, not to mention the murders of Tupac and Biggie, that marks the real end of the Golden Age of rap? While rap in its Golden Age had been one of the few musics to address safe sex directly, whether from the humor of Kool Moe Dee's "Doctor" or Salt-N-Pepa or TLC's safe sex campaigns, Eazy's death isn't enough discussed in its impact, however temporary, on the game.

Hard Knock Life

Jay-Z continues in *Decoded*—its title alone indicating the coded nature of hip-hop—with a discussion and critique of *Scarface*. Among a list of "Lines from that movie [that] are scattered all over hip-hop, including my own songs" is one that might be closest to any code talker's heart: *I always tell the truth, even when I lie.*

Any insistence on authenticity seems to forget—or became necessary exactly because—such authenticity could be appropriated and not earned in hip-hop as it once was in jazz by cutting your chops. Woodshedding is not typically a hip-hop rite of passage. In hip-hop's growing history, all too soon authenticity has become overdetermined; or determined merely by popularity in a tautology of sorts. A cipher. Rap artists are made popular because they are popular; are rich because they show you the money; are gangsta because they say so.

It's a hard knock life—we get kicks. By sampling *Annie,* the musical about an orphan who achieves riches and sings about it—the sample actually coming from the chorus of children in the orphanage—Jay-Z borrows their pluck and plaint, as well as making something so unlikely, something unequivocably white into something black. He also borrows Annie's success story, implying he's not just an orphan (and that "we" are not just a motherless child, far far from home) but also Daddy Warbucks, prosperous and providing.

The kicks we get in the bars of the song are very much the "kicking reality" that NWA used as the intro to "Express Yourself." Kicks can mean "beats" too—but I get the sense of not just kicking reality in the black vernacular of "throwing down reality" but also kicking reality as a vehicle to test to see whether its tires are still sturdy. "Express Yourself" is at times an antidrug song (Dr. Dre announcing *I don't smoke weed or cess*), and at times a message against hypocrisy: both would soon be thrown over by Dre as surely as he had thrown over the costumes of the party-rap group he and Yella had started in for NWA's gangsta drag.

I've started to think the intro to "Express Yourself" means "kicking reality" as in "kicking the bucket"—not in terms of killin' in a performance, but meaning killing reality off. In Jay-Z, *we get kicks* may also mean shoes—and the walking blues. In this one word, *kicks*—from thrills to drugs to sneakers to a hard-luck tale—we see the changing of the guard, again, from the producer who can rap to the rapper who can produce not just records but a record label. The maker as mogul, translating the street game to the corporate one—and making this somehow the stuff of realness (despite his millions few confront Jay-Z on keeping it real) that changes reality (making him richer than God).

Still, hip-hop's many admonitions—to show and prove, to flow, to kick reality—reinforce the idea that what is necessary is not art but fidelity. This is a radical notion, not because fidelity doesn't require invention, but because it speaks of invention as a case of gathering not speed but evidence.

Of being exemplary in all senses. A mogul even. But not, God forbid, a role model.

Gimme the Loot

Ready to Die is the last great hip-hop concept album. There may be others after, notably by Notorious BIG's protégés Jay-Z and Lil' Kim, but in Biggie's debut, you can see the last great collapsing of character and narrative in one danceable form. It is one of the best blues I know.

Straightaway *Ready to Die* gives us the kind of thing usually found on a second rap record: starting with *De La Soul Is Dead,* many a group, especially ones seen as alternative, used their second record to work out their self-perceptions, to reiterate that despite being successful or seemingly soft, they were actually hard. Give a listen to the Pharcyde's second album's single "Can't Keep Runnin' Away"—or even "Check the Rhyme" by Tribe—to see the ways such groups used either hardness or nostalgia (or both) to evoke their authentic origins, mixing danger with desire in recognizing "things done changed."

Biggie's collapsing of history, "spreading love" and even sampling from rap's recent past, established him as just another fan and listener who got lucky. Or, as someone who's good (as on "Juicy"), or dangerous ("Gimme the Loot"), or self-destructive (the whole record). "Things done changed": the record starts by self-consciously insisting on the radical redirection in Biggie's life after getting a record deal. While true, doing so also acknowledges that he's making a record about making a record, and what's more, about making it period. *Blowing up.*

It wouldn't be until De La's underrated, unbelievable third album *Buhloone Mind State* that a group could manage to claim *It might blow up but it won't go pop,* while also declaring on "I Am I Be," a manifesto of self that is expansive, multitudinous, and unapologetic: *I maximize, my soul is the right size.* Biggie's first record charts the largeness of something else—an echo chamber in which death is ever near. If De La Soul is "Dead," Notorious B.I.G. is already "ready to die," death being def in another form.

Biggie's song "Gimme the Loot" is a kind of duet—not like the usual guest appearance, but more like "Bring It on Home to Me" or Big Maybelle's "Gabbin' Blues," where two vocalists trade off, echo, retransmit, and even argue with each other. (This is true even if, as some have argued, and I have come to believe, that it isn't another rapper but

Biggie himself putting on the other voice!) Such dueling is a kind of dualism and embodies all the strategies in the music—simultaneously the code and the decoding, a community and the "I," the longing and "the loot." The imperative found in many of these songs' very titles is a sign of their yearning.

The loot Biggie seeks in his song is also literal: the song is an account of carjacking, and at times a how-to. The result sounds as if he's convincing himself (or us) into doing the deed. Though each song meets a similar end—a shoot-out with police—"Loot" differs from Slick Rick's "Children's Story," which is told by a third-person narrator. In "Gimme the Loot," the storying is done by the jacker. One is a fable with a moral, the other a story Biggie represents as real, or at least as a real wish, even if a death wish. *Ready to Die* is an encounter at the crossroads.

Loot is also the devil's bounty, symbolic of the crossroads encounter, and is ultimately a metonym for Biggie's success as a whole. As in "C.R.E.A.M.," the loot is a stand-in for money that is in turn a stand-in for far more. *Money, power, respect, the key of life.* It is both a call for, and a critique of, cash money.

Gimme the Loot—I'm a bad, bad man, Biggie's chorus says. The second half of that line is a sample, letting us know this braggadocio isn't just Biggie's but a well-worn history. You could call the very sample an example of longing. Certainly the mix of voices, from the vocal to the sample, is part of the whole song's fabric. The real fable it would seem is of the self—even Slick Rick's own morality tale ends in *Knock em out the box Rick, out the box Rick*—the Ruler's ultimate story is one of self-conscious display.

These days we don't bring the pain, we bling it.

History in hip-hop is often fractured, as suggested by the form if not by the rappers themselves. In "Gimme the Loot" this occurs when the second voice declaims

> You don't have to tell me shit
> I been robbing motherfuckers since the slave ships
> With the same clip and the same 4-5.

Besides being bleak and playful, does this transformation differ from Sam Cooke's "Bring It On Home," singing

> I will always be your slave
> Till I'm buried, buried in my grave

itself riffing on the freedom song insisting *Before I'd be a slave I'll be buried in my grave.* As with DMX's "Ruff Ryder Anthem" chanting *Home of the brave, my home is a cave* and *Yo, I'm slave to my home it's the grave,* all these songs contend with the *fact* of slavery through the form of fiction, or storying. We may prefer one tune to the other—one's a love song, another a hymn, the other parables or more—but all wrestle with history as fracture and flux, exactly through the forms of fracture and flux. All discover parts of the groove—they just drop the needle on different places on the same wheel within a wheel.

When you give a good listen, references to slavery in hip-hop are manifold. It is tempting to see gangsta rap or just the gangsta as a delayed response to the trauma of slavery—though I'm not sure how delayed it would be when barely over one hundred years removed from centuries of bondage. *I be the new generation of slaves here to make papes to buy record execs grapes.* It seems more fruitful to view rap music's remembering as exactly that—the process, often physical, of putting the dismembered back together.

The Robot

This re-membered body is on display in b-boying. Or should I say breakin'? Descended from the Robot, the b-boy or b-girl's moves are forms of deformation in defiance of gravity and other seemingly inexorable forces. They are the literal embodiment of what "Planet Rock" sang of—the "body rock" takes the technological desire to be a machine (seen in Kraftwerk) and marries it to liftoff (found in Bambaataa's transformation). All is leavening—not in the lightness of the Lindy Hop, the black dance named for Lindbergh's transatlantic flight, but of the exiled Afronaut. Like history the body is fractured, broken, breaking—it is not always a robot running well, but one running in place or away or at times on empty. At times it just goes backward, moonwalking. Popping and locking, an arm dangling like the Tin Man looking for a heart, out of juice. Or the Scarecrow, all brain all along.

One of the theories being tested on the dance floor is about the self seeming to shatter. If it is not holy, as the body in funk music, then the hip-hop body is not exactly seeking to be whole either. Freakish and an affront, the b-boy or b-girl attempts to do what the body cannot do.

Too soon, this would translate to mean the body in hip-hop would never be divine or funky—merely freaky. And *female,* which hip-hop has unfortunately helped turn from an adjective to a noun, from a description to an objectification. Such devolving is in part due to the corporal becoming corporate: "Mo Money, Mo Problems"; video hos; "Hip Hop Is Dead." No matter its initial innovation, the fish-eye lens from the mid-'90s hip-hop video was symbolic of a kind of broader myopia.

Gone, too, was another form of protest, first found in the music itself (not just the lyrics), which implied all the music's shifts, these breaks and borrowings, were beautiful. This isn't to say that rap isn't still gorgeous, and often, but when realness rules, rap's jazzlike yearning—found, say, in Pete Rock and C.L. Smooth's "They Reminisce over You (T.R.O.Y.)"—becomes rarer and rarer. There is, after all, an alternative universe where gangsta rap and what was once called "acid jazz" shared the stage, and hardness became not the only value. I keep hoping not for more teachers—nor for more liturgy, like KRS-One has produced now, in *The Gospel of Hip Hop*—but for more of the bizarro-rhyme (and buddha-sack-influenced) rap of Gang Starr's "Dwyck," featuring Nice & Smooth, or the jazz tones of Rammellzee's "Beat Bop," with its cover drawn by Basquiat, who also produced it—not to mention the alternative reality where rap kept being alternative.

But maybe I'm just being nostalgic—or hopeful that the recent resurgence of the turntablist and DJing, from Danger Mouse to DJ Rupture to television's DJ Lance Rock, is a sign of rap's return to its origins.

Maybe what we need is not more back in the day. We need less fusion; less poetry trying to be rap, or vice versa; less fiction pretending to be real and more forays into the unfamiliar. Hip-hop needs less prosody and more poetics; less philosophy and more history; less history and far more prophecy, to see the end all these records might make mean. We need the new.

You could say that rap doesn't need a reconstructed past but a fantasy of a future first promised by Bambaataa. Not just the expansiveness and otherworldliness of "Planet Rock" but its wordlessness—*Zuh Zuh Zuh Zuh Zuh ZUH, Zuh Zuh Zuh, Zuh Zuh, Zuh-ZUH, Zuh-ZUH.* Transcribe that.

Pre-Millennium Tension

Rather than a fruitful futurism, we had us some pre-millennium tension. Tricky's album by that name might have best captured the feeling of our millennial moment, whether the feeling stemmed from a fear of a black planet or mourning a lost one. If only we knew the terrorism, war, actual torture, and dissonance that lay around the corner—but this presumes hip-hop's chief form is prophecy rather than history.

For a while there Tricky, not to mention his trip-hop cohort, was the future of hip-hop. He did so by going back to the past on his first solo record, *Maxinquaye,* named for his mother—there he offered up a cover of "Black Steel in the Hour of Chaos" by Public Enemy. The original song, with its depiction of a jailbreak spoken by one of the prisoners—"rebels without a pause"—revolutionized the rap single as Run-DMC had earlier; certainly PE's video was one of the more shocking visual statements even on an unshockable MTV. (We used to call it "WTV" or "White TV" before the Pointer Sisters and Michael Jackson desegregated it.) By recording the song in the voice of his female vocalist and romantic partner, Martina, Tricky's "Black Steel" makes the case for hip-hop as its own original; here, originality is not the standard, or the start of culture, but its end.

Tricky also takes hip-hop's multitude of voices and throws them even further, writing not just autopsychography but an autobiography, as Gertrude Stein did, through the guise of a lover's eyes. This is not a duet with a female vocalist—as is often the case when rappers want to inject soul into their production, ever since at least Snap's "The Power"—but the female mask used to give voice to a male persona. Tricky bends gender and genre too, introducing the frame where there was none. Is Martina speaking about or in the voice of "the black man so I can never be a veteran"? In a sense, both: she is speaking for the veteran, and for

Tricky, as well as for the implied community—not just of prisoners but of antiauthority "fugitives"—created by the jailbreak at the song's end.

Tricky's version of "Black Steel," even darker and far more sped up than the slow, "Message"-like original, returns us to that initial shock of first hearing the song—while also recognizing that the original itself contained other songs. Hip-hop's own standard of stealing—"biting," or "potholes in my lawn," or borrowing without adding one's own flavor—still recognizes that little is new under the sun. PE's version starts with a sample of the spoken interruption (or skit) that appears in Stevie Wonder's "Living for the City." The migratory promise held out and unrealized in Wonder's song eventually lands the song's protagonist in jail. *Get in that cell, nigger:* the clanging of bars in "Living" is a break in the song you cannot dance to, a stand-in for jail—though the ultimate punishment is not incarceration but "living just enough."

In PE's version, the sampled phrase *Get in that cell, nigger* is a metonym for Wonder's full meaning. Tricky's song starts without either the CO's orders or the clanging. The clanging instead is internal, symbolic, loss as a kind of harmony: the chaos found in PE as a sign of the post–civil rights-era promise—already critiqued in Wonder—becomes in turn the backbeat and beginning of Tricky's own "Black Steel." His title doesn't mention "the hour of chaos" that PE's fuller title does—instead of narrative, or time, the repetition of *I got a letter from the government the other day opened and read it, it said they were suckers* becomes a mantra to stave off chaos—as well as a sign of it. More is more: what's being invoked through the voice is not just steel but steeling oneself against the chaos, made all the more poignant knowing Tricky spent time in jail.

Is it also stealing away? Or just stealing? Martina's mantra also means that we never quite reach the jailbreak, at least lyrically. If there's escape in Tricky's formulation—both originals, after all, are about escape; one from the city (and before that, Mississippi), the other from prison—it's well hidden. This is no accident. For Tricky, PE's prison break becomes a broken record, but one we might could dance to.

As a whole *Pre-Millennium Tension* combines social commentary and a music of discomfort to enact heartbreak of the broadest sort: even the opening "Vent" quotes from "The Message," *Don't push me 'cause I'm close to the edge.* Tricky's early solo albums enact many of the journeys one finds in African American culture, whether speaking of how "hell is round the corner" or "suffocated love." Another song also declares "my evil is strong," declaring it better to be a king of hell than a slave in heaven (or at all). His second record's single, "Christiansands," even serves as a manifesto of sorts, back when hip-hop had such things. The song samples "La Di Da Di," that a cappella masterpiece—with its beats made with the human voice, and its voice invoking instruments, or at least its notes—in order to declare the start of a new language. Tricky reminds us that refusing to speak a language is not the same as not being able to. *It means we'll manage, master your language—And in the meantime, I create my own.*

Give Me One More Chance

Not only to sample but to sing another song's chorus, something that happens with great frequency in hip-hop but that I never hear spoken of enough, is to connect not just to that song but to a tradition of riffing, reverb, and rememory. And to mourn it even, not through silence—though there's that—but through the dance. *There's a party at the crossroads.*

It all comes down to recognition and representation. *Recognize* and *represent,* two of hip-hop's favorite terms, acknowledge not just an obsession with origins but with re-ing, with not just seeing and being seen but doing it again. The remix. The dub. Self-awareness is one thing, but what makes hip-hop distinct is the degree of its self-reflexivity—to sample oneself is to participate in the oral tradition, to recognize (as it were) not just your own, but hip-hop's origins in every instant. *We're all self-conscious I'm just the first to admit it.*

Only in hip-hop and house would a term like "the original remix" be necessary. *Let's stay together,* soul music asks, in earnest. *Let's do it again.* In contrast, hip-hop says, *Let's get ready* or *Let's get free:* it is preparation for an action, hibernation as a form of nation building.

Ice Cube uses the Staple Singers' song "Let's Do It Again" in a remix of his "Today Was a Good Day" in order to evoke nostalgia for the very family the singers represent; and for the playfulness of the string of ghetto comedies of the 1970s, starring Sidney Poitier and Bill Cosby, that "Let's Do It Again" was the title song for. There is also the strange fission in the original "Let's Do It Again," where, especially given the Staple Singers' gospel origins and soul's double meanings, the title refers to a kind of resurrection that isn't all physical. The song is about satisfaction—in perpetuity, or a loop. The movie *Let's Do It Again* is about getting over, outwitting the mob; Ice Cube's song may rap about getting over, but is far more about getting through. *Livin just enough.*

The original mix of "Good Day" uses the Isley Brothers' "Footsteps in the Dark (Part 1 & 2)," taking on both its mood and its meanings. Even if we don't recall the lyric, it still lurks behind it all: *Let's look at what's been happening and try to be more aware*; or, *I still care, I still care, what's the sense of going elsewhere?* These questions of a beloved, which might be America, are now the haunting footsteps that haunt "Good Day" both sonically and symbolically. Both ask, What might have been? What if there wasn't an Elsewhere? Cube's song (and video) are one of a life surveyed and under surveillance, of a day going so perfectly because of what all happens—and what doesn't.

No smog, no pigs, no barking dogs, no hog: *Plus nobody I know got killed in South Central L.A. Today was a good day.*

Dear Mama

The hip-hop love song is a genre inaugurated by Spoonie Gee's "Love Rap" (1979), popularized by LL Cool J's "I Need Love," elevated by "Bonita Applebaum," perfected by Mary J. Blige, and wedded in all its contradictions by "Give Me One More Chance" by Biggie Smalls, the most unlikely seducer in the history of radio play. (Or play, period.) But to put that song on at a party—say, at an after-afterparty, dancing in a commandeered hotel room—is to see how Biggie's directness, which is sometimes crass but always clear, can be honest and playful and pleasing. And that ugly, like noise, is not just relative, but something to be redeemed: *Heartthrob never, black and ugly as ever.* The ladies seem to like it.

The hip-hop love song is not a genre in love with prettiness but one of seduction and suspicion, of confession and conflict, even one of testing and testiness; it is, like hard-core rap, which has a surprising number of such songs, about the beginnings of feeling and about the desire to desire. Notorious BIG, and even the hip-hop love song, ain't necessarily for lovemaking—it is not music to make babies by, as with Barry White, Biggie's spiritual big poppa—but for before, for the dance floor, the hustle, the grind.

Bumping uglies. That space, between meeting and making, between a good time and the nostalgia for those times—between "Good Times" and "Delight"—is the one good hip-hop occupies. Being "down" seems to be the larger point of the hip-hop love song. *Real love,* as Mary J. sings. *What's next?* the music asks, like the dancer imploring the cosmic DJ. Just because you make a request, hip-hop says, don't mean you'll get to hear it. But you can hope.

Why do so many hard-core hip-hop songs sample love songs as their basis? Certainly they could use other tunes, protest ones or dance songs—but even PE's "Fight the Power" only borrows its name, not the tune, from the Isley Brothers. The reason: hard-core hip-hop doesn't just borrow the love song's groove but its longing.

Longing in hip-hop is always aspirational. Hip-hop even aspires to *want*—hip-hop charts a preparation for a feeling, not necessarily the feeling itself. *I could really use a wish right now.* In this way hip-hop isn't always useful for, or used to, the idea of being in love or of losing love. "My Girl," soul music sang. "I Feel Love," sang disco. Like its crazy cousin nicknamed New Jack Swing, hip-hop insists, "I *need* love." *You—you got what I* need—*but you say he's just a friend.*

In much the same way, the desire to believe Tupac is still alive despite all evidence to the contrary—including his mother's identifying his body—is a longing to keep alive something larger. To reclaim a kind of invincibility—something that Tupac himself seemed to believe in and promoted after his surviving a first shooting while visiting a studio that also held Notorious B.I.G. Paradoxically this life wish also hopes to maintain Tupac's vulnerability, at least emotionally, something found in his best songs.

It is a wish for rebirth, in other words—a wish for the past not to be past and for the future to be constantly rewritten. *Nostalgia for a past vision of the future.* Tupac's prolificness *after* his death is proof positive not of art's surviving but of life's. To think otherwise admits too much, his contradictions our own: to wish him invincible is to wish ourselves the same, and yet to admit our own mortality in the very face of his immortality. He is in this way half a saint—to be saved, certainly, but also something of a savior, the Black Jesus he regularly invoked.

It is interesting that this rebirth wish is not usually expressed for Notorious BIG, shot less than a year after Tupac—perhaps because Biggie's cortege through Brooklyn provided a kind of state funerary procession, a funeral train of the kind associated with presidents and fallen leaders. Given the lack of such a public funeral for Tupac, belief in his survival is not just a way of keeping him alive but of mourning what wasn't, at least publicly, properly mourned.

Such belief in Tupac's afterlife is one I've heard mostly expressed by women, both in private and in public, as symbolized by poet Nikki Giovanni tattooing Tupac's motto "Thug Life" on her arm. Giovanni's tattoo isn't strictly speaking a belief in his being still alive (or even in thug life), but rather a form of mourning—skin a public memorial to private pain. Both reactions, denial and painful memorial, provide a crucial kind of motherlove—fierce and profound yet, it fears, powerless.

Such motherlove is the opposite of the dozens, which is to say the two are closely related. The dozens end when someone says something too truthful, too close to home, about one's mother; at that point, language stops and actions, even fisticuffs, begin. *Ask Your Mama.* Hip-hop's particular form of mourning and motherlove starts where torture, the dozens, and even the record ends: moving back from truth and action, through the playful taunt and black forms of metaphor toward language itself; a name on an arm.

Life After Death

A leg, a heart, a language, a tongue: the break in hip-hop can be all those at once, staving off what? Some might say the escape hip-hop provides is from death, others an escape from feeling itself, but this ignores the transferring of mourning to the form, to the music and not its maker. If Tricky's song "Black Steel" is a cover, it's the mirror covered when a loved one dies, a beautiful Jewish tradition of mourning; the clothes torn in such a ritual find their way in the breaks of the music. And if the breaks in hip-hop are a wound, they are relished rather than—as in the jazz break—fixed, or covered, up.

Often, the music is the mask in hip-hop—which only connects it to the form of the blues fighting the feeling of the blues. But the mask is sometimes so good it's bad—it seems to revel in its own desire not to feel, even while expressing all feelings wildly.

A song like Biggie's rare first single, "Party and Bullshit," is an interesting example of this. The chorus, sung by B.I.G rather than sampled, riffs off the Last Poets' song "When the Revolution Comes," which like many forms of prophecy, seeks revelation in the present. *Until then, niggers will party and bullshit,* the Last Poets repeat over and over, a critique of those deemed apolitical. Notorious's song seems to be on the side of the apolitical and amoral, wanting only to "party and bullshit." But to hear only this is to mistake the mask for the face—for the song isn't exactly celebratory. While the Last Poets critique something outside the poem, claiming revolution on their side, Biggie's riff contains its critique within its very title. To call your first single "Party and Bullshit" means you are aware of the power of the Party, and of bullshit as a verb—much like the vernacular term *woofin',* such "bullshitting" contains a loving if bemused critique of the self showing out even as it describes the joy of doing so.

To praise the persona is to mourn the self who made it.

All this is not to say that hip-hop is constantly grieving. However aggrieved they are, hip-hop songs don't seem to grieve the break. Rather, hip-hop recognizes that grief differs from mourning, those rituals after a loss that reenact and keep it at bay. Though grief is individual and endless, hip-hop knows mourning has a form that can be borrowed, much like Eliot borrowed sincerity—not as an outward sign of public feeling but as an inner form, the Groove, underpinning the beat, expressing in its emptied-out form all that cannot quite be said.

In hip-hop such mourning is in its very structure, made part of the music. What's so powerful about Biggie is that just as Charlie Parker returned the blues tone to jazz, Notorious BIG returned the blues mood to hip-hop. On *Ready to Die* Biggie is his own executioner, pallbearer, and mourner at once. Yet, he made this moving in all senses, part of the Party. And sometimes, the bullshit.

If the DJ once sought infinity, or the perfect beat, the MC seeks something else. Vengeance, perhaps, that form of fatal looping? It would be easy to say that the MC and hence hip-hop's fascination with death since the get-go—*riding off in a def OJ*—is another way of seeing, or saying, infinity.

But this seems too easy. I think the fascination with death—at times a death wish, at others a revulsion at the same—is a synecdoche for transformation in the music. Just like its insistence on prosperity is often a critique of it, hip-hop's declarations of death, whether Death Row or Def Jam, are veiled protests about *merely* surviving. All are further signs of mourning.

Behind Biggie's rap on "Juicy," "Juicy Fruit" by Mtume loops, heightening the longing—I recall seeing Mtume on *Solid Gold,* along with A Taste of Honey and "Sukiyaki," both songs the kinds of 1980s mid-tempo love songs that the likes of the S.O.S Band perfected and that we don't see enough of anymore. It is no accident that the original love song's tone affects the Biggie version, itself another original that re-establishes and even rethinks the desire therein. The sample is a form of continuity that also represents a break. This is the nostalgia hip-hop is often engaged in: a cipher, a closed loop, a gold rope, the snake eating its tail—and tale—in a kind of furious infinity.

It was all a dream, the rap of the song starts after the dedication intro. Though about living large, the song's American dream actually seems rather small—"lunches, brunches, interviews by the pool"—but this makes Biggie's dream from back in the day only more approachable, and believable.

> I loved that he described what a lot of hustlers were going through in the streets—dissed and feared by teachers and parents and neighbors and cops, broke, working a corner to try to get some bread for basic shit—as more than some glamorous alternative to having a real job. He elevated it to "the struggle." That's a loaded term. It's usually used to talk about civil rights or black power—*the seat where Rosa Parks sat / where Malcolm X was shot / where Martin Luther was popped*—not the kind of nickel-and-dime, just-to-get-by struggle that Biggie was talking about. Our struggle wasn't organized, or even coherent. There were no leaders of this "movement." There wasn't even a list of demands. Our struggle was truly a something-out-of-nothing, do-or-die situation. The fucked-up thing was that it led some

of us to sell drugs on our own blocks and get caught up in the material spoils of that life. It was definitely different, less easily defined, less pure, and harder to celebrate than a simple call for revolution. But in their way, Biggie's words made an even more desperate case for some kind of change.[54]

"Everyday Struggles," the second song on Biggie's album, continues to consider not just struggle, but the feeling that *I don't want to live no mo'.* Any such death wish is belied by the smooth sample, which provides a stark break with the rap—and Puff Daddy's constant cooing in the background. Biggie's are mostly "suicidal thoughts"; all the record's shooting is as directed to the self as against others. In a sense, Biggie is not just one of the last great MCs, his 1997 death signaling the end of yet another era—some might say the real Golden Age, others the start of something even more corporate—but in a real sense, he's the death of the blues tone in hip-hop. *Living every day like a hustle, another drama jungle, every day another struggle.* Nihilism, with a smile.

Real Love

The history of hip-hop is weirder and more wordless than any one book can convey. Former hip-hop soloist and Native Tongues collective member Monie Love has recently turned up again, hosting a show on satellite radio called *Ladies First*—in spots for the show, Love starts off talking with the British accent she rapped in during the Golden Age, only to drop it by way of admitting she never did have one.

Her not being British was actually a story I had long ago heard, back when she was big enough to get a decent amount of airplay, so I was surprised more by her implied admission of her storying than by the fact of her put-on. Plus, even from the get-go, Monie Love's voice was aways put-on so fake it was real—impersonating a version of Britishness actually spoken, though somehow not always thought of, by black people. Her voice in many ways refers to Slick Rick's, which contained many other voices, not only as an émigré from the Caribbean (and London), but also as "the Ruler": sometimes high-pitched, fake feminine as opposed to falsetto; others low and British. These various voices refer to the many Englishes that influenced hip-hop in the first place. Like the post-soul artist knows, the story has many sides—including the story-teller's. *Six minutes, Six minutes, Doug E. Fresh you're on:* the Ruler re-veals that ventriloquist might be as good a name for rapper as player, baller, hustler, or pimp.

Later, when British-raised Neneh Cherry turned punk impresario Malcolm McClaren's hip-hop incursion "Buffalo Dance" into a "Buf-falo Stance," she would interrupt her song midway to say in a kind of Cockney, "What's he like? What's he like anyway?" and then in a more typical African American vernacular, "What'd you expect, the guy's a gigolo, man." She could have been talking about all hip-hop, question-ing the too-often macho, gigolo-lovin' form itself. Male rappers over the years would constantly evoke hip-hop as a woman, from Common's "I Used to Love H.E.R." (1994) to Nas's "Hip Hop Is Dead" (2006), declar-ing their love for "her" almost always in the past tense, calling hip-hop "my first wife." *Hip-hop you're the love of my life.* Cherry and other fe-male artists, often only visible when we expand the idea of the music from rap to hip-hop, talked back to this in many ways: *No money man can win my love.*

Hip-hop flirted not just with other voices but whole genres and sub-genres, theoretically endlessly flexible, but in truth reticent and oddly conservative. But even one's native tongues remained aware there were other voices, not just accents; and Cherry's rap-meets-singing, while hard to sustain—just ask Cherry or Ms. Hill—is something that reap-pears every few years, a country constantly rediscovered.

The singing voice in hip-hop often gets gendered as female and soul-ful, heartfelt but smooth—a heady contrast to the rapper's guttural growl, his "hardness." When done right, such collaboration literally sings, as on "I'll Be There For You/You're All I Need to Get By" by Method Man and Mary J. Blige, which I had on cassingle—a hip-hop form if ever there was one. The most touching, or telling, part of the song is when he says to his boo, *You're my nigger.* Like the word *nigger,* rapping gets mistaken as strictly male; suddenly, Method Man seemed to say, you're not just my girlfriend but my friend girl, my homie, my partner, my one—you're down with me, wherever down is.

But hip-hop's singing ain't always soulful. It's just as often artificial, and rarely raw; one reason Ms. Hill's second solo album *Unplugged 2.0* is less than succesful is that its rawness goes against the "natural" flat quality of her voice, which while powerful, and truly great, ain't exactly soulful. Despite her on-screen debut in *Sister Act 2,* Hill's vocal quality remains far from church—it's far more typically technological. While soul music sings at times in a distorted way—a way we might call analog—this hip-hop singing voice is remarkable because it seeks to render a sound without distortion, decidedly digital. This is a quality Hill shares with other of her fellow female vocalists clearly influenced by Billie Holiday, from Erykah Badu to Macy Gray.

While following Holiday, these singers are not actually mimicking Holiday's voice, but mimicking her wish to make her voice sound like an instrument. Naturally, this instrument is now a different one. At least in the debuts of Hill, Badu, and Gray, or the recent stylings of Rihanna, the hip-hop vocalist seeks to show you a voice that isn't so much affected as it comes to us as if a sonic effect made by a machine. The singers don't evoke a real snare but a fake one; a drum machine met by the voice as machine.

This is in no way a critique but rather a recognition that these artists' debuts actually perform a duet with hip-hop as a whole. It is Mary J. Blige who invented and at times only could sing "hip-hop soul," a genre of one—most other artists are more rightly said to be making hip-hop. Of course Hill raps, Kelis appears on many, and Badu started out rapping; all are descendants of pioneers like Angie Stone, who started out as a member of the old-school group the Sequence and now's a soul singer. Only when we think in terms of hip-hop, rather than the reductiveness of rap, can we witness these singers' full impact and import.

Otherside of the Game

It isn't exactly that Notorious BIG ended the blues tone in hip-hop—songs like 2008's "My Life" by the Game featuring Lil Wayne are essentially blues, wondering not just how bad the singer's luck is, how persecuted, but what has he ever done right to let him live? Rather, it is Biggie who was the last time the tragic and comic sides of the blues remained united.

While the blues has us dance out our despair, and Biggie could be sexy while menacing, hip-hop lately restricts itself to one or the other, or one at a time. With the blues the form fought the feeling, and the form of jazz was its feeling; in hip-hop these two have now split: into pure feeling (often a blues one) on one side; and impure form on the other, flexing or sexing from line to line. Today hip-hop can do the tragic blues or it can do the comic, mostly through the bawdy or dancing side of the blues, but rarely both.

In the Golden Age, gangsta angst had held feelings at bay even while its form was filled with them—sometimes it was the music that expressed emotions, sometimes the lyrics, and when best, both. *My mind's playin tricks on me.* It is no accident that this blues tone circled back to the South where it began, where rappers often pursued it into places familiar yet unexplored. *Southernplayalisticadillacmuzik.* Such loops continued after Biggie's death, with OutKast, Goodie Mob, and the Dungeon Family carrying on crafting an underground set of meanings, now brought above by a *Trans DF Express*; others had echoes in the Southern tone found even in South Central, where the migrant music still kept its accent in ways as deserving of further study and as influential as country music's Bakersfield sound. Snoop's raps called themselves *funky on the mic like an old batch of collard greens* in a way that would echo the Godfather of Soul (and that Snoop would channel into homages to *The Godfather* and Blaxploitation movies).

The split in hip-hop even showed itself in rap from the South (no matter where it is), symbolized by the 2003 double records of the duo OutKast, recording separately as Big Boi and Andre 3000 on *Speakerboxxx* and *The Love Below.* While each record was a brilliant blues in different ways, the emphasis on sound in one and sensuality in the other (and which is which would keep flip-flopping) suggested a split that would continue into hip-hop and even R&B to this day. More and more rappers, from TI to Nelly, would record "two-sided" albums, expressing neatly divided persona. Instead of battling others, rappers now battled themselves; versus became a favorite identifier. *Martians vs. Goblins.* The result is actually a far more limited set of persona than rap once insisted upon, returning to a dichotomy with a whiff of double consciousness not seen since Dunbar embodied and liberated us from it.

As noted of No Wave by Weasel Walter, punk had declared *Fuck them* to anyone outside it; No Wave declared *Fuck you* to its very audience. Hip-hop had first said *Fuck yes,* then *Fuck tha police* and *I don't give a fuck;* now it said *Fuck it,* or simply *Fuck me*—whether seduction or send-off.

Rap would need a savior, it declared over and over, though what it needs are not more saints but a return to forms of hip-hop left behind too soon, many of them found far beyond rap itself and even these shores. Rappers love to refer to themselves as Jesus, embodying their own perceived persecution and also, let's face it, emblemizing their power. Rap's deaths only cemented both. Where Big Baby Jesus and Biggie—who the Game called *Brooklyn's Jesus* in "My Life"—died young, the true tragedy, the song seemed to say, was surviving. The ends of the record were its means: Lil Wayne's multitudinous recordings, his million mixtapes were his message, offering at least another kind of solution to the idea of *"the* message" as something singular: a million missives, unwritten yet still spoken, recorded, leaking. His were messages in a bottle of cough syrup, sent to find a further shore.

If hip-hop has any chance to go beyond the ends of the record, it will be in the hands of women. Whether through their own singing and rapping (Cherry, Missy Elliott), or another's rapping and their singing (Alicia Keys, Rihanna), women hip-hop artists foreground the centuries-old call-and-response qualities of African-influenced music. This is not just musical but philosophical, often seeking a counterpoint to the male MCs and their depictions of women—and themselves—offering up "the otherside of the game." Erykah Badu singing *My cipher keeps going like a rolling stone* couldn't be understood without hip-hop's methodology and incorporation of Five Percenter Black Muslim terminology. But Badu's mention of "a rolling stone" and *You better call Tyrone* suggest that blues correlative and hip-hop thought can't just coexist, but one follows the other.

These sisters refuse to be mere synecdoches for male fantasy—whether as props or signs of making it—instead reminding us that making it means not just making something new but a retracing of tradition, even if only to upend it. *I can't stand the rain.* Not that their work is all nostalgia—rather the nostalgia they seek is a radical one, tied as much to the collective unconscious, "the other side," as the dream of making it. They flip the record, and the script, over.

The tradition female MCs suggest is often far older and deeper—even if "Deeper" becomes the name of a gangsta rap song by the all-female hard-core group Boss. Boss's album starts and finishes with a response that takes into account a countertradition: an obscene outgoing message from a member of Boss herself, declaring the gangsta mantra—*I don't give a fuck, not a single fuck not a single solitary fuck*—followed by a beep after which are outraged messages from a mother and father in turn who've heard all the cursing.

Boss's parents' almost predictable response is to declare their disappointment, if not disgust, with such obscenity: "We raised you better than that" and "I don't like it," even if eventually followed by, "Thanks for the Rolex, baby, call me."

In one fell stroke, the answering machine skit—a subgenre where recordings beget more recordings, even singles like De La Soul's "Hey, How Ya Doin'"—questions the authenticity of her violent, nihilist voice and registers generational difference while noting Boss's connectedness to the tradition. Gangsta angst isn't just the absence of love, after all, but a reckoning with it. The orphaned mode so often portrayed by rappers and suggested by the "Parental Advisory" stickers is belied by paternal affection and unavoidable motherlove.

While at times and at their best interested in a blues mood, however divided, the men are always interested in the ballad form—a form whose start and end are exactly the same. Neither form is interested in narrative progress as such—though at times the ballad contains a tale, such as in "Frankie and Johnny"—but in the ways the meanings change even if the words stay the same. *Damn, why they want to stick me for my paper? Damn, why they want to stick me for my paper? Damn, why they want to stick me for my paper?* Consider too Tupac's "Dear Mama" (though bring a hanky), whose repetition consists of not just the chorus (which is the title) but the sound of "Sadie" by the Spinners. The looping is both emotional and musical.

In hip-hop, the women are interested more in how the response—much like the kicker of the blues—changes the verse's repetition. Male MCs are often interested in an antithesis without thesis; female MCs are interested in exploring many theses, deferring synthesis as long as it may take to reinvent it. You could call this a new kind of blues.

One revels in the unexpected; the other, in the unrestricted: the form's freedoms the female MC takes for her own. But where does such escape end?

99 Problems

The start of the record is where rappers asked to "turn me up in the headphones," including the outtake as an intake of breath—*I'm getting ready to spit,* such intros said, *Let me clear my throat.* Soul usually saved any stage directions for later in the song, for right before the break, as in "Funky Drummer"—but hip-hop had already turned that mother inside out, so why not start before the start?

The end of the record is the place where soul music could get down and where funk found the mothership, where funk and disco called out to the community, waving all its parts—*black people, white people, Puerto Ricans*—as a way of bringing everyone into the fold. It's an altar call that remained unaltered: at the ends of early hip-hop records the call went out to *wave 'em like you just don't* care; a call to ecstasy, communal and familiar. Soul music had used food to serve the same purpose; the Groove had exchanged the church for the club without sacrificing the transcendent. *Throw your hands in the air.*

Soon, the end of the record is where the shots would fall—in song after song, hard-core hip-hop marks the end of the record with a flurry of buckshot, punctuated less by ellipses than an exclamation point. Far more severe than *They don't make no songs like these—period*—of "King of Rock," this end was a means of marking hip-hop's fatalities, sometimes as a monument or worse, a notch on a prize belt. *Talk is cheap, motherfucker.*

Hard-core hip-hop's fatal endings serve two purposes, which are also problems. One is a symbolizing of heartbreak with loss of the most permanent kind, of conflating "def" with death. You see this a lot in the videos of female post-soul singers such as Toni Braxton and Alicia Keys, who can't seem to record a sad song without a video in which heartbreak, which in soul meant *He's leaving,* has been turned into literal death. The blues knew better that the train taking away your sweet mistreater, still breathing, may feel worse than dying—but it wasn't dying. The equating of loss with death in neosoul and even hip-hop, as in Jay-Z's supposedly final video "99 Problems" and Tupac's actually final video "I Ain't Mad at Cha" where they each die in a flurry of buck-shot, is not realness or reenactment but the presence of literalness run rampant. It is a rehearsal, with the emphasis on hearse.

Second, those shots occurring at that formerly sacrosanct, sanc-tified, or communal end of the record are a form of mourning. Not just mourning the self being shot—and by implication, the soul of the shooter—but mourning the loss of the communal. What we witness, or hear, in those shots is the very death of the "I" that had once promised a "we," which is to say, the lyric mode.

For if good hip-hop ultimately seeks the condition and condensation of poetry—what we might call its economy—then too often that poetry isn't lyric poetry but narrative. Sometimes this narrative need works to rap's detriment; at other times, like Slick Rick's "Children's Story" (which also ends with shots), it is the music's chief pleasure. Either way, rap's erosion of lyricism is hard not to notice as we look back over the years—is this the ultimate end of the record?

For the lyric voice does not keep us a bystander as *Straight Outta Compton* does but lets us become the singer—or poet or rapper—and at best even the song itself. For the length of the lyric poem, and a breath or three beyond, we are poem and poet in one; when Whitman says, "I am the man, I suffered, I was there," we stand alongside him. *I am I be.* This blackness of being also connects to a folkloric past Hurston describes as "He who wins from within is in the 'Be' class. *Be* here when the ruthless man comes, and *be* here when he is gone."[55]

Hip-hop's pleasure is often in its Whitmanesque contradictions, em-bodied in the delicate dance between the beats and the bars that the rappers spit; unlike Whitman, the form and the feeling don't often fit. It is a music of breaks, after all: hip-hop's poetry results from the ten-sions and changes in these jarring shifts, as well as the jibing between the lyrics and the music. Poetry can move you, hip-hop can make you move—for my part, I'll take both. But hip-hop and poetry meet not in words but in their frequent wordlessness; not in rhyme, but in reclaim-ing and redefining beauty from the clutches of mere prettiness. *All the ugly people, stay quiet.*

All this ugly beauty, all around us. You could see the shots at the end of the record as a silencer, the noise of menace mixed with hushed mourning—a twenty-one-gun salute. *100 guns going to New York. 99 problems. I'll ask 21 questions, and they all about us.*

Alongside its cousin, hard-core punk, the only other music to embrace such nihilism before hip-hop was jazz. But jazz sees elegy as ecstasy, the second line strutting from the burial ground to the party after. Mournful on the way to what some call homegoing, joyous all the way back. A loop. Duke Ellington's "East St. Louis Toodle-Oo" gives us the ecstatic followed by a funeral march at the record's end; Jelly Roll's "Dead Man Blues" starts with church bells: whatever the order, in jazz there actually seemed an order to be discerned in the universe, and a swing within it.

For the hip-hop artist, the funereal suffuses the ecstatic. The two are no longer separate nor equal—while the blues had shuttled between the two poles rather effortlessly (though not without consequence), hip-hop now requires the creation not just of different sounds but different selves in order to experience them.

This is not an "I" that's a "we" as in the blues or even in old-school rap—with hip-hop we now have a multitude of "I"s. These "I"s sometimes are in third person—*Ice Cube goes crazy when he's full of eight ball*—rappers refer to themselves in the third person almost as much as sport stars. *Sanging* and *slanging,* using invented or borrowed beats, the hip-hop artist insists on a self and a delf, a series of shifting tones taken as one's own. At worst, these multiple "I"s can seem part of a schizo world, as autopsychography rather than as a sign of plenty. But at its best, the self who says "I think therefore I am" simply needs another name, a delf who declares "I Am I Be," knowing full well that to be alive is be multiple. And vast.

It is in "99 Problems" by Jay-Z, as remixed by Danger Mouse, that the DJ once again uses the manifold means of the music, gathers the edges together, as a means to find the communal ends that hadn't been in hip-hop for a long while. The gunshots are gone.

The End of the Record

I've come all this way and only now mentioned the grey pachyderm in the room: the DJ Danger Mouse album that titles this very book. By taking the a cappella vocal tracks of Jay-Z and the beats of the Beatles,

Danger Mouse's *Grey Album* reimagines the original while also insisting on his own. What's more, he does this not for gain, but for the art—not seeking to sell it, knowing the Beatles are protective about samples, he offers it up, recognizing the ways in which the Beatles have suffused the culture, are very much in the air. His *Grey Album* brings the Fab Four down to earth, back among us rather than leaving them in the ether where they mostly reside. Danger Mouse made the Beatles music again.

Taking the record *The Beatles,* better known as "the White Album" (delivered in a plain white wrapper), and mixing it with a black rapper (some, including Jay-Z himself, might say *the* rapper), Danger Mouse achieved a mash-up that was both fission and fusion, its unlikeliness not just a gimmick. The execution was as good as the idea; the part equaled the whole.

Jay-Z intended *The Black Album* to be a final statement, both a declaration of independence and a repudiation of the game: *Never a better time to say good-bye.* Like Michael Jordan retiring young the first time, it never seemed quite believable even as it was happening, and few were surprised when Hova's retirement proved about as permanent as a permanent. But in his repudiation of the game—and later, in his reprisal—Jay-Z echoes not just the Beatles' refusing to include any graphics on their "White Album" after the rumors of death on *Abbey Road,* but also Prince's own *Black Album,* which he was working on in the late 1980s and refused to release—reportedly because he found it too troubling and "negative." Like Prince well knew, at least in his love songs, a little bit of difficulty getting what you want can make it all the more desirable. I myself heard Prince's *Black Album* on a tape a friend made me after he picked up a bootleg vinyl copy while in France for the summer. As with the hip-hop mixtape, it didn't seem that the Prince tracks were necessarily meant to be impossible to find, just underground. Prince in fact reused one *Black Album* track on his subsequent *Lovesexy* album, a record that was meant to be more positive; it seemed fitting that the shared track was "When 2 R in Love"—love, apparently, might be for good or ill.

The Grey Album's distribution alone returned hip-hop not so much to the streets as to its origins—to the informal distribution across the black and blue planet that had circulated Prince's *Black Album,* hip-hop in the form of mixtapes and booming systems, and long before either,

Mamie Smith's "Crazy Blues" and jazz's furious styles. What Danger Mouse's mash-up sought was something beyond the basement or bedroom where it was built: Elsewhere.

By separating the lyrics from the music, and by putting the whole in a lab or a blender, *The Grey Album* emerged from the underground like an Invisible Man or an unnamed slave finding true north. Just as Bob Dylan and the Band's "Basement Tapes"—those equally poorly guarded, once-bootleg recordings—had re-created American folk music and mimicked its informal distribution, Danger Mouse reckoned with pop music, turning it back into the folk forms that begat it. What he discovered was an underground that didn't mean an economy—the download was free—but a subterranean railroad of meaning.

In doing so, Danger Mouse returned the DJ to the center of the groove—not as producer, though certainly Danger Mouse is that now too—but as the spinner of both history and the future. The DJ gathers the edges of the records, the breaks as breakthrough, and makes them the center of the cipher. Looping as a form of retreat—and advance. *Looking for the perfect beat,* the goal of the groove is infinite, transcendent, and transformative. The record, like the world, is round. *It's yours.* It has a long way to go: its sound expands with the known universe, and, like a star exploding or the heavens expanding, we can still see it shine long after it first went *boom,* bass-heavy, hungry.

All such art seeks neither representation nor rehearsal nor reality, but resurrection.

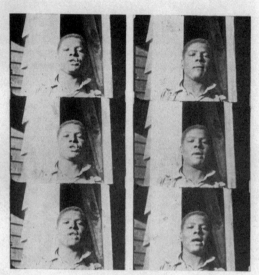

Fig. 15. Burden Down. Left, first sound in *shoutin'*. Right, first
sounds in *burden*.

Deadism

It happens every few years, perhaps oftener: we get the article, widely and usually well published, that declares poetry dead. Usually the accompanying sound is less a lament for this premature pronouncement than a jig on poetry's prepaid grave. Rarely do I hear such an essay sound more like an Irish wake or a New Orleans jazz funeral, two sounds I think poetry should aspire to more often. A raucous solace.

Instead, poetry is dead.

I disagree; I plan wild essays; I respond point by point, debunking and spelunking.

But tonight, why not—poetry is dead. Let it be dead then; let us write as if we are already dead. If poetry is dying, then let's write a poetry pronounced D.O.A.

Perhaps it is just because I have witnessed too many deaths these past few years, but I have tried since to write a poetry of life, against those deaths and even Death in general. Maybe. But it also seems to me some of the same folks who think poetry is dead, or proceed without it, turn to poetry in crucial moments: at a death, or a wedding. Poetry as invocation, as ceremony.

I want an afterparty poetry, a poetry that sings a bit off key, drunk or I never touch the stuff, but sings anyway.

For years I've felt poetry was not ceremony, but the daily thing. The dirt. It is an everyday, not an occasionally. I still think this. But perhaps the only way to make this truly true is to write a poetry that is not like death, but is death: surprising yet inevitable, everyday yet far-off in the future, an ever-present that we still manage to forget. In this, it may resemble jazz—or is this simply because, as Ralph Ellison says, "life is jazz-shaped"? Death may be jazz-shaped too, just ask Gabriel and Satchmo in their cutting contest.

The only way to find out is to write a dead poetry.

I am not taking this lightly: I am not suggesting a poetry of suicide (don't do it), or of homicide (give that up); I am not suggesting a poetry celebrating war, or ignoring war, or a poetry of a war that we celebrated too early our victory in, and now cannot ignore. (The deadening of poetry is celebrated too early and often too.) A dead poetry does not believe in "-cides" of any kind; it believes in insides, in soul and sorrow, in silence and also the singing that is against such.

Deadism believes that poetry should capture a living language; it just knows that we should write in dead languages too.

Write not like something endangered—not like a spotted owl—or reintroduced into the wild, but dead already. (The poetry of "they're coming to get us," the poetry of the horror movie I've seen too much of, the poetry of lament, of victimization—or worse, of declaring the various and nefarious threats to freedom, equality, blackness, or justice—seems to take too much pleasure in watching the killer even as it shouts out warnings in the theater. This poetry is over, but unfortunately not yet dead.) Write not like a coming extinction, but like the extinction already. That said, do not write like a dodo, something rare and flightless—but like the passenger pigeon, a poetry once plentiful and ever-present and so therefore killed off.

Do not write a poetry of rarity, or of rarification, but of *never again*.

Do not even write this poetry but find it, come across it, and step over it. The helpless ant that in the end can lift more than ten times its weight: that is a poetry.

Maybe what we need is an undead poetry—not to take death back from poetry, but to take death back from death itself. A poetry of shambling power, devouring everything in its path. A vampire poetry that will live forever, sexy and dangerous and immortal, shape-shifting when necessary.

That bat in my friend's toilet (true story) a poetry. That dog. That mewling cat caught under my house that left sometime in the night: a poetry. It is hard to find, and harder to coax out, but will one day emerge on its own.

In the meantime, a poetry that speaks from the mouths of those gone that aren't really gone, a poetry of ghosts and haunts. Of haints; not ain'ts. Dead is something you can be, after all, is not itself an *ain't*. The ain'ts I'm afraid are here, among us living.

Instead there's the haints, which our poetry should be: haunting, hard to pin down, glimpsed yet believed. That's a poetry I believe in. A poltergiest poetry that moves things, and us, when we least expect.

Deadism: I did not invent it, it invented me. Paul Celan, Gwendolyn Brooks *(We Real Cool)*, Fenton Johnson ("I'm tired of civilization"—throw the children in the river), the exhaustion of Bob Kaufman, who wrote in order to be forgotten, the ghostly poetry of Larry Levis. The poetry of Alan Dugan seems dead already, a voice from beyond. Toni Morrison's *Beloved*. Kenneth Koch writing a poetry of life that is in the end death.

I used to hope for a poetry of preserving—in my first book, this is what emerged, writing to try and capture the voices of the life I saw that was rapidly disappearing. That of the black rural South of my parents and grandparents.

Some would say they were happy to see it go; what I saw were the good things going too. And worse, nowhere a poetry of it, no poetry either marking or mourning the passing of a way of life—a way folks I knew seemed to mark and remark on, mostly by humor. This was not to me a contradiction, but the paradox back of existence: mournful laughter.

At the same time, my first book seemed almost dictated to me by the ghosts of my family—but a set of ghosts that were my family. My job, in part, to conjure them up—even when they were still alive, as my grandfather (rest in peace) was then. In order to write about him, I had to write about his death, which hadn't happened yet but I knew would; I had to write his funeral, and had as witnesses folks I imagined, remembered, and some who were already dead, like my young cousin who'd recently killed himself. The poem, then, is for the real him, but the living him, made by the poem, also speaks and tells of the funeral of our grandfather, still in real life alive.

While in one way this is preserving, and in another it is merely an insufficient explanation of the vagaries of the imagination; in the main it is to say that I have been a Deadist longer than I remember. So too

William Carlos Williams in *Spring and All* and *The Descent of Winter:* how in the former he must destroy everything before rebuilding, before spring.

Rebuilding is more difficult than we thought.

But if we write a poetry not of ending, but of end, a poetry that is itself unmoving, we may actually move. A poetry not of *if,* but of *when.*

Deadism like those movies with voice-overs that sound not only dead, but by the end you find out are from a dead man: the one not ready for a close-up, but floating in the pool, the one who knows what he can't know but tells us anyway. A poetry not of witness, or of victimhood, or of experience or innocence, but of the moment after: write like a saint, not the picture of a saint. Write like the bone in the box, the relic to be kissed. Better yet, write like the saints that have been officially declared saints no more; write like something once holy, now decanonized and attempted to be forgotten. Write not like remembering, but the forgetting.

This does not mean writing erasures, which has been done (but not, unfortunately, to death). Do not write like the *Erased de Kooning Drawing* by Robert Rauschenberg, brilliant as it is; do not write like the once beautiful thing, ancestral, now gone. Instead, write like de Kooning picking not the ugliest of his drawings for the kid with the good idea to erase him, but instead picking a really beautiful one; write like something you don't mean to be erased but one day know will: then let them try.

Write a poetry unmarked, like Zora Neale Hurston's grave; then write the marker too, like Alice Walker years later.

When I was writing my second book, long before its final title *To Repel Ghosts,* I was aware that its subject—the late painter Jean-Michel Basquiat—was dead the entire book. Even in the earlier poems, where he's painting madly, and living wildly (is there another way to live), he was dead: they are all elegies, and all therefore celebrations of his life. Though dead the whole book, toward the end he died again: it was that point that was particularly maddening, when he did himself in, again, it seemed. I had that anger at him that some save for God when someone they love goes unexpectedly (this is not to say he was a god, or even a saint. He was barely considered acceptable then, though is nearly canonized now).

In other words, like with my first book, I needed to conjure him, as the ghosts of his title and mine—but then later I'd have to perform an exorcism (as I called one early reading), to let him go. You can't really let go, of course, but only by letting go, by writing not to the dead but *as* the dead, can you start to let go and in that way remember. Otherwise you are reliving the death over and over. The dead don't want this for us, though they want to be remembered—which means, if only for a moment, a laugh, an isn't that such-and-such and reaching and then saying it can't be but then realizing, of course it's not but perhaps it can, somehow—only then, in forgetting, can we go on to remember.

The blues know this already—that is why so many of them sing both of death and even, I would argue, *as* death. *Death Letter Blues, See That My Grave Is Kept Clean, Last Kind Words Blues, Fixin' to Die Blues* (*I don't mind dyin', I just hate to leave my children cryin'*—or *behind*, depending how you hear): all imagine oneself dead or dying, dying not as metaphor but as literal thing. In this, then, dying is made more than literal, made metaphor for life itself. *It's so hard to love someone who don't love you*—this is the heart of the blues, but also of life after death for those living, whose love continues just beyond our reach. Who knows, maybe it's like that for the dead too.

Perhaps this is why some folks think if you dream of death it means a wedding, and a wedding, death. Not to court death, mind you—stay away from such a seducer—but to recognize the ways both seem inevitable, inseparable, death is the ultimate affair, the only thing these two may part. Or maybe it's just that like poetry, weddings are a willful ignoring of the odds or the eventualities—and like poems, they don't always work out. But we don't want a poetry of weddings or ceremonies or *I do*'s but of the alone of:

> Grabbed up my suitcase
> Took off down the road
> When I got there
> She was laying on the cooling board.

The blues know that by singing of death, or taxes, or the tolls of the everyday toil, you can know life. I love the blues—I was first attracted to writing through them because they said it all, and said it not in flat-out ways (though they didn't beat around the bush) but by using the everyday, the things around us, the blues correlative, like trains or two-timers or other domestic metaphors, to express emotions. But my longer, deeper love may be their argument over existence, and with existence, with solid notions of what is and what ain't—all the while they don't pretend toward sainthood, not Sabbath but to Saturday night.

Someone I read said that Johnny Cash (bless his heart) didn't write like a saint, but as a sinner, which meant someone who could be redeemed. That's right, it seems to me. And one of the most powerful things was his album *after* the album he thought he'd die in—the sequel to good-bye *(The Man Comes Around)* is just as powerful as, if not more than, the good-bye itself.

We should write a poetry that is after the good-bye, that is not the long farewell but the hello after. The hereafter—a word that in itself is undead, both here and gone at the same time. *I'm a long gone daddy—* and being here, and being gone, seems what we need now.

Film noir, that American form—which, like jazz before it, took the French to help some Americans appreciate—is filled with dead who talk, who tell us secrets and then turn up alive after all. Their Deadism is to be admired, is now, looking back, even more why my next book sought to capture their patter and talk. It's the talk of someone whose time is up, and who knows it—but talks anyway.

Only by writing a dead poetry, a zombie poetry, can the thing come back to life, not so much reborn as born for the first time. Maybe we got it all backward: we die, then we live? Only poetry knows for sure.

Acknowledgments

Thanks to the Graywolf Press Nonfiction Prize, the Guggenheim Foundation, United States Artists (and a James Baldwin fellowship), the Massachusetts Cultural Council, and the Lannan Foundation for support that helped complete work on *The Grey Album*. Thanks too to my agent, Rob McQuilkin, who supported the book and helped me find its true or should I say storying spirit. Thanks to Graywolf Press, especially my editors Fiona McCrae and Jeffrey Shotts for their perceptive comments, and to Katie Dublinski for her steady hand. Thanks too to my graduate student Amy Hildreth who helped fact-check every quote, a daunting task. Major props to Richard Eoin Nash, who helped as only he could with the subtitle; and to the unflappable Julie Delliquanti of the Schatten Gallery, Emory University, whose help with the images was invaluable. A shout-out to the many other friends and far-flung family who allowed and encouraged me to work on this book over the years. Special thanks to Robert Polito, who selected this book for the Graywolf Press Nonfiction Prize and made my work-in-progress a reality. Lastly, endless thanks to my wife, Kate Tuttle, music to my ears.

Thanks too to the editors of journals and reading series who first published parts of *The Grey Album:*

A portion of "The Shadow Book" was first read as a paper at the Association of Writers and Writing Programs conference as part of a Poets House panel.

"It Don't Mean a Thing" appears in *The Poetics of Song Lyrics,* edited by Charlotte Pence (Jackson: University Press of Mississippi, 2012).

Part one of "'If You Can't Read, Run Anyhow!'" appeared in *Conjunctions* 29 as part of a special tribute issue of American writers on American writers.

"Broken Giraffe" began as part of the Passwords Lecture series at Poets House in New York City.

An excerpt of "Moanin'" appeared in *Tin House,* the Ecstasy issue.

"Planet Rock" started life in far different form as a cover review for *Bookforum.*

A portion of "Deadism" first appeared in *American Poets in the 21st Century,* edited by Claudia Rankine and Lisa Sewell (Middletown, CT: Wesleyan University Press, 2007).

Permission Acknowledgments

"Canto LXXIV" by Ezra Pound, from *The Cantos of Ezra Pound,* copyright © 1948 by Ezra Pound. Reprinted by permission of New Directions Publishing Corp.

Images

Photograph of Sojourner Truth, "I sell the Shadow to support the Substance." Original carte de visite portrait is in the Library of Congress Manuscript Division, Sojourner Truth Collection (MMC). Manuscript Division copy negative is LC-MSS-35956-173.

Photographs of girl with flag, "Crazy Blues" sheet music, Mack's Inter-Racial Barbershop, soul singer collage, and Apollo Theater montage from the Robert Langmuir Collection of Historical African American Photographs, Philadelphia. Used with permission.

Glenn Ligon, from *Runaways,* 1993. Suite of 10 lithographs, 11¹³⁄₁₆ x 8¹⁵⁄₁₆ inches (30 x 22.7 cm): image size; 16 x 12 inches (40.6 x 30.5 cm): paper size. Edition of 45, 10 AP. Courtesy Regen Projects, Los Angeles. Copyright © Glenn Ligon.

Photograph of soldier from Paul Laurence Dunbar, *Candle-Lightin' Time* (New York: Dodd Mead & Company, 1901). Illustrated with photographs by the Hampton Institute Camera Club and decorations by Margaret Armstrong.

Langston Hughes postcard to Prentiss Taylor, Bob Kaufman photograph, and tintype photo of a woman from the collection of the author.

Jennie C. Jones, *Two 45 LPs (for Brancusi).* Relief print, 8 x 10 inches, 2010. Courtesy of the artist.

"Burden Down" from Milton Metfessel, *Phonophotography in Folk Music* (Chapel Hill: The University of North Carolina Press, 1928).

Notes

THE SHADOW BOOK

Jean Genet, "Introduction," *Soledad Brother: The Prison Letters of George Jackson* (London: Jonathan Cape and Penguin, 1970), 21; Lucille Clifton, *The Book of Light* (Port Townsend, WA: Copper Canyon Press, 1993), 25; Duke Ellington, "We, Too, Sing 'America'" (1941), *The Duke Ellington Reader,* ed. Mark Tucker (New York: Oxford University Press, 1993). William Carlos Williams, *Asphodel and Other Love Poems* (New York: New Directions, 1994), 18–19; Robert O'Meally, *Jazz Cadence of American Culture* (New York: Columbia University Press, 1998), 389.

HOW NOT TO BE A SLAVE

1. Melvin Dixon, *Ride Out the Wilderness: Geography and Identity in Afro-American Literature* (Urbana: University of Illinois Press, 1987), xi.

2. Henry Louis Gates Jr., "Dis and Dat: Dialect and the Descent," in *Figures in Black: Words, Signs, and the "Racial" Self* (New York: Oxford University Press, 1987), 191–92.

3. Brent Staples, "To Be a Slave in Brooklyn," *New York Times,* 24 June 2001. Staples describes archaeologists' discovery of a slave cosmogram in the attic of the Lott house in Brooklyn, "the first known slave dwelling in what would become New York City":

They pulled up the floorboards in the chimney room and found five corn-cobs arranged in what appeared to be a cross or star shape. New Yorkers renovating old houses may have encountered such things and discarded them. But to experienced eyes, they are more than just debris. The cross formed by cobs suggests a cosmogram, a symbol known to anthopologists as a West African depiction of the cosmos. One line represents the boundary between the living and the dead and the other the path of power that connects these worlds. Archaeologists studying slave quarters in the Deep South have typically found African ritual items buried near fireplaces, which slaves viewed as the way spirits entered or left the house. . . . Scholars have typically argued that West African spiritual life was confined to the Deep South, where slave populations were large enough to sustain their rituals. But the Lott house shows that African religious practices survived, not just in the Deep South and in the border states, but here in New York City.

The cosmogram itself is a "border state" sought by the slave.

4. John Noble Wilford, "Slave Artifacts Under the Hearth," *New York Times,* 27 August 1996. Interestingly, the writings of Frederick Douglass have aided in such excavations, due to the accuracy of his descriptions of plantation life in the Eastern Shore of Maryland. John Noble Wilford, "An Abolitionist Leads the Way in Unearthing of Slaves' Past," *New York Times,* 5 September 2006. See also James Deetz, *Small Things Forgotten: The Archeology of Early American Life,* rev. ed. (New York: Anchor/Doubleday, 1996).

5. Robert Harris Jr. cites this familiar saying in a review of a book on slavery. Robert L. Harris Jr., *African American Review* 29, no. 3 (Fall 1995). Harris starts with a useful reminder: "The question of how much control slaves had over their interior lives is still a matter of debate. As chattel, slaves were property and subject to the complete authority of their owners. But slavery, unlike concentration camps, asylums, or penitentiaries, was never a total institution in which slaveholders governed every moment of the slaves' lives. Although slaves had almost no legal rights, they secured from planters some customary rights. Those customs and practices provided slaves with a degree of autonomy and control over their lives that insulated them against complete dependency on slaveholders" (510). Such lack of complete control should in no way be confused with chattel slavery being in any way mild; rather, it is a measure of the slaves' resistance and ingenuity. Harris in fact goes on to relate, interestingly, how even a nursing child was a means of a slave woman's resisting sexual advances. Rebellion is everywhere, and daily.

6. It is worth noting that often the black author wasn't the same as a black slave; instead "slave narratives" are usually written by a "free" ex-slave or at least an "unbound" fugitive slave. It is tempting to say that since William Wells Brown (the first African American novelist), black authors quite literally are both fugitive, ex-slave narrators. However, this fails to note the ways in which Wheatley, Horton, even Dave the Slave and the "black and unknown bards" who created the spirituals all invented systems of survival and crafted their work while still in bondage.

7. Ralph Ellison, *Shadow and Act* (New York: Random House, 1964), 27–28.

8. Ralph Ellison, "Change the Joke and Slip the Yoke," in *Shadow and Act,* 53.

9. Harriet Wilson ("Our Nig"). *Our Nig; or, Sketches from the Life of a Free Black* (New York: Vintage Books, 1983). *The Bondswoman's Narrative.* We can thank Henry Louis Gates for authenticating the black authors and helping

to publish and republish both of these important early works. Harriet Jacobs (Linda Brent), *Incidents in the Life of a Slave Girl*. In Henry Louis Gates Jr., ed., *The Classic Slave Narratives* (New York: Penguin, 1987). The authentication of this narrative by Jean Fagan Yellin is necessary to consider its current and past readings.

10. Jacobs is not alone in this—her fellow slave Harriet, this one Wilson, pseudo- and eponymously signs her name "Our Nig." With that signing, Wilson signifies on ideas of possession and of naming as name-calling. Such "Signifyin(g)" is defined most theoretically by Henry Louis Gates Jr. in *The Signifying Monkey: A Theory of African-American Literary Criticism* (New York: Oxford University Press, 1988). For a brief summary of the concept, consult pages 64–76. Ralph Ellison defines signifying as "meaning, in the un-written dictionary of American Negro usage, 'rhetorical understatements.'" Ralph Ellison, "Blues People," in *The Collected Essays,* ed. John Callahan (New York: Modern Library, 2003), 281.

11. Douglass, *Narrative of the Life of Frederick Douglass,* in Gates, *The Classic Slave Narratives,* 305.

12. William Andrews, *To Tell a Free Story: The First Century of Afro-American Autobiography, 1760–1865* (Urbana: University of Illinois Press, 1986), 274–75.

13. Ibid., 272. Andrews here quotes Bakhtin.

14. Ishmael Reed, *Flight to Canada* (New York: Random House, 1976), 95.

15. Henry Louis Gates Jr., "Phillis Wheatley on Trial," *The New Yorker,* January 2003.

16. As William Andrews indicates, however bluntly, "She takes the power that comes from the point of a pen to project an alter ego in freedom up North, not a lunatic self raging in rebellion in a psychic attic." Andrews, *To Tell a Free Story,* 259. Andrews here of course is signifying, however unfairly, on several of the white women writers discussed by Sandra Gilbert and Susan Gubar in *The Madwoman in the Attic and the Nineteenth-Century Literary Imagination* (New Haven, CT: Yale University Press, 2000).

17. Robert B. Stepto, *From Behind the Veil: A Study of Afro-American Narrative* (Urbana: University of Illinois Press, 1979), xiii.

18. Frederick Douglass, *Narrative of the Life,* in Gates, *Classic Slave Narratives,* 307.

19. Harriet Jacobs, *Incidents in the Life of a Slave Girl* (New York: Norton, 2001), 104.

20. Ellison, "Blues People," *Shadow and Act,* 249.

21. John F. Callahan, ed., *Trading Twelves: The Selected Letters of Ralph Ellison and Albert Murray* (New York: Modern Library, 2000), 9.

22. Alice Walker, *In Search of Our Mothers' Gardens: Womanist Prose* (New York: Harcourt Brace Jovanovich, 1983), 95. Emphasis in the original.

23. Ibid., 109.

24. Ibid., 110.

25. Zora Neale Hurston, "How It Feels to Be Colored Me," (1928; repr., *Folklore, Memoirs, & Other Writings,* New York: Library of America, 1995), 826–829. Michael North discusses this in his chapter on Hurston in *Dialects of Modernism.*

26. See Carla Kaplan, *Zora Neale Hurston: A Life in Letters* (New York: Anchor Books, 2003).

27. We may also consider Colson Whitehead's *Apex Hides the Hurt* (New York: Anchor Books, 2007), about the naming of a town founded by blacks by a corporate namer, in the end deciding to name it (SPOILER ALERT!) not "Freedom" but "Struggle."

28. James Baldwin, "Introduction: The Price of the Ticket," in *The Price of the Ticket: Collected Nonfiction, 1948–1985* (New York: St. Martin's, 1985), x.

29. Ibid., xi.

30. Douglass, "The Last Flogging," in *My Bondage and My Freedom,* ed. John Stauffer (New York: Modern Library, 2003), 133. This chapter revisits what is found in "chapter 9" of his previous *Narrative of the Life.*

31. Douglass, *Narrative of the Life,* chapter 10, *Norton Anthology of African American Literature,* ed. Henry Louis Gates Jr. and Nellie McKay (New York: W. W. Norton, 2003), 426. Douglass has three distinct, and overlapping autobiographies. I will chiefly refer to the iconic first one, with the fascinating second one for contrast.

30. Thanks to Robert O'Meally's "Introduction" to the twenty-second edition of the *Narrative* for directing me to this text, though I could not locate Morrison's gloss of the scene mentioned there (nor a piece called "Rootedness" that's subtitled "The Ancestor in Afro-American Fiction"). Toni Morrison, "Rootedness: The Ancestor as Foundation," in *Black Women Writers, 1950–1980: A Critical Evaluation,* ed. Mari Evans (New York: Anchor Books, 1984), 343.

33. Robert O'Meally, "Introduction," Douglass, *Narrative of the Life of Frederick Douglass, an American Slave* (New York: Barnes & Noble, 2003), xxviii.

34. In this it echoes Charles Chestnutt's description of "conjure," which appears as a parenthetical in Houston A. Baker's *Modernism and the Harlem Renaissance* (Chicago: University of Chicago Press, 1987): "(. . . in [Chestnutt's] correspondence, the word 'conjure' is always in quotes, protected as a *tricky* or transformative sign—masked)" (47).

35. Douglass, *Narrative of the Life,* chapter 9, in Gates and McKay, *Norton Anthology of African American Literature,* 426.

36. Ibid., 422. The last stanza of the following Negro folk rhyme expresses much the same sentiment about a "master" (here "Mosser"):

Mosser is six foot one way, an' free foot tudder;
An' he weigh five hunderd pound.
Britches cut so big dat dey don't suit de tailor,
An' dey don't meet half way 'round.

Mosser's coat come back to a claw-hammer p'int.
(Speak sof' or his Bloodhound'll bite us.)
His long white stockin's mighty clean an' nice,
But a liddle mo' holier dan righteous.

Thomas Talley, *Negro Folk Rhymes,* ed. Charles K. White, expanded ed. (1922; repr., Knoxville: University of Tennessee Press, 1991), 35. See also Paul Arnett, "Root Sculpture: Tornadoes Inside Eggs," in *Souls Grown Deep: African American Vernacular Art of the South.* Volume 1: *The Tree Gave the Dove a Leaf* (Atlanta: Tinwood Books, 2000). Arnett's history of root sculpture and rootwork helps describe the way that "in the nineteenth century, when beliefs in African spiritual systems were more overt, roots and conjure participated in slave life in often political ways as a means of challenging oppression" (130).

37. Douglass, *Narrative of a Life,* in Gates and McKay, *Norton Anthology of African American Literature,* 427–28.

38. Douglass, *My Bondage,* 140–41.

39. O'Meally, "Introduction," xxix.

40. Zora Neale Hurston, "High John de Conquer," *The American Mercury Reader* (Garden City, NY: Country Life Press, 1944), 106. Emphasis added.

41. Paul Arnett, "Root Sculpture": "Secrecy and invulnerability were among the hallmarks of conjure's specific antebellum incarnation, and set the tone for future applications of conjure to the American challenges of blackness" (130). Albert Murray, *OmniAmericans: Black Experience & American Culture* (1970; repr. New York: Da Capo Press, 1990). The fuller phrase, "the folklore of white supremacy and the fakelore of black pathology" courses thoughout Murray's book.

42. Wilford, "Slave Artifacts Under the Hearth."

43. Sigmund Freud, *Three Essays on the Theory of Sexuality,* trans. James Strachey (1905; repr., New York: Avon, 1972), 43.

44. Ibid., 42.

45. Steele, *Fetish: Fashion, Sex & Power* (Oxford: Oxford University Press, 1996), 5.

46. LeRoi Jones, *Black Magic: Poems 1961–1967* (Indianapolis: Bobbs-Merrill, 1969), 116. Steele's chapter title is in turn quoting critic Robert Stoller.

47. In its very ambiguity, or shall we say indeterminancy, the fetish differs from the stereotype, which as critic James Snead has noted in another context, remains excessively fixed. I explore this further in my essay on Kara Walker:

Kevin Young, "Triangular Trade: Coloring, Remarking, and Narrative in the Writings of Kara Walker," in *Kara Walker: My Complement, My Enemy, My Oppressor, My Love* (Minneapolis: Walker Art Center, 2007).

48. Hal Foster, "The 'Primitive' Unconscious of Modern Art, or White Skin Black Masks," in *Recodings: Art, Spectacle, Cultural Politics* (Seattle, WA: Bay Press, 1985), 181. Emphasis added.

49. Ibid.

50. Ibid., 181–8.

51. I have pulled from the body of the book a long point about "cultural castration" and the fetish, and not just because it seems too theoretical. In the spirit of the shadow book I include it here:

> Where the fetish, then, is for a black creator and keeper of tradition a sign of power, for the white viewer it is often a sign of powerlessness.
>
> The authority that the black viewer or carrier or creator of the fetish achieves is much like that of the counterfeit, as I've mentioned; what the white viewer notices all too often is not black authority but the lack of white authority. Nothing can save you; "Mumbo-Jumbo will hoodoo you": we are rendered powerless against the fetish's power. In this way, the fetish represents blackness disembodied, an authorless black text that seems anonymous (or pseudonymous), and dangerously so. We aren't sure who made the black mask in front of us, or even what tribe: we know only its power, the hands that made it, the face that once wore it (and wore its surface down as it wears us down). We are both transfixed and transported: fetish is pure synecdoche, the part standing in for the whole of unholy blackness.
>
> This is the anxiety at the dark heart of the fetish—not the anxiety of castration from a biologically male perspective, but of emasculation from a cultural one. The fetish seems the virile thing, and a stand-in for the thing itself. No wonder what gets fetishized is often black sexuality, male and female, to stave off fear and satisfy curiosity. The anxiety the fetish fights yet fits might be called *cultural castration* instead of an anxiety of influence; or, to take it out of the sexual realm (a realm staked as male by Freud and then Harold Bloom), fetish represents and reinforces the anxiety over *black* influence. Instead of honoring the tradition on view, this white gaze at fetish (and looking away) cannot easily be resolved: simply put, there is no tradition to fit oneself into, feel connected to in the way a black viewer might, and the white viewer averts the eyes. *Look away, Look away, Look away, Dixieland.*
>
> But the fetish does not just reenact a feeling of white "lack" of authority; it also addresses this anxiety by focusing instead on black "authenticity." Just as the fetish is a far more ambiguous view than a stereotype—which is stable, fixed, natural, "the way things are"—the fetish is not the only way

black folks can be viewed by whites. I view the fetish as a more complex reaction than stereotype—though the latter can cover up the former; that is, stereotypes can contain a desire, a fetish, which the stereotype fights.

Who hasn't seen the typing of a big black buck (or a big black mama), and looked under the hood, to see it driven by a wish unfulfilled?

This may be an inversion of the popular view that the stereotype of black oversexuality leads to fetishizing it; I am saying here that the stereotype, in its negative or mocking assertion, is actually a way of dealing with desire or fetish for blackness. We can see this in the fiction of Margaret B. Seltzer, known as Margaret B. Jones, in her false memoir—just as with Picasso (though without his artistry), the fetish is employed to escape whiteness while simultaneously enforcing it. In this it may be no different than the means to which Ezra Pound and T. S. Eliot used the Uncle Remus tales and dialect, as Michael North notes, to distance themselves from a dominant, all-too-proper literary language, while also retaining their proper English in a pinch.

I want to stress here that if not plenty then many whites have looked objectively at black totemic (and textual) power and not seen simply "object." I want to be clear that the fetish makes up a cultural gaze and not an individual one (though culture can be made up of these selfsame individuals). Many have seen black subjective power and found it inspiring or fruitful, without resorting to making it a thing craved, consumed, made contemptible, but most of all, covered up. There are a host of other examples of white reactions to and enthusiasms for black cultural productions, notably jazz. Some of these we examine in this book.

The careful reader will notice that I am interested throughout this book in black culture as American culture. However, I don't believe that these two things are contradictory, warring in one body, but rather redundant: blackness is Americanness. The question is not, *How white is black culture?*—a concern that comes to a head in many aspects of Black Arts of the 1960s—but *How black is American culture?*

52. Baldwin, "The Discovery of What It Means to Be an American," in *The Price of the Ticket*, 172. Originally published in the *New York Times Book Review*, 25 January 1959, and first collected in *Nobody Knows My Name*.

53. Amiri Baraka (LeRoi Jones), *Dutchman*, scene 2. Reprinted in Gates and McKay, *The Norton Anthology of African American Literature*.

54. James Baldwin, "Notes of a Native Son," in *The Price of the Ticket*, 127. Originally printed in *Harper's* magazine, November 1955, and first collected in *Notes of a Native Son*.

55. Ibid., 145.

56. Quoted in Wilford, "Slave Artifacts Under the Hearth."

57. Walker, *In Search of Our Mothers' Gardens*, 13.

58. Emanuel Swedenborg, *Heaven and Hell: Heaven and Its Wonders and Hell Drawn from Things Heard and Seen* (West Chester, Pennsylvania: Swedenborg Foundation, 2000), 264. Swedenborg notes "the interior sight in which [Africans] excel" after describing what he calls the *interior and the exterior man* in a passage that might serve as another vision of storying: "Internal men are like those who live in the second or third story of a house or palace, the walls of which are continuous windows of clearest glass, who look round about upon the city in its whole extent, and recognize every cottage in it; while external men are like those who live in the lowest story, the windows of which are parchment, who cannot even see a single street outside of the house, but only what is within it, and this only by the light of a candle or of the fire." Emanuel Swedenborg, *The True Christian Religion* (Philadelphis: J.B. Lippincott & Company, 1879), 1094–95.

59. "Usefulness" is discussed widely in Swedenborgian literature. As Swedenborgian thinker Wilson Van Dusen describes, "Swedenborg's 'use' means essentially spiritual function" applied to whatever task is at hand. In doing so, "the basic attitude of uses is a respectful search. *Devotion* would be a better word here." Wilson Van Dusen, *Usefulness: A Way of Personal and Spiritual Growth* (West Chester, PA: The Swedenborg Foundation, n.d.), 2. Thanks to Randall Burkett for his thoughts on Swedenborg and Africa.

60. Richard Wright, "Introduction: How Bigger Was Born," *Native Son* (New York: Perennial Classics, 1998), 433. As the book's acknowledgments indicate, "How Bigger Was Born" appears in the 1 June 1940 issue of *Saturday Review of Literature* and was reprinted later that year by Harper & Brothers.

61. Julia Wright, "Introduction," Richard Wright, *Haiku: This Other World* (New York: Arcade, 1998), viii.

62. Ibid., xii.

63. Cecil Brown, *Stagolee Shot Billy* (Cambridge, MA: Harvard University Press, 2003), 100.

CHORUS ONE: STEAL AWAY

1. Bert Williams, "The Comic Side of Trouble," *American* magazine, January 1918. Reprinted in Gerald Early, ed., *Speech and Power: The African-American Essay and Its Cultural Content from Polemics to Pulpit*, volume 2, (Hopewell, NJ: Ecco Press, 1993), 3–9. The first Williams paraphrase I've heard for years as a folk saying, including from my Aunt Tuddie; the exact quote reads, "In truth, I have never been able to discover that there was anything disgraceful in being a colored man. But I have often found it inconvenient—in America." Likewise, Williams's other saying is usually repeated as "Comedy is when you fall down; tragedy is when I do." Both folk sayings are fair, if rough, approximations of what he did actually say, and I've paraphrased one

and exactly quoted the written version of the other to indicate their continued presence in the folk and literary tradition.

2. W. E. B. Du Bois, *The Souls of Black Folk* (1903), in *The Norton Anthology of African American Literature,* 2nd ed., ed. Henry Louis Gates Jr. and Nellie McKay (New York: W. W. Norton, 2003), 692.

3. Zora Neale Hurston, "How It Feels to Be Colored Me" (1928), in Gates and McKay, *The Norton Anthology of African American Literature,* 1031.

4. Du Bois, *The Souls of Black Folk,* in Gates and McKay, *The Norton Anthology of African American Literature,* 694.

5. Hurston, "How It Feels to Be Colored Me," 1032.

6. Zora Neale Hurston, "Spirituals and Neo-Spirituals," in *Folklore, Memoirs, and Other Writings* (New York: Library of America, 1995), 870. Originally published in Nancy Cunard's *Negro* anthology in 1934.

7. Du Bois, *Souls of Black Folk,* in Gates and McKay, *Norton Anthology of African American Literature,* 695.

8. Frances Foster, *Written by Herself: Literary Production by African American Women, 1746–1892* (Bloomington: Indiana University Press, 1993).

9. The italics, found in the original, seem an important part of Wheatley's naming and equalization of names—yet the italics are dropped in *The Norton Anthology of American Literature* (3rd ed., vol. 1), 729, arguably changing the meaning. The meaning of "black as Cain" is also irrevocably fixed in a footnote to mean "I.e. theological errors, since Africa was unconverted." My restored text, complete with British spelling, comes from Wheatley's original 1773 *Poems.* This version may be most easily found in *The Vintage Book of African American Poetry,* ed. Michael Harper and Anthony Walton (New York: Vintage, 2000), 14. Gates himself dismisses the important questions this poem raises by terming it simply juvenilia.

10. I am thinking here of several of Robert Lowell's most celebrated poems, which we will discuss later in the Pound chapter, including "A Mad Negro Soldier Confined at Munich" and "In the Cage," whose Negroes are clearly symbols of madness, sin, or worse. Even as late as 1974, Jonathan Raban, editor of Lowell's *Selected Poems,* would state that "there is a strong Manichean strain in Lowell's imagination (the heresy of the Manichees lay basically in their belief that the world was a battleground for the equally matched forces of darkness and light), and his Negroes are prone to display *the mark of Cain." Robert Lowell's Poems: A Selection,* ed. Jonathan Raban (London: Faber & Faber, 1974). Emphasis added.

11. Ellison, "Blues People," in *Shadow and Act* (New York: Random House, 1964), 255–56.

12. Thomas Wentworth Higginson, *Army Life in a Black Regiment and Other Writings* (1870; repr., New York: Penguin, 2002). Especially relevant is the "Negro Spirituals" chapter.

13. Ostensibly Wheatley's trip was for her often-ill health—the sea mists

seemed to help, as accounts place her as much healthier in accompanying the family's son (and Wheatley's future "master") to England. In "A Farewell to America," Wheatley herself writes: "Lo! *Health* appears! celestial dame! / Complacent and serene, / with Hebe's mantle o'er her Frame, / With soul-delighting mein," this in contrast with a previous stanza, which states, "We sweep the liquid plain, / And with astonis'd eyes explore / The wide-extended main." In Britannia itself, Wheatley was to meet a powerful woman, for whom the word "patron" is used, but might not accurately indicate her need for *female* help, financial and royal. Interestingly, Wheatley's trip was cut short by the illness of her "mistress," in a kind of doubling: Wheatley's improving health means her mistress's failing health; we can see the ways in which Wheatley serves as a kind of dark double, what Gilbert and Gubar might call the monster abroad, let loose, to her mistress's "angel in the house." See Sandra Gilbert and Susan Gubar, *The Madwoman in the Attic: The Woman Writer and the Nineteenth-Century Literary Imagination* (New Haven, CT: Yale University Press, 2000), chapter 1. There's also an interesting take on Independence in Rita Dove's limited edition "Lady Liberty Among Us," a gorgeous, fine-press production that features a Statue of Liberty with a brown visage.

14. Henry Louis Gates Jr., *The Trials of Phillis Wheatley: America's First Black Poet and Her Encounters with the Founding Fathers* (New York: Basic Civitas Books, 2003): "In 1770, when she was about seventeen, she immortalized the Boston Massacre in her poem, 'On the Affray in King Street, on the Evening of the 5th of March, 1770'" (20).

15. Ibid.

16. Joan Sherman, ed., *The Black Bard of North Carolina: George Moses Horton and His Poetry* (Chapel Hill: University of North Carolina Press, 1997), 56.

17. "Contraband" was the name given to black runaways housed in camps during the Civil War by the Union: "In addition to the black serviceman and the southern slave laborer, there was yet a third role played by the black man during the war years—that of 'contraband of war.' The term was applied to the fugitive slaves who fled by the thousands to the Union army lines, were settled in contraband camps, and placed under the supervision of federal forces. So much confusion resulted from the government's handling of the contrabands that various private elements among the whites organized themselves to assist the refugees." Eileen Southern, *The Music of Black Americans: A History,* 3rd ed. (New York: W. W. Norton, 1997), 206. The contraband camps were also where Colonel Higginson recorded his impressions that led to *Army Life in a Black Regiment* and an important article in the *Atlantic Monthly* that includes information on the Negro spirituals. See ibid., 207. While in some regards an attempt by the Union to prevent returning runaways to slavery, such a term still left the fugitives as property. Contraband could be said to occupy a "border state" between free and refugee—a state Horton at times occupies.

18. Here, editor Joan Sherman's otherwise thoughtful introduction seems to go astray, suggesting that these weekend movements amounted to liberty: "it seems certain that [Horton's] bondage was relatively mild, since he enjoyed much freedom of movement begining in about 1817." *Black Bard*, 3.

19. Ibid., 60.

20. Ibid.

21. Ibid., 55.

22. Ellison, *Collected Essays,* ed. John Callahan (New York: Modern Library, 2003), 458.

23. Frederick Douglass, *Life and Times of Frederick Douglass* (1892; repr., New York: Collier Books, 1962), 159. Quoted in James H. Cone, *The Spirituals and the Blues* (1972; repr., Maryknoll, NY: Orbis, 1999).

24. Hole, *Celebrity Skin,* "Awful." While I sure don't mind some good old-fashioned pastiche, the title of the Hole song may be too accurate.

25. One need only watch, say, Shirley Temple films of the 1930s such as *The Little Colonel* to see the ways in which the spirituals serve entertainment purposes for the whites onscreen (and arguably off), rather than the transformative art of the slave singers. Or a whole host of black church-as-entertainment and rolling that's far less holy than rockin'—including *The Blues Brothers* desecration to more present-day descendants.

26. John Storm Roberts, *Black Music of Two Worlds* (New York: Praeger, 1972). This actual and factual doubleness can at times lead to overreading or overreaching, as in the myth of "freedom quilts," whose revelations as escape routes for slaves have now been widely discredited by scholars. The fact of many of the patterns starting long after slavery, and lack of supporting evidence for claims most fully made by the book *Hidden in Plain Sight: A Secret Story of Quilts and the Underground Railroad* (New York: Doubleday, 1999), would indicate that the quilts were less escape routes than a kind of compelling, if inaccurate, escapism at best and simple tourism at worst. Consult *World of a Slave: Encyclopedia of the Material Life of Slaves in the United States,* ed. Martha B. Katz-Hyman and Kym S. Rice, (Westport, CT: Greenwood, 2010), especially the entry on quilts, for a discussion of the controversy and valuable overviews of the slave's material culture. For an in-depth dissection of the freedom quilt myth, read Leigh Fellner, "Betsy Ross Redux: The Underground Railroad 'Quilt Code,'" available online at ugrrquilt.hartcottagequilts.com.

27. Such a countertradition, it should be noted, may even be found among black creators: the song "Carry Me Back to Ole Virginny" was written by James Bland, the black composer of over seven hundred songs (not all of them minstrelsy). Bland was called "The World's Greatest Minstrel Man" and "The Idol of the Music Halls," and his "songs were sung by all the minstrels—black and white—by college students, and by the American people in their homes and

on the streets. Most of them did not even know that they were singing songs written by a black man. The big white stars of minstrelsy for whom he wrote often published their songs under their own names." Southern, *The Music of Black Americans*, 238. While a common practice, the appropriation of the song "Ole Virginny" by white musicians as their own—its status as authorless contraband—we might say is part and parcel of Ole Virginny. As a false memory, "Ole Virginny" is a sentiment seemingly without a source (and I have left it as such in the body of this book). The song was later adopted as the official state song of Virginia in 1940, Eileen Southern notes: "Few realized that it was the composition of a Negro minstrel who sang his way into the hearts of the public during the turn of the century." The lyrics were modified slightly—not to remove the reference to "that's where this old darkey's heart am long'd to go" (which apparently was in place until 1997 when the song was retired)—but to properly call it "Virginia." This name change alone would seem to indicate the distinction between Virginia the place and Virginny the idea.

28. "As Constance Rourke has made us aware, the action of the early minstrel show—with its Negro-derived choreography, its ringing of banjos and rattling of bones, its voices cackling jokes in pseudo-Negro dialect, with its nonsense songs, its bright costumes and sweating performers—constituted a ritual of exorcism. Other white cultures had their gollywogs and blackamoors but the fact of Negro slavery went to the moral heart of the American social drama, and here the Negro was too real for easy fantasy, too serious to be dealt with in anything less than a national art." Ellison, "Change the Joke and Slip the Yoke,"in *Shadow and Act*, 48.

29. Greg Tate, "Are You Free or Are You a Mystery?" Ellen Gallagher, *Coral Cities*. Catalog to accompany exhibition at Tate Liverpool (2007), 20. Speaking of runaways, "Their maroon imaginations demanded more room to breathe and to conceive. Nor should we be amazed that they would cloak their New Jerusalems in masks and mysteries and riddle them with arcane, esoteric concepts and conceits while simultaneously militarizing their profiles."

30. This verse is inscribed on a jar made in 1857, a few years before Emancipation, by Dave the Slave. Contrast this latter effort's verse with his earlier 1840 one: "Dave belongs to Mr. Miles / wher the oven bakes and the pot biles" [sic]. Jill Beute Koverman, ed., *I made this Jar . . . : The Life and Works of the Enslaved African-American Potter, Dave* (Columbia: McKissick Museum, University of South Carolina, 1998), 38. Whether boiling over or filled with bile, Dave's wondering about his "relations" seems a crucial moment in his development and craft. For a placing of Dave's poetry among early African American verse, including his contemporary George Moses Horton, consult the catalog's essay by James A. Miller, "Dave the Potter and the Origins of African-American Poetry," 53–62.

BROKEN TONGUE

1. For further discussion of the daguerreotype as a function of black representation, see my essay on Kara Walker, "Triangular Trade: Coloring, Remarking, and Narrative in the Writings of Kara Walker," in *Kara Walker: My Complement, My Enemy, My Oppressor, My Love* (Minneapolis: Walker Art Center, 2007).

2. Written in 1905, "Nobody" was recorded by Williams in 1906 on Columbia Records and can be listened to at www.indiana.edu/~jah/teaching/2004_03/sources/ex1_nobodyrecord.shtml. The website also tells us that "the original 1905 published version contained eleven verses, only two of which are heard on the 1906 recording (which also has two verses not in the published version)." Also consult "Nobody" on Johnny Cash, *American III: Solitary Man* (2000).

3. The quote is William Dean Howells's from his review of *Majors and Minors* first appearing in *Harper's Weekly,* 27 June 1896. Howells's review was edited and appeared in the introduction to *Lyrics of Lowly Life* where it has made quite an impact, as I discuss at length in the rest of this chapter. The review's quote might be easily found in Gene Jarrett, "'Entirely *Black* Verse from Him Would Succeed,'" *Nineteenth-Century Literature,* 59 no. 4 (2005), 496.

4. George W. Boswell, "The Neutral Tone as a Function of Folk-song Text," *Yearbook of the International Folk Music Council* 2 (1970), 127. The article also recognizes the modal qualities of folksong; and led me to Milton Metfessel whose *Phonophotography in Folk Music* (Chapel Hill: University of North Carolina Press, 1928) is a fascinating document.

5. Will Marion Cook, "Clorindy, the Origin of the Cakewalk" (1944) *Theatre Arts* (September 1947), 61–65; both quotations are from 61. The lead in *Clorindy* was ultimately performed by Ernest Hogan, comedian with Black Patti's Troubadours, who wrote the unfortunately titled "All Coons Look Alike to Me." A biography of Cook, *Swing Along,* has just appeared.

6. Cook, "Clorindy," 61–62.

7. Ibid., 63–64. To get Hogan to a first practice, Cook engages in a bit of storying: "Hogan, my comedian, could not be reached because, unless he was working (and sometimes even then), he stayed up all night carousing. Consequently he slept all day. Just to play safe, I sent him a note in care of his landlady. 'We were booked!' I exclaimed. That was probably the most beautiful lie I ever told" (63). Such "booking" is another form of storying.

8. I've not seen Dunbar use the language of "coon" and "darkey" much, if at all, in the poems. It would seem a song phenomenon, indicative of other pressures beyond the page. "On Emancipation Day." Words by Paul Laurence Dunbar, music by Will Marion Cook (New York: Harry Von Tilzer Music Pub. Co., 1902). This and other of Dunbar's sheet music may be found on the

Library of Congress website. Thanks to Brown University's Sheet Music Collection, The John Hay Library, for providing the originals for these online sources.

9. This important all-black "whiteface" musical is chronicled in this review in the *New York Times,* 16 April 1898:

> Paul Dunbar, the Negro boy *[sic]* poet, who announced the other day that he was about to collaborate with James Whitcomb Riley and write a comic opera for Negro actors, has been anticipated. At the Third Avenue Theatre this week Cole and Johnson's select company of colored actors is appearing in "A Trip to Coontown" and the plot of the piece bears quite a resemblance to the story which Mr. Dunbar had laid out for his comic opera. This, mind you, is no charge of plagiarism, for the idea of the scallawag who poses himself for a prince was very popular in those days before Mr. Dunbar was born. At the Third Ave., however, the idea has been used to fine advantage and the result is one of the most artistic farce comedy shows that New York has seen in a long time. . . . There is many a white comedian who could sit at the feet of these Negro actors and learn a thing or two. For instance, Bob Cole, who plays Willie Wayside, the tramp, and in a white make-up which makes it almost impossible to guess his particular tint, is quite the equal as a comedian of either Dan Daly or Walter Jones, while he has more distinction than either of them and is funnier than Ward and Vokes. He showed last night that he is capable of playing any white part far better than most Negro comedians play black ones . . . The mere fact that this performance is given entirely by Negro performers would make it interesting in itself. But the excellence of the performance raises it far above any such level. Their lightness of foot, and distinction with which they carry themselves, place these artists high above the average whiteface comedy level.

Quoted in Henry T. Simpson, *The Ghost Walks: A Chronological History of Blacks in Show Business, 1865–1910* (Metuchen, NJ: The Scarecrow Press, 1988), 149–51. There is also here a contemporary illustration of Cole in whiteface as Willie Wayside (150). I don't know of Dunbar's ever collaborating with Riley, the white dialect "Hoosier Poet" most famous for his "Little Orphant Annie." But the notion does suggest something of Bernstein's praise of dialect.

10. After offering a command performance on 20 June 1903 for King Edward at Windsor Castle, Williams & Walker's company for *In Dahomey* was invited back for a birthday matinee performance for "Prince Eddy, the King's Grandson" at Buckingham Palace. A special cable to *New York American* (dated 23 June 1903) indicates that for the occasion, "Walker sang 'The Castle on the Nile.' Williams sang 'I'm a Jonah Man.' Aida Overton Walker did a solo dance, and the company sang a chorus after a cakewalk." We cannot be sure if "Darktown Is Out Tonight" was performed at

the castle, though I would guess it likely the chorus sang at Buckingham Palace. We do have Williams saying, "It was the first time I had appeared in the presence of royalty. The King looks like a jolly good fellow. I hope we entertained the royal family as much as they entertained us." *The Ghost Walks*, 297–98.

11. Letter from Charles Chesnutt to Walter Hines Page, 1898. Quoted in Houston A. Baker Jr., *Modernism and the Harlem Renaissance* (Chicago: University of Chicago Press, 1987), 42. Baker's entire book-length essay provides an interesting counterpoint here: his sense of "mastery of form" and "deformation" could be another way of looking at some of these questions, including the place of oratory and even blackface in black culture; however, Baker himself dismisses Dunbar as neither mastering nor deforming mastery: "Anyone with Dunbar's background who did not realize the guile and game of minstrelsy for what they were, who could in fact whine that the most powerful literary critic of his era had done him 'harm' by praising and ensuring the publication and sale of his dialect poetry—any black writer of this stamp had to be naive, politically innocent, or simply 'spoiled'" (40).

12. Margaret Seltzer [as Margaret B. Jones], *Love and Consequences: A Memoir of Hope and Survival* (New York: Riverhead, 2008). It may be enough to quote some dialect:

> I didn't let his words sting me; I expected it. Really, I didn't' know much about making [drug] deliveries, except that it paid beter than selling weed. I took a step closer to him and looked right at him. That's what my brothers had taught me. Always make people take you sereiously. "What you mean, homie? I'm perfect. Who would ever suspect me?"

This would seem a confession on its own of Seltzer's lying. It is followed by "dialect" that Seltzer's introduction makes clear is integral for her faux memoir ("Please do not confuse the use of slang and *my* replacing *c*'s with *k*'s as ignorance or stupidity"—I suppose she means of the fake speakers, not her own, who after all is supposedly representing black speech she seems ignorant of):

> He thought about it for a minute, then laughed again. "Aiight, sho nuff, you right. Ima take a chance on you. You meet me here tomorrow morning befo skool. You go ta skool, right?"
>
> "Sometimes." I shrugged my shoulders and gave him a half smile. He laughed again. The high school graduation rate, though it varies somewhat from neighborhood to neighborhood, in South Central, hovers somewhere around fifty percent. (3)

The mix of statistics, framing devices, and fictions—all poorly modeled, I might add—meet in her dialect of "replacement," forming exactly the larger frame that Dunbar and the counterfeit fight against.

13. Hurston, "Characteristics of Negro Expression," in *Within the Circle: An Anthology of African American Literary Criticism from the Harlem Renaissance to the Present,* ed. Angelyn Mitchell (Durham, NC: Duke University Press, 1994), 93. "Gwine" or "gwinter" surprisingly comes in for praise from Gates, who claims it is profound. See Gates, "Dis and Dat: Dialect and the Descent," *Figures in Black: Words, Signs, and the "Racial" Self* (New York: Oxford University Press, 1987), 167–95.

14. Edward Kamau Brathwaite, *History of the Voice: The Development of Nation Language in Anglophone Caribbean Poetry* (London: New Beacon, 1984), 13.

15. William Francis Allen, Charles Pickard Ware, and Lucy McKim Garrison, compilers, *Slave Songs of the United States* (New York: A. Simpson, 1867), xxiv–xxv. Reprinted by Dover Publications, 1995.

16. George Steiner, originally in *After Babel.* Reprinted in "On Liars and Lying," special issue of *Salmagundi,* no. 25 (Spring 1975), [5].

17. W. D. Howells, "Introduction," *Lyrics of a Lowly Life* (New York: Chapman and Hall, 1897), xix. Reprinted in *The Complete Poems of Paul Laurence Dunbar* (New York: Dodd, Mead, Company, 1913), ix. Emphasis added.

18. The quote continues: "It was moving from a purely African form to a form which was African but which was adapted to the new environment and adapted to the cultural imperative of the European languages. And it was influencing the way in which the English, French, Dutch, and Spaniards spoke their own languages. So there was a very complex process taking place, which is now beginning to surface in our literature." Brathwaite, *History of the Voice,* 7–8.

19. Houston Baker's writing about the African American use of "standard" might be a defense not just of McKay but also of Dunbar, despite his critique of the latter: "Now [Alain] Locke—and, indeed, the entire Harlem movement—has often been criticized severely for its advocacy of the standard. Yet is seems that such criticism proceeds somewhat in ignorance of the full discursive field marking Afro-American national possibilities. For we may not enjoy or find courageous models of derring-do in the masking that characterizes formal mastery, but we certainly cannot minimize its significant and strategic presence in our history. Furthermore, such masking carries subtle resonances and effects that cannot even be perceived (much less evaluated) by the person who begins with the notion that recognizably *standard* form automatically disqualifies a work as an authentic and valuable Afro-American national production. Analysis is in fact foreclosed by a first assumption of failure." Baker, *Modernism and the Harlem Renaissance,* 86.

20. *Songs of Jamaica* is pictured and discussed in my catalog *"Democratic Vistas": Exploring the Raymond Danowski Poetry Library* (Atlanta: Emory University, 2008).

21. William J. Maxwell, ed., *Complete Poems: Claude McKay* (Urbana: University of Illinois Press, 2008), 311. *The Complete Poems* sadly does not include the *Songs of Jamaica,* those set to music.

22. *Harlem Shadows* (1922). "Author's Word," reprinted in McKay, *Complete Poems,* 314. McKay continues:

> The speech of my childhood and early youth was the Jamaica Negro dialect, the native variant of English, which still preserves a few words of African origin, and which is more difficult of understanding than the American Negro dialect. But the language we wrote and read in school was England's English. Our text books then, before the advent of the American and Jamaican readers and our teachers, too, were all English-made. The native teachers of the elementary schools were tutored by men and women of British import. I quite remember making up verses in the dialect and in English for our moonlight ring dances and for our school parties. Of our purely native songs the jammas (field and road), shay-shays (yard and booth), wakes (post-mortem), Anancy tales (transplanted African folk lore), and revivals (religious) are all singularly punctuated by meter and rhyme. And nearly all my own poetic thought has always run naturally into these regular forms. (314)

Note the double meaning in "British *import*" given his own colonial status; and the "difficult of understanding" that may be all the more purposeful.

23. Gene Jarrett, "'Entirely *Black* Verse,'" 503. Jarrett continues: "Let us be clear about how realism can be racial. Realism is generally a 'pseudo-objective *version* of reality,' according to Raymond Williams, 'a version that will be found to depend, finally, on a particular phase of history or on a particular set of relationships.' Racial realism likewise suggests that racialism arbitrates the accuracy or truth of cultural representations of the African Diaspora. The cultural pervasion of minstrelsy across the United States connected racialism and realism in such a way that a hybrid cultural genre, minstrel realism, formed and defined its own racial verisimilitude through the exploits of minstrelsy to romanticize or sentimentalize race" (503). See also Henry B. Wonham, *Playing the Races: Ethnic Caricature and American Literary Realism* (New York: Oxford University Press, 2004).

24. The black poem/photo-essay, from Langston Hughes and Roy DeCarava's *The Sweet Flypaper of Life* to Amiri Baraka's *In Our Terribleness,* is a topic worthy of further investigation than I can give here—a shadow book of sorts, to this one—but may address the ways in which the poems or often poetic language that accompany the photos are another instance of storying.

25. James Weldon Johnson, "Preface," *The Book of American Negro Poetry* (1922). Quoted from Gates and McKay, *Norton Anthology of African American Literature,* 2nd ed., 902.

26. While I enjoy the cleaned-up version of this song, its second stanza originally ran:

I jumped on board de Telegraph,
And floated down de riber,
De electric spark it magnified,
And killed five hundred nigger.
De bulgine bust, de horse run off,
I really thought I'd die,
I shut my eyes to hold my breat,
Susannah don't you cry.

Swaggering Farmers and *Susannah Don't You Cry* (Durham [England]: Walker, Printer, ca. 1850). Broadside, collection of the author.

27. Malcolm Bradbury notes: "In literary and artistic matters, the America of the early twentieth century was still dominated by the Genteel Tradition, the lineage of Bryant, Longfellow and Lowell, by Mark Twain and Howells, provincialism and 'innocence' . . ." Bradbury relates that the sense and shock of the new, while brewing in Europe, were relatively silent on our shores at the end of the century when Dunbar was writing; I would add that we are also in the midst of the postbellum, of Southern "Redemption" and rolling back of the clock for African Americans, politically and socially. Bradbury, "The American Risorgimento," in *The Penguin History of Literature: American Literature since 1900,* vol. 9, ed. Marcus Cunliffe (London: Penguin, 1993), 3. Charles Bernstein offers another reading of the fin de siècle, as referenced below.

28. See Wonham, *Playing the Races*: "According to this logic, the art of caricature is ethically and aesthetically incompatible with American realism, as Howells insisted, and yet in practice these purportedly antithetical categories of representation remain intimately related, as a glance through Harris's Uncle Remus collections will confirm beyond a doubt. One reason for this curious overlap of representational practices may be that, for all their theoretical antipathy, realism and caricature pursue strikingly similar aesthetic aims. Indeed, both programs understand their function in terms of 'penetration' and 'exposure,' and both claim a unique capacity to lay bare the 'essence' of the human subject" (9).

29. This assessment comes from Robert B. Stepto in his important "I Rose and Found My Voice: Narration, Authentication, and Authorial Control in Four Slave Narratives," *The Slave's Narrative* (New York: Oxford University Press, 1985), ed. Charles T. Davis and Henry Louis Gates Jr., 225–41.

30. Dunbar's first book actually does not contain as many dialect poems—at least black dialect poems—as one might expect. Johnson said he was more a poet in the vein of Riley in this book. Dunbar's fiction, by many accounts,

remains committed to melodrama, and is out of bounds of our discussion; but note that Dunbar wrote fiction about a white family both as a way of avoiding these questions, and possibly, addressing or seeking the popular.

31. For a discussion of the troubling nature of Harris's Uncle Remus, consult Alice Walker—who came from Eatonton, Georgia, the same town as Harris. Walker, "The Dummy in the Window: Joel Chandler Harris and the Invention of Uncle Remus," *Living by the Word: Essays* (New York: Mariner Books, 1989).

32. Quotations from Dunbar, "Blue," "Compensation," and "A Death Song," in *Complete Poems,* 416, 256, and 228–29

33. bell hooks, *Talking Back: Thinking Feminist, Thinking Black* (Boston: South End Press, 1989), 11.

34. Rita Dove, "Elevator Man, 1949," in *New American Poets of the '90s,* ed. Jack Elliott Myers and Roger Weingarten (Boston: David R. Godine, 1991), 63–64. The protagonist gets his revenge on the segregated success of his colleagues "by letting out all the stops, / jostling them up and down / the scale of his bitterness / until they emerge queasy, rubbing / the backs of their necks, / feeling absolved and somehow / in need of a drink."

35. Natasha Trethewey, "Speculation, 1939," in *Domestic Work* (Saint Paul: Graywolf Press, 2000), 14.

36. Gates, "Dis and Dat," in *Figures in Black,* 172.

37. Gilles Deleuze and Félix Guattari, *A Thousand Plateaus: Capitalism and Schizophrenia,* trans. Brian Massumi (Minneapolis: University of Minnesota Press, 1987), 97. Emphasis in the original.

38. Dunbar, "We Wear the Mask," in *Complete Poems,* 112–13. Continuing his critique of Dunbar, Baker's *Modernism and the Harlem Renaissance* quotes this same passage, describing it thus: "The poem rolls through solemn, Christian meters with the breast-forward stoicism of William Ernest Henley's *Invictus:* 'In the fell clutch of circumstance / I have not winced nor cried aloud.' Rather than recognize that the black soul's eternal indebtedness is a result of *white* guile, the speaker *accepts* an indebtedness to 'guile' as a force—not unlike a cosmic spirit making life bearable—that enables stoicism. In other words, it is as though Dunbar's speaker plays the masking game without an awareness of its status as a game. It seems that he does not adopt masking as self-conscious gamesmanship in opposition to the game white America has run on him. And he surely does not have as one of his goals the general progress of the Afro-American populace" (39). Surely this is a lot for any one poem to bear—what's more, it seems to reemphasize my point about Dunbar's lack of personal language; Baker seems to wish Dunbar and his speaker (a "we," after all) were one and the same.

39. William Dean Howells, "Introduction to *Lyrics of Lowly Life,*" in *Complete Poems,* viii–ix.

40. Dunbar, "An Ante-bellum Sermon," in *Joggin Erlong* (New York: Dodd, Mead and Company, 1906), 73–81.

41. Henry Louis Gates reminds us of this fact in *Signifying Monkey*. Rita Dove, "Canary," in *Grace Notes* (New York: W. W. Norton, 1989), 64.

42. Charles Bernstein, *A Poetics* (Cambridge, MA: Harvard University Press, 1992), 107.

43. Ibid. Emphasis added. Later, Bernstein puts it thisaway: "The Island English verse tradition is only one of many streams feeding non-Island English poetry, and for many contemporary poets it has little or no importance, and need have none. But then even Island English is a misnomer since there is no one imperial standard for all the English-speaking people of England, with its dozens of dialects, much less for all of Britain and Ireland. (By *imperial* I mean a single, imposed standard for correctness of speaking or writing or thinking or knowing; I mean a unitary cultural canon, an artifice denying its artificiality)." Ibid., 117–18.

44. Ibid., 111.

45. Ibid.

46. See Aldon Lynn Nielsen, *Reading Race: White American Poets and the Racial Discourse in the Twentieth Century* (Athens: University of Georia Press, 1990), for information about William Carlos Williams.

47. Ralph Ellison quoted by James Alan McPherson, "Gravitas," in *A Region Not Home: Reflections from Exile* (New York: Simon & Schuster, 2000), 130–31. Emphasis added.

CHORUS TWO: IT DON'T MEAN A THING

1. Fredric Jameson. "The Cultural Logic of Late Capitalism," in *Postmodernism* (Durham, NC: Duke University Press, 1991), 11.

2. See my introduction to Kevin Young, ed., *Blues Poems* (New York: Everyman's Pocket Poets, 2003).

3. Taken from Woolf's essay "Mr. Bennett and Mrs. Brown" (1924). Questions of proper dating and periodization swirl around the Harlem Renaissance, usually with political implications, both large and small. In her terrific *Women of the Harlem Renaissance* (Bloomington: Indiana University Press, 1995), Cheryl Wall effectively argues that ending the Renaissance in 1932 is not just a question of accuracy but bias: if we don't expand either the start or end, we leave out many of the important works by Hurston and other women writers. Others say by not dating the Renaissance earlier than the 1920s, we miss the connectedness to what might be called the New Negro movement that can even be seen before the turn of the century. In his *Modernism and the Harlem Renaissance,* Houston Baker opens with a discussion of Woolf's quote, countering it by establishing "the commencement of Afro-American

modernism" to September 18, 1895, and "Washington's delivery of the opening address at the Negro exhibit of the Atlanta Cotton States and International
Exposition." Baker, *Modernism and the Harlem Renaissance* (Chicago: University of Chicago Press, 1987), 15.

4. Just as I have not provided here an endpoint of modernism, I do not
provide one for the Harlem Renaissance—in part to provide for a broader
inclusiveness and avoid problems of periodization (see previous note). For a
description of the *Opportunity* parties (and a good gossipy overview), consult
Steven Watson, *The Harlem Renaissance: Hub of African American Culture,
1920–1930* (New York: Pantheon, 1995).

5. For a look at some of the Harlem or New Negro Renaissance's publishing history and visual impact, consult Kevin Young, *"Democratic Vistas":
Exploring the Raymond Danowski Poetry Library* (Atlanta: Emory University,
2008). Note that I have retained Hurston's spelling of "Niggerati" with one *t*,
as the term is supposedly her coinage. However, in his fine book on Richard
Bruce Nugent, Thomas H. Wirth notes that he adopts "the spelling of Nigger-
atti used by Nugent (and by Thurman in *Infants of the Spring*). That spelling
self-consciously emphasizes the 'ratty' aspects of the group and is consistent
with Nugent's pronunciation. Langston Hughes, however, spelled the word
'Niggerati' in his autobiography, *The Big Sea*. Hughes's version renders the
irony more genteel." Thomas H. Wirth, ed., *Gay Rebel of the Harlem Renaissance: Selections from the Work of Richard Bruce Nugent* (Durham, NC: Duke
University Press, 2002), 273 n. 7.

6. Peter Brooker, ed., "Editor's Preface," *Modernism/Postmodernism* (London: Longman, 1992), xi. I have had some debates about whether "Anglo" here
means "white, English speaking" (as the dictionary and current usage would
have it) or merely British, but at best this is badly worded, at worst poorly considered. Why not say "British"? Perhaps unsurprisingly, it seems white critics
often refer to "Anglo" to mean "British"; African American and Afro-British
writers often use it to indicate "white" or "white American." Anglo, of course,
means something entirely different in a Chicano/a context.

7. Thomas McEvilley, *FUSION: West African Artists at the Venice Bien-
nale*. The Museum for African Art (New York). (Munich: Prestel-Verlag,
1993), 10–11. The catalog goes on to view history in four phases of identity:
"the pre-Modern period"; "the colonial or modernist period, [where] the idea
of cultural identity became a weapon or strategy used by the colonizers both
to buttress their own power and to undermine the will and self-confidence
of the colonized"; a third stage in which "the colonized not only negated the
identity of the colonizers, but also redirected their attention to their own,
perhaps abandoned, certainly altered identity. This is the phase of resistance,
which leads to the end of colonialism. In Africa it is reflected in the *Négritude*

movement"; and lastly "a fourth stage" whose artists are "secure in their sense of identity, formed by whatever blends of African and European influences, they want to get beyond questions of identity and difference and to move into the future" (11). Such a development has interesting if too simple contrasts to the four sections and phases of this study.

8. Stephen Vincent Benét, "American Names," in *Poems and Ballads 1915–1930* (Garden City, NY: Doubleday, Doran, 1931).

9. T. Bowyer Campbell, *Black Sadie* (Boston: Houghton-Mifflin, 1928), front inside flap of a very deco, if clumsy and stereotypical, cover by Jack Perkins. I must confess the text seems more of the same; the book starts: "Black Sadie's father was hanged several months before she was born. Lightfoot Mose died on the gallows for raping an old white woman. He descried her one evening in her cowshed milking her cow." Downhill from there.

10. Michael North notes the ways Eliot, in *Sweeney* and in other poems, uses the Negro image. See *The Dialect of Modernism: Race, Language and Twentieth-Century Literature* (New York: Oxford University Press, 1994). Such a placelessness is different from the rootlessness found in the blues—where the blues provide a grim hope, a stoic yet funny resistance, Eliot provides us with a mask in which death and despair meet, blackface meeting a death mask, a literal cenotaph that is our and his modern hero's fate.

11. Recently an advertisement for the reality show *Survivor Gambon* advertised "In Exotic Africa—Earth's Last Eden—Temptation is Everywhere." Only in the West would televised starvation be part of entertainment, and living in Africa be about mere "survival" that provides a path to riches.

12. With Douglas, his silhouettes form a kind of mask, a visual ritual often literally perched between Jungle and skyscraper, nature and modernity. Caroline Goeser describes Douglas's "in-betweenist" strategy: "Douglas developed a new American primitivism, which became his multifaceted strategy to complicate the ways in which Euro-Americans had codified such categories as civilization to exclude black America. By collapsing the Western polarity between the civilized primitivist and the 'savage' primitive, he subversively held a role as both primitivist and primitive. In his graphic art, primitivism no longer constituted a longing for what was outside civilization or what had been lost. It connoted instead that black Americans could contribute to modern American culture by reconnecting the primitive and civilized, the past and present, from a strategically interstitial position as a welcome 'compound of the old and new.'" Caroline Goeser, *Picturing the New Negro: Harlem Renaissance Print Culture and Modern Black Identity* (Lawrence: University Press of Kansas, 2007), 25.

13. *American Heritage College Dictionary,* 3rd ed. (New York: Houghton Mifflin, 1993), 736.

14. Ronald Takaki, *A Different Mirror: A History of Multicultural America* (New York: Little, Brown, 1993), 59. This passage has been reworked in the revised edition of *Different Mirror,* where it appears on page 50. I have retained the version I first encountered in Takaki's first edition.

15. Melvin Dixon, *Ride Out the Wilderness: Geography and Identity in Afro-American Literature* (Urbana: University of Illinois Press, 1987), 17–18.

16. Eileen Southern, *The Music of Black Americans: A History,* 3rd ed. (New York: W. W. Norton, 1997), 179.

17. Black thought contested such notions by seeing the States, chiefly Southern, as Eden *after* the Fall, Greene notes. J. Lee Greene, *Blacks in Eden: The African American Novel's First Century* (Charlottesville: University Press of Virginia, 1996). The first chapter is particularly useful for the history of the Garden and Wilderness concepts. For a contrast and deepening with the black notion of wilderness, consult Dixon, *Ride Out the Wilderness.*

18. Jean-Paul Goude, *Jungle Fever* (New York: Xavier Moreau, 1982), 4–5.

19. Ibid., 102.

20. Ibid., 105. Deleuze and Guattari writing on "becoming" could be talking about Goude's view of Jones instead: "Of course, the child, the woman, the black have memories; but the Memory that collects those memories is still a virile majoritarian agency treating them as 'childhood memories,' as conjugal, or colonial memories. It is possible to operate by establishing a conjunction or collocation of contiguous points rather than a relation between distant points: you would then have phantasies rather than memories. For example, a woman can have a female point alongside a male point, and a man a male point alongside a female one. The constitution of these hybrids, however, does not take us very far in the direction of a true becoming (for example, bisexuality, as the psychoanalysts note, in no way precludes the prevalence of the masculine or the majority of the 'phallus')." Gilles Deleuze and Félix Guattari, *A Thousand Plateaus: Capitalism and Schizophrenia,* trans. Brian Massumi (Minneapolis: University of Minnesota Press, 1987), 293. This conjugation continues in Goude's imagined photos of Jones's "brother," a twin identical to her except for a giant phallus.

21. "Wild Things" series accessed on Goude's homepage: www.jeanpaul goude.com, 4 August 2010. It apparently also ran in *Harper's Bazaar* in 2009.

22. Jean-Michel Basquiat, "Interview," conducted by Demosthenes Davvetas. Originally appeared in *New Art International* (Lugano), no. 3, October–November 1988. Reprinted in *Basquiat* (Milan: Edizioni Charta, 1999), lxiii. I love the switch of pronouns from "we" to "you" here, indicative of community and memory's shifts and acceptances.

23. *African Americana,* Swann Gallery (New York) auction catalog, February 2009.

24. Randall K. Burkett, *Garveyism as a Religious Movement: The Institutionalization of a Black Civil Religion* (Metuchen, NJ: Scarecrow Press and American Theological Library Association, 1978), xii.

25. Houston Baker, quoting Professor Robert Hill, *Modernism,* 96. Dixon too helps us see Harlem as part of "the black writer's use of memory": "By calling themselves to remember Africa and/or the racial past, black Americans are actually re-membering, as in repopulating broad continuities within the African diaspora. This movement is nonlinear, and it disrupts our notions of chronology. If history were mere chronology, some might see Africa as the beginning of race consciousness—and racial origin—rather than the culmination or fulfillment of ancestry." Dixon, "The Black Writer's Use of Memory," in *A Melvin Dixon Critical Reader,* ed. Justin A. Joyce and Dwight A. McBride (Jackson: University Press of Mississippi, 2006), 59.

26. Quoted in Watson, *The Harlem Renaissance,* 66.

27. Wall, *Women of the Harlem Renaissance,* 31.

28. Ibid., 28.

29. Baker, *Modernism,* 89.

30. With *Black Sadie* we do see modernity's fetishization of blackness—and that this fetishization is a crucial part of modernism ("Her story is modern, elemental, compelling") and of history (despite the story being called "hers"). More important, notice how the fetish is used to establish white authenticity, and in turn, authority: the author was "brought up on a Southern plantation," so he knows what he's talking about. The power of his authority comes from his proximity to blackness. The fetishization, then, of an elemental blackness has a purpose: to make the whiteness both clearer and the blackness more containable. Keep 'em down on the plantation where *he* was raised! And also, to empower the white writer himself, to make his "negro novel" part of the Harlem vogue, both in publicity and plausibility.

31. Langston Hughes, "Songs Called the Blues," *Phylon* 2, no. 2 (2nd Qtr., 1941), 143–45.

32. Langston Hughes to Carl Van Vechten, 17 May 1925, *Remember Me to Harlem: The Letters of Langston Hughes and Carl Van Vechten,* ed. Emily Bernard (New York: Vintage, 2002), 12.

33. Bessie Smith, composer and singer, "Backwater Blues," transcribed by Angela Davis in *Blues Legacies and Black Feminism: Gertrude "Ma" Rainey, Bessie Smith, and Billie Holiday* (New York: Vintage, 1999). Reprinted in Young, *Blues Poems,* 72–73.

34. See Hazel Carby, "It Jus Be's Dat Way Sometime: The Sexual Politics of

Women's Blues," *The Jazz Cadence of American Culture,* ed. Robert O'Meally (New York: Columbia University Press, 1998), 474.

35. Hurston, *Their Eyes Were Watching God* (1937; New York: Harper-Collins, 2000), 1. We may also read this alongside Paul Gilroy's *Black Atlantic: Modernity and Double-Consciousness* (Cambridge, MA: Harvard University Press, 1993).

36. W. E. B. Du Bois, *The Souls of Black Folk* (1903), in *The Norton Anthology of African American Literature,* 2nd ed. Henry Louis Gates and Nellie Y. McKay (New York: W. W. Norton, 1997), 694.

37. Albert Murray, *Stomping the Blues* (New York: Da Capo, 1976), 254.

38. One recent critic noting the relation of the minstrel show to *The Waste Land* amazingly manages to discuss it while avoiding race altogether.

39. Ralph Ellison, "On Bird, Bird-Watching, and Jazz," *Living with Music: Ralph Ellison's Jazz Writings,* ed. Robert G. O'Meally (New York: Modern Library, 2001), 69. Originally published in *Saturday Review,* 18 July 1962, and collected in *Shadow and Act.*

40. For Ellison, this connection continues in recognizing "the poetry of Countee Cullen and Langston Hughes had a connection with the larger body of American poetry. . . . Given the racial stereotypes Negroes must learn to recognize the elements of their own cultural contribution as they appear in elements of the larger American culture." "Ralph Ellison's Territorial Vantage," in *Living with Music,* 29. Interview originally conducted by Ron Welburn in 1976. In another essay, "Hidden Name and Complex Fate," Ellison describes how "*Wuthering Heights* had caused me an agony of unexpressible emotion, and the same was true of *Jude the Obscure,* but *The Waste Land* seized my mind. I was intrigued by its power to move me while eluding my understanding. Somehow its rhythms were often closer to those of jazz than were those of the Negro poets, and even though I could not understand then, its range of allusion was as mixed and as varied as that of Louis Armstrong." *The Collected Essays,* ed. John Callahan (New York: Modern Library, 2003), 203.

41. Edward Kamau Brathwaite, *History of the Voice: The Development of Nation Language in Anglophone Caribbean Poetry* (London: New Beacon, 1984), 30.

42. Ibid., 30–31. Brathwaite's terrific point appears in the footnote to the sentence cited above.

43. This transcription, done by Adam Gussow, can be found with several other blues songs, in Young, *Blues Poems.*

44. Richard Pryor has an ironic reading on the idea of "crazy," not only through his own album *That Nigger's Crazy,* but also through a monologue as recorded in a painting by Glenn Ligon, *Beautiful Black Men* (1995):

In my neighborhood there used to be some beautiful black men that would come through the neighborhood dressed in African shit you know, really nice shit, you know, and they'd be "Peace. Love. Black is beautiful. Remember the essence of life. We are people of the universe. Life is beautiful."

My parents go "That nigger's crazy."

Glenn Ligon—Some Changes, curated by Wayne Baerwaldt and Thelma Golden (Toronto, Ontario, Canada: The Power Plant Contemporary Art Gallery at Harbourfront Centre, 2005).

45. These can be seen in my own small collection, and the large collections at Indiana University's Lilly Library; some of the "blues" sheet music graced the printed hardcover case of my third book, *Jelly Roll: A Blues* (New York: Knopf, 2003). Such borrowed blues may be symbolized by "High Society Blues" (1930), lyrics by Joseph McCarthy and music by James F. Hanley, that I have the sheet music for—it apparently was also a "William Fox Musical Movietone." The song's chorus seems unintentionally telling of the larger "society" and its attitude toward the cover: *I guess we've got what they can't use / We've sort o' got those high society blues.*

46. Quoted in Toni Morrison, *Playing in the Dark: Whiteness and Literary Imagination* (Cambridge, MA: Harvard University Press, 1992), vi–vii. A contemporary novel, *Strange Brother* by Blair Niles (New York: Horace Liveright, 1931), starts with the description of a singer doing "Creole Love Call"—its title rendered without quotes, as if it is less a song than a state of being. This book, which explores a white male (who the flap copy calls "an intermediate man") attracted to Harlem and the black men there, is an important and interesting novel worthy of further study. Thanks to A. B. Christa Schwarz's *Gay Voices of the Harlem Renaissance* (Bloomington: Indiana University Press, 2003) for calling attention to the novel.

47. Niles, *Strange Brother,* 9–10.

48. Harvey G. Cohen writes of Ellington's negotiation of the world of the Cotton Club, discussing "longtime Ellington drummer and friend" Sonny Greer: "Greer remembered that George Gershwin coined the term 'jungle music' to describe the Cotton Club–era music of the Ellington orchestra. According to Greer, Gershwin and Paul Whiteman used to be 'in awe of the things Duke used to do, so they were sitting up at the Cotton Club and George Gershwin said to Paul, I know what that is, that's jungle music. And it stuck with us . . . but . . . they would never say that [to members of the Ellington band because] they were scared to offend a guy's feelings.' Barney Bigard, Ellington's famous clarinetist, recalled that Gershwin wanted to collaborate with Ellington as 'a partner' on songwriting while the band was at the Cotton Club, but Ellington refused the offer." Harvey G. Cohen, *Duke Ellington's America* (Chicago: University of Chicago Press, 2010), 55.

"IF YOU CAN'T READ, RUN ANYHOW!"

1. This, despite the fact that there has emerged a "Topeka School of Poetry," including me, Ben Lerner, Ed Skoog, Eric McHenry, and most recently, Gary Jackson—all publishing and writing from their origins in the Kansas capital.

2. Langston Hughes, "Too Blue," in Kevin Young, ed., *Blues Poems* (New York: Everyman's Pocket Poets, 2003), 25.

3. Arnold Rampersad, "Introduction," Langston Hughes, *The Big Sea: An Autobiography* (New York: Hill and Wang, 1996), xvii. Even a contemporary review of *The Big Sea* takes up this theme of Hughes's surface simplicity: "Engrossing as the book is in event and illuminating as commentary, 'The Big Sea' is essentially an individual evocation of life, in sentiment response and penetrating clarity; and it is as literature, thus, that it is to be read, in all its vivid complexity of situation and *simplicity* of phrase." Katherine Woods, "A Negro Intellectual Tells His Life Story," *New York Times*, 25 August 1940. Emphasis added.

4. Hughes, *The Big Sea*, 263.

5. See Rampersad on "Goodbye Christ," *The Life of Langston Hughes*, volume 1, 252–54.

6. See Hughes's "That Boy LeRoi" for a cheeky response from Hughes about Baraka.

7. Hughes, *The Big Sea*, 3 and 98.

8. A variation on this phrase is found in Keith E. Byerman, *Fingering the Jagged Grain: Tradition and Form in Recent Black Fiction* (Athens: University of Georgia Press, 1986): "These writers reject the Black Arts notion that blackness and humanity are fixed, clearly definable qualities. Instead, identity becomes a process, a continual creation partly in negation of those forces that deny individuality and self-determination and partly in affirmation of the disorderly, vital history they see as the black experience. Thus, the black self in recent fiction grows out of a *negative dialectics* in making an identity from this tension. It must be understood that 'negative' here implies neither that the self or the culture is somehow a poor imitation of white society nor that either is a simplistic reaction to that society. . . . Moreover, that negation constitutes an affirmation to the extent that black culture rejects dehumanization" (5). Emphasis in the original.

9. Houston Baker Jr., "Caliban's Triple Play," in *"Race," Writing, and Difference*, ed. Henry Louis Gates Jr. (Chicago: University of Chicago Press, 1987), 394.

10. Seamus Heaney, "Sounding Auden," *The Government of the Tongue: Selected Prose, 1978–1987* (New York: Farrar, Straus and Giroux, 1989), 110.

11. Cornelius Eady describes Johnson's possible emotions in a terrific poem, "Jack Johnson Does the Eagle Rock," *Hardheaded Weather: New and Selected*

Poems (New York: G. P. Putnam's Sons, 2008), 102–3. (Originally appeared in Eady, *Victims of the Latest Dance Craze,* 1986.)

12. Houston Baker's *Long Black Song: Essays in Black American Literature and Culture* (1972; repr., Charlottesville: University Press of Virginia, 1990) also reminds us of what he calls the "repudiation" involved in black folklore (10–14).

13. Discussed by Plimpton in the documentary *When We Were Kings,* about the Ali–Foreman fight Ali dubbed "The Rumble in the Jungle." Together with the technique he used to win, the "rope-a-dope," such sayings may qualify as another kind of Ali's poetry, and of storying.

14. This is unlike Auden, who arguably overemphasized truth, as Seamus Heaney discusses in his 1987 *London Review of Books* essay "Sounding Auden." Reprinted in Heaney, *The Government of the Tongue.*

15. Hughes, *The Big Sea,* 7.

16. Ibid.

17. Heaney continues "she usually limited herself to a note that would not have disturbed the discreet undersong of conversation between strangers breakfasting at a seaside hotel." Heaney, "Government of the Tongue," 101. Hughes replaces the seaside hotel with a Tempest, and Caliban's undersong for the café, yet manages to sound notes equally subtle—both in the sense of musical and written notes.

18. Hughes, *The Big Sea,* 11.

19. Let us be reminded that blackness was traditionally thought of as negative (often literally) and even by African Americans; this fact goes a long way to further explaining the black notion of "negation as affirmation" traced by critic Keith Byerman, prefiguring the 1960s adoption of the term "Black" itself.

20. Bob Kaufman, *Solitudes Crowded with Loneliness* (New York: New Directions, 1972), 28.

21. Hughes, *The Big Sea,* 50.

22. Ibid., 51. This refusal is an interesting contrast to the letters, where Hughes recounts playing at "passing" with Richard Bruce Nugent. Consult *Remember Me to Harlem: The Letters of Langston Hughes and Carl Van Vechten,* ed. Emily Bernard (New York: Vintage, 2002), which has this exchange from Hughes on 24 June 1925, writing to Van Vechten:

> I've met a couple of interesting fellows about my own age,—one a pianist and the other an artist, and we have been amusing ourselves going downtown to the white theatres "passing" for South Americans and walking up Fourteenth Street barefooted on warm evenings for the express purpose of shocking the natives. The artist boy has had some of his sketches taken by Harper's Bazaar. They are not at all Negro but very good for one who has had so little training. I'd like to have you meet him. He has some

amusing ideas for a Negro ballet and some clever ideas for short stories if he weren't too lazy to write them. Like myself—But I am going to try to do the book because you want me to. (22)

23. For a print version of Baldwin's critiques consider his damning review of the *Selected Poems of Langston Hughes:*

Every time I read Langston Hughes I am amazed all over again by his genuine gifts—and depressed that he has done so little with them. . . . There are poems which almost succeed but which do not succeed, poems which take refuge, finally, in a fake simplicity in order to avoid the very difficult simplicity of the experience!

Baldwin, "Sermons and Blues," *New York Times,* 29 March 1959. Needless to say, Baldwin's idea of simplicity I find neither permanent nor "fake" in Hughes—unless it is the fruitful fakery of storying.

24. The phrase "absence of direct reproach" is taken from Pound's own footnote to "The Jeweled Stair's Grievance," and might be thought of as one definition of modernism. Indeed, Pound's poem itself could be said to be related to the subtle protest of Hughes's own "Mother to Son" with its refrain of "Life for me ain't been no crystal stair."

25. Ralph Ellison, *Collected Essays,* ed. John Callahan (New York: Modern Library, 2003), 368.

26. Hughes, *The Big Sea,* 139.

27. For two contrasting, black-authored views on the numbers writer, consult Julian Mayfield and Etheridge Knight in Gerald Early, ed., *Speech and Power: The African-American Essay and Its Cultural Content from Polemics to Pulpit* (Hopewell, NJ: Ecco, 1992). Knight's "The Poor Pay More, Even for Their Dreams" in particular is forceful in its assertion of the dream deferring even the numbers "racket" provides: "The benefits to a black community from a numbers operation is a mouse's tit compared to the elephant's udder suckled by the syndicate and politicians. And, perhaps some scholar on the collective dream of an oppressed people could explain to those who argue for the numbers operation why it is that three of the constantly played combinations are 6-6-60, 5-10-15, and 2-19-29, which, according to the dream books, are respectively sexual intercourse, clear water, and money. And also why the two most often played combinations of all are: 3-6-9 and 7-11-44. The former is shit; the latter is blood" (150).

28. Hughes, *The Big Sea,* 287.

CHORUS THREE: UGLY BEAUTY

1. Amiri Baraka (as LeRoi Jones), "The Modern Scene," *Blues People: Negro Music in White America* (New York: William Morrow and Company, 1963),

212–13. One of the problems with Baraka's otherwise brilliant book is found in its familiar subtitle: America wasn't always or everywhere "white." Rather than the weight of sociology critiqued by Ellison's famous review of the book, it may be that this is its limitation. Baraka himself has provided a kind of footnote that says as much about his book's limits, quoted in "Chorus Four: Planet Rock."

2. *Othering* is a useful word Mackey uses to describe both black invention and the hindering of that imagination: "Artistic othering has to do with innovation, invention, and change, upon which cultural health and diversity depend and thrive. Social othering has to do with power, exclusion, and privilege, the centralizing of a norm against which otherness is measured, meted out, marginalized. My focus is the practice of the former by people subjected to the latter." Nathaniel Mackey, "Other: From Noun to Verb," in *Discrepant Engagement: Dissonance, Cross-Culturality, and Experimental Writing* (1993; repr., Tuscaloosa: University of Alabama Press, 2003), 265.

3. Stephen Spender, *The Struggle of the Modern* (London: Hamish Hamilton, 1963), 17.

4. "Conceptually, not much separates jazz from the (post)modernist avant-garde," critic Craig Werner observes. "Both harbor a fierce desire to make it new, to shatter the idols of the marketplace, to explore the deepest recesses of human experience." Craig Werner, *A Change Is Gonna Come* (Ann Arbor: University of Michigan Press, 2006), 135.

5. Cornel West, "On Afro-American Music: From Bebop to Rap," in *The Cornel West Reader* (New York: Basic Books, 1999), 475.

6. Donald Allen, ed., "Preface," *The New American Poetry* (New York: Grove, 1960), xi. The difference in focus, between bebop ("modern jazz") as Afro-American by West, and "American" by Allen, is instructive.

7. A phrase suggested by any number of sources. See Peter Brooker's 1992 anthology *Modernism/Postmodernism* and West's interview in it (Harlow, UK: Longman, 1992). Several of these postmodern starting points are suggested by David Perkins's fine two-volume *A History of Modern Poetry* (Cambridge, MA: Harvard University Press, 1976, 1987).

8. Quoted by Susan Gubar in her crucial *Poetry after Auschwitz:* "the 1949 judgment of Theodor Adorno was taken to be as axiomatic as the biblical commandment against graven images: 'To write poetry after Auschwitz is barbaric.' Even as the word 'poetry' expanded and contracted in meaning—it was understood to signify any and all forms of representation, poetry as a genre, or aesthetic work about the Shoah—the sentence sometimes was taken to be an admonition (beware of writing poetry), sometimes a directive (poetry ought not be written), sometimes simply a diagnosis (poetry cannot be written)." Gubar, *Poetry after Auschwitz: Remembering What One Never Knew* (Bloomington: Indiana University Press, 2003), 4.

9. Hurston, "Characteristics of Negro Expression," in *Folklore, Memoirs, and Other Writings* (New York: Library of America, 1995), 833–34.

10. I first heard this idea in a paper presented at a *Callaloo* conference in Cuba in 2001. Reprinted in Edwards, "Rendez-vous in Rhythm," *Connect* 1 (Fall 2000): 183–90. Thanks to Prof. Edwards for this article.

11. The phrase "hornlike" comes from Albert Murray: "Charlie Christian, 1919–42, who attained world prominence during his two years (1939–41) as a sideman with Benny Goodman, the so-called King of Swing, was an instrumentalist who not only mastered all of the soulful nuances of traditional blues-idiom statement but also made of the guitar a hornlike solo vehicle with orchestral rank equivalent to the trumpet, the trombone, and the saxophone. Christian was born in Texas, grew up in the Oklahoma City of the Blue Devils and, like Lester Young and Charlie Parker, was a product of the territory dance circuit and Kansas City style after-hours jam sessions. His best-known records include *Solo Flight, Air Mail Special, Blues in B, Seven Come Eleven, A Smooth One,* and *Till Tom Special.*" Murray, *Stomping the Blues* (New York: De Capo, 1976), 207. For a fuller treatment of Christian, consult *A Biography of Charlie Christian, Jazz Guitar's King of Swing* by Wayne E. Goins and the inestimable Craig R. McKinney (Lampeter, UK, and Lewiston, NY: Mellen Press, 2005).

12. The recent discourses on cool are too many to name, but would include Dick Pountain and David Robins, *Cool Rules: Anatomy of an Attitude* (London: Reaktion, 2000), and Lewis MacAdams, *Birth of the Cool: Beat, Bebop, and the American Avant-Garde* (New York: Free Press, 2001). In a useful preface MacAdams nicely traces other meanings and mentions of cool.

13. A recent catalog traces West Coast cool more broadly. See Elizabeth Armstrong's *Birth of the Cool: California Art, Design, and Culture at Midcentury* (Newport Beach, CA, and New York: Orange County Museum of Art/ Prestel Publishing, 2007).

14. Ralph Ellison, "On Bird, Bird-Watching, and Jazz" (1964), in *Shadow and Act* (New York: Random House, 1964), 223. Note how Ellison's words echo yet importantly alter—one could say burlesque—the difficulties James Weldon Johnson spoke of with dialect's full stops: pathos and humor.

15. Ibid.

16. Larkin, *All What Jazz: A Record Diary 1961–1971,* 2nd ed. (London: Faber and Faber, 1985), 22–23. The quote continues: "My own theory is that it [modernism] is related to an imbalance between the two tensions from which art springs: these are the tension between the artist and his material, and between the artist and his audience, and that in the last seventy-five years or so the second of these has slackened or even perished. In consequence the artist has become over-concerned with his material (hence an age of technical experiment), and, in isolation, has busied himself with the

two principal themes of modernism, mystification and outrage." Note that Larkin does not mean the jazz of Armstrong and Kid Ory and Jelly Roll Morton as that is roughly contemporaneous with literary modernism, as I argue earlier. He means the postwar products typically called "modern jazz," which he sees as commiserating with the whole of modernism, before and after the war.

17. Ibid., 16.

18. Ibid., 24. You could say Larkin and Ellison are not far apart in their view of the shift in entertainment after the way, and the ways "hating" the audience had become part of the bebop audience's experience and even expectation. But Ellison doesn't write of this as the same kind of fault that Larkin does.

19. Ellison, "On Bird," 226. See Brent Hayes Edwards, "Louis Armstrong and the Syntax of Scat," *Critical Inquiry* 28, no.3 (Spring 2002): 618–49, for an unpacking of the meaning of "mugging" by Armstrong and others in the jazz tradition, and its relation to scat.

20. For more on asymmetry and the connections between modern and African American culture, see my essay "Visiting St. Elizabeths: Ezra Pound, Impersonation, and the Mask of the Modern Artist," in *Ezra Pound and African American Modernism*, ed. Michael Coyle, 185–204 (Orono, ME: National Poetry Foundation, 2001).

21. Armstrong caught such flak over being King of the Zulus, a real local honor, he swore never to be buried in New Orleans, a request summarily denied. For a discussion of the meanings of King Zulu, consult Albert Murray's *Stomping the Blues;* for a poetic riff, consult my "King Zulu" in *To Repel Ghosts,* based on a painting by Basquiat. Indeed, Murray's caption for a photograph of Satchmo serves as an epigraph to the poem-sequence. Young, "King Zulu," *To Repel Ghosts: The Remix* (New York: Knopf, 2005), 159.

22. Ellison, "On Bird," 226–27.

23. Blue Monday means not only the Monday before Lent but also according to the *Oxford English Dictionary,* "a Monday spent in dissipation by workmen." It is also a term that courses throughout blues and jazz compositions.

24. Ellison, "On Bird," 228.

25. The phrase "picaresque saint" is taken by Ellison from R. W. B. Lewis in his discussion of contemporary novels. Ellison, "On Bird," 228.

26. Ellison, "The World and the Jug," in *Shadow and Act,* 111, 112.

27. Despite the dedication Ellison was notoriously nasty about Hughes, who had helped early on, later in his life—pretending even not to recall being the dedicatee of Hughes's book. Consult Arnold Rampersad's biography of Ellison for his subject's treatment of other writers.

28. Langston Hughes, *Montage of a Dream Deferred* (New York: Henry Holt, 1951).

29. "Sunday by the Combination" and "Casualty," in Langston Hughes, *Selected Poems of Langston Hughes* (New York: Vintage Classics, 1990), 259.

30. Yusef Komunyakaa, "To Have Danced with Death," *Dien Cai Dau* (Middletown, CT: Wesleyan University Press, 1988), 46. The poem ends:

I wanted him to walk ahead,
to disappear through glass,
to be consumed by music

that might move him like Sandman Sims,
but he merely rocked on his good leg
like a bleak & soundless bell.

31. Hughes, *Selected Poems,* 259–61.

32. Gwendolyn Brooks, "kitchenette building," in *A Street in Bronzeville* (New York: Harper and Brothers, 1945), 2.

33. Langston Hughes, *The Best of Simple* (New York: Hill and Wang, 1961), 118. Adam Gussow mentions this quote in the context of his study of violence in the blues, *Seems Like Murder Here: Southern Violence and the Blues Tradition* (Chicago: Univesity of chicago Press, 2002), 7.

34. Edwards, "Louis Armstrong and the Syntax of Scat," 618. As Edwards indicates, rejecting other parallels, "In this complex metaphorical mix, the Armstrong scat aesthetic is equally a strategy of catharsis and physical (erotic) regulation. . . . It is something more akin to James Joyce's identification of creativity with excretion—or, as he calls it, 'chamber music'" (632). We may also think of Stein's notion of Alice B. Toklas having a "cow," a code recently revealed to mean a bowel movement. See Kay Turner, ed., *Baby Precious Always Shines: Selected Love Notes Between Gertrude Stein and Alice B. Toklas* (New York: St. Martin's Press, 2000).

35. Zora Neale Hurston, "Spirituals and Neo-Spirituals" (1934), in *Folklore, Memoirs and Other Writings,* 872. Emphasis added.

36. Gilles Deleuze and Claire Parnet, *Dialogues II,* rev. ed. (New York: Columbia University Press, 2007), 132. This quote also appears as part of the epigraph for my first book, *Most Way Home* (1995).

37. *Oxford English Dictionary,* 2nd ed., 1989; online version September 2011.

38. See also Thomas Brothers, ed., *Louis Armstrong, in His Own Words: Selected Writings* (New York: Oxford University Press, 1999). Brothers also suggests similar: "I will leave for others the task of analyzing Armstrong's syntax and his use of African-American dialect. But I would like to suggest that there is something similar about the flow of many jazz solos, in which phrases may routinely lack a firm ending point, and the verbal flow that Armstrong cultivates with his dashes and ellipses. It would be interesting to look

for literary antecedents that Armstrong may have known. The dash is occasionally used in combination with comma and with period, forming what Nicholson Baker dubs 'dash-hybrids' in a discussion of nineteenth-century styles of punctuation" (xxiii). For the artwork, see *Steven Brower, Satchmo: The Wonderful World and Art of Louis Armstrong* (New York: Abrams, 2009).

39. A sample "translation," itself a recasting of an ode first rendered in more "standard" English:

Aliter

Ole Brer Rabbit watchin' his feet,
Rabbit net's got the pheasant beat;
    When I was young and a-startin' life
    I kept away from trouble an' strife
But then, as life went on,
Did I meet trouble?
        Aye, my son;
Wish I could sleep till life was done.

Ezra Pound, *The Confucian Odes: The Classic Anthology Defined by Confucius* (New York: New Directions, 1959), 5.

40. MacAdams, *Birth of the Cool,* 38. MacAdams continues with another well-known anecdote: "One night, in September 1941 he was conducting the band but facing the audience, and somebody hit the back of his conk with a spitwad. Calloway accused Gillespie of the deed, precipating a fight that ended with Gillespie pulling a carpet cutter out of his trumpet case and stabbing Calloway in the butt. Calloway took ten stitches and Gillespie was out of there" (38).

41. Andrew F. Jones, *Yellow Music: Media Culture and Colonial Modernity in the Chinese Jazz Age* (Durham, NC: Duke University Press, 2001), 1.

42. For more on Pound's often racial impersonation, consult Young, "Visiting St. Elizabeths."

43. I've not seen them till only recently, and only in the bookstore. But they both are in Italian, which raises some interesting questions about language and Pound—who translated Canto 72, included in recent editions.

44. Canto 74/434. Pound's engagement with black folks and symbolic darkness may be said to have occurred earlier. For *The Cantos* begin not just with Odysseus but with a reference to the "Kimmerian lands," not necessarily a view of hell, but one of darkness. I have always been fascinated by the "dark lands" Odysseus visits and avoids—Kimmeria seems in some crucial ways a metaphor for blackness itself, for an unnamed nation that falls somewhere between Scylla and Charybdis, as it were. Canto 1 also navigates the start of Pound's attempt at epic, one for which the notion of hiding is crucial—the

journey is one of escape, of close calls, and concealment. The destination may be paradise. Or the darkness Pound evokes yet tries like Odysseus to avoid.

45. This isn't merely a function of its being a persona, as other poems don't use it. In Lowell's "The Banker's Daughter," which appears just two poems earlier in the *Collected Poems* (New York: Farrar, Straus and Giroux, 2003), Marie de Medici speaks without quotation marks.

46. Robert Lowell, "A Mad Negro Soldier Confined at Munich" (1959), in *Collected Poems*, 118.

47. Pound–Hughes correspondence is found in *Paideuma: Journal of Pound Studies* (Fall 2001). Reprinted in Coyle, *Ezra Pound and African American Modernism*.

48. Till is "mythologically associated with Zeus's ram, whose golden fleece Jason and the Argonauts hunted in the kingdom of Colchis." Ezra Pound, *The Pisan Cantos* (New York: New Directions, 2003), 122, footnote 74.171–73. This edition, while not where I first encountered the poem, is invaluable for its introduction and notes, which synthesize the criticism surrounding the poem. The notes also identify Louis Till as the father of Emmett Till, confirming a fact I am thankful to the Library of America's Geoffrey O'Brien for bringing to my attention.

49. For more on the lynching photograph, consult *Without Sanctuary: Lynching Photography in America* (Santa Fe, NM: Twin Palms, 2000).

50. Farah Jasmine Griffin, *If You Can't Be Free, Be a Mystery: In Search of Billie Holiday* (New York: Free Press, 2001), 19.

51. Ibid., 17.

52. Ibid., 50.

53. Clarence Major, *Juba to Jive: A Dictionary of African-American Slang* (New York: Penguin, 1994), 164. The full implications of the black mask might be seen on the definition of "face" on the same page: "a stranger, especially an unknown white person."

54. Griffin, *If You Can't Be Free, Be a Mystery*, 50–51.

55. The *Oxford English Dictionary* has two relevant definitions of *refuge*: one, dating from 1822, "An establishment providing accommodation, and typically some supervision, for people who have been discharged from prison. Also: a similar institution for homeless people, young offenders, etc." and another of more recent vintage, "An establishment offering protection to women who have suffered or are considered likely to suffer domestic violence; a women's shelter"(3rd ed., September 2009; online version March 2011).

56. Major, *Juba to Jive*, 111.

BROKEN GIRAFFE

1. "A Conversation with Kevin Young," *Indiana Review* 23, no. 1 (Spring 2001).

2. An unholy hybrid, barely black and awfully modern, jazz could even be dispraised by someone otherwise sympathetic to black culture, like Waldo Frank:

> Jazz is not so much a folk music—like the Negro spirituals—as a folk accent in music. It expresses well a mass response to our world of piston rods, cylinders and mechanized laws. . . . Jazz expresses a personal maladjustment to this world, righted by sheer and shrewd compliance. And this, doubtless, is why the races at once most flexible and most maladjusted— the Negro and the Jew—give the best jazz masters. Since the rhythm of our age is not transfigured in jazz, as in truly creative art, but is assimilated, the elements of the age itself which we may disapprove will appear also in jazz. In other words, a folk art—being so largely an art of reaction and of assimilation—will contain the faults of the adult minorities that rule the folk, as well as the pristine virtues of the people.

Waldo Frank, *In the American Jungle (1925–1936)* (New York: Farrar & Rinehart, 1937), 122–23.

While Frank praises elsewhere the broader "American jungle," here he can't bring himself to see the "rhythm of the age" in jazz the way that Hughes did— that "the rhythm of life is a jazz rhythm, honey"—or at least not to see this rhythm as a good thing. Instead, more noise than music, jazz provides further evidence of society's decay, embodied in the idea of the Negro (with a bit of Jew thrown in for good measure). Mechanized and flexible, passive and maladjusted, jazz is worse off for its assimilation—rather than transfiguration—of modern life. The corrupt origins of jazz, which extend to the unclear lineage of the very word "jazz," are troubling.

This view, inadvertently or not, echoes how the Nazi party in Germany before the war labeled what it called "degenerate art and music," making such depravity's mascot a stereotypical black figure with a yellow star on his chest, a gypsy earring, and a saxophone almost as big as his lips. And while Frank, mentor to Jean Toomer, passed for black when they traveled the South, Frank's clearly black no longer. (Some may say neither was Toomer, but Toomer's works—even his later works—say otherwise.) Though Waldo's is largely a view of culture largely in opposition to Nazism, both share a view of culture dependent on purity that neither jazz nor I share.

3. Bob Kaufman, "Jail Poems," in *Solitudes Crowded with Loneliness* (New York: New Directions, 1971), 56, 60, 61.

4. Kaufman, *Solitudes,* 10. This poem, one of Kaufman's finest, is inexplicably left out of *Cranial Guitar.*

5. The quote continues: "When not African [the nickname] is likely to be an English word indicating something regarding the nature of the weather at the

time of the child's birth (such as *Snow, Snowy, Storm, Rain, Freeze, Hightide*); or the appearance, temperament, or health of the child (such as *Ugly, Egghead, Frogeyes, Badboy, Sick, Laydead, Death, Bigboy, Bigchild, Lookdown, Mammasweet, Livefine*); or the time of birth (such as *Harvest, Evening, Night, October, Saturday*); or some particular incident or object with which the child or his parents were associated at the time of the child's birth or later (such as some superstition, or a place, person, animal, or plant). In many instances both the given-name and surname are African words. Some of my ex-slave informants explain this by saying that during slavery they used for their surname (which they called *trimmin'*) the surname of their owner. After slavery, many of them refused to use any longer the name of their former enslavers. Likewise, many former slaveholders refused to allow the freedmen to use their names. Thereupon, the former slaves chose their nickname for their surname and gave themselves another nickname. This also is frequently an African word." Lorenzo Dow Turner, *Africanisms in the Gullah Dialect* (1949; repr., Columbia: University of South Carolina Press, 2002), 40.

6. Edward Kamau Brathwaite, *History of the Voice: The Development of Nation Language in Anglophone-Caribbean Poetry* (London: New Beacon, 1984), 13.

7. Hurston, "Shouting" (1934), in *Folklore, Memoirs, and Other Writings* (New York: Library of America, 1995), 851–82.

8. Kaufman, *Cranial Guitar* (Minneapolis: Coffee House Press, 1996), 80–81.

9. Kaufman, "Fragment," *Solitudes*, 12.

10. Kaufman, *The Ancient Rain: Poems 1956–1978* (New York: New Directions, 1981), ix. See also "Repetition as a Figure of Black Culture" by critic James Snead, in *The Jazz Cadence of American Culture*, ed. Robert G. O'Meally, 62–81 (New York: Columbia University Press, 1998).

11. Kaufman, "Ginsberg (for Allen)," *Solitudes*, 23.

12. Afaa M. Weaver, "The Bop According to Afaa M. Weaver," unpublished essay (Somerville, MA: 2 October 1997). Thanks to Sean Hill for providing this early important unpublished essay that circulated among the early Cave Canem fellows (and other black writers). Weaver's manifesto opens with a bit of the bop's inspiration:

> In the second year of Cave Canem, many of us expressed a need to make manifest a new dimension, acknowledging all that has gone before, understanding our varying sense of the politic in Black poetry, not the least of which is that our very persistence as poets is a resistance to the dictating mind of racism and its economic and political constructs. In the beginning of our week at Mt. St. Alphonsus in nineteen ninety-seven, I set out

to initiate the beginning of our collective effort to create new forms by making the first draft of a form I named "The Bop," and I brought the first Bop poems to the workshop in raw draft, having since revised them extensively. The African-American poetic at Cave Canem is a collective effort, as there are other forms in development in the hands of other poets. Renee Moore is working on a form called "The Double Dutch," and Stephanie Byrd is working on a form called tentatively "The Hot Comb," as we are looking to be proactive on the subject of African women's hair.

I am not entirely sure whether the other forms were created; certainly they haven't had the effect that this crucial, African American form has had on contemporary poetics. As the phrase "In the second year of Cave Canem" suggests, soon we'll be speaking of dates as ACC: After Cave Canem.

13. Kaufman, "Battle Report," *Solitudes,* 8.

14. You could say that Kaufman's even as orchestral as Ray Charles, or proves a kind of percussive group sound as John Cage's prepared pianos—two innovators and rough contemporaries in music. Of course, Cage himself would compose using silence in his *4'33"*—if only to force us to realize, as a recent study of Cage has it, "no such thing as silence." Consult David Hadju on Ray Charles in *Heroes and Villains: Essays on Music, Movies, Comics, and Culture* (New York: Da Capo, 2009) and Kyle Gann's *No Such Thing as Silence: John Cage's 4'33"* (New Haven, CT: Yale University Press, 2011).

15. Kaufman, *Solitudes,* 28.

16. This was Neeli Cherkovski. I wrote a long, far more theoretical essay about Kaufman years back, never published, that serves as a shadow to this chapter. It may be worth excavating one day, though certainly not here.

17. Bob Kaufman, "Oregon" and "Untitled," in *Ancient Rain,* 58, 59.

18. James H. Cone, *The Spirituals and the Blues: An Interpretation* (New York: Seabury Press, 1972), 95.

19. Countee Cullen, "For a Lady I Know," *Color* (New York: Harper and Brothers, 1925), 50.

20. Kaufman, "Crootey Songo," *Cranial Guitar,* 74.

CHORUS FOUR: MOANIN'

1. Craig Werner, *A Change Is Gonna Come: Music, Race, and the Soul of America* (Ann Arbor: University of Michigan Press, 2006), 120.

2. *Curtis/Live,* "Rap" (track 4).

3. Lyn Hejinian, *The Language of Inquiry* (Berkeley: University of California Press, 2000), 148. The classic example may be "The White House" to mean the presidency, which, no doubt, funk and recent events would dare to paint black.

4. J. A. Cuddon, *A Dictionary of Literary Terms* (Garden City, NY: Doubleday, 1977), 386: "A figure of speech in which the name of an attribute or a thing is substituted for the thing itself. Common examples are 'The Stage' for the theatrical profession; 'The Crown' for the monarchy; 'The Bench' for the judiciary system; 'Dante' for his works."

5. Aretha's nickname. In it we hear, fascinatingly, the powerful chorus of her "Respect": "Re, Re, Re, Re, Re, Re, Re, Re, Respect / just a little bit."

6. Of course, in the hands of David Bowie and Mick Jagger—who said at the time of its recording, it was cynically done in one night—"Dancing in the Street" becomes a banal party anthem again. It is only with "Racing in the Street" by Bruce Springsteen, with its chorus that riffs off the original "Dancing," that the power of the original sentiment, and desire for change, is fully realized.

7. At least according to VH-1. Aretha's "Respect" was number three, as I recall.

8. This trait they share with the Beatles, who began also with Chuck Berry et al. The Stones' focus on covers is often unacknowledged, at least by listeners unaware of their invariably black origins: I recall once playing Robert Johnson's "Love in Vain" to my poetics class, and a woman in the front row (older and with kids) sang every word: afterward, she said she wasn't aware that it was not by the Stones. (I myself was not aware it was covered by someone not Robert Johnson!) The argument that the Stones are exposing this music to others (i.e., whites) seems to me specious, and indeed, to reinscribe the need for a cover process, implying that black culture requires an interpreter (instead of the white audience requiring one). However, with British artists, such black origins are at least treated with reverence—though at times, with a romance reminiscent of Larkin's view of jazz as better in its more "primitive," earthy, prewar form.

9. I engage these issues more fully in my essay "Cover Song," found in the retrospective catalog for the artist Sam Durant. Note that this is not merely a function of color but culture: Durant himself is white, but in his fearlessness indicates how comfortable he is with these ideas, even taking on the Stones' "Brown Sugar."

10. Lott, *Love and Theft: Blackface Minstrelsy and the American Working Class* (New York: Oxford University Press, 1995), 56–57.

11. Cornel West, "On Afro-American Music," *The Cornel West Reader* (New York: Basic Civitas Books, 1999), 476.

12. Werner, *A Change Is Gonna Come.*

13. Important here is Thadious Davis's notion of falsetto found in male soul singers, and her arguments about its particular resonance in black culture and what it does to questions of gender. Certainly there is irony in the fact that it takes a deep voice to render such a high-pitched holler. Davis's

critique, given as a paper at the centennial Langston Hughes conference at the University of Kansas (Lawrence, Kansas, 2001), is a crucial one that I hope sees print soon.

14. See Baraka, "Blues People Addendum," in *Digging: The Afro-American Soul of American Classical Music* (Berkeley: University of California Press, 2009), 27. It is unclear what date this piece is, but the essay the "Addendum" follows is dated "90/91." Emphasis in original.

15. Soul is defined in many different forums. A good place to start is *Soul,* ed. Lee Rainwater (Chicago: Trans-action Books, 1970).

16. Mel Watkins, "The Lyrics of James Brown: Ain't It Funky Now, or Money Won't Change Your Licking Stick," *Amistad 2: Writings on Black History and Culture* (New York: Vintage Books, 2001), 23. We may also consult Zora Neale Hurston's "Shouting," in *Folklore, Memoirs, and Other Writings* (New York: The Library of America, 1995).

17. Watkins, "Lyrics of James Brown," 32.

18. Ibid., 27

19. Vertamae Smart-Grosvenor, *Vibration Cooking; or, The Travel Notes of a Geechee Girl* (1970; repr., Athens: University of Georgia Press, 2011). Quotations in text are from the 1992 Ballantine Books edition, 49. Those who might doubt the persistent problems of "Geechee" as a term may consult the current *OED*, which seems particularly tin-eared in defining the word: not only in the etymology, which the dictionary places from "the name of the *Ogeechee* River, Georgia" but I think is far more likely from the "Gissi" people; but also in the dated examples which help restrict it to what they call "a derogatory term for a black person of the southern United States." To wit:

> 1926   *National Geographic* Sept. 278   Among the negroes living on the Ogeechee River a patois, developed in ante bellum days, has persisted. The origin of 'Geechee', as the patois is called, is explained by the fact that slaves employed on the old rice plantations were more or less isolated and rarely conversed with their white owners, with the result that their knowledge of English words was slight and the pronunciation of them was bizarre. The 'Geechee' negro speaks in a sort of staccato and always seems excited when talking.

> 1934   *Webster's New Internat. Dict. Eng. Lang.*   *Geechee.* A dialect, originally of Negro slaves on the Ogeechee river, Georgia, formed of English and native African words. 2. One who speaks Geechee.

> 1940   E. Caldwell *Trouble in July* xiii. 208   He sounds like one of those Geechee niggers. That breed'll do anything to keep them from working.

> 1945   *New Yorker* 8 Sept. 20/2   Creecy was a Geechee blacker than the soot in the fireplace.

Oxford English Dictionary, available online; or *Compact Oxford English Dictionary,* 2nd ed. (Oxford: Oxford University Press, 1987). The definition remains unchanged from 1987, or should we say from the 1945 quotation taken from the *New Yorker.*

20. Smart-Grosvenor, *Vibration Cooking* (Ballantine Books, 1992), 31.

21. Ibid., 32.

22. Ibid., 6. See also the chapter "I Love . . . Bon Voyage Parties," 119–25.

23. Zadie Smith. *Changing My Mind: Occasional Essays* (New York: Penguin Press, 2009), 12–13.

24. Ibid., 13.

25. After reading part of this chapter at the Southern Foodways Alliance in the keynote to the 2011 symposium on the Cultivated South, I was reminded of a couple other examples of white songs that mention food (rather than use it as metaphor, which is plentiful in all traditions), including Hank Williams's "Jambalaya." Still, the sheer number pales besides those in soul food and jazz, and this question still lingers, suggestive of other notions of plenty.

26. Hurston, "Shouting," 851–52.

27. Ralph Ellison, "What America Would Be Like without Blacks." Originally appeared in *Time,* 6 April 1970. Reprinted in *Going to the Territory* (1986). *The Collected Essays of Ralph Ellison,* ed. John Callahan (New York: Modern Library, 2003), 582.

INTERSTELLAR SPACE

1. Not everyone sees this in the same successful light as I do. In his monograph *Electric Ladyland* (New York: Continuum, 2004), John Perry describes Band of Gypsys: "In later years, after Jimi's Band of Gypsys experiment foundered and left him drifting in a sea of excess freedom, [producer Chas] Chandler's disciplined approach would again be sought, but in mid-1968 all Hendrix needed was *space*" (3). Perry's emphasis in the original on *space* is a nice foreshadowing of our arguments for space as the dominant mode of the post-soul era.

2. For a good discussion of postfeminism (and the fallacy of post meaning "anti") consult Sarah Gamble, ed., *Dictionary of Feminism and Postfeminism* (New York: Routledge, 1999). Gamble's own separate chapter titled "Postfeminism" is particularly insightful.

3. "Putting Gertrude on the Mothership: An Interview with Thomas Sayers Ellis by Philip Metres (February 8, 2002)." *Combo* magazine, vol. 10 (Spring 2002): 42–53.

4. See my interview with Laylah Ali in *Laylah Ali: Note Drawings* (deCordova Museum and Sculpture Park, Lincoln, Mass., 2008) for her insight into the term *post-black.* Ali was included in *Freestyle,* a catalog for the exhibition of young black artists curated by Thelma Golden, who helped coin the

term "post-black" in the catalog's introduction. Interestingly, post-black was also resurrected in Touré's cover review of Colson Whitehead's *Sag Harbor:* "Visible Young Man," *New York Times Book Review,* 1 May 2009.

5. Jeff Chang, *Can't Stop Won't Stop: A History of the Hip-Hop Generation* (New York: Picador, 2005), 13.

6. Seamus Deane, *Strange Country: Modernity and Nationhood in Irish Writing since 1790* (Oxford: Oxford University Press, 1997), 2–3.

7. Cornelius Eady, "The Supremes," in *Hardheaded Weather* (New York: Putnam's Sons/Penguin, 2008), 136.

8. Rita Dove, "Ö," in *The Yellow House on the Corner* (Pittsburgh: Carnegie-Mellon University Press, 1989).

9. Audre Lorde, "The Master's Tools Will Never Dismantle the Master's House." Originally read as a paper in 1979. In *Sister Outsider: Essays and Speeches* (Berkeley, CA: Crossing Press, 1984), 110–13.

10. Melvin Van Peebles, *Ain't Supposed to Die a Natural Death* (New York: Bantam, 1973), 2–5. In 2008, the play underwent a revival in Harlem, celebrating its 1971 debut.

11. Perry, *Electric Ladyland,* 11. The whole book is a wonderful, sophisticated introduction to the heights of Hendrix's artistry, as well as a firsthand witnessing of his live playing. Thanks to Perry for articulating some of the more technical aspects of what I had been hearing in Hendrix all along.

12. Susan Willis, *Specifying: Black Women Writing the American Experience* (Madison: University of Wisconsin Press, 1987), 108.

13. Toni Morrison, *The Bluest Eye* (New York: Holt, Rinehart and Winston, 1970), 64.

14. The latter song provides critic Farah Jasmine Griffin with ample example of the migration narrative. Griffin, *"Who Set You Flowin'?" The African-American Migration Narrative* (New York: Oxford University Press, 1995).

15. Cornel West, "On Afro-American Music: From Bebop to Rap," in *The Cornel West Reader* (New York: Basic Civitas Books, 1999), 478.

16. Piper's "Notes on Funk I–IV" are some of the best writings on funk, based on her 1980s series of small- and large-group performances in which she taught participants funk dances and then music, recording their often strong reactions—many of which she describes usefully (and sensitively) not just in terms of racism but xenophobia. She also gets how fun funk is and that the result was "LISTENING by DANCING," which I take up here. Adrian Piper, "Notes on Funk I–IV," in *Out of Order, Out of Sight.* Volume I, *Selected Writings in Meta-Art, 1968–1992* (Cambridge, MA: The MIT Press, 1996), 214.

17. Robert Hayden, "[American Journal]," in *Collected Poems of Robert Hayden,* 2nd ed., ed. Frederick Glaysher (New York: Liveright, 1996), 192–93.

18. Leslie Fiedler, "Cross the Border—Close the Gap" (1970), in *A New Fiedler Reader* (Amherst, MA: Prometheus Books, 1999), 287.

19. Any number of recent articles and exhibitions such as *Alien Nation* feature black takes on this idea of outer space.

20. Lester Bangs, *Psychotic Reactions and Carburetor Dung: The Work of a Legendary Critic; Rock 'N' Roll as Literature and Literature as Rock 'N' Roll*, ed. Greil Marcus (New York: Knopf, 1987), 75.

21. See Brian Coleman, *Check the Technique: Liner Notes for Hip-Hop Junkies* (New York: Villard, 2007), for a discussion of the case.

22. Louis Menand, *Discovering Modernism: T. S. Eliot and His Context,* 2nd ed. (1987; repr., New York: Oxford University Press, 2007), 23.

23. Don't take my word for the brilliance of "Buddy": consult *Ego Trip's Book of Rap Lists,* "Hip Hop's 25 Greatest Remixes," where "Buddy" ranks number 10. Sacha Jenkins, Elliott Wilson, Chairman Mao, Gabriel Alvarez, and Brent Rollins, *Ego Trip's Book of Rap Lists* (New York: St. Martin's Griffin, 1999), 74. Note too that the collective sprung not just spiritually but literally from the example of Afrika Bambaataa, who first took Jungle Brothers under his wing.

24. Lyrae Van Clief-Stefanon made this statement during a panel discussion on "The Future of Southern Poetry" conducted at Emory University and moderated by me as part of the Poetry Society of America's Centennial Celebration, 7 October 2010.

FINAL CHORUS: PLANET ROCK

1. Jeff Chang, *Can't Stop Won't Stop: A History of the Hip-Hop Generation* (New York: Picador, 2005), 122.

2. Colson Whitehead, *Sag Harbor* (New York: Doubleday, 2009), 61–62.

3. Northrop Frye, *Anatomy of Criticism: Four Essays,* 3rd ed. (Princeton, NJ: Princeton University Press, 1973), 125.

4. Dieter Lesage and Ina Wudtke, *Black Sound White Cube* (Vienna: Löcker, 2010), 29. This book provides a useful overview of these issues. Thanks to Jennie C. Jones for putting this book on my radar, and for her work's incursions into this area. For a good example of scratching as percussion, consult "Fantastic Freaks at the Dixie" by DJ Theodore and other cuts on the *Wild Style* soundtrack.

5. Legs McNeil and Gillian McCain, *Please Kill Me: The Uncensored Oral History of Punk* (New York: Penguin, 1997); Dick Hebdige, *Subculture: The Meaning of Style* (London: Methuen, 1979). See the "Lester Bangs" entry, Nicholas Rombes, *A Cultural Dictionary of Punk, 1974–1982* (New York: Continuum, 2009), 20–22. See also, Lester Bangs, "The White Noise Supremacists" from 1979, reprinted in Lester Bangs, *Psychotic Reactions and Carburetor Dung: The Work of a Legendary Critic,* ed. Greil Marcus, 272–82 (New York:

Vintage, 1988). Though I may disagree with his notion that New Wave was "sheer" or "white," Simon Reynolds nicely summarizes Legs McNeil's "segregationist" beliefs this way:

> Factor in the sheer whiteness of New Wave music, and you had a situation where, for the first time since before the 1920s hot jazz era, white bohemians were disengaged from black culture. Not only that, but some of them were *proud* of this disengagement. Just a week before Bangs' essay, *Village Voice* profiled Legs McNeil of *Punk* magazine. Writer Marc Jacobson discussed how McNeil and his cohorts consciously rejected the whole notion of the hipster as "white Negro" and dedicated themselves to celebrating all things, white, teenage and suburban. Years later, McNeil candidly discussed this segregationist aspect of punk in an interview with Jon Savage: "We were all white: there were no black people involved with this. In the sixties hippies always wanted to be black. We were going: 'Fuck the Blues; fuck the black experience.'" McNeil believed that disco was the loathsome musical child of an unholy union of blacks and gays.

Simon Reynolds, *Rip It Up and Start Again: Post-Punk 1978–1984* (London: Faber & Faber, 2005), 67.

  6. Quoted in Chang, *Can't Stop Won't Stop*, 259.

  7. D. A. Powell, *Tea* (Hanover, NH: Wesleyan University Press, 1998), 11.

  8. For several of these meanings, consult Nicholas Rombes's *Cultural Dictionary of Punk*. The entries "Punk, alternate meanings of" and "Punk rock is a put on" are especially cogent, and relevant to Rombes's stated wish: "One of the goals of this book is to go back to that moment in time when the term 'punk' was unstable, ambiguous, loaded with so many suggestions" (199). Though he quotes Geneva Smitherman on "punk" in her *Black Talk,* he only quotes the first definition. Far more useful is Tavia Nyong'o, "Punk'd Theory," which relates how "the figure of the punk in Anglo-American culture is a venerable but mercurial one" but reads the "punk as African American slang for a gay man" to consider the intersection of queer theory and punk:

> No source I consulted could definitively trace the origin of the word *punk,* but a representative etymology reports that "the word originated in British slang around the end of the 17th century when it was used to denote a *whore* and later a precursor to the modern *rent boy*." Although this account does not preclude an African origin for the word, I read the evidence as indicating that *punk'd* emerges from within what Dick Hebdige has called "the frozen dialectic between black and white cultures," that is, a word for which the memory of its English provenance has been surrogated by the imagination of a black resonance. Telltale evidence of this faux-African origin is the use of "eye dialect," ungrammatical spell-

ings indistinguishable in audible speech from grammatical ones (e.g., "punk'd" for "punked"). Such a graphic practice has characterized white transcriptions of black speech since slavery times, so MTV's eye dialect notifies us that we are in the presence of what the novelist Toni Morrison has termed an "American Africanism."

Tavia Nyong'o, "Punk'd Theory," *Social Text* 23, nos. 3–4. (Fall–Winter 2005), 84–85.

9. See the *New York Times Magazine,* 25 July 2010, for a consideration of sissy bounce: Jonathan Dee, "New Orleans's Gender-Bending Rap."

10. "Contrivance" comes from *American Heritage Dictionary.* The fuller definition comes from Robert L. Chapman and Barbara Ann Kipfer, *The Abridged Edition of the Dictionary of American Slang* (New York: HarperPerennial, 1998).

11. Elizabeth Alexander, *The Black Interior* (St. Paul: Graywolf Press, 2004).

12. Chang, *Can't Stop Won't Stop,* 130–131.

13. Pras of the Fugees, quoted in Brian Coleman, *Check the Technique: Liner Notes for Hip-Hop Junkies* (New York: Villard, 2007), ix.

14. Even this line from NWA's "Gangsta Gangsta," which admittedly deliberately plays with image and the idea of a role model—the ultimate synecdoche, that—is countered by the BDP sample in the chorus: *It's not about a salary it's all about reality.*

15. Such looping is inadvertently described by film critic Roger Ebert in his fascinating review of *Synecdoche, New York:* "Sometimes the most unlikely-seeming films will slot right into *this groove* of projection, strategy and coping, as they involve the achievement of our needs and desires. You could put Harold Ramis' 'Groundhog Day' (1993) on the same double bill with 'Synecdoche.' Bill Murray plays a weatherman caught in a time loop. As I wrote at the time: 'He is the only one who can remember what happened yesterday. That gives him a certain advantage. He can, for example, find out what a woman is looking for in a man, and then the 'next' day he can behave in exactly the right way to impress her.' Not science fiction. How the world works. On 'I Love Lucy,' even ditzy Lucy understood this process. I will act as if I am the kind of woman Cary Grant would desire. We all live through 'Groundhog Day,' but it is less confusing for us because one day follows another. Or seems to." Roger Ebert, "O Synecdoche, my Synecdoche!" From the blog *Roger Ebert's Journal* at the *Chicago Sun-Times* website. Originally reviewed 10 November 2008. Accessible at blogs.suntimes.com/ebert/2008/11/o_synecdoche_my_synecdoche .html. Emphasis added.

16. Mark Costello and David Foster Wallace, *Signifying Rappers: Rap and Race in the Urban Present* (Hopewell, NJ: Ecco Press, 1990), 38–39. Emphasis in original.

17. Albert Murray, *Stomping the Blues* (New York: DaCapo, 1976), 254.

18. "When I first heard the track for 'Empire' I was sure it would be a hit. It was gorgeous. My instinct was to dirty it up, to tell stories of the city's gritty side, to use stories about hustling and getting hustled to add tension to the soaring beauty of the chorus. The same thing happened with another big hit, 'A Hard Knock Life.'" Jay-Z, *Decoded* (New York: Spiegel & Grau, 2010), 130.

19. Greil Marcus, *Lipstick Traces: A Secret History of the Twentieth Century* (Cambridge, MA: Harvard University Press, 1990), 8–9. Emphasis added.

20. I lived on the West Coast then, and there was an independent radio station that regularly played hip-hop, including Ice Cube and Digital Underground's "Freaks of the Industry," a perfect example of a song whose raunchiness contains no "obscene" words. The radio station's unfortunate demise at the hands of Clear Channel is recalled in Chang, *Can't Stop Won't Stop.*

21. While he mistakes the crossroads for a place of fertile individuality rather than of exit, transport, and last resort, DJ Spooky that Subliminal Kid (a.k.a. Paul Miller) writes about collage and fragmentation:

> A deep sense of fragmentation occurs in the mind of a Dj. When I came to Dj-ing, my surroundings—the dense spectrum of media grounded in advanced capitalism—seemed to have already constructed so many of my aspirations and desires for me; I felt like my nerves extended to all these images, sounds, other people—that all of them were extensions of myself, just as I was an extension of them. . . . By creating an analogical structure of sounds based on collage, with myself as the only common denominator, the sounds came to represent me.
>
> No matter how much I travel, how much the global nomad, the troubadour, or the bard I become, this sonic collage becomes my identity. Blues musicians speak of "going to the crossroads"—that space where everyone could play the same song but flipped it every which way until it became "their own song." In jazz, it's the fluid process of "call and response" between the players of an ensemble. These are the predecessors of the mixing board metaphor for how we live and think in this age of information.

Paul D. Miller aka DJ Spooky that Subliminal Kid, *Rhythm Science* (Cambridge, MA: Mediawork/The MIT Press, 2004), 23–24.

22. Tricia Rose, *Black Noise: Rap Music and Black Culture in Contemporary America* (Middletown, CT: Wesleyan University Press, 1994), 47.

23. Jay-Z, *Decoded*: "Our fathers were gone, usually because they just bounced, but we took their old records and used them to build something fresh" (255).

24. Chang, *Can't Stop Won't Stop.* Dieter Lesage and Ina Wudtke, *Black Sound White Cube,* have an interesting take on 1989's import in the art world,

using Richard Powell's exhibition from that year as a reification of the Blues Aesthetic.

25. Many recent articles have reconsidered the case, most prominently Lyn-Nell Hancock's "Wolf Pack: The Press and the Central Park Jogger," *Columbia Journalism Review,* January/February 2003, 38–42. The *Village Voice* also took close looks at the case, as in Sydney H. Schanberg, "A Journey through the Tangled Case of the Central Park Jogger: When Justice Is a Game," 19 November 2002; and "Rivka Gewirtz Little's 'Rage Before Race': How Feminists Faltered on the Central Park Jogger Case," *Village Voice,* 15 October 2002. Also useful is Hancock's sidebar, "False Confessions: How They Happen," 40–41.

26. Both Schanberg and Hancock point this out; Hancock relates too that the case had real-world implications far from the young men, as "The case set the stage for the reinstatement of New York's death penalty."

27. Quoted in Hancock, "Wolf Pack," 38.

28. W. Joseph Campbell, in *Getting It Wrong: Ten of the Greatest Misreported Stories in American Journalism* (Berkeley: University of California Press, 2010), traces some key journalistic errors—including the crack baby phenomenon, "the epidemic that wasn't" (132)—that still persist. Shockingly, while the crack baby controversy is well reported, the book manages to avoid race assiduously in its discussion of what clearly had, if not racial motivation, then racist implication.

29. The website Gawker.com has an interesting set of posts about "flash mobs" as a form of racist worry, revealing that the so-called mobs of Philly youth were actually started by "breakdance crews." Fascinatingly, an image from one of their flyers advertises the group by the phrase "Wild 'N Out."

30. Hancock, "Wolf Pack," 42.

31. Oddly Chang misrecords the "wildin'" lyric quite differently: as "I go wild and . . ." Both Adam Bradley and Andrew Dubois's *The Anthology of Rap* (New Haven, CT: Yale University Press, 2010) and I hear it as "wildin'."

32. June Jordan, "More Than You Ever Wanted to Know about Vertical Rhythm." In *June Jordan's Poetry for the People: A Revolutionary Blueprint,* ed. Lauren Muller (New York: Routledge, 1995), 38. Emphasis added.

33. Martha Cooper and Henry Chalfant, *Subway Art* (1984; repr., New York: Owl Books, 2005). The definition appears on page 27, in a useful "Vocabulary" list, but many of the photographs illustrate the technique better than a description can. Of particular interest are the *Two-man window-down wild-style burner by Shy 147 and Kel, 1980* shown on pages 30–31.

34. Lester Bangs, "From Notes on PiL's Metal Box, 1980," in *Psychotic Reactions and Carburetor Dung,* 315.

35. The RZA, with Chris Norris, *The Wu-Tang Manual* (New York: Riverhead Freestyle, 2005), 22.

36. A dialogue from "Can It Be All So Simple," Enter the Wu-Tang (36 Chambers).

37. The RZA, *The Wu-Tang Manual,* 90–91.

38. Ronald Takaki, *Strangers from a Different Shore: A History of Asian Americans,* updated and revised ed. (New York: Little, Brown, 1998), 251 and 253. Emphasis added.

39. The RZA, *The Tao of Wu* (New York: Riverhead Books, 2007).

40. Raekwon's "Simple" remix is an angry refutation of all that memory seeks to soothe in the original; though of course like the original it asks the ultimate question—*Can it be all so simple?*—it starts with a skit planning an assault that ends with a shooting. This is quite a contrast from the reminiscent stoop talk that starts out the first version on Wu-Tang's *36 Chambers.*

41. Louis Menand, *Discovering Modernism: T. S. Eliot and His Context,* 2nd ed. (New York: Oxford University Press, 2007), 27.

42. "The distinction the criterion of sincerity wants us to make between a private feeling and its public expression—the distinction that enables us to judge the degree of their congruence—is no longer of any use, since the poet has chosen to regard his own feelings from the outside, as it were. He seems to suggest, in fact, not that the form for his feeling is artificial or inadequate (a perfectly conventional literary decorum), but that the feeling itself is as much a public thing, a construct, as its literary form." Menand, ibid., 16.

43. Mayfield was always aware his song was a disguised prayer, as discussed in Paul Gilroy, *The Black Atlantic* (Cambridge, MA: Harvard University Press, 1993).

44. For more on the history of Gee's Bend, and the mixed legacy of the New Deal efforts, consult *The Quilts of Gee's Bend: Masterpieces from a Lost Place* (Atlanta: Tinwood Books, 2002).

45. William Arnett and Paul Arnett, "On the Map," in ibid., 35–36.

46. David Shields, *Reality Hunger: A Manifesto* (New York: Knopf, 2010), 99. Shields quotes Brian Goedde, "Fake Fan," Experience Music Project Annual Pop Conference.

47. John L. Austin, *Sense and Sensibilia* (1962), quoted in Arnett's artwork, on view at Tate Britain, October 2010.

48. See Sacha Jenkins, Elliott Wilson, Chairman Mao, Gabriel Alvarez, and Brent Rollins, *Ego Trip's Book of Rap Lists* (New York: St. Martin's Griffin, 1999).

49. Fernando Pessoa, translated by Edwin Honig and Susan M. Brown, *Poems of Fernando Pessoa* (San Francisco: City Lights, 2001), 167.

50. Antonin Artaud, *The Theater and Its Double* (New York: Grove Press, 1958), 24–25. Emphasis added.

51. Ibid., 25.

52. Kelefa Sanneh, quoted in Bradley and Dubois, *The Anthology of Rap*, 128. Originally in "Rapping about Rapping: The Rise and Fall of a Hip-Hop Tradition," *This Is Pop: In Search of the Elusive at Experience Music Project*, ed. Eric Weisbard (Seattle: Experience Music Project, 2004), 224, 226.

53. Jay-Z, *Decoded*, 292.

54. Ibid., 23–25.

55. Zora Neale Hurston, "High John de Conquer," *The American Mercury Reader* (Garden City, NY: Country Life Press), 107.

Afterword: Fission and Fusion

"There are terrible spirits, ghosts, in the air of America," D. H. Lawrence announced in *Studies in Classic American Literature* (1923), much as Kevin Young in *The Grey Album: On the Blackness of Blackness* summons "a poetry that speaks from the mouths of those gone who aren't really gone, a poetry of ghosts and haunts." Few books of cultural history since Lawrence have dared anything approaching his intellectual adventurousness before America's spectral past—and fewer still have risked Lawrence's stylistic bravura in reclaiming criticism as a form of experimental literature. Here I am thinking of a small, probative tradition of dynamic critical writing as rare and original as William Carlos Williams's *In the American Grain* (1925), Thomas Beer's *The Mauve Decade* (1926), Constance Rourke's *American Humor: A Study of the National Character* (1931), Greil Marcus's *Invisible Republic: Bob Dylan's Basement Tapes* (1997), and, most recently, *The Grey Album*, winner of the 2010 Graywolf Press Nonfiction Prize.

Back in the third decade of the twentieth century, Lawrence was aiming to revitalize mainstream American literature as modernist. "The furthest frenzies of French modernism or futurism," Lawrence proposed, "have not yet reached the pitch of extreme consciousness that Poe, Melville, Hawthorne, Whitman reached. The European moderns are all *trying* to be extreme. The great Americans I mention just were it. Which is why the world has funked them, and funks them today." Now, during the second decade of the twenty-first, Kevin Young twists the radio dial again on that mainstream American cultural funk, shifting the frequencies as well of modernism and postmodernism.

Young's observations in *The Grey Album* prove as alive and vivid as his vision is expansive, his tonalities generous, and his arguments persuasive. By revisiting "what I read, heard, and saw at the crossroads of African American and American culture," Young tracks an "alternative system of literary currency and value, so to speak, functioning both within and without the dominant, supposed gold-standard system of American culture." In the personae, disembodied voices, and "anonymity" of Paul Laurence Dunbar's poems, for instance, "we have modernism's not-so-modest beginnings." The 1920 recording of "Crazy Blues" by Mamie Smith "provides the first full expression, still overlooked, of a black modernist presence previously hinted at by the dialect of Dunbar." T. S. Eliot and Ezra Pound echo Louis Armstrong, and hip-hop folds modernist collage inside out, such that "the seams are meant to show." Re postmodernism: "We could say that with the cakewalk, as with blackface, white folks projected back onto blacks the kind of pastiche or 'blank copy' that Fredric Jameson saw as one of the fundamental qualities of postmodernism—a full century before the idea took hold." Similarly, Young recalls that listening to Public Enemy's *It Takes a Nation* "was the first time I heard what postmodernism sounded like. Loud, layered, filled with longing and language—not just self-conscious but self-referential." Finally, as he advances in his elegant scrutiny of soul music, "I believe it is black culture (which is distinct) that transforms American culture (making it more black, and thereby more distinct). . . . American culture is black culture—and it is this unique African American culture that in large part makes American culture popular the world over."

Early on, Young, the capacious poet of *To Repel Ghosts* and *Ardency: A Chronicle of the* Amistad *Rebels,* references William Carlos Williams's *Paterson* and Ezra Pound's *Cantos*—books that "seemed to wonder, if only by their form, can the poem, can any one book, contain everything?" But as comprehensive prose with an accent on storying, or "the artful dodge," *The Grey Album* might find a closer analogue in the all-embracing modernist encyclopedic fictions: Joyce's *Ulysses,* Stein's *The Making of Americans,* Reed's *Mumbo Jumbo,* and Pynchon's *Gravity's Rainbow.* Across his great reckoning Young finds room for artists as various as Afrika Bambaataa, Louis Armstrong, Jean-Michel Basquiat, James Brown, Sterling A. Brown, Gwendolyn Brooks, Countee Cullen, Rita Dove, W. E. B. Du Bois, Paul Laurence Dunbar, T. S. Eliot, Duke Ellington, Ralph Ellison, Grandmaster Flash, Robert Hayden, Jimi Hendrix, Lauryn Hill, Elton John, Langston Hughes, Jay-Z, Fenton Johnson, Robert Johnson,

Bob Kaufman, Gladys Knight, Robert Lowell, Claude McKay, OutKast, Charlie Parker, Parliament/Funkadelic, NWA, Pablo Picasso, Ezra Pound, Public Enemy, Otis Redding, Run-DMC, The Sugarhill Gang, Phillis Wheatley, Colson Whitehead, Bert Williams, and Wu-Tang Clan. Rereading *The Grey Album,* I kept asking who can't, or who *won't,* this radical, far-reaching chronicle take on—Isaac Hayes, Bowie, the Sex Pistols, disco? Well, they're all here, as along the way Young provocatively improvises on such topics as Topeka (Kansas), Muhammad Ali, punk, Black Bohemia, glamour, space music, and—inevitably—montage, scat, and story. His stylish investigations of Wheatley, Hughes, and Kaufman amount to intensive, self-contained nonfiction novellas.

Young occasionally tags himself a collector, curator, and preservationist, but *The Grey Album* invokes history to project the future. In his propulsive retrospect, "tradition is not what you inherit, but what you seek, and then seek to keep." One emblem for this book of choruses, licks, bridges, solos, ensembles, and breakdowns is jazz:

> Standing as it does between blues gossip and spiritual thunder, jazz offers not just freedom but another, radical tradition— instead of progress, jazz emphasizes *process*. Most interested in the past only as a way of riffing toward the future, jazz seems to say we "make it new" only when we make it our own.

Another emblem for *The Grey Album* can be discovered along the borders of jazz and hip-hop—or, as on the Danger Mouse mash-up that furnished Young his cunning title, at the convergence ("both fission and fusion") of Jay-Z and the Beatles:

> Both jazz and hip-hop seek the song within the song. That is, they often take older songs—and, indeed, song itself—and bend, stretch, and riff it till it almost rips at the seams. In jazz, however free, the desire is to see how far the song can go without breaking; in hip-hop, the wish is to find the breaks, to break on it, to divide and conquer and reconfigure. In our own image.

Our own . . . In our own image. Ultimately, then, for all its volatile erudition, *The Grey Album* is a personal, even autobiographical study.

I don't only mean Young's account of the Dark Room Collective and his days as a DJ on WHRB, or the private worlds within such disclosures as the "first record I bought with my own money was *King of Rock* on vinyl," and Langston Hughes's *The Big Sea* "changed my life," but an impulse here at once vaster and bolder. By dividing, conquering, and reconfiguring the tradition, he is showing us how he turned into the poet he is today. As he implicitly conjures up *The Grey Album* in his sly recapitulation of Ralph Ellison, coded languages, storying, and shadow books, "It also may provide one map to being a writer."

Robert Polito
New Paltz, New York
August 2011

Index

The Graywolf Press Nonfiction Prize is funded in part by endowed gifts from the Arsham Ohanessian Charitable Remainder Unitrust and the Ruth Easton Fund of the Edelstein Family Foundation.

Arsham Ohanessian, an Armenian born in Iraq who came to the United States in 1952, was an avid reader and a tireless advocate for human rights and peace. He strongly believed in the power of literature and education to make a positive impact on humanity.

 Ruth Easton, born in North Branch, Minnesota, was a Broadway actress in the 1920s and 1930s. The Ruth Easton Fund of the Edelstein Family Foundation is pleased to support the work of emerging artists and writers in her honor.

Graywolf Press is grateful to Arsham Ohanessian and Ruth Easton for their generous support.

KEVIN YOUNG is the author of seven books of poetry, most recently *Ardency: A Chronicle of the* Amistad *Rebellion*. His *Jelly Roll: A Blues,* was a finalist for the National Book Award and the *Los Angeles Times* Book Prize, and winner of the Paterson Poetry Prize. He is the editor of six volumes, including *The Art of Losing: Poems of Grief and Healing.* His first book of critical nonfiction, *The Grey Album: On the Blackness of Blackness,* won the 2010 Graywolf Nonfiction Prize. He is the Atticus Haygood Professor of Creative Writing and English and Curator of Literary Collections and the Raymond Danowski Poetry Library at Emory University in Atlanta. For more information, visit his website: kevinyoungpoetry.com.

Book design by Ann Sudmeier. Composition by BookMobile Design and Publishing Services, Minneapolis, Minnesota. Manufactured by Versa Press on acid-free 100 percent postconsumer wastepaper.

Atlanta-Fulton Public Library